Cognitive Behaviour Therapies

SAGE has been part of the global academic community since 1965, supporting high quality research and learning that transforms society and our understanding of individuals, groups, and cultures. SAGE is the independent, innovative, natural home for authors, editors and societies who share our commitment and passion for the social sciences.

Find out more at: **www.sagepublications.com**

Cognitive Behaviour Therapies

Edited by Windy Dryden

Los Angeles | London | New Delhi
Singapore | Washington DC

Editorial arrangement, preface and Chapter 9 © Windy Dryden 2012
Chapter 1 © Sarah Marks 2012
Chapter 2 © Frank Wills 2012
Chapter 3 © Rebecca Crane 2012
Chapter 4 © Eric Morris and Joe Oliver 2012
Chapter 5 © Michaela Swales 2012
Chapter 6 © Peter Fisher 2012
Chapter 7 © Paul Gilbert 2012
Chapter 8 © Vartouhi Ohanian and Rana Rashed 2012
Chapter 10 © John Rhodes 2012
Chapter 11 © Joe Curran, David Ekers, Dean McMillan and Simon Houghton 2012
Chapter 12 © Warren Mansell 2012

SAGE Publications Ltd
1 Oliver's Yard
55 City Road
London EC1Y 1SP

SAGE Publications Inc.
2455 Teller Road
Thousand Oaks, California 91320

SAGE Publications India Pvt Ltd
B 1/I 1 Mohan Cooperative Industrial Area
Mathura Road
New Delhi 110 044

SAGE Publications Asia-Pacific Pte Ltd
3 Church Street
#10-04 Samsung Hub
Singapore 049483

Library of Congress Control Number: 2011926256

British Library Cataloguing in Publication data

A catalogue record for this book is available from the British Library

ISBN 978-0-85702-118-2
ISBN 978-0-85702-119-9 (pbk)

Typeset by C&M Digitals (P) Ltd, Chennai, India
Printed by MPG Books Group, Bodmin, Cornwall
Printed on paper from sustainable resources

MIX
Paper from
responsible sources
FSC® C018575

Contents

List of Figures and Tables

Figures

Tables

About the Editor and Contributors

The Editor

Windy Dryden is Professor of Psychotherapeutic Studies, Goldsmiths, University of London. He is a Fellow of the British Psychological Society and of the British Association for Counselling and Psychotherapy. He began his training in rational emotive behaviour therapy (REBT) in 1977 and became the first Briton to be accredited as an REBT therapist by the Albert Ellis Institute. In 1981, Windy spent a six-month sabbatical at the Center for Cognitive Therapy, University of Pennsylvania, one of the first British psychologists to do an extended training in cognitive therapy. He is a Fellow of the Albert Ellis Institute and a Founding Fellow of the Academy of Cognitive Therapy.

While his primary therapeutic orientation is REBT, Windy has been very much influenced by his cognitive therapy colleagues and by the working alliance theory of Ed Bordin. His research interests are in the historical and theoretical roots of REBT (with Arthur Still) and the phenomenology of hurt, the study of which is informed by REBT theory.

Windy is perhaps best known for his voluminous writings in REBT/CBT and the wider field of counselling and psychotherapy. To date he has authored or edited over 185 books, making him probably the most prolific book writer and editor currently alive in the field today. He has also edited 20 book series including the best-selling 'Counselling in Action' series.

Windy was the founding editor of the *British Journal of Cognitive Psychotherapy* in 1982, which later merged with the *Cognitive Behaviorist* to become the *Journal of Cognitive Psychotherapy: An International Quarterly*. Windy was co-founding editor of this journal with E. Thomas Dowd. In 2003, Windy became the editor of the *Journal of Rational-Emotive and Cognitive-Behavior Therapy*.

The Contributors

Rebecca Crane is an occupational therapist who works as a teacher and trainer in mindfulness-based interventions at the Centre for Mindfulness Research and Practice, Bangor University. She has written *Mindfulness-Based Cognitive Therapy* in the CBT Distinctive Features Series; Routledge, 2009.

Joe Curran works as a Consultant Cognitive Behavioural Psychotherapist for Sheffield Health and Social Care NHS Foundation Trust. He is course leader for a Postgraduate Diploma in CBT and has an interest in the theory and practice of contextual CBTs, such as behavioural activation and acceptance and commitment therapy.

David Ekers is a Consultant Nurse and Clinical Lead for 'Talking Changes' Improving Access to Psychological Therapies service in Co Durham and Darlington. This role is split between clinical leadership service development and research with the mental Health Research Unit at Durham University. David's main research interests are focused upon primary care mental health provision and in particular improving delivery of effective treatments for anxiety and depression. In particular he is involved in the development and dissemination of behavioural activation for depression across the age bands and provision of collaborative care.

Peter Fisher is a Senior Lecturer in Clinical Psychology, University of Liverpool and is a supervisor and tutor for the Metacognitive Therapy Institute. He has published over 40 articles and book chapters on metacognitive therapy and cognitive therapy. Currently, his main research interests focus on the development and evaluation of metacognitive therapy for emotional disorders in adult mental health and physical health populations.

Paul Gilbert is a Professor of Clinical Psychology at the University of Derby. He has published a number of books and over 150 academic papers in the areas of mood disorders, shame and self-criticism. He is a fellow of BPS and a former president of BACBP. He is the founder of the charity the Compassionate Mind Foundation (www.compassionatemind.co.uk) and is currently developing and researching the efficacy of compassion focused therapy.

Simon Houghton is Consultant Cognitive Behavioural Psychotherapist and Clinical Lead for the Obsessive Compulsive Disorder Specialist Team of Sheffield Health and Social Care NHS Foundation Trust. He is also the visiting Consultant Psychotherapist for Riverdale Grange, an independent sector residential clinic for people with eating disorders in Sheffield. Until recently Simon was the Clinical Advisor to the Improving Access to Psychological Therapies programme for Yorkshire and the Humber.

Warren Mansell is a Reader at the University of Manchester, a clinical psychologist and an accredited cognitive behavioural therapist. He has been the co-chair of the annual conference of the British Association of Behavioural and Cognitive Psychotherapies (BABCP) since 2008 and has authored over 80 publications. In 2011, he received the May Davidson Award from the British Psychological Society for outstanding contribution to clinical psychology in the 10 years since qualifying. His books include: *Cognitive Behavioural Processes Across Psychological Disorders: A Transdiagnostic Approach to Research and Treatment*, *The Oxford Guide to Metaphors in CBT*, *Coping with Fears and Phobias: A Step-by-Step Guide to Understanding and Facing Your Anxieties* and *The Bluffer's Guide to Psychology*.

Sarah Marks is a historian and Research Associate at the Wellcome Trust Centre for the History of Medicine at University College London. Her work ranges across the history of psychology and psychiatry in the British and European contexts, from the 19th century to the present day. Her current research focuses upon the historical development of cognitive and behavioural therapies in the UK, and their place in wider political debates surrounding wellbeing, welfare and governance.

Dean McMillan is a senior lecturer in Mental Health Services Research at the University of York. He has a background in clinical psychology and a Diploma in cognitive behaviour therapy. His research interests include the development and evaluation of cognitive-behavioural interventions.

Eric Morris works as a consultant clinical psychologist for the South London and Maudsley NHS Foundation Trust, and has practised acceptance and commitment therapy (ACT) for the past ten years, as well as providing teaching and training in ACT and other contextual behavioural therapies. He is involved in developing and researching mindfulness-based group and individual interventions for psychosis at the Institute of Psychiatry, King's College London.

Vartouhi Ohanian is a consultant clinical psychologist and Head of Psychology Services in Hounslow, West London Mental Health Trust. Vartouhi has trained extensively in schema therapy since 1991 with Dr Jeffrey Young and Dr Mary Anne Layden. She has been instrumental in introducing and disseminating schema therapy in the UK by organising national workshops since 1996. She is a long-standing member of the International Society for Schema Therapy and is certified by them as a schema therapist and schema therapy training and supervision provider. She is also trained in group schema therapy with borderline personality disorder. She teaches widely in the UK and has presented on schema therapy at the British Association of Behavioural and Cognitive Psychotherapy and eating disorder conferences. She established the first ISST-approved advanced certification training programme in schema therapy in the UK, which has now been running for many years. She has also been invited to run schema therapy training programmes abroad. Vartouhi is co-author of a number of publications on schema therapy with eating disorders and has particular expertise in the use of imagery to bring about schema change.

Joe Oliver is a clinical psychologist working in the South London and Maudsley NHS Foundation Trust. He works within an early intervention for psychosis team in South London. He has clinical and research interests in the use of acceptance and commitment therapy in working with people with psychosis.

Rana Rashed is a principal clinical psychologist who currently works in a community mental health setting with clients with severe and enduring mental health problems. She has a specialist interest in working with clients with diagnoses of psychosis and personality disorders. She is a certified schema therapist and is a supervisor on the Schema Therapy Certification Programme.

John Rhodes is a consultant clinical psychologist in the NHS (Brent, CNWL), working in a service for clients diagnosed as having psychosis and long-term mood disorders. For many years he has used solution focused, narrative and CBT approaches. Publications include *Solution Focused Thinking in Schools* (1995) with Yasmin Ajmal and *Narrative CBT for Psychosis* (2009) with Simon Jakes. He is a visiting lecturer at the University of Hertfordshire and honorary lecturer at University College London.

Dr Michaela Swales is Consultant Clinical Psychologist, Betsi Cadwaladr University Health Board and Senior Lecturer in Clinical Psychology, School of Psychology, Bangor University. She runs a DBT programme for adolescents with a history of chronic suicidal behaviour in a Tier IV inpatient service in North Wales. She is co-author with Dr Heidi Heard of *Dialectical Behaviour Therapy* in the 'CBT Distinctive Features Series' published by Routledge (2009). In November of the same year she was awarded the Cindy Sanderson Outstanding Educator Award by the International Society for the Improvement and Training in DBT at their conference in New York.

Dr Frank Wills is an independent CB therapist, trainer and author, living in Bristol. He comes originally from the Wirral and supports Tranmere Rovers FC and the England cricket team – activities that have made him so skilled in dealing with anxiety and depression.

Preface

In 1986 I co-edited a book with Bill Golden entitled *Cognitive-behavioural Approaches to Psychotherapy* (1986). In the preface of that book we noted that a recent survey at that time showed that cognitive approaches to psychotherapy, while making their initial mark in the 1950s and early 1960s, were in the mid-1980s one of the leading forces in psychotherapeutic practice. Bill Golden and I began work on that book in 1984, three years after I had returned from a six-month sabbatical at the Center for Cognitive Therapy in Philadelphia. I had edited the first edition of my textbook entitled at that time *Individual Therapy in Britain* (1984) and wanted to edit a companion volume entitled *Cognitive Behaviour Therapy in Britain*. The problem was that there were very few British practitioners of CBT at that time, and those that did exist practised mainly cognitive therapy and rational-emotive therapy. I soon learned that if I was going to edit an 'approaches to CBT' book it would have to rely heavily on contributors from North America. Of the 18 contributors to the 1986 volume, 15 were from the USA, one was from the Netherlands, one from Italy and one from Britain – me! It made sense, then, for me to team up with an American co-editor, Bill Golden.

Twenty-six years after the publication of that book, the situation has changed markedly in Britain. There are many more CBT therapists and most of the CBT approaches have British proponents. Indeed, in this book, a number of approaches were pioneered in Britain (e.g. compassion-focused therapy and meta-cognitive therapy). All of the chapters in this book are written by British authors and therefore I decided to edit the volume without an American co-editor. Also, as Sarah Marks shows in Chapter 1, CBT has its own British history. This therapeutic tradition has taken a firm foothold in British counselling and psychotherapy. Thus this volume, as can be seen from Table 0.1, is very different in content from its 1986 predecessor. Indeed, only two approaches (Beck's cognitive therapy and REBT) feature in both volumes.

Having noted the differences between this book and its predecessor, the major similarity can be found in the chapter structure of both volumes. The following appeared in the preface of the 1986 book, but equally applies to this one:

> Contributors were asked to write to a common chapter structure emphasizing the distinctive features of their approach. First, they were asked to address themselves to the historical development and theoretical underpinnings of their approach. Under this rubric, major theoretical concepts are considered and issues of conceptualizing clients' problems are detailed. Second, the contributors were invited to focus on practical applications. Here, the relationship between therapist and client is outlined and major treatment strategies and techniques are presented. In addition, contributors were asked to address themselves to the issue of obstacles to client progress, how they are conceptualised and what tactics are used to overcome them. Finally, a case example is

Table 0.1 Comparison of chapters in the 1986 and 2012 volumes

1986	2012
• Cognitive Behaviour Modification	• Beck's Cognitive Therapy
• Cognitive Therapy	• Mindfulness-based Cognitive Therapy
• Structural Cognitive Therapy	• Acceptance and Commitment Therapy
• Rational-Emotive Therapy	• Dialectical Behaviour Therapy
• Rational Behaviour Therapy	• Metacognitive Therapy
• Cognitive Appraisal Therapy	• Compassion-focused Therapy
• Personal Construct Therapy	• Schema Therapy
• Interpersonal Cognitive Problem-Solving Therapy	• Rational Emotive Behaviour Therapy
• Cognitive-Behavioural Hypnotherapy	• Narrative Cognitive Behaviour Therapy
• Multimodal Therapy	• The Transdiagnostic Approach to Cognitive Behaviour Therapy

presented to show how each approach is applied to clinical problems. (Dryden and Golden, 1986: xi–xii)

In addition to the above instructions, contributors to the 2012 volume were asked to make clear the research status of their approach and to provide five suggested further readings.

I was tempted to write a concluding chapter in the current volume speculating on the likely future direction of CBT. I have resisted this temptation for one major reason. There was no way Bill Golden and I could have foreseen the developments that have taken place in CBT in Britain and in the world over the 26 years since the original book was published. Should I be around to edit this book again in 26 years' time (I will be 87 then!), then my guess is that CBT as it exists then will be as unrecognisable to me now as today's CBT would have been to Bill and I back then.

Let me close by thanking all contributors for their excellent work and for the dignified way in which they responded to my feedback and to my continual promptings for them to keep to the chapter structure.

References

Dryden, W. (Ed.) (1984) *Individual Therapy in Britain*. London: Harper & Row.

Dryden, W. and Golden, W.L. (Eds) (1986) *Cognitive-behavioural Approaches to Psychotherapy*. London: Harper & Row.

ONE Cognitive Behaviour Therapies in Britain: The Historical Context and Present Situation

SARAH MARKS

The rise in the profile of cognitive behaviour therapy (CBT) is an international phenomenon, with theoretical and clinical contributions coming from across the European and anglophone world, but cognitive and behavioural interventions have a particularly significant – and sometimes controversial – position in contemporary Britain. Whilst the genealogy of many of the cognitive techniques used by current practitioners originates in the USA, there has been a strong tradition in evidence-based psychotherapeutic interventions on this side of the Atlantic. Much of the early impetus for the development of behaviour therapies originated with clinical psychologists and psychiatrists at the Maudsley Hospital from the 1950s onwards, and cognitive-behavioural interventions have become established practices across public sector fields, from the health services and social work through to education (Baistow, 2001). This chapter will chart some of the key moments in the development of cognitive behaviour therapies in Britain, from the first wave of behaviour therapies in the 1950s, through the second wave of the 1980s and 1990s associated with the 'cognitive revolution', and up to the recent third wave of approaches that draw from eclectic traditions. It will also explore the broader social and political aspects of the British context, in which CBT has become the dominant form of 'talking therapy' in the National Health Service (NHS), with significant political and economic backing.

The origins and professionalisation of behaviour therapies in Britain

Histories of CBT frequently cite Ellis and Beck as the original founders. While this is true of the cognitive component, a number of behavioural approaches were advanced by a group of clinical psychologists and psychiatrists at the Institute of Psychiatry and the Maudsley Hospital in

London, providing the foundations for an evidence-based therapeutic movement that underpinned the later development of cognitive-behavioural therapies.

The institutional setting of the newly amalgamated Bethlem and Maudsley Hopsitals, forming a home for the University of London Institute of Psychiatry, provided a professional and experimental space for the development of psychotherapeutics in post-war Britain. Headed by Sir Aubrey Lewis, the imperative for critical experimentalism in research, along with a broad education in the philosophy of science, laid the foundations for a move away from traditional psychoanalytic approaches in Britain. This emergence of behavioural therapy as an experimental science at the Maudsley has been credited as one of the single most important developments in the international psychology community for facilitating the development of Behaviour Therapy as a distinct movement (Krasner, 1971). But how did this theoretical space emerge?

Shalumit Ramon argues that there was a rise in public interest, and sympathy, with those suffering from mental distress in after the Second World War, with a congruent rise in media coverage of the activities of psychiatrists (Ramon, 1985: 134). The inclusion of mental health services within the remit of the NHS had not been a given, and had not featured in early drafts of the implementation plans, until the integration of psychiatry into general medical services was guaranteed by Aneurin Bevan's insistence in 1944 (Busfield, 1998: 16).

The creation of state-funded hospital psychiatry resulted in a widening of hospital services for individuals suffering from distress categorised under the label of 'neuroses', who would previously have been treated by their family doctor and would not have been referred for secondary or tertiary care (Busfield, 1998: 16). The need for a training centre for the newly nationalised profession soon became apparent, which is how the Institute of Psychiatry originally came in to being, with research being essentially secondary to its role as a teaching hospital (Waddington, 1998: 188). For Keir Waddington, a significant outcome of the organisational structure of the Institute, split as it was over the Maudsley and Bethlem Royal Hospitals, was the ability to nurture a truly multidisciplinary approach to the treatment of mental distress, allowing the resources and scope for research across the full breadth of interventional techniques (Waddington, 1998: 188). Thus, both a department of psychiatry and a separate department of clinical psychology were established.

The institutional state of mental health services in the immediate post-war period was unfavourable to the recently professionalised clinical psychologist (Hall, 2007: 29), who was viewed primarily as a diagnostic assistant to the psychiatrist, operating within a traditional framework which regarded behavioural disorders within a medicalised disease model (Fishman and Franks, 1992: 166). Cyril Franks, a psychologist who trained at the Institute of Psychiatry, has argued retrospectively that the dissatisfactory status of the psychological profession was one of the catalysts for the shift towards a new theoretical basis for psychotherapeutics (Fishman and Franks, 1992: 167). The development of behavioural psychology demanded a paradigm shift away from Cartesian dualism towards an acceptance of a more materialistic basis of psychological disorder – from treatment of the mind to treatment of the nervous system (Wolpe, 1963: 23). For Eysenck: 'there is no neurosis underlying the symptom but merely the symptom itself. Get rid of the symptom and you have eliminated the neurosis' (Eysenck, 1960). To quote Jan Ehrenwald's broad summary:

> Behaviour modification as a therapeutic tool is an offspring of a philosophy and a technique. The philosophy is frankly materialistic, positivistic, causal-reductive, and is based on Pavlovian, Watsonian, and Skinnerian principles of conditioned reflexes, operant reinforcement, and learning theory ... Behaviour is determined by genetic and environmental factors such as operant reinforcements, aversive or punitive interventions, and their consequences. The self – or the sense of self – is merely a product of our sociocultural environment generating self-knowledge and self-control. Freedom and dignity are illusions and autonomous man is a mythical animal. (Ehrenwald, 1991: 445)

A landmark publication for post-war behaviour psychology is Hans Eysenck's 1952 paper 'The effects of psychotherapy: An evaluation', published in the *Journal of Consulting Psychology*. The study stemmed from Eysenck's own criticism of a recommendation of the American Psychological Society that all trainee clinical psychologists should be schooled in psychoanalytic psychotherapy, employing an argument based on the 'social need' for psychotherapeutic skills. Looking to dispute this 'social need', Eysenck sought to question the efficacy of the psychoanalytic approach through an examination of data from various other studies, concluding that the evidence did not support the efficacy of therapy, to the extent that there actually appeared to be 'an inverse correlation between recovery and psychotherapy; the more psychotherapy, the smaller the recovery rate' (Eysenck, 1952). Jack Rachman, a PhD student of Eysenck who trained at the Maudsley, argued that patients treated with psychoanalysis were highly selected, based on the likelihood of their 'suitability' for treatment: specifically in terms of their level of education and social status (Eysenck, 1973). His primary piece of research was based on 'spontaneous remission', the phenomenon of patient recovery from depression or neurosis as a result of natural, non-interventional causes. When the statistics for spontaneous remission are analysed, he argued, it is difficult to make a case for the efficacy of psychoanalytic therapy beyond the normal base-level of recovery through spontaneous remission (Eysenck, 1997: 179).

   This critical engagement with psychoanalysis can be seen as laying the foundations for the reconceptualisation of psychotherapeutics, and the growth of a behavioural approach arrived at through clinical experimentation. Isaac Marks' thesis, later published as a Maudsley Monograph under the title

Patterns of Meaning in Psychiatric Patients (Marks, 1965), falls into this tradition, as a study whose initial object was to test psychoanalytic methods (Marks, 2009, personal communication). Marks offers the quip that 'we were Popperians before we even knew of Popper' (Marks, 2009, personal communication), referring to Karl Popper's *Conjectures and Refutations*, in which he argued that psychoanalysis was a pseudoscience as it was not falsifiable (Popper, 1963). Subsequently, the first 'behaviour therapy' paper is deemed to have been that published by the clinical psychologist H.S. Jones, from studies at the Maudsley in 1956, entitled 'The application of conditioning and learning techniques to the treatment of a psychiatric patient' (Jones, 1956).

While experimentation was being carried out in the psychology department of the Institute of Psychiatry, Aubrey Lewis was simultaneously encouraging members of the department of psychiatry to clinically evaluate the efficacy of the methods being carried out by the psychologists (Gelder, 1968: 111), which challenges Maarten Derksen's assertion that psychiatrists at the Institute of Psychiatry were ambivalent about the developments being made by the clinical psychologists (Derksen, 2001: 275). This analysis began with J.E. Cooper's small-scale control study of de-conditioning treatments published in the *Lancet* in 1963; 'A study of behaviour therapy in thirty psychiatric patients' (Cooper, 1963), and was soon followed by an extended collaborative study by Cooper with Isaac Marks and Michael Gelder (Cooper et al., 1965). This paper, along with further studies by Marks and Gelder, suggested that patients suffering from phobias responded more rapidly to desensitisation techniques than patients suffering from other neurotic disorders, and that desensitisation, along with psychotherapy, could offer a significant improvement in patients' symptoms across the anxiety disorders (Gelder et al. 1967).

It was not only the Maudsley Hospital that was involved in pioneering behaviour therapy techniques. Victor Meyer was simultaneously developing therapeutic interventions for obsessive-compulsive disorder (OCD) at the Middlesex Hospital, where he founded a Behavioural Psychotherapy Unit in 1962 (Bruch, 2002). Meyer developed exposure-and-response-prevention therapy (ERP) for patients suffering from OCD by exposing them to the stimuli that provoked their anxieties and preventing them from performing their anxiety-reducing rituals. For example, one of Meyer's first patients to undergo this treatment had a severe fear of dirt: she was gradually exposed to dirty objects whilst being denied access to water and cleaning agents over a period of eight weeks, and her anxiety and compulsive cleaning behaviour began to wane (Meyer, 1966). Stanley Rachman cites this research as a key turning point for psychotherapeutic practice:

> What he did was very brave. Dr. Meyer applied to humans what studies had shown applied to frightened animals: if they were exposed to what scared them for a prolonged period of time and prevented from leaving the situation, they became less scared. Therapists were scared to do it with patients ... he had broken the ice. (Rachman, 2005)

Given the budget constraints of the post-war nationalised healthcare service, investment into the rates of efficacy of treatments in psychology and psychiatry can be seen in part as a rational consequence of the economics of healthcare. As a result of this shared interest in the evidence-base of psychotherapeutic treatments, clinical psychologists and psychiatrists working on behaviour therapies were able to make a strong case for the use of their approaches over others in the NHS, even at such an early stage in the service's development.

The coming of age of behaviour therapy as a professionally recognised field in the UK can be best dated as 1963, with the establishing of the journal *Behaviour Research and Therapy* (referred to by the acronym *BRAT*). In the absence of an association or society to represent the interests of the field, the founding of the journal fell to Hans Eysenck and Jack Rachman to initiate, which was essentially done by arranging a personal meeting with Robert Maxwell to persuade him to take up the cause and publish the journal under Pergamon Press (Eysenck, 1960: 149). The editorial to the first edition invited, among various types of study, 'experimental investigations (animal or human) of mechanisms involved in abnormal behaviour' (Eysenck, 1963: 1), illustrating the continuation of the position of earlier behaviourists that there was essentially no difference in the psychological mechanisms of animals and humans.

The first textbook for training in behaviour therapy in Britain was authored by Eysenck with S. Rachman in 1965, *The Causes and Cures of Neurosis: An Introduction to Modern Behaviour Therapy Based on Learning Theory and the Principles of Conditioning*. Victor Meyer and Edward Chesser established a formal training course in behaviour therapy at the Middlesex Hospital in the 1970s, which later became a higher degree diploma course in 1979 (Bruch, 2002). A further significant textbook for training, *Clinical Psychology: Theory and Therapy* was published by Dougal MacKay in 1975. MacKay, based at the University of Bristol, was not only a key figure in the 1970s and 1980s in terms of training a new generation of clinical psychologists and therapists, but also contributed to the development of behavioural therapies for a broad variety of disorders including sexual dysfunction, insomnia and assertion problems (Dryden, 1985: 113).

With the quantity of publications in the field rising, and the number of qualified practitioners in psychiatry and psychology increasing by the early 1970s, a professional association was founded in 1972 in the form of the then British Association for Behavioural Therapy (BABP), after a meeting of various interested delegates at the Middlesex Hospital in London (Lomas, 2008). The following year the association founded its own journal, initially the *BABP Bulletin*, later to become the journal *Behavioural Psychotherapy*. Four years later, the European Association for Behaviour Therapy (EABT) was officially founded, but there had already been an informal association between the BABP with its analogues in the Netherlands and Germany for several years (EABT, 2009).

At its conception, the membership of the BABP was spread across several professions, although it was still dominated by the traditional fields of psychiatry and psychology (Lomas, 2008): This situation was to change dramatically over the next 30 years as therapeutic treatments were deployed by a much wider range of practitioners in the NHS, particularly in primary care community mental health teams. From the early 1970s, efforts were made to expand the practise of behaviour therapy outwards, from the traditional professions to nursing staff. Isaac Marks identified a problem in the restriction of access to therapies, given that only a few hundred psychologists practised in the UK at the time. In order to widen the availability of behavioural treatments, a course was set up at the Maudsley to train nurse therapists. Marks chose nurses as a target group for pragmatic reasons: they constituted a large section of the NHS workforce across the country and there was no shortage in numbers. But he was also motivated through his experiences of working in developing countries with non-qualified practitioners who had limited training but were capable of performing required medical procedures effectively; borrowing from the Chinese term 'barefoot doctor', denoting rural farmers trained in basic paramedic procedures, Marks coined the term 'barefoot therapists' for the new generation of nurses qualifying at the Maudsley (Gournay, 2000: 370). The widening of behaviour therapy practices from the traditional professions must also be seen in the context of the rise of community mental healthcare since the 1950s, with the majority of patients suffering from mental illness now being treated as outpatients by community mental health teams, incorporating the nursing and social work professions (Busfield, 1998: 18).

By the beginning of the 1980s, therefore, behavioural therapy had become an established paradigm, with a high demand for the services, and a professionalised workforce. But it was still controversial, having gained adversaries within other forms of psychotherapy, and providing a target for the anti-psychiatry movement (Thomson, 2006: 274). Its identity as a coherent, scientifically and philosophically grounded approach began to wane, however, as therapists began to adapt their clinical practice to include techniques guided by different models.

BT, CT and CBT

CBT as it is practised now in Britain is by no means an unmediated product of the behaviour therapies developed at the Maudsley in the 1950s and 1960s. Approaches to psychotherapy underwent a so-called 'cognitive revolution' during the 1970s, drawing on therapeutic techniques developed in the USA.

The invention of the cognitive therapies is classically attributed to two psychotherapists: Albert Ellis and Aaron Beck. As therapist Meir Stolear argues, the history of cognitive therapy has been heavily biased towards the Beckians, with Ellis having been somewhat marginalised (Stolear, 2009, personal communication). In response to this, and in consideration of the fact that Ellis' writings pre-dated Beck's, I will deal with Albert Ellis's theories first.

Ellis's rational-emotive therapy departs from the Eysenckian approach in quite a dramatic way, although it, too, was formulated through a negative response to Freudian psychoanalysis (Hoffmann, 1984). Ellis's first work on rational emotive behaviour therapy dates to 1955, when he first began to practice it after conducting a systematic review of available forms of psychotherapy (Ellis, 2007: 14). For Ellis, the personal story of the patient was crucial to understanding the formation of the neurosis – in direct contrast to Eysenck's dismissal of the patient's personal life as having any significance to his or her treatment (Ramon, 1985: 198). For Ellis, the psychoanalytic notion of suppression was flawed: instead of the effects of childhood being manifested through unconscious processes, rational-emotive therapy identified a conscious, active 'self-indoctrination' process, in which the patient reiterates pathogenic thoughts and inner-monologues borne out of childhood experiences (Ellis, 1962). Similarities are present in Beck's cognitive model of depression, which explicitly draws upon Ellis's work and dates to 1976 (Beck, 1976/1991: 240). Both have since agreed that the fundamentals behind their theories of emotional disorder are largely similar, with only a few 'differences in technique and style' (Beck and Ellis, 2000). Aaron T. Beck's most widely read book *Cognitive Therapy and the Emotional Disorders* was first published in 1976 and provides a step-by-step targeted approach to the specific problem areas associated with depression. These techniques primarily involve deconstructing and challenging the client's 'maladaptive' beliefs (Beck, 1976/1991). The therapist's primary role, then, is to explore how the client's belief system came to be so, and gradually pull these beliefs apart, providing alternative, more positive ways of thinking, which are then reinforced through 'cognitive rehearsal'. This latter technique – the role-playing of difficult situations and preparing a positive reaction, then rewarding oneself for accomplishing the positive reaction when the situation actually arises – does have similarities with behavioural conditioning, but the explicit exploration of the origins of the emotional disorders as *a fundamental part of the therapeutic process itself* is at odds with the approaches of more traditional behaviour therapies.

At first glance, it appears difficult to see how the behavioural and cognitive world-views could be compatible – the former, after all, frequently rejects the relevance of the latter in the aetiology of psychopathology. As G. Terence Wilson states, in traditional behaviour therapy 'cognitive approaches are rejected as improper targets of experimental study or relegated to the status of epiphenomenal events that are merely the by-products of physical actions in the body and/or the external environment; they exert no causal effect on a person's behaviour or subjective state' (Wilson, 1978: 8). Further incompatibilities are apparent in the interest of cognitive psychologists in how experience becomes organised and structured by the mind, whereas traditional behavioural psychologists rejected the possibility of the mind possessing innate organisational ability (Schulz and Schulz, 2004: 492). The most significant disparity between the two theoretical systems is perhaps their view of volition: for behaviourists, free will is purely epiphenomenal, whereas cognitive psychology allows for volition and ascribes volition agency in particular cognitive processes, such as the selection of experiences to commit to memory (Schulz and Schulz, 2004: 493). However, therapeutic integration *did* occur, and it has indeed been argued that the cognitive revolution came about as a development within behavioural therapy, or was to some extent 'implicitly' influenced by it (Hoffmann, 1984: 5).

The extent to which cognitive processes could be completely excluded from explaining the efficacy of behavioural therapy was doubtful – the effect of the patient's expectation of positive results, for example, is a cognitive process *as distinct from* a behavioural one (Hoffmann, 1984: 5). Therapeutic strategies such as verbal conditioning, as developed by Luria (1961) and Staats (1963), and subsequently taken up in Britain by Michael Gelder (1965), are particularly similar to a cognitive approach, to the extent that it is seems peculiar to categorise it as a solely behavioural intervention (Eifert, 1987: 176). Self-instruction techniques, in which 'clients are taught to emit self-statements that are incompatible with, and opposite in emotional content to, the negative self-statements they have employed previously' (Eifert, 1987: 176), had marked similarities to the semantic reinforcement techniques in Beck's cognitive therapy for emotional disorders (Beck, 1976/1991).

The boundaries between the categories of cognitive and behavioural interventions are evidently unclear, yet the incorporation of cognitive models remained highly contentious for many self-professed behavioural therapists. From a practical perspective, Hoffmann argues persuasively that the integration of cognitive and behavioural techniques was in part a result of consideration of time and economics: *in-vivo* treatment of neuroses was a long and costly process whereas simulation thereof, through use of symbolic stimuli and through verbally-induced 'cognitive rehearsal', can reduce the time required for treatment to take effect (Hoffmann, 1984: 5).

A key text that brought together behavioural and cognitive approaches was Albert Bandura's work on self-efficacy which dealt with the cognitive aspects of fear alleviation and their impact upon the patients' behaviour modification – challenging the traditional behavioural models of the treatment of phobia (Bandura, 1977). It is important to reiterate that this development, as with most of the significant texts which contributed towards the cognitive shift in psychotherapy, came about through the clinical observations by therapists of their patients, rather than a 'trickle down' diffusion of applied methods from the theoretical developments in cognitive science.

In terms of charting the rise of the integrated 'cognitive behavioural' approach in psychotherapy, it would be worthwhile to take a nomological approach, identifying instances of the term in the literature to create a historical map of the growth of CBT. According to David Clark and Christopher Fairburn, 'cognitive behaviour therapy can be found [although they state this without reference] in the first instance in the literature of the mid 1970s, with the first clinical trials coming at the end of the same decade' (Clark and Fairburn, 1997: ix). This is a roughly accurate pronouncement: an inaugural conference on CBT was held in New York in 1976 (Wilson, 1978: 7), with Mahoney's *Cognition and Behaviour Modification* appearing in 1974. A 1978 book, published in the USA and edited by Foreyt and Rathjen, includes the rather amusingly titled introduction: 'Cognitive behaviour therapy: Paradigm shift or passing phase?' (Wilson, 1978). Arguably, the first serious 'cognitive behaviour' text came as far back as 1969 with A. Bandura's *Principles of Behaviour Modification,* which argued that certain therapeutic processes, such as covert modelling, were better conceived of as cognitive processes rather than behavioural conditioning (Bandura, 1969).

Philip C. Kendall and Steven D. Hollon, in the introduction to their 1979 *Cognitive-Behavioural Interventions: Theory, Research and Procedures*, emphasise that CBT 'is not yet another new exotic therapy. Rather it is *a purposeful attempt to preserve the demonstrated efficiencies of behaviour modification within a less doctrinaire context and to incorporate the cognitive activities of the client in the efforts to produce therapeutic change.'* (Kendall and Hollon, 1979: 1). The same authors argue that the 'hyphenation' of the two terms came about through bilateral movements, as behaviour therapists turned their research to mediation techniques (such as symbolic stimuli, as discussed above), and a certain degree of interest shown by cognitive therapists towards the more established field of behaviour modification (Kendall and Hollon, 1979: 2).

In terms of institutional integration in Britain, the key turning point didn't occur until the 1990s, when the alliance of the cognitive and the behavioural approaches became institutionally recognised through the renaming of the BABP to the British Association of Behavioural and Cognitive Psychotherapies in 1992. In the same year the authors of the *Handbook of Psychotherapy and Behaviour Change* documented that:

> Most of the people who used to consider themselves behavioural therapists now identify themselves as cognitive-behavioural. Also, most people who once considered themselves strictly cognitive practitioners are now willing to take on the cognitive-behavioural label as well. Although many influences have produced these changes, it is pleasing to note that the effect of the research has been substantial. (Bergin and Garfield, 1994: 824)

The following year, the second edition of *Behaviour Modification,* a handbook of behavioural therapy interventions which was aimed primarily at social workers and originally published in 1982, was issued under the new title *Cognitive Behaviour Therapy: Research, Practice and Philosophy*. The author, Brian Sheldon, argued that it was only with moderate enthusiasm that the addition of the cognitive framework to more traditional behavioural techniques had been adopted in social work, but that positive outcomes in effectiveness research, particularly for probation, had led to a shift in practice: 'this is a difficult field and we need all the help we can get' (Sheldon, 1995: xiii).

It is perhaps no accident that the integration of the cognitive and behavioural approaches became dominant during the 1980s and throughout the 1990s, as there was a concurrent movement for the integration of therapies. This was not by any means an attempt to create 'grand unified theory' of mental illness and therapy, but rather as an acceptance of the value of the diversity of approaches to psychotherapy and a positive attitude towards pluralism. Indeed, this was a period in which interdisciplinarity became common across the academic social sciences. This development within psychotherapy occurred primarily in the USA, as an attempt to develop a 'rapprochement' between the competing approaches to psychotherapy, but had an influence across the anglophone world, and a movement for integrative psychotherapy has gained considerable popularity in the UK (Dryden, 1992; Evans and Gilbert, 2005; Norcross and Goldfried, 2005).

CBT Research and Training in the UK

As mentioned above, the Maudsley Hospital and Middlesex Hospital pioneered early research and training in behaviour therapy, but Michael Gelder's move to Oxford led to a further research group being founded at the University of Oxford's Department of Psychiatry in 1970, initially specialising in research on agoraphobia and depression. In later years, with the addition of David Clark, Paul Salkovskis and Anke Ehlers to the centre's staff, research expanded to the application of CBT approaches to post-traumatic stress disorder, the anxiety disorders, hypochondriasis and obsessive compulsive disorder (Gelder and Mayou, 1997: 328). After the retirement of Professor Isaac Marks from the Institute of Psychiatry at King's College London, Salkovskis and Clark were appointed as professors of clinical psychology at the Institute of Psychiatry, acting as clinical directors of the Centre for Anxiety Disorders and Trauma at the Maudsley Hospital. This move re-established the Institute of Psychiatry as one of the primary centres for CBT, with Anke Ehlers following in 2005 to act as the Centre's research director.

A further school for CBT training and research is that centred around Windy Dryden at Goldsmiths, University of London, which specialises in rational emotive behaviour therapy. Dryden has been a particularly significant figure for updating and popularising Ellis's REBT approach for a British audience, and was part of the 'second wave' of CBT theorists, influenced by cognitive therapy techniques which came to the fore on the cusp of the 1970s and 1980s. Following substantial training and co-therapy practice with Ellis in the late 1970s, and a six-month sabbatical with Aaron Beck in 1981, Dryden went on to start one of the first ever CBT training programmes at Aston University in 1982–83. This later expanded to become the basis of a Diploma in Cognitive Approaches to Counselling and Psychotherapy at Goldsmiths, University of London in 1988, and later an MSc programme in rational-emotive and cognitive-behaviour therapy in 1995. Dryden is also the patron of the Association for Rational Emotive Behaviour Therapy (AREBT) (Dryden, 2010, personal correspondence). The AREBT is an important professional association, founded in 1993 by counsellors and REBT practitioners. The Association publishes a professional journal, *The Rational Emotive Behaviour Therapist*, as well as co-ordinating conferences and workshops, and has developed a comprehensive accreditation pathway for training therapists. In addition, the AREBT played a joint role with the BABCP in setting up the CBT Register UK, providing a public-access database of accredited CBT and REBT therapists (AREBT, 2010).

The Centre for Rational Emotive Behaviour Therapy, based at the University of Birmingham, also provides primary and advanced certificate training in REBT, along with peer supervision. The Centre was founded by Peter Trower and Jason Jones, based on the same model as the Albert Ellis Institute, New York, which accredits its courses (Centre for Rational Emotive Behaviour Therapy, 2011).

Other significant centres for CBT in the UK include the University of Exeter's Mood Disorders Centre, led by Professor David Richards. The Exeter group focuses upon major depressive disorder and bipolar disorder, taking a transdiagnostic approach to understanding the relationship between these and their co-occurring psychiatric disorders and physical health problems (Mood Disorders Centre, 2010). The University of Edinburgh's Health in Social Sciences department offers clinical training, with Kenneth Laidlaw's research being quite unique in its specialisation on CBT with older people (Laidlaw et al., 2003). Paul Salkovskis' move to the Department of Psychology at the University of Bath in September 2010 signals the beginning of a further centre for training and research in CBT.

While there are currently 37 universities providing training courses in cognitive and behavioural approaches to counselling and psychotherapy (BABCP, 2010), training is by no means restricted to university departments. The Association for Psychological Therapies provides training to the NHS and social services in CBT for specific disorders, as well as a number of 'new wave' approaches, such as schema-focused therapy and acceptance and commitment therapy, employing clinical psychologists as course leaders on a consultancy basis. The Centre for Stress Management, directed by Professor Stephen Palmer, has also offered accredited training since its foundation in 1987, with diplomas and advanced certificates in both CBT and REBT in association with the Centre for Cognitive Behaviour Therapy and the UK Centre for Rational Emotive Behaviour Therapy. Among the most popular and long-running training workshops are those of Christine Padesky, co-author of the bestselling self-help book *Mind Over Mood* (Greenberger and Padesky, 1995).

Self-help material such as *Mind Over Mood* plays a key role in CBT in the UK, particularly in the low-intensity interventions associated with IAPT and the NHS Books on Prescription scheme. A significant figure in the early development and popularisation of self-help material was Robert Sharpe, whose book *Self Help for Your Anxiety: The Proven 'Anxiety Antidote' Method* was published in 1979 (Sharpe, 1979). Sharpe also made a series of CBT-based self-help television programmes for ITV under the title 'Lifeskills', dealing with issues such as stress, agoraphobia, assertiveness and relaxation techniques (Sharpe, 2010). In more recent years, the *Overcoming* ... series of self-help books has perhaps been one of the most important in enabling access to CBT to a wide audience, covering over 30 different conditions (Overcoming Ltd, 2010).

CBT in Practice: Mental Health Policy, IAPT and Community Settings

Writing in the early 21st century, it has been evident for at least 20 years that, although still controversial, CBT has become the most dominant form of therapy, and recent policy developments have rendered it by far the most dominant form of psychotherapy now available through the NHS. The advent of the Labour Government's Increasing Access to Psychological Therapies scheme in 2007 is one of several policy attempts to improve mental health services, and one which has been continued by the Coalition Government (HM Treasury, 2010).

One avenue of explanation that must be explored in this context is the rise of evidence-based medicine in British healthcare, followed shortly after by a growth in evidence-based psychology. The term was coined in the early 1990s; according to the MEDLINE database of international publications in the life sciences, collated by the US National Library of Medicine, the term was cited only once in 1992, rising to 2,957 citations by February 2000 (Straus and McAlister, 2000: 837). Those lobbying for an increase in funding for CBT services readily engaged with the evidence-base agenda. David Clark, along with many other academic psychologists, and specifically those who speak in favour of CBT in policy, underline its evidence base as demonstrated through randomised control trials, review articles and meta-analyses. This is by no means a new trend in clinical psychology, as the early behaviour therapy control trials at the Maudsley illustrate (Buchanan, 2010).

In England and Wales, evidence-based practice became institutionalised with the foundation of the National Institute for Health and Clinical Excellence (NICE) in 1999, which provides guidelines to NHS practitioners for best clinical practice and evaluates the cost-benefits of particular treatments within the framework of a state-funded healthcare system (Dobson, 1999).The NICE Guidelines on Depression and Anxiety, published in December 2004, advised that 'When considering individual psychological treatments for moderate, severe and treatment-resistant depression, the treatment of choice is CBT' (National Collaborating Centre for Mental Health, 2004).

Evidence-based medicine is not without its cogent critiques, however, particularly in psychiatry. Concerns have been raised that published evidence is skewed towards positive outcomes because negative results tend not to be published. This problem, referred to as 'publication bias', is a long-term feature of publishing in science and medicine. It occurs when a journal with a particular editorial agenda in favour of a treatment reject negative results for publication, and in terms of authorial selection as to which studies are or are not included in meta-analyses, resulting in negative results not being included in studies, biasing overall statistical results towards the agenda of the author (Begg and Berlin, 1988). Pim Cuijpers has argued that the efficacy of psychotherapies, CBT included, is 'considerably overestimated' in the treatment of depression in adults as a consequence of publication bias in meta-analyses (Cuijpers, 2010: 178).

Even representatives of the CBT community itself have demonstrated reservations about the effects of the guidelines on effective practice. Paul Salkovskis, editor of *Behavioural and Cognitive Psychotherapy*, published an article criticising NICE's guidelines, arguing that their explicit focus on the randomised control trial as the fundamental knowledge base for governance did not reflect the true developmental process which had underpinned CBT. He argued that the implementation of the guidelines would lead to a narrowing of the scope of CBT in practice, which would counteract the productive developments gained through the pluralist, integrative approach developed in the 1990s (Salkovskis, 2002).

Despite the recommendations contained within the NICE guidelines, it took at least three years for the cause to be taken up by politicians, and then only as a result of considerable lobbying. The key figure for initiating this process was the Labour peer, Lord Richard Layard of Highgate. An economist and director of the LSE's Centre for Economic Performance, Layard had been the primary policy architect of the New Deal under the Labour Government after 1997. His motivations for improving access to psychotherapies were, in part, in keeping with the wider project of the New Deal, as it recognised the detriment caused to the national economy by incapacity through mental distress. Layard has a longer-standing interest in mental health, related to his interests in the economics of subjective wellbeing (Layard, 2009, personal correspondence). This is illustrative of a wider intellectual shift towards a concern with the subjective in the late 20th century, growing out of the overall problematic of the disparity between increased economic wealth and the incongruous lack of growth in individuals' happiness in Western society. Layard's book, *Happiness: Lessons from a New Science*, is a popular exemplar of such concerns; combined with a simplified explication of recent neurobiological sciences demonstrating the 'reality' of subjective emotion through use of imaging technologies which demonstrate positive and negative affect in brain function (Layard, 2005).

Concerted efforts to implement the NICE guidelines began with Layard's success in getting a pledge to improve care for mental illness included in the Labour Party Manifesto for the 2005 general election – in which, through accident, the pledge was to improve 'behavioural, as well as drug therapies' (Labour Party, 2005), neglecting to include the 'cognitive' aspect. Layard was advised that expert confirmation of the evidence base for the efficacy of psychotherapeutics would be required in order to persuade policy-makers of the importance of investment. Consequently, David Clark, Professor of Psychology at the Institute of Psychiatry, was called in to conduct a question-and-answer session. Clark has continued to play a key role in authoring policy documents and acting as a national adviser to the Improving Access to Psychological Therapies (IAPT) initiative (Layard, 2009, personal communication).

The implementation of IAPT, with the institution of less orthodox forms of low-intensity therapy, has raised concerns among therapists at the level of competency with which they will be carried out, representing a concern with the de-professionalisation of psychotherapy delivery. With the concurrent growth in the number of therapists in the NHS as a result of IAPT, with 3,600 therapists being required to implement to policy, there has been a corresponding development towards regulation of the practice (Laurance, 2009). Draft standards of proficiency were released by the Health Professionals' Council in 2009 (HPC, 2009). Responses from the psychotherapy community displayed dissatisfaction with the medical model of regulation; with the client seen as a 'passive object who receives treatments and procedures' (Association of Independent Psychotherapists et al., 2009). Further criticisms have been levelled by the British Association of Psychotherapists (BAP) who state that:

> Many if not most practitioners see their work as more an art than a science. Any attempt to impose a quasi-objective framework of standards and competencies not only stifles creativity but also damages therapeutic work with the client. Applying a predetermined set of external principles means overriding the client's individuality. This is ethically unacceptable as well as therapeutically ineffective. (Laurance, 2009)

The integration of psychotherapy into an NHS framework has raised particular tensions with regard to the imposition of a medical model of governance that practitioners see as misplaced. This is echoed again in Salkovskis's critique of evidence-based medicine as a means of selecting treatments:

> Evidence Based Medicine may be appropriate as a way of making coherent sense of dozens of studies in which thousands of patients are administered identifiable doses of medication, or in treatments such as most psychotropic medications, which have been stumbled upon rather than developed and refined. It seems unlikely that it will ever be appropriate to exclusively consider the management of psychosocial problems in this way; to do so would be to endorse a one-dimensional approach to science. CBT has thrived because, from the earliest days, it has been both evidence based and empirically grounded. This grounding is in a range of different types of evidence, including but definitely not confined to randomised controlled trials. (Salkovskis, 2002)

The professionalisation of CBT has perhaps reached an apex, but increasing integration into the healthcare system has led to a perceived challenge to the therapy profession, with low-intensity practitioners with short-term training covering part of the workload that would previously have been the remit of therapists. It has also led to questions as to where the profession should stand within the NHS: as fully integrated into medicine or as a practice with separate modes of clinical governance and regulation.

While access to CBT in the NHS has courted the most media attention, the health services are not the only area of public service in which CBT-based interventions play a key role. Techniques are now widely used within social work, criminal justice and education. Within the criminal justice system there has been substantial investment in the use of cognitive behavioural techniques in rehabilitation programmes. These are a key feature in the rehabilitation programmes of young offenders, with training aimed at reducing substance misuse, drink-driving, violence and sexual offending (Sheldon and MacDonald, 2008: 269). Such programmes were originally developed by Canadian criminal psychologist Robert Ross in the 1980s, based on the theory that offenders experience 'cognitive deficit', tending towards concrete thinking rather than abstract, egocentricity, impulsiveness and lack of empathy. If offenders could be taught the necessary 'cognitive skills' they were lacking by means of creative problem solving, non-aggressive assertiveness training, role playing and social perspective training, their offending behaviour should consequently be reduced (Hawkins, 1996: 119). A number of trial programmes were carried out in the UK between 1992 and 1998, with Home Office evaluations carried out in 2002 and 2003. Two of the three studies found the programmes reduced reconviction rates, with one showing a marked reduction of reoffending among adult male sexual offenders (House of Commons Home Affairs Committee, 2005: 228–9). In the last decade a proliferation of cognitive behaviour programmes have been introduced in both custodial and community contexts, and such approaches have become an integral part of offender rehabilitation in the British criminal justice system (Robinson and Crow, 2009).

The social work profession has adopted cognitive behavioural approaches across several areas of practice, including parenting programmes in family services, substance abuse and harm reduction, anger-management training and social care of children. The latter in particular has not been without controversy, after the 'pindown' scandal in the 1980s in which children in residential care in Staffordshire were physically restrained for long periods of time, with the perpetrators justifying their actions as a form of behaviour training (Levy and Kahan, 1991). This example is one used in the training of contemporary social workers to reflect upon the ethical aspects of cognitive and behavioural interventions in their work, encouraging students to reflect upon the boundaries between intervention and coercion with vulnerable service users, particularly in relation to 'punishment' and 'reward' techniques (Wilson et al., 2008: 358).

Karen Baistow has described the rise in behaviour modification approaches in primary and secondary education. Before 1980 such techniques had been widely adopted in special schools, but increasing political attention to the effectiveness of school in the 1980s led behavioural approaches to become normal practice in mainstream education, particularly given the perceived increase in problems of discipline and pupil disruption. As well as 'classroom management' techniques, teachers were encouraged to increasingly use positive reinforcement strategies both to modify behaviour and to raise self-esteem (Baistow, 2001: 325). Baistow goes on to argue that the extension of cognitive and behavioural techniques into the wider community context has been surrounded by a political discourse of 'empowerment' and 'self-management' that has made it popular with both New Labour and the New Right (Baistow, 2001: 327). This aspect of CBT has been the focus of much controversy (House and Loewenthal, 2008), with some critics going so far as to claim that it is essentially government-sponsored 'personal spin doctoring' (James, 2007).

The 'Third Wave' Therapies

Despite the concerns raised by the consequences of IAPT for the profession and the very public criticisms of the philosophical and political thinking underpinning the practice of CBT, the actual range of cognitive behavioural approaches to psychotherapy and counselling in practice remains diverse and draws upon a broad range of theoretical frameworks.

Many new and eclectic approaches have been established through engagement with techniques from other schools of psychotherapy, drawing from a variety of philosophical perspectives. Other approaches, such as meta-cognitive therapy (MCT), have been developed in response to the limitations of traditional cognitive therapy with particular client groups. MCT departs from the Beckian focus on the *content* of cognitions, and looks instead at the pathological effects of thought *processes* and *styles* of thinking (Fisher and Wells, 2009: 5). In addition, some long-standing CBT approaches have been updated for contemporary clinical practice. Behavioural activation, which focuses on mood improvement through increasing client engagement in pleasurable activities, has been a behaviour therapy technique since the 1970s (Lewinsohn and Graf, 1973). It was revived and further expanded in the early 2000s by Hopko and Lejuez, who also blended the approach with more recent concepts such as mindfulness-based therapies (Hopko et al., 2003).

More recent therapies have included interventions that have been developed with specific conditions or groups in mind. Dialectical behaviour therapy (DBT), for example, provides a framework of techniques and skills training primarily directed towards individuals suffering from chronic suicidal thoughts, and has a strong evidence base for clients with a diagnosis of borderline personality disorder (Dimeff et al., 2007: 1). Schema therapy, which also draws on Gestalt, psychoanalytic and constructivist schools, focuses on treatments for clients with chronic issues, such as the personality disorders, which do not respond well to more traditional CBT techniques (Young et al., 2003: 1–2). Similarly, the limitations of available approaches to treating eating disorders through CBT led to the development of the 'transdiagnostic approach'. This model, associated with Christopher Fairburn, focuses upon the behaviours and cognitions which tend to be common across the individual diagnostic categories of the eating disorders, paying attention to the common psychopathological beliefs and how these cognitions are maintained (Waller et al., 2007: 7).

Individuals with emotional difficulties associated with self-criticism and shame, many of whom may have suffered abuse or neglect, are the primary focus of compassion-based therapies. Compassion-focused techniques seek to activate experiences of safety, reassurance and self-compassion that, in turn, help to 'counter' maladaptive self-criticism (Gilbert, 2009: 211). As well as being significant for putting a strong emphasis upon the therapeutic relationship above and beyond the efficacy of the techniques in themselves, the theoretical foundations that underpin compassion-based therapy is notable for its basis in the cognitive neurosciences. This approach was developed in response to research in neuroscience that suggested that

> there are in fact different affect processing systems that provide information on threat and safeness. It is possible, therefore, that people can experience affective arousal in threat systems (based on fast threat processing) but lack accessibility to affect systems that process information in terms of safeness and help regulate threat. (Gilbert, 2009: 205–206)

This is indicative of an emerging trend in CBT research, in which evidence from the neurosciences is beginning to inform the development of, as well as serve as a justification for, new therapeutic methods. A further example of this trend is eye movement desensitization and reprocessing (EMDR), which is used as a treatment for post traumatic stress disorder (PTSD). While this was initially discovered by a chance experience on the part of Francine Shapiro, she has since developed it in clinical practice with reference to 'neuro-network' concepts and the working model of 'adaptive information processing' (Shapiro, 2001: 29).

Neuroscientific concepts are not the only theoretical frameworks to guide new techniques, however. The rise of constructivist and post-modernist perspectives in recent years have seen an alternative strand within the 'third wave' of cognitive behavioural approaches. Some of these, such as acceptance and commitment therapy (ACT) and mindfulness-based CBT are characterised by a shift away from an emphasis of first-order change and didactic approaches, towards more contextual and experiential change strategies (Hayes, 2004: 6). Mindfulness-based therapies refer to a broad base of techniques influenced by the Buddhist philosophical tradition, enabling clients to 'pay attention in the present moment to whatever arises internally or externally, without becoming entangled or 'hooked' by judging or wishing things were otherwise' (Roemer and Orsillo, 2009: 2). The associated acceptance and commitment therapy also correlates with the Eastern philosophical tradition in that it takes as a foundation the acceptance of suffering as part of the normal human condition. ACT advocates actively challenge the binary notions of health/illness and normal/pathological, arguing that the mainstream mental health community has wrongly adopted these categories from medical models (Hayes et al., 1999: 4). It also draws from assumptions associated with the linguistic turn, seeing language as a tool for therapeutic intervention precisely because it can itself be at the core of psychological distress (Hayes and Strosahl, 2004: 4). A similar constructivist epistemology is present in the narrative therapy approaches of Michael White and David Epstein, focusing upon client's personal histories as a basis for therapeutic interventions (Payne, 2006: 8). While narrative therapy has broad-based theoretical origins, it has become adopted as an approach for cognitive behavioural therapists, particularly for use with clients experiencing psychosis (Rhodes and Jakes, 2009).

Cognitive behavioural approaches to therapy and counselling certainly remain eclectic. Recent years have seen CBT practitioners embracing theoretical approaches from across different schools of psychology, providing a wide range of techniques for clients experiencing a broad range of emotional difficulties, across the spectrum of psychiatric disorders. These approaches have become valued techniques not only in the psychology and healthcare communities, but are increasingly used also across the fields of social work, education and criminal justice. The chapters in this book further demonstrate the breadth and depth of approaches available, and provide an opportunity to reflect on the present and future state of CBT in the British context.

References

Association for Rational Emotive Behaviour Therapy (2010) Available at: www.arebt.org/index.html.

Association of Independent Psychotherapists et al. (2009) *Response to the HPC Draft Standards of Proficiency for Psychotherapists and Counsellors from AIP, AGIP, Arbours, CFAR, The College of Psychoanalysts-UK, Guild of Psychotherapists, The Site for Contemporary Psychoanalysis, Philadelphia Association.* Unpublished document.

BABCP (2010) List of training courses in CBT in the United Kingdom. Available at: www.babcp.com/training/cbt-training-courses.

Baistow, K. (2001) 'Behavioural approaches and the cultivation of competence', in G. Bunn, A.D. Lovie and G.D. Richards (Eds), *Psychology in Britain: Historical Essays and Personal Reflections.* Leicester: BPS Publishing.

Bandura, A. (1969) *Principles of Behaviour Modification.* New York: Holt, Rhinehart and Winston.

Bandura, A. (1977) 'Self-efficacy: toward a unifying theory of behavioural change', *Psychological Review*, 84: 191–215.

Beck, A.T. (1976/1991) *Cognitive Therapy and the Emotional Disorders.* London: Penguin.

Beck, A.T. and Ellis, A. (2000) Address to the American Psychological Association Convention, 8th July. Available at: www.fenichel.com/Beck-Ellis.shtml.

Begg, C.B. and Berlin, J.A. (1988) 'Publication bias: A problem in interpreting medical data', *Journal of the Royal Statistical Society*, 151(3): 419–63.

Bergin, A.E. and Garfield, S.L. (1994) *Handbook of Psychotherapy and Behaviour Change.* Chichester: Wiley.

Bruch, M.H. (2002) Edward Stuart Chesser. *Munks Roll*, Vol. XI. Available at: http://munksroll.rcplondon.ac.uk/Biography/Details/5231.

Buchanan, R.D. (2010) *Playing With Fire: The Controversial Career of Hans J. Eysenck.* Oxford: Oxford University Press.

Busfield, J. (1998) 'Restructuring mental health services in twentieth-century Britain', in M. Gijswijt-Hofstra and R. Porter (Eds), *Cultures of Psychiatry and Mental Health in Post-war Britain and the Netherlands.* Amsterdam: Rodopi.

Centre for Rational Emotive Behaviour Therapy, University of Birmingham (2011) Available at: www.rebt.bham.ac.uk/index.shtml.

Clark, D.M. and Fairburn, C.G. (Eds) (1997) *Science and Practice of Cognitive Behaviour Therapy.* Oxford: Oxford University Press.

Cooper, J.E. (1963) 'A study of behaviour therapy in thirty psychiatric patients', *Lancet*, 411–415.

Cooper, J.E., Gelder, M.G. and Marks, I.M. (1965) 'Results of behaviour therapy in 77 psychiatric patients', *British Medical Journal*, 1222–25.

Cuijpers, P. (2010) 'Efficacy of cognitive-behavioural therapy and other psychological treatments for adult depression: Meta-analytic study of publication bias', *British Journal of Psychiatry*, 196: 173–8.

Derksen, M. (2001) 'Science at the clinic: Clinical psychology at the Maudsley', in G.C. Bunn, A.D. Lovie and G.D. Richards (Eds), *Psychology in Britain: Historical Essays and Personal Reflections*. Leicester: BPS Books.

Dimeff, L.A., Linehan, M.M. and Koerner, K. (Eds) (2007) *Dialectical Behaviour Therapy in Clinical Practice: Applications Across Disorders and Settings*. New York: Guilford Press.

Dobson, F. (1999) *The National Institute of Health and Clinical Excellence (Establishment and Constitutional) Order. Statutory Instruments 1999 no. 220*. London: NHS England and Wales.

Dryden, W. (1985) *Therapists' Dilemmas*. London: Sage.

Dryden, W. (Ed.) (1992) *Integrative and Eclectic Therapy: A Handbook*. Milton Keynes: Open University Press.

EABT (2009) *About EABCT*. Available at: www.eabct.com/.

Ehrenwald, J. (Ed.) (1991) *The History of Psychotherapy*. Lanham, MD: Jason Aronson.

Eifert, G.H. (1987) 'Language conditioning: Clinical issues and applications in behavioural therapy', in H. Eysenck and I. Martin (Eds), *Theoretical Foundations of Behaviour Therapy*. New York: Plenum Press.

Ellis, A. (1962) *Reason and Emotion in Psychotherapy*. New York: Lyle Stewart.

Ellis, A. (2007) *Overcoming Resistance: A Rational Emotive Behaviour Therapy Integrated Approach*. New York: Springer.

Evans, K. and Gilbert, M. (2005) *An Introduction to Integrative Psychotherapy*. Basingstoke: Palgrave.

Eysenck, H. (1952) 'The effects of psychotherapy', *Journal of Consulting Psychology*, 16: 319–24.

Eysenck, H. (1960) *Behaviour Therapy and the Neuroses*. New York: Pergamon.

Eysenck, H. (1963) Editorial. *Behaviour Therapy and Research*, 1: 1.

Eysenck, H. (1973) 'Evaluating Psychoanalysis', *Medical Tribune*, 4 April.

Eysenck, H. (1997) *Rebel With a Cause: The Autobiography of Hans Eysenck*. Edison, NJ: Transaction Press.

Eysenck, H. and Rachman, S. (1965) *The Causes and Cures of Neurosis: An Introduction to Modern Behaviour Therapy Based of Learning Theory and the Principles of Conditioning*. London: Routledge.

Fisher, P. and Wells, A. (2009) *Metacognitive Therapy: Distinct Features*. New York: Routledge.

Fishman, D.B. and Franks, C.M. (1992) 'Evolution and differentiation within behaviour therapy: A theoretical and epistemological review', in D.K. Freedheim (Ed.), *History of Psychotherapy: A Century of Change*. Washington, DC: American Psychological Association.

Gelder, M. (1965) *Verbal Conditioning in Psychiatric Patients*. Unpublished D.M. thesis, University of Oxford, Oxford.

Gelder, M. (1968) 'Psychological treatments', in M. Shepherd and D.L. Davies (Eds), *Studies in Psychiatry: A Survey of Work Carried out in the Department of Psychiatry of the Institute of Psychiatry, Under the Chairmanship of Sir Aubrey Lewis, 1945–66*. London: Oxford University Press.

Gelder, M., Marks, I.M. and Wolff, H.H. (1967) 'Desensitization and psychotherapy in phobic states. A controlled enquiry', *British Journal of Psychiatry*, 113: 53–73.

Gelder, M. and Mayou, R. (1997) 'The Oxford University Department of Psychiatry', *The Psychiatrist*, 21: 328–30.

Gilbert, P. (2009) 'Developing a compassion-focused approach in cognitive behavioural therapy', G. Simos (Ed.), *Cognitive Behaviour Therapy: A Guide for the Practicing Clinician*. New York: Routledge.

Gournay, K. (2000) 'Nurses as therapists (1972–2000)', *Behavioural and Cognitive Psychotherapy*, 28: 369–77.

Greenberger, D. and Padesky, C. (1995) *Mind Over Mood: Changing the Way You Feel by Changing How You Think*. New York: Guildford Press.

Hall, J. (2007) 'The emergence of clinical psychology in Britain from 1943 to 1958, Part 1: Core tasks and the professionalisation process', *History and Philosophy of Psychology*, 9(1): 29–55.

Hawkins, D. (1996) *Delinquency and Crime: Current Theories*. Cambridge: Cambridge University Press.

Hayes, S.C. (2004) 'Acceptance and commitment therapy and the new behaviour therapies: Mindfulness, acceptance and relationship', in S.C. Hayes, V.M. Follette and M. Linehan (Eds), *Mindfulness and Acceptance: Expanding the Cognitive-Behavioural Tradition*. New York: Guilford Press.

Hayes, S.C. and Strosahl, K. (2004) *A Practical Guide to Acceptance and Commitment Therapy*. New York: Springer.

Hayes, S.C., Strosahl, K. and Wilson, K.G. (1999) *Acceptance and Commitment Therapy: An Experimental Approach to Behaviour Change*. New York: Guilford Press.

Health Professionals Council (2009) *Draft Standards of Proficiency – Practitioner Psychologists*. Available at: www.hpc-uk.org/publications/standards/index.asp?id = 198.

HM Treasury (2010) *Spending Review 2010*. London: The Stationery Office.

Hoffmann, N. (1984) 'Cognitive therapy as the result of a turnabout from psychoanalysis', in N. Hoffman (Ed.), *Foundations of Cognitive Therapy: Theoretical Methods and Practical Applications*. New York: Plenum.

Hopko, D.R., Lejeuz, C.W., Ruggiero, K.J. and Eifert, G.H. (2003) 'Contemporary behavioural activation treatment for depression: procedures, principles and process', *Clinical Psychology Review*, (23): 699–717.

House, R. and Loewenthal, D. (Eds) (2008) *Against and For CBT: Towards a Constructive Dialogue*. Ross-on-Wye: PCCS Books.

House of Commons Home Affairs Committee (2005) *Rehabilitation of Prisoners, First Report of Session 2004–5, Volume I*. London: The Stationary Office.

James, O. (2007) 'It's a mad world', *Guardian Online*. Available at: www.guardian.co.uk/commentisfree/2007/feb/16/itsamadworld.

Jones, H.S. (1956) 'The application of conditioning and learning techniques to the treatment of a psychiatric patient', *Journal of Abnormal and Social Psychology*, 52: 414–20.

Kendall, P.C. and Hollon, S.D. (1979) *Cognitive-Behavioural Interventions: Theory, Research and Procedures*. New York: Academic Press.

Krasner, L. (1971) 'Behaviour therapy', *Annual Review of Psychology*, 22: 483–532.

Labour Party (2005) *Labour Party Manifesto 2005: Britain Forward Not Back*. London: Labour Party.

Laidlaw, K., Thompson, L.W., Gallagher-Thompson, D. and Dick-Siskin, L. (2003) *Cognitive Behavioural Therapy with Older People*. Chichester: Wiley.

Laurance, J. (2009) 'Psychotherapists in turmoil over plans to start regulation', *The Independent*, 11 April.

Layard, R. (2005) *Happiness: Lessons from a New Science*. London: Penguin.

Levy, A. and Kahan, B. (1991) *The Pindown Experience and the Protection of Children: The Report of the Staffordshire Care Inquiry 1990*. Stafford: Staffordshire Social Services Department.

Lewinsohn, P.M. and Graf, M. (1973) 'Pleasant activities and depression', *Journal of Consulting and Clinical Psychology*, 41: 261–8.

Lomas, H. (2008) *The Development of the BABCP*. Available at: www.babcp.com/about-babcp/the-development-of-the-babcp/.

Luria, A. (1961) *The Role of Speech in the Regulation of Normal and Abnormal Behaviours*. New York: Liveright.

MacKay, D. (1975) *Clinical Psychology: Theory and Therapy*. London: Methuen.

Mahoney, M.J. (1974) *Cognition and Behaviour Modification*. Cambridge, MA: Ballinger.

Marks, I.M. (1965) *Patterns of Meaning in Psychiatric Patients: Semantic Differential Responses in Obsessives and Psychopaths*. Oxford: Oxford University Press.

Meyer, V. (1966) 'Modification of expectations in cases with obsessional rituals', *Behaviour Research and Therapy*, 4: 273–80.

Mood Disorders Centre (2010) *University of Exeter Mood Disorders Centre Research Profile*. Available at: www.exeter.ac.uk/mooddisorders/research/.

National Collaborating Centre for Mental Health (2004) *Depression: Management of Depression in Primary and Secondary Care, National Clinical Practice Guidline No. 23*. London: BPS and Gaskell.

Norcross, J.C. and Goldfried, M.R. (Eds) (2005) *Handbook of Psychotherapy Integration*. Oxford: Oxford University Press.

Payne, M. (2006) *Narrative Therapy: An Introduction for Counsellors*. London: Sage.

Popper, K. (1963) *Conjectures and Refutations*. London: Routledge and Keagan Paul.

Rachman, S. (2005) Keynote Address to the 12th Annual OCF Conference, San Diego, 30 July 2005. Available at: www.ocdhistory.net/20thcentury/behaviortherapy.html.

Ramon, S. (1985) *Psychiatry in Britain: Meaning and Policy*. London: Croom Helm.

Rhodes, J. and Jakes, S. (2009) *Narrative CBT for Psychosis*. New York: Routledge.

Robinson, G. and Crow, I. (2009) *Offender Rehabilitation: Theory, Research and Practice*. London: Sage.

Roemer, L. and Orsillo, S.M. (2009) *Mindfulness- and Acceptance-Based Behavioural Therapies in Practice*. New York: Guilford Press.

Salkovskis, P. (2002) 'Empirically grounded clinical interventions: Cognitive-behavioural therapy progresses through a multi-dimensional approach to clinical science', *Behavioural and Cognitive Psychotherapy*, 30(1): 3–9.

Schulz, D.P. and Schulz, S.E. (2004) *A History of Modern Psychology*. Belmont, CA: Thomson.

Shapiro, F. (2001) *Eye Movement Desensitization and Reprocessing: Basic Principles, Protocols and Procedures*. New York: Guilford Press.

Sharpe, R. (1979) *Self Help for Your Anxiety: The Proven 'Anxiety Antidote' Method*. London: Souvenir Press.

Sharpe, R. (2010) *About Lifeskills*. Available at: www.lifeskillsdirect.com/pages/about_us.html.

Sheldon, B. (1995) *Cognitive-Behavioural Therapy: Research, Practice and Philosophy*. London: Routledge.

Sheldon, B. and MacDonald, G. (2008) *A Textbook of Social Work*. Abingdon: Routledge.

Staats, A.W. (1963) *Complex Human Behaviour*. New York: Holt, Rinehart and Winston.

Straus, S.E. and McAlister, F.A. (2000) 'Evidence-based medicine: A commentary of common criticisms', *Canadian Medical Association Journal*, 163(7): 837–41.

Thomson, M. (2006) *Psychological Subjects: Identity, Culture and Health in Twentieth-Century Britain*. Oxford: Oxford University Press.

Waddington, K. (1998) 'Enemies within: Postwar Bethlem and the Maudsley Hospital', in M. Gijswijt-Hofstra and R. Porter (Eds), *Cultures of Psychiatry and Mental Health in Post-War Britain and the Netherlands*. Amsterdam: Rodopi.

Waller, G., Cordery, H., Corstorphine, E., Hinrichsen, H., Lawson, R., Mountford, V. and Russell, K. (Eds) (2007) *Cognitive Behavioural Therapy for Eating Disorders: A Comprehensive Treatment Guide*. Cambridge: Cambridge University Press.

Wilson, G.T. (1978) 'Cognitive behaviour therapy: Paradigm shift or passing phase', in J.P. Foreyt and D.P. Rathjen (Eds), *Cognitive Behaviour Therapy: Research and Application*. New York: Plenum.

Wilson, K., Ruch, G., Lymbery, M. and Cooper, A. (2008) *Social Work: An Introduction to Contemporary Practice*. Harlow: Pearson Education.

Wolpe, J. (1963) 'Psychotherapy: The non-scientific heritage and the new science', *Behaviour and Research Therapy*, 1(1): 23–8.

Young, J.E., Klosko, J.S. and Weishaar, M.E. (2003) *Schema Therapy: A Practitioner's Guide*. New York: Guilford Press.

TWO Beck's Cognitive Therapy

FRANK WILLS

This chapter will begin with a brief account of Aaron Beck's personal history as it intertwines with the development of his therapeutic approach. It will then describe his model's main theoretical ideas, followed by a review of its main practical aspects. After giving a case example, the chapter will conclude with an assessment of its efficacy, effectiveness and status as a model of therapy.

Historical Development of the Approach

Beck was a somewhat sceptical recruit into both psychiatry and psychoanalysis (Wills, 2009a). His open and enquiring mind has served the generation of cognitive behaviour therapists who followed his work well. He was particularly interested in trying to establish the validity of psychoanalytic concepts by empirical research and set out to test the hypothesis that depression was caused by anger turned in on the self. His research found that this theme was *not* reflected in the content of dreams reported by depressed patients. At the same time he discovered the existence of a constant stream of non-conscious negative thoughts in depressed clients. Eventually he concluded that the content of the dreams of depressed patients was better explained by the nature of this negative thought stream than by any unconscious 'need to suffer' – a completely extraneous concept, he suggested. Furthermore, studies of the behaviour of depressed clients showed them as no less keen to succeed in life than the non-depressed (Weishaar, 1993).

At first he hoped to interest analysts into taking the concept of negative thinking into psychoanalysis as 'cognitive therapy' with a small 'c'. He found his fellow analysts unreceptive and began to develop his own independent style of therapy – *the* cognitive model. He found younger colleagues more receptive and his writings frequently refer to these colleagues as 'my group' (Wills, 2009a). The excitement over the efficacy of cognitive therapy became increasingly international. Britain, especially psychologists based in Oxford, responded particularly well to Beck's work, perhaps because of the pronouncedly pragmatic behavioural tradition in British psychiatry (Rachman, 1997). One can in fact draw a direct

Table 2.1 Cognitive specificity

Thoughts (cognitive theme)	Emotions	Behaviours
I am useless, a loser (loss/defeat)	Sad, depressed	Withdrawn, giving up
There is danger (threat)	Fear, anxiety	Safety seeking
He wronged me (transgression)	Irritation, anger	Protest, aggression
I've done wrong (self-transgression)	Guilt, remorse	Contrition

line from Beck to the Increasing Access to Psychological Therapy (IAPT) project via David. M. Clark, who did a residency in Philadelphia and played a key role in developing cognitive therapy in Oxford between the 1980s and 2000s. Beck's publishing record is immense and he is now the second most cited author in the psychotherapy field. Approaching 90 years old, he is still producing many high-quality papers and books. Known as a generous and friendly man, he, unlike Freud, has been willing to let others develop his model. The model has evolved at a continuously rapid rate, so that it is a considerable task to corral its main elements into a single chapter.

Theoretical Underpinnings

Major Theoretical Concepts

Discovering negative thoughts amongst his clients initially by chance, Beck went on to test the role that 'negative automatic thoughts' (NATs) played in clients' psychological problems. He found that the effects showed a high degree of cognitive specificity, that is, specific negative cognitions showed a close 'fit' with specific negative emotions and behaviours (see Table 2.1).

An early part of cognitive behaviour therapy (CBT) assessment often consists of assembling a range of 'vicious cycle' examples showing how specific thoughts, feelings and behaviours relate to each other (see Figure 2.1).

Although the arrows shown in Figure 2.1 are unidirectional so as to emphasise the cognitive mediational stance of the model, it is generally recognised that thoughts, feelings and behaviours interact with each other in a mutual way. Cognitive therapy and CBT have been criticised for downplaying environmental effects (Weishaar, 1993). As a man brought up in Birkenhead[1] I would not wish to be understood as failing to appreciate the aversive effects of environment on mental health! Epictetus' famous dictum – 'People are not disturbed by events but by the view they take of them' – does not preclude the fact that some things are exceptionally

---

[1]Like Philadelphia, Birkenhead, home of Lily Savage, is 'one tough town'! Scousers (Liverpudlians) for some reason call it the 'one-eyed city'.

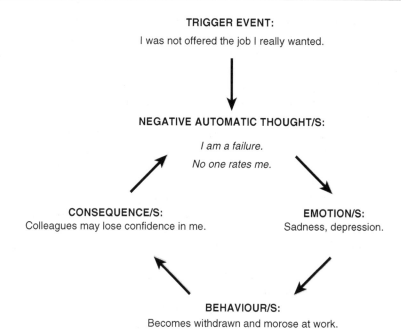

TRIGGER EVENT:
I was not offered the job I really wanted.

NEGATIVE AUTOMATIC THOUGHT/S:
I am a failure.
No one rates me.

CONSEQUENCE/S:
Colleagues may lose confidence in me.

EMOTION/S:
Sadness, depression.

BEHAVIOUR/S:
Becomes withdrawn and morose at work.

Figure 2.1   A simple vicious cycle

difficult to take another perspective on. Therapists should not therefore discount the importance of social/environmental aspects of triggers: suffering abuse from a bad employer may really indicate that the client should take out a grievance procedure or is in the wrong job, so that 'changing jobs' or 'changing boss' or 'fighting to change the system' may be better goals than changing appraisals of the boss – at least in the longer term.

Although I have referred to 'negative' emotions and behaviours, not all of these cycles are dysfunctional – in Table 2.1 taking the example of anxiety shown, there really may be a danger, in which case it is sensible to seek safety. Anxiety sufferers, however, tend to 'catastrophise' and therefore have many 'false alarms'. Whilst these over-reactions may have survival advantage at first, they eventually have negative feedback effects on functioning; for example, causing tiredness and poor concentration. In many instances, other factors need to be added to the client's typical vicious cycle. Physiology, for example, plays a prominent role in many psychological problems – one of several significant factors that may encourage cognitive therapists to take an increasingly 'trans-diagnostic' approach (Harvey et al., 2004). Clients vulnerable to panic attacks seem to apply 'catastrophic misinterpretations' to relatively normal physical reactions. These appraisals then raise anxiety and, ironically, increase physiological reactions (Clark, 1996). Clients often then use 'safety behaviours' (Salkovskis, 1996a); for example, during a panic attack they may have the thought 'I am losing control' and may sit down to stop the panic attack. Clients may consequently not learn that they would not actually have lost control whilst on their feet. They may come to believe that sitting down has prevented the attack – again confirming and maintaining the vicious cycle pattern. Negative thoughts may sometimes be submerged in negative images – a client with panic disorder may, for example, have images of themselves becoming ill and dying – and these images then play the same role in the cycle as actual thoughts (Stopa, 2009).

It has become increasingly clear that negative patterns are not abnormal or pathological per se. All people seem to show such reactions quite often. Even the puzzling thinking that can go with obsessive compulsive disorder (OCD) is reported as being experienced at least sometimes by large numbers of people (Rachman, 2003). There is, however, a 'tipping point' beyond which negative functioning becomes predominant. Even this may not become problematic until it stops people doing what they want or need to do in pursuit of their cherished life goals. The 'tipping point' may relate to underlying vulnerabilities, such as childhood traumas, but also to the sheer weight of negative thoughts and the quality of the attention that is afforded them. Depressed clients often begin to ruminate on how difficult their lives are. The effects of negative attentional bias (Ingram et al., 1998) will ensure that the increased amount of thinking will also be negative. Negative attention bias is one key maintenance factor in depression; cognitive distortion is another (Beck et al., 1979). Clients often have characteristic distortions such as 'personalising' ('It is all my fault') and 'catastrophising' ('It is a complete mess'), and these processes play a part in maintaining the negative cycle. Metacognitive factors – how we think about our thinking – also play a role in maintaining problems (Wells, 2008; Fisher and Wells, 2009). Wells describes, for example, how people often have 'positive' beliefs about worrying, such as 'If I didn't worry about x, I'd never remember to do y', so it is unsurprising that such thinking will maintain worry even though the client may see many other problems with it.

It seems that metacognitive aspects of problematic functioning are also linked to the issue of how clients pay attention to their negative thoughts. Problematic forms of attention seem to have a 'fixated' quality. Further discussion of this follows in the treatment section.

Beck's (1970) paper on integrating behavioural elements into cognitive therapy played an important role in the integration of the behavioural and cognitive therapies into CBT. Behaviours play a significant part in cognitive formulation because they often lock the vicious cycle in place. Depressed clients have a tendency to withdraw, and this means that they have less contact with potentially supportive aspects of their environments and also have far more time to engage in ruminative thoughts. Safety behaviours in anxiety often show similar effects. Socially anxious clients, for example, exhibit increasingly self-conscious behaviours that may attract the very negative attention they most fear.

Beck 'and his group' have spawned a rich tradition of empirical research that can prove a very helpful starting point for any therapist. Research on social anxiety, for example, clarifies the thinking styles and behaviour patterns worth exploring with clients, offering a generic (nomothetic) formulation. It is important, however, that cognitive therapists are not seduced by the plausibility of a generic formulation into assuming that it will apply exactly in an individual case (Persons, 2008).

Similarly, therapists should not assume that knowledge of a generic cognitive formulation for one problem can be easily applied to another: for example, the thinking that goes with social anxiety may not fit with other types of anxiety. Clark (1996) outlines the very careful process that has guided the development of applications of the model. This process begins with careful testing of the psychological processes upon which formulation and treatment are subsequently developed. Treatment guidelines are not published until rigorous clinical trials have demonstrated efficacy. The rigour of this process may explain the status of the model in effectiveness research.

Cognitive therapy theory has assumed that negative schemas underpin negative thoughts and the other elements of 'vicious cycle' functioning. A schema is 'hypothesised to be a general cognitive structure in which experiences, memories, attitudes and beliefs connected with a cluster of generalised meaning gather' (Wills, 2009a: 28). Though schemas can be positive and negative, in cognitive therapy literature the term is usually reserved for beliefs and assumptions connected with problematic functioning and are usually represented by negative core beliefs and unhelpful assumptions (see Figure 2.3 in the case example below). Core beliefs and unhelpful assumptions generally occur in simple declarative language and thus have a rather inflexible nature. This may be because they were learnt in childhood and have been encoded in the type of 'black and white' language that typifies the earlier stages of child development. Schemas are probably best understood as networks of psychological response and are usually reckoned as less conscious than thoughts. If they were encoded in very early experience, they may have little linguistic content. Clients sometimes report associated body sensations; for example, one client whom, it turned out, had been abandoned in a wet nappy found that she was unaccountably triggered by wet skin. These reactions are therefore harder to track down and identify. They may also be very difficult to change. They may not be amenable to change by methods that use language developed at a later developmental stage than when encoding took place. Though the schema concept seems highly plausible and evidence for it may be inferred, it has been problematic to show that schemas exist in other than state-dependent form (Wills, 2009a). If the emergence of depressive schemas is dependent on the person being depressed, they cannot therefore be demonstrated as *pre-existing* phenomena and therefore a vulnerability factor for depression. Young et al. (2003) have developed a longer-term version of cognitive therapy that can be applied to 'schema-driven problems' – a term with many advantages over 'personality disorder'. They describe how they established the existence of the schemas described in their approach from clinical insight and questionnaire development. Young et al. (2003) have also pointed out that their 'early maladaptive schemas' often cluster into 'modes' – a concept with some similarities to and differences from that described by Beck (1996). Arntz and van Genderen (2009) offer an intriguing analysis of how Young's modes of 'Critical Parent', 'Detached Protector', 'Abandoned Child', 'Angry Child' and the weaker 'Healthy Adult' interact in borderline personality disorder. Now that solid evidence has emerged for the efficacy of schema therapy with borderline clients (Arntz and van Genderen, 2009), there are likely to be renewed efforts to demonstrate how these schemas and modes actually operate. It is, however, not the first time that cognitive therapists might say that they know much more about how rather than why their treatments work (see later comments on research status). In the absence of firmer validation, it may be wise to regard any hypothesised negative schema with caution. There is a real danger of reification; that is, a therapist may imply that schemas have a 'thing-like' reality so that clients could easily assume they 'have them', thus therapy may reinforce aspects of the client's negative beliefs.

Cognitive therapy and CBT are sometimes criticised for lacking a grand narrative underpinning its theory. Beck has actually been happy to call himself a 'pragmatist' (Goode, 2000). I have argued elsewhere that a possible candidate for a grand narrative role may lie in an evolutionary perspective (Wills, 2009a). An evolutionary perspective underpins Beck's (1996) approach to personality disorders and Gilbert's (2009) to self-compassion, but we still await a comprehensively developed evolutionary perspective on CBT.

How Client Problems are Conceptualised

A case formulation – shown as a 'map'-style longitudinal diagram in Figure 2.3 in the case example below – aims to provide a chart of the client's problems based on the theoretical principles described above. This chart then serves to guide goals for therapy and treatment (Wills, 2009a: 87–91). Different ways of mapping out and presenting formulations have developed but they mainly consist of the same essential elements, described by Dudley and Kuyken (2006) as the 'five Ps':

1 Presenting issues.
2 Predisposing factors: underlying historical factors, e.g. childhood and other trauma.
3 Precipitating factors: triggers for current problems, e.g. difficulties in relationships or at work.
4 Perpetuating factors: e.g. 'vicious cycles' patterns.
5 Protective factors: e.g. strengths.

The most commonly used tradition for presenting formulations is the longitudinal diagram (Beck, 1995). The other main tradition is that of a written 'narrative' formulation, either in a short 'snapshot' format (Persons, 2008) or in the form of a longer 'story' (Johnstone and Dallos, 2006). The choice of format usually depends on the context of use; for example, notes for a file, a longer report for an academic or other presentation. For everyday work I personally favour a combination of diagrammatic and short narrative format, with occasional resort to longer narrative form. Diagrammatic and narrative formats related to the case study are presented in the case example below.

A written narrative can make explicit what is implicit in a diagram, especially when as a process it is usually abbreviated by the representation of an arrow. It may be easier for a client to challenge a more explicit notion so that the formulation can be made subject to modification. A client may agree that her childhood experiences have influenced the current problem but may see *how* that has happened differently from the therapist.

The Concept of Applications of Cognitive Therapy

Cognitive therapy varies depending on what it is applied to. One can now readily find generic formulations, treatment guidelines and protocols for specific, often DSM (*Diagnostic and Statistical Manual of the American Psychiatric Association*)-based, psychological problems. This has led to a common misunderstanding that cognitive therapy is based on psychiatric 'labelling' and narrow treatment options. The diagnostic guidelines themselves, however, are consensually derived lists of common symptoms that occur together. The danger again lies in reification – taking that list to mean more than it actually does – rather than in the list itself. Readers may be surprised by the passages where the DSM describes its exhaustive and careful processes of consultation. Diagnostic categories are tested to see how much commonality of outlook is generated when therapists look at the same cases. Even the best agreement levels, however, are around 80 per cent – that means that a lot of people do not fit them so well. In most situations where they are used – other than in highly controlled research studies – these formulations and protocols are offered as starting points from which therapists can find ideas for understanding and addressing clients' problems. Formulation and treatment must be tailored to the individual client (Persons, 2008). There is no 'CBT Stasi' that tells therapists how they should achieve the resulting idiographic treatment.

Practical Applications

The Therapeutic Relationship

The seemingly simple phrase 'therapeutic relationship' is the seed of much misunderstanding within the therapy field. The root meaning of 'therapy' is that of 'making things better' or 'healing'. When it becomes an adjective – therapeutic – however, two meanings – a relationship linked to therapy, and, a relationship that is in itself healing – that are often confused seem to emerge, as described below.

A Relationship Linked to Doing Therapy

Surveying the current psychotherapy field one is immediately struck by a great diversity of concepts and practices. Most practices, but not all (e.g. self-help), involve a treatment agent and a client/clients. The diversity of methods, however, makes it difficult to craft a definition of the relationship that is robust enough to cover them all. This can make it all too tempting to assert that how others see that relationship is 'wrong', or in some cases that other therapy models 'have no therapeutic relationship'. Beck and Emery (1985: 173) are clear that 'a sound therapeutic relationship' is an essential principle of cognitive therapy without which 'the techniques and procedures of cognitive therapy are unlikely to work' (Beck and Emery, 1985: 173). Beck et al.'s (1979: 45) early[2] description of the therapeutic relationship uses Rogerian language: 'The general characteristics of the therapist that facilitate the application of cognitive therapy ... include warmth, accurate empathy and genuineness.' Beck agrees with Rogers that such therapist qualities are necessary but argues that they are not sufficient for therapeutic change. The therapeutic relationship in cognitive therapy should be collaborative. Collaboration is probably best seen as combining the therapist's 'expertise about people in general ... with the client's expertise about her own life' (Wills, 2009a: 123). Expertise is not arrogance. I once worked in a medical setting seeing some clients with rare illnesses of which I knew little. I came to see my 'expertise' in this situation as 'wanting to know' about their condition and how it felt to them so that we might work things out together.

Some have criticised cognitive therapy for its supposedly unsophisticated concept of the therapeutic relationship, for example not including a notion of transference. Beck et al. (1979: 58–60) did include a brief discussion of 'transference' and 'counter-transference' in which they note that such transactions can be treated as cognitive distortions. Later publications (Beck et al., 2004) have, however, mainly used the term when considering the treatment of personality problems. Other authors have continued to use the transference and counter-transference in relation to all types of cognitive therapy (Safran and Segal, 1990; Leahy, 2001; Sanders and Wills, 2005; Gilbert and Leahy, 2007). It would be true to say that they have tended to do this in terms different from standard psychodynamic accounts. Cognitive therapists have been more inclined to see that client 'resistance' is quite widespread and the best way to deal with it is via an understanding of the therapist's own schema-driven counter-transference reaction to them

---

[2]The book was actually based on the manual used for the first trials of cognitive therapy.

(Leahy, 2001). This does not, however, add up to a view that all therapy is ultimately about 'working through' the client's transference to the therapist. Even psychodynamic therapists have quite wide differences on the nature and extent of transference effects (Safran and Muran, 2000). If we follow Strupp and Binder's (1984: 143) definition that it is the client's 'proclivity for enacting emotional conflicts through the relationship to the therapist' and do not require that it be seen in all therapeutic interaction or that it only stems from early childhood, there is no barrier to reconceptualising these effects in cognitive terms and using cognitive therapy to deal with them. It might be less complicated to subsume the concepts of transference and counter-transference under a generally interpersonally sensitive and informed version of cognitive therapy (Wills, 2008).

A Relationship that is in Itself Healing

When I began work in the medical context discussed above, I was at first worried by my lack of medical knowledge. However, I found that the patients responded very well to my willingness to find out *with* them. They often experienced a 're-moralisation' effect similar to that observed early in successful therapy (Ilardi and Craighead, 1994). My intervention was healing for them in a way that was different from, but compatible with, that of the doctors. As cognitive therapy has developed, it has paid increasing attention to these more interpersonal aspects of practice (Wills, 2008). Leahy (2001) highlights aspects of CBT itself that can disrupt therapy, for example inflexible agenda setting. If 'caught' these disruptions can be worked through in a way that then actually improves the therapeutic relationship. Some clients, for example, are vulnerable to criticism and may be hurt by an inadvertently clumsy therapist intervention. The therapist may then focus on the sense of awkwardness that may arise between him and the client and use 'immediacy' to explore that awkwardness (Wills, 2008). Sensitively handled, this is a type of valuable learning experience that is much less likely to occur in everyday social life. Gilbert and Leahy (2007) have emphasised how attachment theory can inform the interpersonal perspective in CBT – in a sense, clients can explore these awkward but valuable moments from the 'secure base' of the relationship. Wills (2008) has shown how vital interpersonal material is often contained in formulations and can be used to good therapeutic effect. Clients vulnerable to criticism may well see other people as hostile but may be able to find evidence to disconfirm that belief in the sensitive therapist's open behaviour. Readers may note that this interpersonally sensitive perspective on cognitive therapy does not necessarily imply departing from using relatively traditional cognitive therapy techniques.

Strategies for Treatment

Strategies for treatment can be regarded as general treatment aims that are operationalised by more specific treatment techniques. We have seen above how the interventions are guided and informed by his formulation. All cognitive therapy interventions should in fact be *formulation-driven* so that the formulation becomes a working document that informs all aspects of the case (Persons, 2008). As the focus of therapy often shifts and develops, the formulation must be regarded as both provisional and amendable. Cognitive therapy aims, initially at least, to be *relatively short term* – that is, less than 20 sessions (for a longer discussion, see Wills, 2009a: 105–108). This aspiration has important knock-on effects on other aspects of the model – towards relatively pronounced foci on being *goal-oriented, problem-solving, structured, directional*[3] and *present time-oriented*. I have made liberal use of the word 'relatively' here because cognitive therapists have increasingly argued for the desirability of flexible responses to individual clients (Beck, 1995; Wills, 2008). Even Beck et al.'s early publication, for example, noted that 'exquisite sensitivity' is needed to 'titrate' structure according to the individual needs of clients (1979: 556). Beck has also stressed the desirability of eliciting feedback on how the client is experiencing therapy on an ongoing basis. He also derived the well-known measure of the Beck Depression Inventory (BDI) as another way of keeping therapy on track. The BDI also offers sound ways of monitoring hopelessness and suicidal intent – an area where Beck's work has made a strong contribution (Wills, 2009a). Beck has also devised a number of other important measures, for example, on anxiety and obsessive-compulsive disorder. Two final and related strategies come in the uses of *educational input* and *homework*. Beck has said that he hopes a distinct cognitive therapy will eventually 'melt away' leaving only its most effective features behind for all psychotherapy (Salkovskis, 1996b). This development may already be happening in the instance of the homework principle as the argument grows for regarding homework as a 'common factor' increasingly seen in virtually all models (Kazantzis and Ronan, 2006).

Major treatment techniques

Cognitive therapy is known as having an extensive range of techniques and methods. Listing them all here would make for dull reading. I therefore propose to cover the main *areas* of method, exemplified by representative techniques and relating to the case example below.

Turning to *cognitive interventions* first, various ways for lessening the hold of negative thinking and helping the client to access more functional thinking styles have been developed (Leahy, 2003). Traditional techniques for doing this usually follow a sequence of identifying, evaluating and modifying such thoughts (Beck, 1995). As identification has been covered in the theory section, we proceed here by looking at evaluation and modification. We should start by realising that cognitive therapy is best seen as a constructivist enterprise because the evidence pertinent to human experiences is seldom fully

---

[3]For an argument supporting this term, see Wills (2009a: 111).

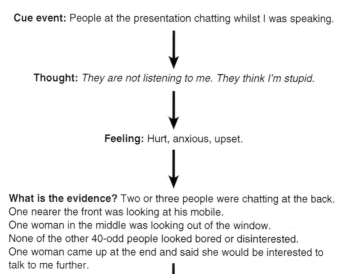

Cue event: People at the presentation chatting whilst I was speaking.

Thought: *They are not listening to me. They think I'm stupid.*

Feeling: Hurt, anxious, upset.

What is the evidence? Two or three people were chatting at the back.
One nearer the front was looking at his mobile.
One woman in the middle was looking out of the window.
None of the other 40-odd people looked bored or disinterested.
One woman came up at the end and said she would be interested to
talk to me further.

Review of original thought: The feedback from the meeting was actually
quite mixed. They mostly were listening and I don't really know what they
thought of me but there is no real evidence that they thought I am stupid.

Outcome: Feel much less hurt. Next time – I can try to stay with it more.

Figure 2.2   Reviewing a negative thought

available. Leahy (2003: 2) puts it well when he says: 'The therapist asks the patient to look at the preponderance of the evidence to reach tentative conclusions and to remain sceptical about all ways of knowing ... the cognitive therapist should not become a "cheer leader" for positive thinking.'

The process of reviewing a negative thought – in this case written on a white board – is shown in Figure 2.2.

Some of my clients now take mobile phone photographs of white board reviews, but a more usual format would be to use one of the many available 'thought records' or 'mood logs' (Wills, 2008). Whilst I often find it helpful to suggest that clients simply look at negative thoughts written on a white board to begin with, thought records and other cognitive interventions can usefully reinforce such work. These written methods usually offer ways of collecting a wider degree of evidence pertaining to the trigger event or situation. The client's currently available evidence may be restricted by the narrowing effects of schema-driven processing, general cognitive biases or deficits in concentration brought on by problems such as depression. It is very important that the evidence collected is credible and emotionally convincing to clients. Attempts to gather evidence can be hampered when cognitive restructuring is focused on a reaction that the client does not particularly want to change, in which case goals may need reconsideration. In practice, cognitive restructuring may be harder and may require more persistence and over-learning than was sometimes described in early cognitive therapy texts. Judith Beck (1995: 128) has a useful checklist of common problems and solutions for improving working with thought records. For some, however, cognitive restructuring is becoming a less favoured intervention in CBT and there has been a lively debate about whether methods for changing the content of thoughts are really very effective (see Wills, 2009a: 163). In my view, the answer to this question is likely to be complicated; it may well be that thought records work by helping clients to 'decentre' their thinking from negative thoughts, the act of 'playing' with the content of thoughts may loosen attention to them. Neither is it yet clear whether the ineffectiveness of cognitive restructuring shown in some studies is because they really are not effective or because too little attention has so far been given to developing good practice and training guidelines for implementing it.

As noted above, cognitions may sometimes be more easily identified and modified via imagery techniques. Images based on current functioning or the client's history can be 'unpacked' for their underlying meaning. Sometimes simple methods of merely closing down and replaying images can lead to significant shifts in feelings associated with them (Beck et al., 1985). Sometimes more elaborate exercises to restructure images are used to offer alternative perspectives on experiences such as childhood trauma, and imagery work may become part of wider efforts to modify maladaptive core beliefs and schemas, for example, empowering a child to take self-protective steps in a traumatic scene (Stopa, 2009).

A new dimension has been added to cognitive interventions by techniques to help clients change the way they pay attention to thoughts. Although Beck noted the role of 'fixation' (problematic attention) in cognitive processing in his early work, a more elaborated view of the role of attention in psychopathology and treatment has only emerged relatively recently. Development of ways of working with attention has followed research showing that it is attention to thoughts rather than their content that is more problematic in problems such as rumination and obsessions (Wells, 2008). Wells describes how ways of learning to detoxify thoughts by paying 'detached mindfulness' (DM) to them can effectively lessen their negative impact. DM overlaps with the concept of mindfulness used elsewhere in CB and other therapies but also has some important differences: it focuses on meta-awareness rather than on present-moment awareness. DM is closer to using specific techniques (Wells, 2008: 71–88) than to adapting ongoing practice of meditation. It does, however, have the same general aim as other mindfulness perspectives: helping clients to not only change the content of their negative thoughts but also the way they pay attention to them (Baer, 2006; Crane, 2009).

Different methods have been advocated for working with deeper levels of cognition such as unhelpful assumptions, core beliefs and schemas (Padesky and Greenberger, 1995). Essentially, these methods use adapted forms of Guided Discovery through Socratic Dialogue (Wills, In press). Such methods usually work by 'stretching out' inflexible belief statements that are in any case quite mood dependent. Behavioural experiments have great utility in many areas of cognitive therapy (Bennett-Levy et al., 2004) and to some extent stand at the crossroad between cognitive and behavioural interventions. Cognitivists argue that they work by facilitating cognitive change and, to no one's surprise, behaviourists argue for facilitation of behavioural change. Pragmatists tend to think that they can work quite nicely as one or the other or both (Wills, 2009a).

Though *behavioural intervention* methods such as activity scheduling have been included in cognitive therapy from the start, there is a new interest in behavioural methods as they have been revived in wider CBT in the previously unlikely territories of mindfulness (Linehan, 1993) and interpersonal factors (Tsai et al., 2008). Activity scheduling has been widened and deepened by contemporary approaches to behavioural activation (Martell et al., 2001), and is especially important in the context of IAPT (Richards, 2010). Most behavioural interventions are ultimately underpinned by traditional functional analysis focused on what maintains behaviour in a rewarding (or unrewarding) environment (Wills, 2008). Functional analysis can also be used to examine the benefit to effort ratio involved when clients have adopted compulsive ways of coping with work – often involving 'workaholic' hours – helping them to establish a better-balanced week and improved sleep. Other behaviourally based interventions may also be relatively easily integrated into cognitive therapy. Assertiveness techniques are useful in both goal achievement and in building self-concept. Exposure methods help clients to accept and work through anxiety feelings. They can also be conceptualised as behavioural experiments testing the cognition 'I can't stand it'. Alford and Beck (1997) have argued that behavioural techniques in cognitive therapy are primarily used to disconfirm negative cognitions and beliefs. This seems a slightly inflexible approach to me, and I perhaps prove myself even more of pragmatist than Beck by suggesting that they can serve behavioural and/or cognitive goals equally well.

Overcoming Obstacles to Client Progress

One of the best pieces of advice that I was given in my teenage years was 'Never believe your own propaganda'. There has occasionally been a propagandistic image of CB therapists with smart methods carrying all before them – smart technicians who can 'retrain' brains like servicing machines. When talking with experienced CB therapists, I have not found anything like this self-confidence – most admit that the work is hard and full of twists and turns. Obstacles and 'resistance', it turns out, are normal. In my supervision work, I find that there are two main areas of difficulty that regularly crop up: the way that clients react to either the techniques or the structure of CBT, and in the form of interpersonal problems within the therapeutic relationship.

First, different types of clients respond differently to different CB techniques and methods. Some will take up and run with thought records almost straight away, whereas others just never seem to get them. It is a mistake to give up too soon on any particular method, and sometimes non-response should be taken as a cue for persistence. Problems like depression really do disrupt normal problem-solving routines so that over-practice may be needed to establish normal practice. Another reason for being careful to avoid premature abandonment of a technique is that what works on one day may not work on another and vice versa. Indeed, clients often benefit from having a variety of things they can try in difficult situations: I sometimes offer clients the metaphor that 'if you are going round St Andrew's, you may need more than a putter' (Wills, 2008).[4] Persistence can, of course, be overdone so that at some stage we just have to recognise that 'different strokes suit different folks'.

Some clients react badly to structure so that it is generally wise to 'wear structure quite lightly' and as noted before be prepared to titrate the dose accordingly. From another angle some clients may get too comfortable with the structure and may even use it to avoid certain issues and emotions from arising.

Because time for therapy may be short, the structured elicitation of feedback can be very helpful. This sets up a rolling review system that aims to detect and overcome obstacles to client progress at the earliest stage. It is difficult for clients to criticise therapists or therapy and the feedback system should be reinforced by regular reviews, say after 6 and 12 sessions. Persons (2008) offers a useful review format that allows the therapist to establish a parsimonious statement on the mechanisms underpinning the client's problems and then explore such questions as are shown in Table 2.2; the answers are supplied in relation to the short narrative formulation shown in Table 2.3 as part of the case example below.

The therapist's interpersonal sensitivity is crucial in overcoming obstacles and 'resistance' to change. Leahy (2001) has written powerfully on resistance and how an understanding of 'counter-transference' is especially helpful in overcoming it. A problematic situation can arise when clients are especially looking for the 'validation' that comes from empathic listening and therapist sensitivity before they are ready for change. This may look like resistance or unwillingness to change to a therapist and additionally may play straight into a 'therapist schema' such as 'I have to succeed with all my clients'.

---

[4]Or similar age and gender appropriate equivalents!

Table 2.2   Review questions

Review Questions
Is the client accepting current interventions?
Is/are the hypothesised underlying mechanism/s changing as expected?
Does/do the mechanism/s and symptoms co-vary as expected?
Are symptoms remitting?
Is the therapy relationship working?

The interpersonal perspective on therapy has been particularly helpful in understanding how 'therapeutic ruptures' can actually enhance therapeutic progress if handled sensitively. The problems that clients bring to therapy can obviously be reflected in the therapeutic process itself at times. The case example illustrates how the client's sensitivity to criticism showed itself in sessions and required the therapist to monitor for its occurrence and to handle it appropriately at times. The necessary sensitivity can be particularly well fostered by supervision, as interpersonal rather than technical problems may more regularly feature in cognitive therapy supervision (Wills, 2009b). As a final thought to this section, I wish to agree with Persons (2008) that treatment failure is more common and normal than is often reported. As the Cognitive Therapy Scale (Young and Beck, 1988) notes, the therapist can do all the right things and still not be successful. Human change processes retain an aspect of mystery and we would all do well to remember that.

Case Example: Alan

Assessment

Presenting issues: Alan was a 44-year-old married man and worked as an IT specialist in a college. He had always worried about work but had recently become very anxious and depressed about a real threat of redundancy. He had gone 'off sick' from work for three weeks but had just returned and now wanted help with settling back into work. It proved difficult to return his referral call because, it turned out, he was staying late at work most days. At assessment he met the criteria for both Major Depressive Episode and Generalised Anxiety Disorder, scoring as 'severe' on the Beck depression and anxiety measures. He did not like his job and berated himself for moving from another college where he had a 'cushy number'. Despite this he continued to ruminate over losing the job and to work very late, with resulting fatigue and poor sleep.

(Continued)

(Continued)

Formulation

Precipitating factors: Alan's wife had wanted to be nearer her ageing mother. He agreed to move from his 'cushy number' job for her but then blamed her for the way things had worked out. When problems arose at work Alan threw lots of energy at them, worked extra hours and went more than the extra mile to find solutions. He had a promotion but this had made him nervous because he felt 'at the edge of his competence' in his new post. He said that 'IT is a young man's game' and found his younger peers at his new level to be more competitive – sometimes resorting to 'bullying' to get their way. He thought that 'there are a lot of predators where I work – I don't think anyone would tell me if some one were sneaking up on me.' He'd felt this even before the possibility of redundancies emerged, and when this was announced it fuelled new fears, finally tipping him into excessive anxiety, chronic worry and depression.

Predisposing factors: Alan was the only child of older parents who were both in their 40s when he was born. He described his parents as 'easy going', but it became increasingly clear that this really meant 'laissez-faire'. When Alan was struggling academically and being bullied at primary school, he did not experience his parents as helping in any way. He eventually concluded that 'No one will help me much' (core belief) and 'I'll be OK as long as I can sort out all my own problems' (assumption). He did gradually manage to get on top of his schoolwork and found ways of deflecting the bullies. The problems repeated themselves at secondary school but this was a time when Alan's strengths as a science student were emerging and once again he overcame his problems by 'keeping my head down and doing sheer hard work.' This hard-working style served him well, but he also suffered from dysthymic periods and a full-blown depression in his early 20s. However, he had been well, with a stable marriage and two children, until the recent threat of redundancy.

Perpetuating factors: Tracing out a vicious cycle for an incident in his office worked well in socialising Alan to the CB model. Going over an incident when he'd felt criticised at a meeting revealed that only two out of ten people at the meeting had said things that could be construed as critical, whereas others at the meeting had said neutral or positive comments that he hadn't taken on board (Wills, 2008: 44). Alan had originally construed this situation as 'they were out to get me' and his behavioural response was escape. By 'storming out' of work he may well have been putting himself more at risk of what he feared (see Figure 2.3). When stressed he tended to catastrophise and then go into 'over-response' mode. He could take this strategy to extremes, working late into the night but only really succeeded in tiring himself out and making himself more vulnerable to anxiety, worry and depression.

Protective factors: Alan had two major environmental protective factors: his home situation and his achievements at work. Despite the way things had worked out with the job, he realised that it had been unfair to blame his wife, who loved him and was supportive of him. In addition, he was naturally reflective, psychologically minded and was eventually motivated to work on his situation by reading self-help material and completing homework assignments. (See Figure 2.4 for Alan's short narrative formulation.)

EARLY AND LATER EXEPRIENCE:

'Laissez-faire' parents; Did not offer encouragement in relation to his schooling; Did not offer protection when he was bullied at both primary and secondary school; 'They could have done much more'; Alan was able to succeed due to his own efforts but has also now been 'bullied' at work too.

SCHEMAS AND CORE BELIEFS:

VULNERABILITY SCHEMA: *I AM WEAK; PEOPLE WILL NOT HELP ME MUCH; THE WORLD IS COMPETITIVE AND HOSTILE.*

UNHELPFUL ASSUMPTIONS:

I SHOULD RELY ON MYSELF; IF I CAN SOLVE MY PROBLEMS BY MYSELF, I WON'T HAVE TO RISK THE HELP OF OTHERS; IF I RELY ON OTHERS, I WILL BE VUNERABLE.

TRIGGERS: Threat of redundancy (distal);

Critical comments at meeting (proximal)

Negative thought: They are out to get me.

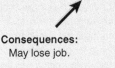

Consequences:
May lose job.

Emotions:
Fear, sadness, anger.

Behaviour: Storms out of the meeting.

Figure 2.3 Alan's longitudinal formulation

Treatment

Therapeutic interventions: Alan's initial reaction to the cognitive model was uncertain. This was partly because he disliked his job so much that he felt ambivalent about striving to cope with it. This led to a refinement of the goals for treatment by redefining 'coping at work' as a short-term strategy and adding a new longer-term goal of searching for a new job. He was able to use material from David Burns' book

(Continued)

(Continued)

Alan's problems are underpinned by strategies of excessive reliance on himself that were fostered by being an only child of 'laissez-faire' parents. When his parents seemed unable to help him during crucially difficult phases at school – like when he was bullied – he gradually came to believe that only he himself could be relied on to get him through difficult situations. He learnt that by 'sheer hard work' he could overcome many of his difficulties. This strategy of relying on himself to work very hard works well whilst things are 'going well' but can backfire at times of crisis – such as the current threat of redundancy since which he has gone into 'overdrive' exhausting himself to the point where he feels tired and depressed. The strategy can also have counterproductive effects on his work performance – he can become 'touchy' and 'tetchy' with colleagues – and on his social support networks – he has a few good friends but at these times sees much less of them. All these factors increase his sense of insecurity and of having no one to turn to. This is a bit hurtful to his wife who feels that he seems to underestimate her capacity to help and support him.

Figure 2.4   Short narrative formulation for Alan

The Feeling Good Handbook (1999) to help him cope better at work by learning to use assertiveness techniques such as the 'broken record'. Whilst he was still absorbing this book, we used a modified form of behavioural activation (Martell et al., 2001) to re-balance his daily schedule by reducing his pattern of overworking and by including regular small pleasurable activities in each day, such as spending more time with his children. As his mood lifted he seemed more open to trying cognitive interventions and began to use the 'mood log' (Burns, 1999), a modified version of the thought record, to help him deal with negative moods. At first he said his alternative balanced thoughts made intellectual sense but did not change his feelings much. Towards the end of the 17-session treatment, the therapist encouraged him to look at some of his deeper assumptions and core beliefs (Sanders and Wills, 2005), particularly focusing on 'No one will help me'. Therapist and client devised behavioural experiments ranging from easy to more difficult tasks to request help to test this belief. These tasks seemed not to help much until they focused on the context of approaching work peers for help. One colleague was unexpectedly frank and told him that he thought that Alan would lose his job but gave some advice on how to 'get out in good order'. Though deeply shocked, Alan liked the honesty of this response and also found that the advice proved helpful. The incident marked a 'turning point' after which both mood logs and experiments seemed to make much more sense to him. At the end of therapy he filled out a 'blueprint' (Sanders and Wills, 2005) to remind him of what he'd learnt in therapy. He summed up his learning about asking for help as follows: 'It's not that some people will help and others won't. Most people will help at least a bit, but how much depends on a lot of other things, what the situation is or how they are that day. You just have to ask for what you want as clearly as you can and then work with what you get.' The blueprint also asked how he would react to problems in the future – he wrote that he would first use mood logs and then if they proved insufficient he would call the therapist.

CONCLUSION

Cognitive therapy with Alan consisted of two sessions of assessment and formulation, followed by 14 treatment sessions and one follow-up session six months after the last treatment session (see Table 2.3 for Alan's review questions). Alan's Beck scores improved quickly at first but then reached a plateau and only reached non-problematic levels towards the end of therapy. He had an unsurprising resurgence of anxiety at the time of the redundancy announcements but was pro-active in searching for work and eventually found a more sympathetic employer. His wife was exceptionally supportive at this time. She attended some sessions and helped Alan formulate various plans for the future. They felt that their relationship had been 'tested in the fire' and survived. He reported continued better functioning at home and work at six-month follow up and was known to be neither anxious nor depressed three years after treatment.

Table 2.3   Review questions for Alan

Review questions	Review for A after session 6
Is the client accepting current interventions?	A has sometimes taken on too much homework and needs to 'peg back' at times. On the plus side he has the capacity to persist with the 'mood logs' even though he has found them only partially helpful so far.
Is/are the hypothesised underlying mechanism/s changing as expected?	A has been able to modify his negative thinking somewhat and goes into 'overdrive' somewhat less than before.
Does/do the mechanism/s and symptoms co-vary as expected?	As negative thinking and being 'too busy' have lessened, BDI scores have reduced – though medication may also be a factor.
Are symptoms remitting?	See above – BDI scores initially dropped (from 30+ to 20+) but then have 'flat lined' in recent weeks.
Is the therapy relationship working?	Yes – though we need to keep working on the difference between collaboration and deference.

Research Status

Psychotherapy research is rarely defined as a 'user-friendly' branch of knowledge. Psychological change is subject to many variables and is therefore highly complex. Findings are often contested, especially from the standpoint of opposing models and ideologies, often giving the impression that almost all models can assemble some evidence but none can land a killer blow to suggest superiority over the others. In a sense, most writers end up devising a narrative on research efficacy and then try to fit what evidence is available to it – hopefully in a way that at least excludes the worst kind of bias. This is my aim here. The headline news on the efficacy of Beck's cognitive therapy is, in my view, that *the initial explosion of positive reports has given way to a more complex view that includes continuing generally good but more mixed results in many areas and also a number of important theoretical and practical challenges.*

Butler et al. (2006) present a recent and high-quality meta-analytic review of the model's efficacy. The overall review is of CBT, though results are sometimes broken down into behavioural and cognitive elements. The meta-analysis pulls together other high-quality meta-analytic studies across 16 different psychiatric disorders. The results 'suggest that cognitive therapy is highly effective for adult and adolescent unipolar depression, generalised anxiety disorder, panic with and without agoraphobia, social phobia, PTSD, and childhood depressive and anxiety disorders' (Butler et al., 2006: 28). Comparisons with other forms of treatment, including medication, generally show cognitive therapy or CBT as equivalent or slightly superior – though the limitations of meta-analysis are accepted in relation to these findings.

Although Beck's model has spread to other areas, depression may still be regarded as its essential testing ground and will therefore be the main focus of this brief review. The research story shows interesting twists and turns as the model strives to demonstrate effectiveness in everyday practice as well as in clinical trials.

Beck et al.'s (1979) seminal book on the cognitive therapy of depression reported studies that showed the therapy had efficacy equal to that of anti-depressant medication after treatment and had a better relapse prevention record at follow-up. The results of such studies can, however, be contaminated by 'allegiance' effects (all the researchers want them to succeed) and by the 'Hawthorne effect' (the excitement and specialness of an intensive study transfers to its participants). Large-scale clinical trials aim to bypass these problems. When the well-known US National Institute for Mental Health (NIMH) study of the 1980s tested cognitive therapy against interpersonal therapy (originally designed as a placebo) and anti-depressant medication; few differences in effectiveness emerged. As might be expected, this was a disappointing result for cognitive therapists, and the evidence has been much chewed over. Beck withdrew support for the project before its commencement because he was not satisfied with the arrangements for therapist training. The NIMH trial was multi-site and there is evidence that where cognitive therapy training was better developed, its results were superior to the other conditions (Hollon et al., 1996). Larger-scale, especially meta-analytic, studies tend in any case to show humble results because aggregation tends to flatten the differences between approaches. Although some critics glory in the finding that 'all therapies are equally effective' the small effect sizes of many meta-analytic studies would also justify the statement that all are equally ineffective! This raises the interesting question of why the findings of trials frequently do not generalise to everyday practice? One factor could be the specialised training element already mentioned; another is that everyday practitioners cannot usually exercise the degree of control over entry into therapy that clinical trials do. Nevertheless, in the real world one can argue that the most serviceable models of practice will be the ones that can be disseminated most easily. This surely is the justifiable gamble of IAPT to democratise therapy (Bennett-Levy et al., 2010).

The IAPT project is, however, a context in which another challenge to cognitive therapy may be tested. Most researchers do regard the evidence for cognitive therapy effectiveness as quite strong, though there are still large questions over *how* it works. Like most models, cognitive therapy has a number of elements so it could be that some elements are more effective than others. This doubt about change mechanisms partly reflects another aspect of research status: the extent to which there is research backing for fundamental concepts. One problematic theoretical aspect of Beck's model – the schema concept – was noted above. On the practical side, efforts have been made to 'dismantle' the different elements of cognitive therapy so that its most effective elements can be distinguished (Gortner et al., 1998). The bad news for cognitive therapy was that in these reviews behavioural interventions of the cognitive therapy of depression achieved as much change as the whole package of cognitive therapy and requires less training. Some have gone on to argue that it may not be necessary to modify negative thoughts (Longmore and Worrell, 2007) – an argument potentially fatal to cognitive therapy. Needless to say, this argument has not been uncontested (Carey and Mansell, 2009). I personally believe that de-emphasising cognitive restructuring is just the sort of wrong conclusion that can so easily be drawn from large-scale studies where the richness of variation in therapeutic exchanges is rolled flat. Another challenge to cognitive restructuring interventions such as thought records has come from those who argue that they are less effective than 'behavioural experiments' because the latter are more experientially based (Bennett-Levy et al., 2004). It has also been pointed out that there has been very little process research on how cognitive therapy techniques – like thought records – work or do not work (Wills, 2010), so that even basic heuristic 'good practice' rules for using techniques are usually only supported by anecdote. As the official CBT research field seems entirely absorbed by big grant-backed randomised control trials, it seems to me that if CBT practitioners are ever to benefit from process research, they themselves will probably have to do that research. A clarion call for cognitive therapists to be more pro-active in testing and owning their own model seems a good note to end this chapter on.

Suggested Further Reading

Beck, A.T. (2005) 'The current status of cognitive therapy: A 40-year retrospective', *American Psychologist*, 62(9): 953–59.

Beck, A.T., Shaw, B., Emery, G. and Rush, A.J. (1979) *Cognitive Therapy of Depression*. New York: Guilford.

Persons, J.B., Gross, J.J., Etkin, M.S. and Madan, S.K. (1996) 'Psychodynamic therapists' reservations about cognitive behavior therapy: Implications for training and practice', *Journal of Psychotherapy Practice and Research*, 5: 202–212.

Weishaar, M.E. (1993) 'Criticisms and rebuttals', in M.E. Weishaar (Ed.), *Aaron T. Beck*. London: Sage. pp. 99–132.

Wills, F. (2009) *Beck's Cognitive Therapy: Distinctive Features*. London: Routledge.

References

Alford, B. and Beck, A.T (1997) *The Integrative Power of Cognitive Therapy*. New York: Guilford.

Arntz, A. and van Genderen, H. (2009) *Schema Therapy for Borderline Personality Disorder*. Chichester: Wiley.

Baer, R. (2006) *Mindfulness-based Treatment Approaches*. San Diego, CA: Elsevier.

Beck, A.T. (1970) 'Cognitive therapy: Nature and relation to behavior therapy', *Behavior Therapy*, 1(2): 184–200.

Beck, A.T. (1976) *Cognitive Therapy and the Emotional Disorders*. Harmondsworth: Penguin.

Beck, A.T. (1996) 'Beyond belief: A theory of modes, personality and psychopathology', in P. Salkovskis (Ed.), *Frontiers of Cognitive Therapy*. New York: Guilford Press. pp. 1–25.

Beck, A.T., Rush, A.J., Shaw, B.F. and Emery, G. (1979) *Cognitive Therapy of Depression*. New York: Guilford Press.

Beck, A.T. and Emery, G., with Greenberg, R. (1985) *Anxiety Disorders and Phobias: A Cognitive Perspective*. New York: Basic Books.

Beck, A.T., Freeman, A.M., David, D.D. and Associates (2004) *Cognitive Therapy of Personality Disorders*, 2nd Edn. New York: Guildford.

Beck, J. (1995) *Cognitive Therapy: Basics and Beyond*. New York: Guilford Press.

Bennett-Levy, J., Butler, G., Fennell, M., Hackman, A., Mueller, M. and Westbrook, D. (2004) *Oxford Guide to Behavioural Experiments*. Oxford: Oxford University Press.

Bennett-Levy, J., Richards, D.A., Farrand, P., Christensen, H., Griffith, K.M., Kavanagh, P.J., Lau, M.A., Proudfoot, J., Ritterband, L., White, J. and Williams, C. (2010) *Oxford Guide to Low Intensity CBT Interventions*. Oxford: Oxford University Press.

Burns, D.D. (1999) *The Feeling Good Handbook*, 2nd Rev. Edn. New York: Penguin.

Butler, A.C., Chapman, J.E., Forman, E.M. and Beck, A.T. (2006) 'The empirical status of cognitive behavioral therapy: A review of meta-analyses', *Clinical Psychology Review*, 26(1): 17–31.

Carey, T.A. and Mansell, W. (2009) 'Show us a behaviour without a cognition and we'll show you a rock rolling down a hill', *The Cognitive Behaviourist*, 2: 123–133.

Clark, D.M. (1996) 'Panic disorder: From theory to therapy', in P.M. Salkovskis (Ed.), *Frontiers of Cognitive Therapy*. New York: Guilford Press. pp. 318–344.

Crane, R. (2009) *Mindfulness-based Cognitive Therapy: Distinctive Features*. London: Routledge.

Dudley, R. and Kuyken, W. (2006) 'Formulation in cognitive-behavioural therapy: There is nothing good or bad but thinking makes it so', in L. Johnstone and R. Dallos (Eds), *Formulation in Psychology and Psychotherapy*. London: Routledge. pp. 17–46.

Fisher, P. and Wells, A. (2009) *Metacognitive Therapy: Distinctive Features*. London: Routledge.

Gilbert, P. (2009) *Compassion-focused Therapy: Distinctive Features*. London: Routledge.

Gilbert, P. and Leahy, R.L. (2007) *The Therapeutic Relationship in the Cognitive Behavioural Psychotherapies*. London: Routledge.

Goode, E. (2000) 'Scientist at work: Aaron. T. Beck: Pragmatist embodies his no-nonsense therapy', *New York Times*, 11 January.

Gortner, E.T., Gollan, J.L., Dobson, K.S. and Jacobson, N.S. (1998) 'Cognitive behavioral treatment for depression: Relapse prevention', *Journal of Consulting and Clinical Psychology*, 62: 377–384.

Harvey, A., Watkins, E., Mansell, W. and Shafran, R. (2004) *Cognitive-behavioural Processes across Psychological Disorders*. Oxford: Oxford University Press.

Hollon, S.D., DeRubeis, R.J. and Evans, M.D. (1996) 'Cognitive therapy in the treatment and prevention of depression', in P.M. Salkovskis (Ed.), *Frontiers of Cognitive Therapy*. New York: Guilford Press. pp. 293–317.

Ilardi, S.S. and Craighead, E.W. (1994) 'The role of non-specific factors in cognitive behavior therapy of depression', *Clinical Psychology: Science and Practice*, 2(1): 138–155.

Ingram, R.E., Miranda, J. and Segal, Z.V. (1998) *Cognitive Vulnerability to Depression*. New York: Guilford Press.

Johnstone, L. and Dallos, R. (2006) *Formulation in Psychology and Psychotherapy*. London: Routledge.

Kazantzis, N. and Ronan, K.R. (2006) 'Can between session (homework) activities be considered a common factor for psychotherapy?', *Journal of Psychotherapy Integration*, 16(2): 189–192.

Leahy, R.L. (2001) *Overcoming Resistance in Cognitive Therapy*. New York: Guilford Press.

Leahy, R.L. (2003) *Cognitive Therapy Techniques*. New York: Guilford Press.

Linehan, M.M. (1993) *Cognitive Behavioral Treatment for Borderline Personality Disorder*. New York: Guilford Press.

Longmore, R.J and Worrell, M. (2007) 'Do we need to challenge thoughts in cognitive behaviour therapy?', *Clinical Psychology Review*, 27: 173–187.

Martell, C., Addis, M.E. and Jacobson, N.S. (2001) *Depression in Context: Strategies for Guided Action*. New York: Norton.

Padesky, C. and Greenberger, D. (1995) *A Clinician's Guide to Mind Over Mood*. New York: Guilford Press.

Persons, J.B. (2008) *The Case Formulation Approach to Cognitive Behavior Therapy*. New York: Guilford.

Rachman, S. (1997) 'The evolution of cognitive behaviour therapy', in D.M. Clark and C.G. Fairburn (Eds), *Science and Practice of Cognitive Behaviour Therapy*. Oxford: Oxford University Press. pp. 27–46.

Rachman, S. (2003) *The Treatment of Obsessions*. Oxford: Oxford University Press.

Richards, D. (2010) 'Behavioural activation', in J. Bennett-Levy, P. Farrand, H. Christensen, K. Griffiths, D. Kavanagh, B. Klein, M.A. Lau, J. Proudfoot, L. Ritterband, J. Whiteand and C. Williams (Eds), *Oxford Guide to Low Intensity Interventions*. Oxford: Oxford University Press. pp. 141–150.

Safran, J.D. and Muran, J.C. (2000) *Negotiating the Therapeutic Alliance*. New York: Guilford.

Safran, J.D. and Segal, Z.V. (1990) *Interpersonal Processes and Cognitive Therapy*. New York: Guilford.

Salkovskis, P. (1996a) 'The cognitive approach to anxiety: Threat beliefs, safety seeking behavior, and the special case of health anxiety and obsessions', in P. Salkovskis (Ed.), *Frontiers of Cognitive Therapy*. New York: Guilford. pp. 48–74.

Salkovskis, P. (1996b) 'Cognitive therapy and Aaron T. Beck', in P. Salkovskis (Ed.), *Frontiers of Cognitive Therapy*. New York: Guilford Press. pp. 532–539.

Sanders, D. and Wills, F. (2005) *Cognitive Therapy: An Introduction,* 2nd Edn. London: Sage.

Stopa, L. (Ed.) (2009) *Imagery and the Threatened Self: Perspective on Mental Imagery and the Self in Cognitive Therapy*. London: Routledge.

Strupp, H.H. and Binder, J.L. (1984) *Psychotherapy in a New Key: A Guide to Time-limited Dynamic Psychotherapy*. New York: Basic Books.

Tsai, M., Kohlenberg, R.J., Kanter, J.W., Kohlenberg, B., Follette, W.C. and Callaghan, G.M. (2008) *A Guide to Functional Analytic Psychotherapy: Awareness, Courage, Love and Behaviorism*. New York: Springer.

Weishaar, M.E. (1993) *Aaron T. Beck*. London: Sage.

Wells, A. (2008) *Metacognitive Therapy for Anxiety and Depression*. New York: Guilford Press.

Wills, F.R. (2008) *Skills for Cognitive Behaviour Counselling and Psychotherapy*. London: Sage.

Wills, F.R. (2009a) *Beck's Cognitive Therapy: Distinctive Features*. London: Routledge.

Wills, F.R. (2009b) 'Crossing the great divide: Supervising CBT counsellors from a non-CBT perspective', in F. Inskipp and B. Proctor (Eds), *The Art, Craft and Tasks of Supervision*, Rev. Edn. Twickenham: Cascade. pp. 193–200.

Wills, F.R. (2010) 'Yada, yada, yada: The missing bit of CBT research'. Paper given at the Annual Conference of the British Association of Behavioural and Cognitive Psychotherapies, Manchester, July.

Wills, F.R. (In press) 'CBT skills', in W. Dryden and M. Townend (Eds). *The Sage CBT Handbook*. London: Sage.

Young, J.E. and Beck, A.T. (1988) *The Cognitive Therapy Scale (Revised)*. Philadelphia, PA: Center for Cognitive Therapy.

Young, J.E., Klosko, J.S. and Weishaar, M.E. (2003) *Schema Focused Therapy: A Practitioners' Guide*. New York: Guilford Press.

THREE   Mindfulness-Based Cognitive Therapy

REBECCA S. CRANE

Historical Development of the Approach

Mindfulness-based cognitive therapy (MBCT) was developed during the late 1990s by cognitive scientists in the UK and Canada (Zindel Segal, Mark Williams and John Teasdale). The decade of clinical and research interest in MBCT since the results of the first MBCT trial were published (Teasdale et al., 2000) have been marked by an international upsurge of interest in clinical approaches based on mindfulness meditation. Developments in the field of MBCT research and clinical practice have been a significant part of this expansion.

The pioneer of integrating mindfulness meditation into contemporary approaches to managing life challenge and developing psychological well-being is Jon Kabat-Zinn, who developed mindfulness-based stress reduction (MBSR) from the late 1980s on, as an approach to complement participants' existing medical care. MBSR is an eight-session skills training course involving intensive training in mindfulness meditation for people with a wide range of physical and psychological conditions. MBSR reached public attention in the late 1990s through the dissemination of research demonstrating its effectiveness (e.g. Kabat-Zinn et al., 1985, 1992, 1998), via a high-profile television programme which followed a group of patients through an MBSR course (Moyers, 1993) and through Kabat-Zinn's first impactful book describing the potential of mindfulness and the MBSR programme (Kabat-Zinn, 1990). All this triggered a groundswell of interest from both the general public and healthcare professionals.

MBSR caught the attention of Segal, Williams and Teasdale as they engaged together in a collaboration to design and develop an approach to target the vulnerability processes which cognitive research has identified as triggering and maintaining depression. Their aim was to design a relapse prevention programme for people who are vulnerable to depression recurrence which could be taken while in remission. Although their original intention had been to develop a group-based cognitive behavioural programme, the MBCT developers became curious about the way in which skills gained through training in mindfulness meditation seem to overlap with the very skills which they deduced would enable participants to work skilfully with the psychological processes causing depression. Furthermore, Kabat-Zinn had a track record in successfully translating mindfulness into an accessible format for ordinary American people. In 1993 Segal, Williams and Teasdale therefore made contact and spent time with Kabat-Zinn and his colleagues at the Center for Mindfulness, Massachusetts.

In the seminal book on MBCT (Segal et al., 2002), the MBCT developers transparently describe the personal and theoretical journey they took as they followed the trail of developing understanding of the aetiology and mechanisms underlying the vulnerabilities they were intending to target, identifying methodologies through which participants could recognise and work with these, evolving all this into a form which could be offered to groups of participants and then testing the efficacy of this new approach in reducing vulnerability and lowering recurrence of depression. Through this process MBCT evolved as a manualised, theoretical integration of mindfulness meditation and cognitive behavioural theory and practice. The form, structure and teaching style of MBCT are closely aligned with MBSR, whist the CBT contribution to the integration informs the way in which the curriculum and learning are fine tuned towards gaining skills in depression prevention. The MBCT developers in collaboration with Jon Kabat-Zinn later published a popular account of the approach for the general public (Williams et al., 2007).

On the basis of the two first randomised controlled trials of MBCT (Teasdale et al., 2000; Ma and Teasdale, 2004) the approach was recommended in 2004 by the UK's best practice advisory board for the NHS – the National Institute for Health and Clinical Excellence (NICE, 2004) – as a treatment of choice for preventing future depression in those individuals who have experienced three or more episodes. There are currently three UK universities (Bangor, Exeter and Oxford) offering Master's level training in delivering MBCT.

Theoretical Underpinnings

Problem Formulation

The development of MBCT is an example of a problem formulation approach to treatment development (Teasdale et al., 2003). The integration of mindfulness with cognitive therapy followed a clear rationale of what the developers expected would be helpful given current data on depression and mindfulness. An account is given below of this in relation to the development of MBCT for its original target: prevention of depressive relapse. It is helpful to bear in mind that using this same problem formulation approach (i.e. programme adaptations made on the basis of understanding the ways in which the MBCT teaching process and curriculum elements interface with the critical variables underlying vulnerability for particular populations and conditions), new versions of MBCT have been developed (see research section below). Whilst there are some specifics which are tailored to working with people vulnerable to depression in the original programme, the broad thrust of the training process is relevant to and has the potential to influence the universal human experience of mental pain.

Depression Recurrence

Major depression is predicted to become the second leading cause of disability worldwide by the year 2020 (Murray and Lopez, 1996). Like other chronic conditions, a key feature of major depression is the likelihood that sufferers will experience repeated episodes. Research has found that the risk of relapse after a first episode of depression is approximately 50 per cent, despite the individual appearing to have made a full recovery. After a second or third lifetime episode, the risk of recurrence rises to between 70 and 90 per cent (Judd, 1997; Mueller et al., 1999). Key to understanding this increasing vulnerability is the observation that negative life events play an increasingly smaller part in triggering depression in later episodes compared to earlier episodes. Later episodes of depression are more likely to be triggered autonomously or by relatively minor stressors.

How Depression Recurrence is Conceptualised

MBCT does not put forward elaborate theories explaining how psychological disturbance historically develops; it does, though, present an in-depth understanding of how difficulties are triggered and perpetuated on which the treatment model is based. Cognitive science explains vulnerability to depression through the framework of *differential activation* (Segal et al., 1996; Teasdale et al., 1995). The theory of differential activation suggests that across depressive episodes learned associations are formed between low mood and the characteristic feelings, thoughts, body sensations and behaviours that are part of depression. Typical examples of this depressed 'mode' are:

- *Feelings* – persistent sadness, anxiety, fear, irritability, anger, hopelessness and despair.
- *Thoughts* – pattern of negative, self-critical and blaming thoughts; rumination; a pattern of repetitive, abstract-analytical thinking.
- *Body sensations* – dysregulation of eating and sleeping habits; decrease in energy levels; increase in tiredness and fatigue; bodily aches and pains; increased muscle tension.
- *Behaviour* – pattern of giving up the things in life that are enjoyable but seem optional; tendency to avoid challenging situations; increased passivity; withdrawal.

The particular patterns of experiencing vary between individuals, forming the individual's unique 'relapse signature', but are relatively stable and predictable for the same individual over time. Over repeated episodes of depression the association between these different aspects of experience are strengthened (due to co-activation) such that the threshold for activation is lessened (Barnhofer and Crane, 2009).

For people who have experienced depression in the past, the experience of sadness or slightly lowered mood is highly threatening and aversive. Consequently, it tends to trigger strong reactivity typically characterised by an increase in ruminative thinking (an attempt to 'problem solve' and 'fix' lowered mood) and in avoidant patterns (an attempt to not feel the physical sensations of emotional pain which manifest in the body and to suppress or push away unwanted thoughts). Continued risk of relapse and recurrence is hence brought about by aversive reactions to the unpleasant experience of the symptoms of lowered mood.

The elements of experiencing which characterise depressive 'mode' thus become a pattern of interconnected cyclical reactivity which are evoked by the experience of depression in an attempt to ward off or manage lowering mood, and instead they tragically serve only to activate and perpetuate the condition – a mechanism known as 'depressive interlock' (Teasdale et al., 2000). Thus it is that for an individual who has experienced recurrent depression, the 'arrival' of what for many would be a fleeting experience of the emotion of sadness can easily, through a cascade of internal reactivity, become the trigger to the reactivation of old habitual patterns of thinking and experiencing and so to the re-emergence of a new episode of depression.

The intention of relapse prevention is thus to pre-empt the establishment of reactive cycles of self-perpetuating negative thinking and experiential avoidance that are triggered during states of mild depressed mood, or at other times of potential relapse.

Reactivity to Threats

A key process that MBCT is seeking to influence is the way in which challenging internal experience such as sadness is acknowledged and processed. Human patterns of reactivity to threat are shaped by a combination of old, hardwired evolutionary tendencies which switch on and off depending on contingencies (e.g. the automatic physical leap away from a fast approaching car followed by a physiological settling once the threat is no longer there); *and* by the ability of our conceptual mind to operate strategically and to create representations of experience and symbolic reactions (e.g. the brooding which goes on long after the car is out of sight about what *could* have happened, what *should* be done by way of redress etc.) (Williams, 2010). This tendency of our conceptual mind to work 'off-line' is, from an evolutionary perspective, a more recent development and is less dependent upon contingencies (i.e. the mind's reactivity does not always cease once the trigger has subsided). The human mind/body does not therefore generally distinguish between threats originating externally (e.g. a wild animal chasing us) and threats originating internally (e.g. the arising of sadness). In individuals who have experienced repeated depression, the characteristic body sensations, emotions, thoughts, memories and images that occur at times of lowered mood become linked though repeated experience to a sense of threat. These internal experiences thus trigger a threat reaction characterised by the automatic urge to get away from the aversive experience by endeavouring to remain out of contact with it – a process known as 'experiential avoidance' (Hayes et al., 1996).

'Doing' Mode of Mind

The theory underpinning MBCT posits that the mind has two characteristic modes of operation through which we experience the world – 'doing' mode and 'being' mode. Both are functional and adaptive, but psychopathology arises from overuse of doing mode of mind processes. In particular, the use of doing mode to suppress or elaborate emotional expression serves to increase the emotional disturbance that it was intended to fix (Williams, 2010).

Doing mode of mind: the experience of 'discrepancy' between how things are (or our perception of how things are) and our ideas of how we want things to be or not be. A mode of conceptual focus.

Doing mode of mind enables us to build simulations and mental models, to use language, to operate in the abstract, to draw from past experience, to project into the future, to analyse and problem solve. These abilities are crucial to the way humans operate in the world and central to our success as a species. They also create our vulnerability to emotional distress. When applied to our emotional experience this ability to recognise discrepancies between our *perception* of our current experience and our *ideas about* our desired (or feared) experience leads to a heightened awareness of the gap between the two triggering a further lowering of mood. Typically this lowering of mood leads the individual to redouble efforts to analyse, problem solve, suppress and do battle with difficult emotions, so perpetuating doing-mode ruminative cycles. The main problem becomes the escalation of despair and hopelessness caused by the strategies that are triggered at times when challenging emotions are registered (Crane, 2009). Crucially, mindfulness training is not about trying to get rid of the aspects of doing mode of mind that create and perpetuate emotional distress; it enables recognition of where adaptive automatic reactions stop and unhelpful elaboration and avoidance processes begin (Williams, 2010).

'Being' Mode of Mind

An underlying premise of MBCT is that in order to live a healthy and balanced life we need to be able to cultivate and know both being and doing modes of mind so that we can be flexible and responsive to what is needed in each moment. The term 'being or doing mode of mind' describes our relationship to our experience and our state of mind rather than being descriptive of the activity we are engaged in.

> **Being mode of mind:** the experience of direct, present moment and non-judgemental connectedness with sensory experience. A mode of experiential focus.

Being mode of mind is an experiential mode of self-focus (as contrasted with the conceptual mode of self-focus employed during doing mode) in which one settles into the actual experience of the moment and allows it to be a focus for exploration. Through cultivating familiarity with being mode of mind, participants are enabled to encounter the reactive patterns that potentially trigger depression, in a way which provides extra time and distance to make skilful choices (McCown et al., 2010).

For a summary of the features of doing and being modes of mind, see Table 3.1.

Table 3.1   A summary of the features of doing and being mode of mind

'Doing' mode of mind	'Being' mode of mind
Goal or problem orientation. The mind is engaged in trying to change experience. There is an absence of acceptance – the judging mind is highly active.	Experience is seen as it is rather than judged as a problem. Orientation of acceptance towards experience.
Attention is focused on concepts and thoughts about experience (labelling, elaborating, analysing, judging, comparing, remembering, self-reflecting).	Attention is placed on the direct sensations that arise in the place of contact between sensory organs and sense impressions: seeing, hearing, smelling, feeling, tasting, visceral sensations, proprioceptive sensing.
Absence of attention on direct sensory experience.	
Attention primarily focused on ideas about the past and future. These thoughts become reality, the 'lens' through which the world is seen.	Attention primarily focused on present moment.
The mind is frequently on 'autopilot' – processing of experiencing is habitual and beyond conscious awareness.	The choice of focus for attention is consciously made.
Attention becomes automatically 'caught' by detailed aspects of the content of experience (e.g. the thought 'nobody values me' becomes a fixed idea).	Attention is placed on the 'process' of experience rather than the details of the content (e.g. recognition of the flux of thoughts, emotions and sensations).

Acceptance Orientation

Paradox is intrinsic to mindfulness-based teaching. Participants engage with an MBCT programme because they want things to be different. The teaching aims to facilitate recognition that this urge to push away unwanted internal experience and the drive towards experience other than what is happening in the moment creates the patterns which fuel emotional distress. Mindfulness trains one to notice the immediacy of experience (including the urge to try to get rid of it) without attempting to alter or avoid it. Acknowledging experience does not hold any promise that it will make it better – sometimes intensity is increased. The value it holds is twofold. First, acceptance offers an intentional and deeper connection with the actuality of experience, thus increasing tolerance to aversive experience (such as the emotion of sadness which was previously perceived as threatening) and thereby decreasing the likelihood of the activation of habitual reactive patterns. Second, acceptance of experience seems to clear the way for accessing our intuitive (as contrasted with rational and logical) responses to experience.

Attentional Control

MBCT holds that much of our emotional distress is created through the ways in which our attention is habitually and automatically 'taken' by ruminative thought processes. Although, attention is often 'caught' so that beyond our awareness the ruminative thinking mind has become active, it is also clear that attention can be deliberately redirected to varying aspects of experience (body sensations, emotions and thoughts) – a skill which can be developed and refined through mindfulness meditation practice. Deliberately bringing attention to the detail of physical sensations in the body (experiential being mode of mind) has the effect of disengaging attention from the mind's self-generated information (conceptual doing mode of mind) because the conscious attention has a limited capacity (Williams, 2010).

Relationship with Experience

People who engage in CBT during a depressive episode are less likely to experience future relapse than those who don't. Understanding why this is was important to the developers of MBCT because it offers understanding of the psychological processes that offer protection. It became clear that through the explicit CBT emphasis on challenging belief in the content of negative thoughts, an implicit process of relationship change with these thoughts emerges. Development of this 'decentered' perspective towards challenging thoughts is seen to be a key protective mechanism in preventing depressive relapse. Thus in MBCT there is a central focus on facilitating a shift from a position of being 'caught' inside the content of negative thoughts to a stance within which there is a perspective on their process – they are seen as passing events in the mind which are not necessarily valid representations of reality or truth.

Universal and Specific Vulnerability

The unique nature of the human mind that creates our success as a species also makes us vulnerable to experiencing layers of internal reactivity which create distressing emotions. In addition to this universal vulnerability, individuals also carry specific vulnerabilities: patterns, traits or tendencies which incline the individual towards particular forms of suffering (Williams, 2008). The core intention of MBCT is to empower the individual to work skilfully with both these universal and specific vulnerabilities through developing a fine-tuned awareness of their nature, and through learning to work with them consciously rather than habitually.

Practical Applications: Strategies of Approach and Treatment Techniques

The Eight-session Programme

MBCT is a short-term intensive approach. It is taught over eight weekly 2–2.5 hour sessions, each with its own theme and curriculum; follow-up sessions are frequently scheduled during the year after the class to reinforce continuation of practice and integration of learning into daily life. Prior to the course the instructor meets individually with participants to orient them to the intentions of the approach, to answer any questions and to mutually explore whether the course is suitable for the participant at this particular point in their life. The group size is typically up to 12 participants, currently in recovery or remission. There is a structured schedule of home practice involving 45 minutes per day of formal meditation, daily informal mindfulness practice and some recordings of observations of experiences. Many programmes include a whole day of guided mindfulness practice during the sixth week.

During sessions 1–4 the emphasis is on developing skills in bringing attention to experience, familiarity with habitual patterns of mind and an experiential understanding of the nature of experience (e.g. seeing that experience in each moment is made up of a constellation of thoughts, emotions, body sensations and behaviours). Participants have repeated practice in working with the wandering mind through bringing the attention back to its intended focus (e.g. the breath). This offers opportunity to practice the skill of letting go of thoughts and emotions which seem compelling. During sessions 5–8 the emphasis shifts towards choosing to deliberately remain with challenging thoughts and feelings, by bringing a kindly, accepting and investigative awareness to them rather than trying to eliminate or get entangled in them.

Therapeutic Relationship

The literature on the practice of mindfulness-based teaching places considerable emphasis on the importance of the instructor embodying the spirit and essence of mindfulness (e.g. McCown et al., 2010). Along with the participant's direct personal experience of the practice, this opportunity to witness mindfulness in action is seen as a key vehicle though which the instructor communicates the potential of bringing mindfulness to personal experience.

Mindfulness-based teaching processes emphasise the shared experience of being human. The processes of mind that are under investigation fall under a continuum of experience that everyone can relate to. During sessions the instructor guides participants in meditation from a position of full participation, and just like the participants, engages in a regular personal mindfulness practice outside the sessions. The class dialogues are led from a position of shared inquiry into the nature of experience. The emerging ethos is one of shared possibilities.

MBCT is delivered in a group format so that the therapeutic relationship is both with the instructor and with fellow participants in the group. The group 'container' for the teaching process if skilfully managed can offer a community within which individuals can have an experience of 'co-journeying', thereby reinforcing the learning that the patterns of mind under investigation are universal rather than personal.

Mindfulness Meditation

The MBCT programme is based on mindfulness practice and principles. Mindfulness training is a systematic methodology through which we learn to recognise doing mode of mind patterns and intentionally cultivate being mode of mind. It is taught through formal mindfulness meditation in which a period of time is set aside to engage in a specific practice and through informal mindfulness practice in which we bring mindful attention to our daily life experience. In MBCT the formal practices taught are the body scan (learning to systematically attend to direct physical sensations in the body), mindful movement (attending to sensations in the body while engaged in movement and stretches) and sitting meditation (attending in turn to different aspects of internal experience – breath sensations, wider body sensations, sounds, thoughts, emotions).

Mindfulness practice enables the individual to see patterns of reactivity in the mind and to learn to respond in new ways. For example, as we pay attention to the sensations of breath movement in the abdomen a range of reactions are likely to occur. Our experience might be unpleasant: thoughts of what else I could be usefully doing, wondering when this will end; physical sensations of restlessness and agitation; and emotions such as boredom or worry. Or our experience might be pleasant: thoughts of how well I am doing, how peaceful this is; physical sensations of warmth, relaxation; and emotions such as ease and contentment. Our innate tendency is to react to the unpleasant by endeavouring to push it away and the pleasant by holding on to it. Through mindfulness practice we learn that it is possible to non-judgementally recognise all these reactions for what they are, repeatedly returning the attention to direct experience rather than reactions to direct experience. The attention is thus brought back to present-moment experiencing and is not carried away into a stream of simulation about experience and so imbuing it with extra implications (Williams, 2010).

Cultivating the Attitudinal Underpinnings to Mindfulness Practice

A key intention of the MBCT teaching process is to enable participants to experientially taste the effects of coming towards experience through a radically different attitudinal framework. Doing mode of mind patterns are characterised by judgemental, critical, goal orientated, closed and fixed ways of perceiving experience. Particularly, for people who are vulnerable to depression these modes of processing can easily become the predominant way of processing emotional experience. Mindfulness skills enhance the possibility of recognising when these patterns recur, deliberately redirecting attention to direct experience and infusing this attention with a particular attitudinal framework. This includes bringing to experience a quality of kindly acceptance, an interest and curiosity in the detail of experience in the present moment, and an attitude of non-striving and allowing experience to be as it is. Participants have the opportunity to experientially experiment with bringing these qualities to experience during mindfulness practice and also to witness the embodiment of them in action in the instructor during the sessions.

Working with Obstacles

MBCT intentionally invites a new relationship with processes which might usually be perceived as obstacles to progress or barriers to learning. Core to the learning process is the understanding that it is the habitual reactive patterns that emerge when difficulty presents itself which perpetuate and escalate challenge. In essence, the learning fosters an 'approach' rather than an 'avoidance' mode towards all experience – and in particular (because of its tendency to trigger unhelpful reactive patterns) towards difficult, 'problematic' experience. Therefore, from the pre-course interview onwards the instructor will encourage the participant to expect that the learning process will present challenges, and that these challenges are particularly important because the exploration of how to approach them will offer important learning opportunities. The instructor will repeatedly invite participants to step back from the well-practiced tendency to analyse experience (because this leads into a doing mode of mind conceptual style of processing) and instead will invite them to direct attention to present moment experience without judgement (because this leads into a being mode of mind experiential style of processing).

Case Example: Emma[1]

Emma is a 42-year-old mother of three teenage daughters. She teaches outdoor pursuits in a further education college. Her GP recommended that she take an MBCT course following recovery from a recent episode of major depression. This had developed over a period of months in which her college work had been particularly demanding and Emma had a perceived sense that her colleagues and boss did not value her contribution to the team. This had led to an increasing sense of uncertainty, isolation and rejection; and to agitation which she channelled into extra time spent on her college work, leading to a withdrawal from her family which in turn led to feelings of guilt about her role as a mother and wife. Over time, Emma became deeply exhausted with a persistent low mood and an escalating sense of desperation and worthlessness.

By the time of referral to MBCT, Emma had been back to work on a part-time basis for three months, having had four months of sick leave, antidepressant medication treatment and a period of brief counselling. Although she was continuing to experience periodic episodes of anxiety and low mood and occasional suicidal thoughts, she felt that on the whole things were more stable – she did, however, feel that her recovery was fragile. She described how she easily moved into downward spirals of low mood typically triggered by an internal sense of uncertainty about whether someone at work or in her personal life liked or approved of her. This would easily trigger feelings of rejection and worthlessness; cascades of ruminative thoughts casting doubt on her value as a colleague or friend; a physical response of tightness in her chest and abdomen; and a behavioural tendency to pull back from making contact with people around her.

In the individual pre-class interview the instructor invited Emma to share her experience of depression over the years, with a particular emphasis on the factors involved in relapse and maintenance. The class instructor supported Emma in looking at her experience alongside a wider understanding of how depression is understood to be triggered and perpetuated, which in turn led to a discussion about the background and intentions of the MBCT course and the potential benefits and challenges of the programme. The interview concluded with discussion about practical arrangements and the importance of the home practice element of the programme.

Session 1: Automotive Pilot

Two weeks later Emma, along with ten other participants, arrived for the start of the course. The early part of the session was spent establishing the ground rules for the group, offering the opportunity for participants to introduce themselves and their hopes for participating in the programme. Although Emma felt anxious

(Continued)

---

[1]The case example is structured around the progression of the client through the eight-week MBCT programme. Within this the theoretical underpinnings and practical applications of the approach are highlighted.

(Continued)

speaking within the group, she found this process reassuring, realising that others had experienced similar challenges. The teaching process in this first session is intended to help participants to recognise the tendency we have to operate on automatic pilot, hardly aware of what we are doing or thinking. The session highlights the difference between mindful awareness and automatic pilot; how often routine activities such as eating are carried out in automatic pilot; how paying detailed attention changes the way we experience; and how the mind makes rapid associations from sensory information. The guided mindfulness practices within the session are eating one raisin and the Body Scan meditation, both offering detailed guidance on paying attention to the direct experience of physical sensations. This foundational skill supports participants in interrupting and disengaging from habitual ruminative thought patterns through anchoring attention in the body.

Emma found the session very revealing – she hadn't previously realised that her mind was so active, and hadn't connected the pattern of autopilot to the potential recurrence of 'depression mind'. She was aware of her tendency to miss out on the detail of present moment experiencing, but had not previously seen this as a process she had influence over.

Emma left the first session with handouts summarising the session's themes and a Body Scan CD which she used for guidance for her daily mindfulness practice over the following week. She was also invited to bring moment-to-moment attention to the sensory experience of doing one routine activity each day (such as brushing teeth).

Session 2: Dealing with Barriers

As is the case for many, Emma's first experience of sustained meditation practice had been challenging and she came to the next session with a lot of questions. Rather than moving straight into exploration of these, the instructor started the session (and all subsequent sessions) with a guided meditation practice – at this point in the programme a Body Scan. This was followed by a dialogue exploring experiences of this practice and then experiences of the previous week's home practice. Emma felt disappointed with herself for seemingly not having 'succeeded' in the task set her. She recalled the discussion in the pre-class interview about engaging in the programme whilst being open to outcome, but had nevertheless developed a clear image in her mind of what she 'should' be experiencing during meditation (stillness, calm, relaxation), which was some distance from her actual experience (distracted mind, waves of anxiety which triggered sensations of agitation and tension). The instructor acknowledged her experience and invited her to describe the body sensations that had accompanied the experience of anxiety. Emma was able to describe global experience (panicky, on edge) and the cascade of thoughts 'about' her experience but not the detail of physical sensation. The instructor offered guidance and encouragement to Emma and others to continue to practice while approaching the detail of sensations in the body with interest and curiosity. There was also an exploration of the effect of the 'doing' mode of mind reactive patterns that had emerged for Emma and for others in the group: the desire to have a certain sort of experience; the endeavour to try and get it right; the judging that arises when experience does not match our ideas about how it 'should' be. The instructor emphasised to the whole group that there is no right way to experience a body scan (and the divergence of experience within the room underlined this point) and invited throughout a spirit of allowing experience to be as it is rather than one of trying to achieve a particular goal or outcome.

The cognitive model was introduced in the second part of the session by guiding participants to imagine themselves in an ambiguous scenario. This illuminates how emotions are strongly influenced by the meaning that we attach to experience and how in turn this is influenced by our underlying mood. Emma was struck by the range of potential interpretations from the group to one scenario.

For home practice through the next week Emma continued to practise the Body Scan and to bring daily attention to a routine activity. An additional practice of a 10-minute sitting meditation (bringing attention to sensations of breathing) was introduced and participants were invited to record in detail one pleasant experience each day.

Session 3: Mindfulness of the Breath

Emma enjoyed the guided mindful movement at the start of this session, feeling particularly in touch with the pleasure of moving her body. The practice also highlighted her increasing ability to recognise and stay with body sensations. Over the previous week Emma had continued to experience waves of anxiety both during and outside the formal practice sessions and was uncharacteristically tearful at various moments during the week. This was accompanied at times by surges of ruminative thinking that things were getting worse. This is often a challenging phase in the programme when heightened levels of noticing create greater levels of awareness of challenging thoughts, sensations and emotions. However, there is also an increasing recognition of how the processes of rumination and avoidance tend to 'fuel' negative spirals. Emma was discovering that there were moments when she could become aware of difficult aspects of experience (particularly ruminative thinking), attend to them briefly and then redirect attention to body sensations. During meditation practice she noticed that she was letting go of trying to control her experience – experiencing a greater willingness to allow things to be as they are.

Through recording the detail of a pleasant experience each day and the exploration of this that followed in the session, Emma discovered a habitual pattern of not paying attention to pleasant experience. Through the week she had deliberately noticed the experience of being outside with her dog on early morning walks, sensing the wind and sun on her skin, the smells, the sights – particularly the irrepressible joy of her dog as he ran. She also was beginning to recognise that in each moment her experience is made up of the elements of thoughts, emotions and sensations and that these are continually interacting with each other.

A new practice is introduced in the third session – the 3-minute breathing space, a 'mini-meditation' which encourages the integration of mindfulness practice into everyday life. For home practice Emma alternated mindful movements done on the floor with standing stretches followed by a sitting meditation using CDs for guidance. Additionally, she practiced the 3-minute breathing space daily at three prescheduled times and kept a diary of one unpleasant experience every day.

(Continued)

(Continued)

Session 4: Staying Present

This session commenced with the introduction of the full sitting meditation in which participants were invited to bring attention to different aspects of their experience in turn: breath, the whole body, sounds, thoughts and emotions. Emma experienced repeated mind wandering, and recognised a recurrent pattern of slipping into worrying about the future. Through direct experiential engagement with her own process and through hearing others within the group, she was becoming increasingly able to see the active mind as inherent rather than a problem, and to stay with the process of bringing the attention back again and again to its intended focus. She was gradually changing her relationship with her thoughts towards recognising them as passing phenomena that she did not have to engage in. In so doing she was learning to interrupt spiralling patterns of rumination that would historically have led to low mood.

The exploration of the 'unpleasant experiences' diary illuminated to Emma the characteristic patterns and tendencies which take place in the face of unpleasant experience, in particular the tendency to 'think about' rather than feel. This led Emma to notice that whilst she tended to experience pleasure in the present and then let it go, unpleasant experiences were maintained long after the event through ongoing rumination. The strong example of unpleasant experience particularly well known to people who are vulnerable to depression is the painful and judgemental thoughts that are a universal feature of persistent low mood. The potential of cultivating a new relationship to them in which they are seen as symptoms of depression and as thoughts rather than representations of reality was explored. Emma and her fellow participants had been practicing this over the previous weeks in relation to 'everyday' thoughts, and this discussion opened the potential of bringing this 'decentered' relationship even to the most highly charged thoughts.

At home Emma practiced a 40-minute sitting meditation each day using a CD for guidance, and the 3-minute breathing space (both at prescheduled times and when unpleasant experience was present).

Session 5: Allowing and Letting be

By this stage in the programme participants have usually developed some foundational skills and insights which include using the breath and sensations in the body as an anchor to the present moment, and recognition of the activity and patterns of their minds. This now becomes the basis for exploring the development of a radically different relationship with experience – one of allowing and opening to difficult experience as it is. This is introduced in the sitting practice through inviting participants to deliberately bring their attention to difficult experience (thoughts, emotions or body sensations); to become aware of how this is expressing itself in the body and to bring gentle investigative attention to this experience.

Emma had come to session five fresh from an argument with her 16-year-old daughter who was pushing her parents to give her a greater degree of autonomy than they felt she was ready for. As Emma settled into the opening sitting meditation practice she was experiencing considerable physical agitation in her body and cascades of ruminative thoughts which were feeding an emotional experience of doubt, inadequacy and a sense of incompetence as a mother. The instructor's initial guidance invited her to place her attention in the physical feel of her posture and the sensations of contact of her body with the chair; she was then invited to settle her attention on the sensations of breath movement in the abdomen and next to open her attention to the whole body. Although feeling 'scattered' she was able to repeatedly redirect her attention in these ways and experienced a gradual settling. The subsequent invitation to turn attention towards a challenging aspect of experience felt highly unwelcome to Emma. Despite the resistance, she did experiment with recalling the argument and experienced an immediate resurgence of feelings of failure and worthlessness. The instructor guided participants to turn attention towards the sensations that were showing in the body in connection with the challenging thoughts and feelings. Emma noticed that the sensations were most intense around the upper part of her abdomen – a cluster of sensations characterised by the feeling of a tight band, which pulsed, leaving her feeling nauseous. Within the practice Emma was encouraged to approach these sensations with interest and curiosity; to gently explore the elements that make up the sensations, whether they change moment by moment, and the reactions they triggered. Whenever the intensity of 'staying with' these sensations became overwhelming, participants were invited to return attention to their breathing as a way of taking care and 're-anchoring' to the present moment, before returning again if appropriate to notice without judgement the way this challenge showed itself within the body. Through this process, Emma was introduced to the potential for using her mindfulness practice as a way of staying with intensity and challenge without engaging in patterns which further 'fuel the fire'. In the dialogue which followed Emma shared her discovery that 'it is OK for things to not feel OK'. She was beginning to experientially taste alternatives to habitual reactive patterns of rumination and experiential avoidance.

For home practice Emma continued with the sitting meditation and with the use of the 3-minute breathing space at prescheduled times and as a response to troubling situations.

Session 6: Thoughts are not Facts

The theme that thoughts are merely thoughts and that we have choices about how we respond and work with them now becomes explicit. Developing the capacity to decenter from thoughts – particularly those that are emotionally charged – is a crucial skill in preventing downward mood spirals. In addition to this theme being highlighted through the sitting meditation practice and class dialogue, participants are guided in an exercise which reveals the impact of mood on thought patterns. By this stage Emma was feeling more familiar with the practices and with the potential they offered. In daily life, she felt in touch with physical experience in her body – the discovery that this added a new dimension to her role as an outdoor pursuit's teacher was creating a new interest, enthusiasm for and ease with her work. The curriculum in session six enabled her to consolidate and integrate new learning.

In preparation for the end of the course, work begins on developing a 'relapse prevention action plan' through careful mapping out of individual relapse signatures. Emma spent time with her husband during the week hearing from him what

(Continued)

(Continued)

changes he noticed in her during moments of spiralling low mood. This in turn supported him in recognising that the time that Emma was investing in practice (although making her unavailable to the family temporarily) was strengthening her ability to be present within the family.

For home practice Emma was given a further CD with a range of different lengths of meditations. In preparation for the end of the course, participants were invited to structure their own practice by meditating for 40 minutes each day using different combinations of the core practices that have been learned as well as continued use of the 3-minute breathing space.

Session 7: How can I Best take Care of Myself?

This session highlights the effects of daily life activities on our mood and wellbeing. Participants are guided in a detailed investigation of daily activity and of the potential for mindfully influencing choices. Emma noticed that the largest proportion of her days was given over to her work and to her family, leaving little time to dedicate to activities which improved her wellbeing or lifted her mood. She also recognised that the times that she did have to herself were often clouded by guilt about what else she could be doing with her time – this was particularly true when her mood was low, leading to a tendency to give up the very things which might support her in difficult times.

Time is spent in session seven building on last week's work on the relapse prevention action plan by considering and listing skilful responses to the recognition of warning signs of relapse. For home practice Emma chose from all the formal practices experienced during the programme a form of practice that she could sustain beyond the end of the course.

Session 8: Using What has been Learned to Deal with Future Moods

The final session invites participants to reflect back on the course and to look forward to the future, exploring how new skills and understandings can be maintained and strengthened. Emma was able to look back over the eight weeks and recognise some key areas in which she had shifted. She had a new orientation in her life that prioritised taking care of and being kind to herself which showed itself both in how she conducted her days (less pressure to achieve, more spaces to pause and gather herself) and how she related to internal experience (greater tendency to be gentle with herself during difficult times; recognition of the recurrence of negative judgemental thoughts and a capacity to see them for what they are).

Research Status

The publication of the first MBCT trial (Teasdale et al., 2000) was shortly followed by a further randomised control trial (Ma and Teasdale, 2004) replicating the result that MBCT approximately halves the expected relapse rate in recovered patients with three or more episodes of depression over a year long follow-up period. In Teasdale et al. (2000), 145 patients were randomised to treatment as usual or MBCT and subsequently followed up over 60 weeks; 66 per cent of those with three or more episodes in the treatment-as-usual group experienced a relapse during the period, compared with 37 per cent in the MBCT group. The Ma and Teasdale (2004) trial randomised a smaller sample of 55 patients with three or more episodes of depression; 78 per cent of those in the treatment-as-usual group relapsed, compared to 36 per cent in the MBCT group.

The early research on MBCT was in relation to its effectiveness not in treating acute depression but in preventing depression for those known to be vulnerable to recurrence. Subsequent research has shown that MBCT produces outcomes comparable to maintenance antidepressants in this group (Kuyken et al., 2008). Two further open trials indicate that it may be effective for people who have been found to be resistant to antidepressants (Eisendrath et al., 2008) and for those who are resistant to antidepressants and cognitive therapy (Kenny and Williams 2007). Kingston et al. (2007) have found that MBCT reduced residual symptoms of depression and Barnhofer et al. (2009) have found that it may be helpful for those with chronic depression. Williams and colleagues are currently investigating MBCT for people with suicidal depression (Williams et al., 2006, 2010). Some promising preliminary research has been conducted in the effects of MBCT in bipolar affective disorder (Williams et al., 2008).

Research on MBCT is beginning to focus on hypothesised mechanisms of action. For example, in 2000, Williams et al. published research indicating that MBCT reduces overgeneral autobiographical memory recall, a mechanism thought to be implicated in depression recurrence; Crane et al. (2008) investigated how MBCT reduces the perceived discrepancy between actual self and ideal self, and Barnhofer et al. (2007) investigated the effects of MBCT on prefrontal α-asymmetry in resting electroencephalogram with findings suggesting that MBCT can help individuals at high risk for suicidal depression to retain a balanced pattern of baseline emotion-related brain activation. Kuyken et al. (2011) found that changes in self-rated mindfulness and in self-compassion mediated the relapse-preventing effect of MBCT.

The effectiveness of this integration of MBSR with cognitive behavioural approaches into a mindfulness-based approach tailored for a specific population has set the stage for the adaptation of the MBCT-based curricula for a range of other populations including chronic fatigue (Surawy et al., 2005), children (Lee et al., 2008), binge eating (Baer et al., 2005), insomnia (Heidenreich et al., 2006; Yook et al., 2008), oncology (Foley et al., 2010), generalised anxiety disorder (Evans et al., 2008) and childbirth and parenting (Hughes et al., 2009).

Suggested Further Reading

Crane, R. (2009) *Mindfulness-Based Cognitive Therapy: Distinctive Features.* London: Routledge.

Kabat-Zinn, J. (1990) *Full Catastrophe Living:Using the Wisdom of Your Body and Mind to Face Stress, Pain and Illness*. New York: Delacorte.

McCown, D., Reibel, D.C. and Micozzi, M.S. (2010) *Teaching Mindfulness: A Practical Guide for Clinicians and Educators*. New York: Springer.

Segal, Z.V., Williams, J.M.G. and Teasdale, J.D. (2002) *Mindfulness-based Cognitive Therapy for Depression: A New Approach to Preventing Relapse*. New York: Guilford.

Williams, J.M.G., Teasdale, J.D., Segal, Z. and Kabat-Zinn, J. (2007) *The Mindful Way Through Depression: Freeing Yourself from Chronic Unhappiness*. New York: Guilford.

References

Baer, R.A., Fischer, S. and Huss, D.B. (2005) 'Mindfulness-based cognitive therapy applied to binge eating: A case study', *Cognitive and Behavioral Practice*, 12: 351–158.

Barnhofer, T. and Crane, C. (2009) 'Mindfulness-based cognitive therapy for depression and suicidality', in F. Didonna (Ed.), *Clinical Handbook of Mindfulness*. New York: Springer.

Barnhofer, T., Duggan, D.S., Crane, C., Hepburn S., Fennell, M.J.V. and Williams, J.M.G. (2007) 'Effects of meditation on frontal [alpha]-asymmetry in previously suicidal individuals', *Neurorepor*, 18: 709–712.

Barnhofer, T., Crane, C., Hargus, E., Amarasinghe, M., Winder R. and Williams J.M.G. (2009) 'Mindfulness-based cognitive therapy as a treatment for chronic depression: A preliminary study', *Behaviour Research and Therapy*, 47: 366–373.

Crane, R. (2009) *Mindfulness-Based Cognitive Therapy: Distinctive Features*. London: Routledge.

Crane, C., Barnhofer, T., Duggan, D.S., Hepburn S., Fennell, M.J.V. and Williams, J.M.G. (2008) 'Mindfulness-based cognitive therapy and self-discrepancy in recovered depressed patients with a history of depression and suicidality', *Cognitive Therapy Research and Practice*, 32: 775–787.

Eisendrath, S.J., Delucchi, K., Bitner, R., Fenimore, P., Smit, M. and McLane, M. (2008) 'Mindfulness-based cognitive therapy for treatment-resistant depression: A pilot study', *Psychotherapy and Psychosomatics*, 77: 319–320.

Evans, S., Ferrando, S., Findler, M., Stowell, C., Smart C. and Haglin, D. (2008) 'Mindfulness-based cognitive therapy for generalized anxiety disorder', *Journal of Anxiety Disorders*, 22: 716–721.

Foley, E., Baillie, A., Huxter, M., Price, M. and Sinclair, E. (2010) 'Mindfulness-based cognitive therapy for individuals whose lives have been affected by cancer: A randomized controlled trial', *Journal of Consulting and Clinical Psychology*, 78: 72–79.

Hayes, S.C., Wilson, K.G., Giffor, E.V., Follette, V.M. and Strosahl, K. (1996) 'Experiential avoidance and behavioural disorders: A functional dimensional approach to diagnosis and treatment', *Journal of Consulting and Clinical Psychology*, 64: 1152–1168.

Heidenreich, T., Tuin, I., Pflug, B., Michal, M. and Michalak, J. (2006) 'Mindfulness-based cognitive therapy for persistent insomnia: A pilot study', *Psychotherapy and Psychosomatics*, 75: 188–189.

Hughes, A., Williams, J.M.G., Bardacke, N., Duncan, L.G., Dimidjian, S. and Goodman, S.H., (2009) 'Mindfulness approaches to childbirth and parenting', *British Journal of Midwifery*, 17: 630–635.

Judd, L.L. (1997) 'The clinical course of unipolar major depressive disorder', *Arch. Gen. Psychiatry*, 54(11): 989–991.

Kabat-Zinn, J. (1990) *Full Catastrophe Living:Using the Wisdom of Your Body and Mind to Face Stress, Pain and Illness*. New York: Delacorte.

Kabat-Zinn, J., Lipworth, L. and Burney, R. (1985) 'The clinical use of mindfulness meditation for the self-regulation of chronic pain', *Journal of Behavioral Medicine*, 8: 163–190.

Kabat-Zinn, J., Massion, M.D., Kristeller, J., Peterson, L.G., Fletcher, K.E. and Pbert, L. (1992) 'Effectiveness of a meditation-based stress reduction program in the treatment of anxiety disorders', *American Journal of Psychiatry*, 149: 936–943.

Kabat-Zinn, J., Wheeler, E., Light, T., Skillings, Z., Scharf, M.J. and Cropley, T.G. (1998) 'Influence of a mindfulness meditation-based stress reduction intervention on rates of skin clearing in patients with moderate to severe psoriasis undergoing phototherapy (UVB) and photochemotherapy (PUVA)', *Psychosomatic Medicine*, 50: 625–632.

Kenny, M.A. and Williams, J.M.G. (2007) 'Treatment-resistant depressed patients show a good response to mindfulness based cognitive therapy', *Behaviour Research and Therapy*, 45: 617–625.

Kingston, T., Dooley, B., Bates, A., Lawlor, E. and Malone, K. (2007) 'Mindfulness-based cognitive therapy for residual depressive symptoms', *Psychology and Psychotherapy: Theory, Research and Practice*, 80: 193–203.

Kuyken, W., Byford, S., Taylor, R.S., Watkins, E R., Holden, E.R., White, K., Barrett, B., Byng, R., Evans, A., Mullan, E. and Teasdale, J.D. (2008) 'Relapse prevention in recurrent depression: Mindfulness-based cognitive therapy versus maintenance anti-depressant medications', *Journal of Consulting and Clinical Psychology*, 76: 966–978.

Kuyken, W., Watkins, E., Holden, E., White, K., Taylor, R.S., Byford, S., Evans, A., Radford, S., Teasdale, J.D. and Dalgleish, T. (2011) 'How does mindfulness-based cognitive therapy work?', *Behaviour Research and Therapy*, 48: 1105–1113.

Lee, J., Semple, R.J., Rosa, D. and Miller, L. (2008) 'Mindfulness-based cognitive therapy for children: Results of a pilot study', *Journal of Cognitive Psychotherapy*, 22: 15–28.

Ma, S.H. and Teasdale, J.D. (2004) 'Mindfulness-based cognitive therapy for depression: Replication and exploration of differential relapse prevention effects', *Journal of Consulting and Clinical Psychology*, 72: 31–40.

McCown, D. Reibel, D.C. and Micozzi, M.S. (2010) *Teaching Mindfulness: A Practical Guide for Clinicians and Educators*. New York: Springer.

Moyers, B. (1993) *Healing and the Mind: Vol. 3 Healing from Within*. Co-produced by David Grubin Productions, Inc. and Public Affairs Television, New York.

Mueller, T.I., Leon, A.C., Keller, M.B., Solomon, D.A., Endicott, J., Coryell, W., Warshaw, M. and Maser, J.D. (1999) 'Recurrence after recovery from major depressive disorder during 15 years of observational follow-up', *The American Journal of Psychiatry*, 156: 1000–1006.

Murray, C.J.L. and Lopez, A.D. (1996) *The Global Burden of Disease: A Comprehensive Assessment of Mortality, Injuries and Risk Factors in 1990 and Projected to 2000*. Cambridge, MA: Harvard School of Public Health and the World Health Organisation.

National Institute for Clinical Excellence (2004) *Depression: Management of Depression in Primary and Secondary Care* (Clinical Guideline No. 23). Geneva: NICE. Available at www.nice.org.uk/CG023NICEguideline.

Segal, Z.V., Williams, J.M.G., Teasdale, J.D. and Gemar, M. (1996) 'A cognitive science perspective on kindling and episode sensitization in recurrent affective disorder', *Psychological Medicine*, 26: 371–380.

Segal, Z.V., Williams, J.M.G. and Teasdale, J.D. (2002) *Mindfulness-based Cognitive Therapy for Depression: A New Approach to Preventing Relapse*. New York: Guilford Press.

Surawy, C., Roberts, J. and Silver, S. (2005) 'The effect of mindfulness training on mood and measures of fatigue, activity and quality of life in patients with chronic fatigue syndrome on a hospital waiting list: A series of exploratory studies', *Behavioral and Cognitive Psychotherapy*, 33: 103–109.

Teasdale, J.D., Segal, Z. and Williams, J.M.G. (1995) 'How does cognitive therapy prevent depressive relapse and why should attentional control (mindfulness) training help?', *Behaviour Research and Therapy*, 33: 25–39.

Teasdale, J.D., Segal, Z.V., Williams, J.M.G., Ridgeway, V.A., Soulsby, J.M. and Lau, M.A. (2000) 'Prevention of relapse/recurrence in major depression by mindfulness-based cognitive therapy', *Journal of Consulting and Clinical Psychology*, 68: 615–623.

Teasdale, J.D., Segal, Z.V. and Williams, J.M.G. (2003) 'Mindfulness training and problem formulation', *Clinical Psychology: Science and Practice*, 10: 157–160.

Williams, J.M.G. (2008) 'Mindfulness, depression and modes of mind', *Cognitive Therapy and Research*, 32: 721–733.

Williams, J.M.G. (2010) 'Mindfulness and psychological process', *American Psychological Association, Emotion*, 10: 1–7.

Williams, J.M.G., Teasdale, J.D., Segal, S. and Soulsby, J.G. (2000) 'Mindfulness-based cognitive therapy reduces over-general autobiographical memory in formerly depressed patients', *Journal of Abnormal Psychology*, 109: 150–155.

Williams, J.M.G., Duggan, D.S., Crane, C. and Fennell M.J.V. (2006) 'Mindfulness-based cognitive therapy for prevention of recurrence of suicidal behavior', *Journal of Clinical Psychology*, 62: 201–210.

Williams, J.M.G., Teasdale, J.D., Segal, Z. and Kabat-Zinn, J. (2007) *The Mindful Way Through Depression: Freeing Yourself from Chronic Unhappiness.* New York: Guildford Press.

Williams, J.M.G., Alatiq, Y., Crane, C., Barnhofer, T., Fennell, M.J.V., Duggan, D.S., Hepburn, S. and Goodwin, G.M. (2008) 'Mindfulness-based cognitive therapy (MBCT) in bipolar disorder: Preliminary evaluation of immediate effects on between-episode functioning', *Journal of Affective Disorders*, 107: 275–279.

Williams, J.M.G., Russell, I.T., Crane, C., Russell D., Whitaker, C., Duggan, D., Barnhofer, T., Fennell, M.J.V., Crane, R. and Silverton, S. (2010) 'The staying well after depression study: Trial design and protocol', *BMC Psychiatry*, 10: 23.

Yook, K., Lee, S., Ryu, M., Kim, K., Choi, T.K., Suh, S.Y., Kim, Y., Kim, B., Kim, M.Y. and Kim, M. (2008) 'Usefulness of mindfulness-based cognitive therapy for treating insomnia in patients with anxiety disorders: A pilot study', *Journal of Nervous and Mental Disease*, 196: 501–503.

FOUR   Acceptance and Commitment Therapy

ERIC MORRIS AND JOSEPH E. OLIVER

Acceptance and commitment therapy (ACT) is a modern radical behavioural approach to psychotherapy that emphasises active acceptance and a mindful stance toward experiences, to enable people to commit to actions guided by their personal values.

ACT (pronounced as one word) is based upon a functional contextual philosophy, and draws upon a basic account of language (relational frame theory) that has emerged from research into verbal behaviour. Compared to other cognitive behavioural psychotherapies, the ACT stance emphasises working on the way people *relate* to their thinking and feeling, rather than directly trying to challenge or change the form or frequency of these experiences. This has been suggested as a key feature of the 'third wave' in the development of behaviour therapies (Hayes, 2004).

Historical Development of the Approach

ACT is situated philosophically and scientifically in the behavioural tradition of CBT and can be considered as a radical behavioural response to the challenge of working with cognition (verbal behaviour). Providing a behavioural analytic model of verbal behaviour was a key challenge to behaviourism (Cullen, 2008), and in the late 1950s the cognitive revolution in psychology was spurred by Chomsky's criticism of Skinner's account of verbal behaviour (Chomsky, 1959), leading to the emergence of the computer as a metaphor for the human mind. In this era, cognitive models of disorder were developed (e.g. by Meichenbaum, Mahoney, Beck), and early promising results for cognitive therapies suggested that behaviour therapy could be enhanced by interventions that directly focused on helping the client to identify and modify irrational, unhelpful patterns of thinking. The cognitive models relied less on operant and respondent accounts of learning, and gave primacy to information processing and the role of biases in appraising situations as a key process in explaining psychopathology. Although a number of key behaviour therapists shifted to cognitive accounts for learning, radical behaviourists rejected this development as it violated a number of founding assumptions of the philosophy (i.e. eschewing mentalistic accounts for behaviour, emphasising structure over function, reliance on hypothetical constructs like schemas as causal explanations).

No longer the mainstream of psychology, radical behavioural researchers continued to study verbal behaviour, particularly stimulus equivalence and the effects of rule-governance. Steven Hayes, the founder of ACT, was one of these researchers, studying the effects of verbal rules upon human performance in a series of experiments (summarised in Hayes, 1989). This work demonstrated that verbal rules produced a relative insensitivity to changes in the environmental contingencies. Furthermore, verbal reinforcers could be developed that were abstract and derived (not directly trained).

The research had implications for the focus of psychotherapy; it suggested that many psychological problems were a result of following unhelpful rules to receive social approval (pliance), or inaccurate rules about how private experiences work (tracking). It seemed that more effective behaviour could be developed through contingency shaped procedures; however, the problem was that psychotherapy can be a largely verbal enterprise, which could result in further rule-following (e.g. to please the therapist).

Similarly, verbal behaviour appeared to play a large role in distress/dysfunction, with clients describing problems with private experiences, particularly efforts to try to control and eliminate them (inaccurate tracking), and that reason-giving became a barrier to engaging in effective behavioural methods such as exposure (Hayes, 1989). It appeared that it was not presence of particular cognitions that was problematic, but rather the *function* of these experiences; cognitive therapists recognise this, in helping people challenge unhelpful cognitions, by sometimes asking them to consider the functional utility of thoughts (e.g. Beck, 1995).

Hayes and his student Rob Zettle studied the differential effects of an approach that took such a functional stance to private events, called 'comprehensive distancing', by comparing it with cognitive therapy in a small-scale trial in the treatment of depression (Zettle and Hayes, 1986). This study was done at the University of Pennsylvania, with Zettle supervised in cognitive therapy by Beck as well as supervised by Hayes in comprehensive distancing. The results of this trial demonstrated equivalent results between CT and comprehensive distancing, and interesting differences about the way that clients reported changes in unhelpful thoughts. In CT clients reported a reduction in the frequency of thoughts and later decreases in their conviction about these thoughts, while with comprehensive distancing it appeared that there were early changes in the conviction of unhelpful thoughts, and these thoughts continued with some frequency. This was suggested to be a difference in the change process, and argued to be theoretically consistent with rule-governance (Zettle and Hayes, 1986).

Basic research on an operant account of language eventually led to the explication of relational frame theory (RFT) (Hayes et al., 2001). RFT represents a *post-Skinnerian* account of human language and cognition, suggesting that the behaviour of framing relationally ('arbitrary applicable relational responding') represents a special class of operant behaviour. Relational responding is a basic and learned aspect of language (e.g. Barnes-Holmes et al., 2004; Berens and Hayes, 2007; Devany et al., 1986), which serves important functions in the outside world but can cause distress when applied to private experiences (Hayes et al., 2001). Importantly, relational responding transforms the functions of stimuli and modifies other behavioural processes such as classical and operant conditioning (e.g. Dymond and Barnes, 1995).

RFT relates to ACT by providing an internally consistent, behaviour-analytic account of cognition and how this influences other behaviours. It also provides an account for why people suffer, through experiential avoidance and cognitive fusion/literality with private experiences. More recent RFT research suggests that the development of perspective taking 'deictic frames' (the contextual sense of self, that of 'I-Here-Now'; McHugh et al., 2004) is important in fostering acceptance, compassion and mindfulness, and can be developed through experiential exercises and language training.

The term 'acceptance and commitment therapy' was not used until the early 1990s, first appearing in print in 1994 (Hayes and Wilson, 1994). In that decade conference presentations about ACT started gaining interest, with a number of behaviourally inclined psychologists attending workshops and a draft form of a treatment manual being distributed. The first randomised controlled trial of ACT was published by Frank Bond and his supervisor David Bunce. The study reported on a group-based ACT intervention for stress management (Bond and Bunce, 2000). Crucially, in Europe Steven Hayes presented keynote speeches at the European EABCT conference in Granada, Spain in 1998, as well as at the International Congress of Cognitive Therapy at Catania, Italy in 2000. ACT came to mainstream attention with the publication of the 1999 treatment manual, the first book-length description of the model and ACT techniques (Hayes et al., 1999).

Theoretical Underpinnings

There are several features of ACT that distinguish it from other approaches to psychotherapy.

Major Theoretical Concepts

Functional Contextualism

Fundamentally, ACT is based upon a functional contextualistic philosophy (a modern statement of radical behaviourism) which describes the goal of the science behind ACT as the prediction-and-influence of behaviour, with precision, scope and depth. This pragmatic stance leads to the goal of any analysis of problems as being *successful working*. Thus a formulation of a client's problems is only considered 'true' if it leads to effective changes and valued outcomes. Similarly, it is important to understand behaviour in the context that it occurs, influenced by the current environment as well as the historical circumstances that shaped it (Hayes et al., 1999).

Contextualism, therefore, views psychological events (such as thinking, feeling, remembering etc.) as ongoing actions of the whole organism interacting in, and with, historically and situationally defined contexts. Actions are whole events that can only be broken up for pragmatic purposes, not ontologically. Therefore, from a functional contextualist stance, the therapist does not confuse the analysis with the way reality 'is'; an analysis is only judged in terms of its capacity for successful working. Clarifying analyses in terms of successful working means that the focus is about finding manipulable environmental variables available in the current context, as these are the only means with which the therapist can have influence over behaviour. What this also implies for psychotherapy is that the therapist is part of the context of the client, and only has control over his or her behaviour in that context, verbal and non-verbal.

Theory of Suffering: Unhealthy Normality

The ACT model suggests it is normal for human beings to experience emotional pain, which can be amplified to lead to suffering by our capacity of language. Normal language processes that allow humans to derive meaning, relate two concepts together and respond psychologically to novel stimuli based on familiar stimuli, can also amplify our pain and lead to suffering when we make decisions and take actions that limit our lives, reducing meaning and vitality.

The ability to arbitrarily relate events can lead humans to become fearful of things never directly experienced, to persist with strategies that are ineffective but make sense (to the degree that being logical/coherent is privileged over learning from experience), and to remain haunted by their own histories despite current circumstances providing safety and comfort. These language processes are also adaptive in some contexts, such as persisting toward long-term, abstract goals despite aversive experiences (e.g. completing a course of study; writing a book), to problem-solve, be creative, learn from the experiences of others even if they are separated from us by geography and time (e.g. reading books by long-dead authors).

Clinical problems are considered to be contextually determined, with a major context being language itself. Thus, for example, anxiety may be considered a problem because anxiety is believed to be bad, frequently used as a cause (reason) for behaviour (e.g. when a person describes not being able to leave the house 'because' of anxiety), and because verbal formulations can suggest that anxiety must be changed before a meaningful, effective life is possible (Hayes and Batten, 2000). Language may support the relationship between presence of the experiences that make 'anxiety' and life restriction, and suggest unworkable solutions for fixing this problem (e.g. 'just get over it', 'don't think about it').

ACT aims to increase *psychological flexibility*, which is 'contacting the present moment fully as a conscious human being, and based on what the situation affords, changing or persisting in behaviour in the service of chosen values' (Hayes et al., 2006). The treatment targets of ACT are the processes of language/cognition considered to be involved in limiting psychological flexibility. Two key processes supported by language and culture are suggested to lead to suffering: *experiential avoidance* and *cognitive fusion* (contexts of literality with psychological events). Experiential avoidance has been defined as 'when a person is unwilling to remain in contact with particular private experiences (e.g. bodily sensations, emotions, thoughts, memories, behavioural predispositions) and takes steps to alter the form or frequency of these events and the contexts that occasion them, even when this process is unhelpful' (Hayes et al., 1999). Experiential avoidance is associated with many psychological disorders (Hayes et al., 2004a). Hayes and Gifford (1997) review research that suggests that poorer clinical outcomes for people who frequently use coping strategies aimed at avoiding or suppressing negative emotions and thoughts, rather than solving problems by overt behaviour change. There is a wide range of descriptive and experimental evidence that demonstrates the unhelpful life-restricting effects of experiential avoidance (Hayes et al., 1996; Strosahl et al., 2004), which links with the empirical literature about the ironic effects of mental control (Wegner, 1994; studies suggest that acceptance-based treatments are effective in reducing experiential avoidance (Hayes et al., 2004a). Due to its language-based origin, experiential avoidance can be difficult to modify through methods of direct instruction; rather, more experiential methods are needed to help clients to notice the *process* of thinking, instead of just the content.

A person is engaged in *cognitive fusion* when their behaviour is inflexible, and influenced more by verbal networks than by experienced environmental consequences (Bach and Moran, 2008). Cognitive fusion refers to situations when people are unhelpfully guided by the literal content of thoughts, rather than by direct experience. The ACT therapist helps the client to notice the process of thinking, rather than changing the thought content directly. By using mindfulness and other 'defusion' exercises, the client is encouraged to notice the difference between what their mind is saying about a situation (evaluations and judgements that they can be 'fused' to) and what their experience is of the situation (descriptions, noticing contingencies).

ACT was developed to emphasise experiential learning, helping the client to contact the effects of their choices and actions, and to discriminate these effects from how their minds say it should be. The functional contextualist focus on successful working requires a prior description of a value or goal; the client is encouraged to consider the workability of their actions from the perspective of whether this helps them to move forward in valued directions. Thus, there is a concordance between the philosophy underlying ACT and the therapeutic approach. This also means that ACT emphasises different

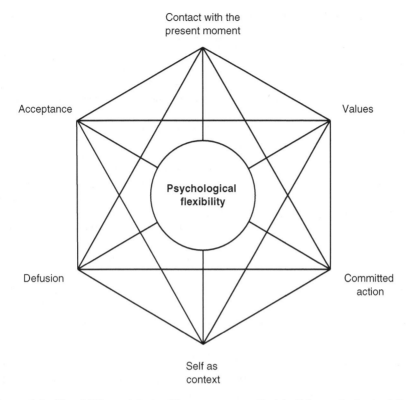

Figure 4.1 The ACT model: positive processes that build psychological flexibility (adapted from Hayes et al., 2006)

outcomes from many mainstream therapies, with a primary focus on quality of life, functioning and meaning, rather than symptom elimination.

The ACT model appears in Figure 4.1, the model is a set of interrelated processes to build psychological flexibility. A set of definitions for these processes appears in Table 4.1.

These ACT processes are 'mid-level terms', not be taken literally, but a useful clinical language to orientate the therapist to important features in the therapeutic context; there is a more technical behaviour-analytic account that sits underneath (outlined by Hayes, Barnes-Holmes and Roche, 2001). For example, cognitive fusion is defined as 'the domination of behavior regulatory functions by relational networks, based in particular on the failure to distinguish the process and products of relational responding' (Hayes et al., 2006).

Frequently, clients present in sessions with concerns related to presence, absence or intensity of psychological events; for example, the depressed client who wants to be rid of feelings of sadness, who would like to have positive thoughts or finds the intensity of sad memories to be overwhelming. In ACT terms what is of interest is how these experiences act as barriers to valued

Table 4.1   Central ACT processes (from Luoma et al., 2007)

Process	Definition
Acceptance	The active and aware embrace of private events that are occasioned by our history, without unnecessary attempts to change their frequency or form, especially when doing so would case psychological harm.
Defusion	The process of creating non-literal contexts in which language can be seen as an active, ongoing relational process that is historical in nature and present in the current context.
Self as context	A continuous and secure 'I' from which events are experienced, but is also distinct from those events.
Contact with the present moment	Ongoing, non-judgmental contact with psychological and environmental events as they occur.
Values	Verbally-constructed, global, desired and chosen life directions.
Committed action	Step-by-step process of acting to create a whole life, a life of integrity, true to one's deepest wishes and longings.

actions, as well as the personal values of the client. It is suggested that suffering comes from the presence of painful experiences plus the cost of life meaning/vitality in trying to control these. Early on, the client is encouraged to reflect on the personal cost of efforts to control experiences, and whether these efforts at control are working in the way that was expected. The client is validated for the effort to find a solution to their problems, while also encouraged to trust their own experience of the efficacy of control.

Similarly explored are the ultimate outcomes of these efforts at control. The client is asked: If they had a choice, what would they want their life to be about? This exploration of personal values provides an important direction for therapy, as well as helping the therapist to understand the client's pain, as suffering comes from the sacrifices made in not taking valued actions while trying to control experiences. This reflection is designed to help the client come into contact with the unworkability of the control agenda, and to learn to use their own experience as a guide (be more contingency shaped).

How Client Problems are Conceptualised

The ACT case formulation approach is dimensional and functional (Bach and Moran, 2008). The focus is upon how a particular behavioural repertoire can interfere with valued life goals, and how a person can develop a more psychologically flexible approach to what life offers. Consistent with a behavioural approach, therefore, is that ACT does not place importance on diagnosis to understand a client's problems. Rather the therapist engages in a *functional analysis*, considering the functional relationships observed between the client's behaviour and the environmental variables that support problems or influence clinical improvements (Bach and Moran, 2008).

The ACT therapist is interested in what the client wants their life to be about (values), what they are currently doing and the environments in which they occur, and the purpose of actions (whether behaviours are serving the purpose of escape or avoidance, rather than approach, i.e. guided by values).

The six domains in the ACT model (Figure 4.1) can be useful to consider as *skills* that build psychological flexibility; each domain can describe processes that narrow client behaviour, leading to unworkable solutions to problems (Bach and Moran, 2008). Some example questions to aid conceptualisation are given below (based on Lillis and Luoma, 2005).

Experiential Avoidance

1   What private experiences is the client attempting to control and avoid? (Outline unwanted thoughts and feelings, and in which contexts they occur).
2   What avoidance behaviours are being used and how pervasive are they? Consider levels of:

   • overt behavioural avoidance (activities, situations, people the client has stopped doing or avoids);
   • internal and external emotional control strategies (distraction, suppression, dissociation, drug use, self-harm, over-eating, suicide etc.);
   • in-session emotional control or avoidance (changing topic, argumentativeness, risk of drop-out).

Cognitive Fusion

1   Is the client overly attached to beliefs, expectancies, evaluations? Consider the effects of:

   • judgements of good–bad/right–wrong even when harmful;
   • needing to work things out before action;
   • having certainty, having 'reasons';
   • comparisons and critical attitudes toward self and others.

Attachment to a Conceptualised Self

1   Is the client's identity defined in judgemental, simplistic terms, by problematic content or a particular life story?
2   Can the client notice the distinction between the content of their experience and themselves as the container of these experiences (a transcendent self)?

Out of Contact with the Present Moment

1 Is the client preoccupied with thoughts about the past or future?
2 Does the client dissociate or lose track of the current moment?
3 Does the client engage in lifeless story-telling or seem disconnected from things happening in the session?
4 Does the client find it difficult to describe current feelings and thoughts, or have a lot of 'don't know' responses?

Out of Contact with Values

1 Is the client able to describe personal values across a range of life domains?
2 Does the client see a discrepancy between their current actions and personal values?
3 Does the client describe tightly held but unexamined goals, such as making money, as though they are values?

Inability to Build Patterns of Consistent Action

1 Does the client engage in self-control problems, such as procrastination, impulsivity, poor health behaviours, under-performance etc.?
2 Is the client engaged in actions that promote successful working? And able to change strategy when actions are not working?
3 Is the client exhibiting a specific, step-by-step pattern of action?

Consideration of the above can point to what skills to emphasise in treatment. Some clients will require the development of several domains, while for others the ACT work may be focused on one or two areas. As the ACT processes are inter-related, progress in one domain will facilitate the strengthening of others (e.g. values work may contact present-moment awareness, acceptance and defusion, as the client takes actions that evoke previously avoided feelings).

Practical Applications

The Therapeutic Relationship

The therapeutic relationship is seen as the central context of ACT. Overall, there is an emphasis on viewing problems that clients bring to therapy as generally applicable, including with the therapist. This flows directly from the model, in which client problems are understood not as indicative of dysfunction or disorder but as understandable (although unhelpful in terms of moving towards valued life outcomes) responses to difficult internal experiences. This results in a levelling of the therapeutic relationship, as the therapist approaches the relationship with warmth, compassion, genuineness and vulnerability that comes from a recognition that the client is another human who similarly struggles with thoughts and emotions. A metaphor for the ACT therapeutic relationship is that of the client and therapist both climbing separate mountains. Instead of the therapist being at the top of the mountain, having already succeeded in the climb, telling the client how to reach the top, the therapist is climbing her or his own mountain beside the client. From the benefit of perspective, the therapist can help the client find good footholds to help them on their journey upwards (the two mountains metaphor, adapted from Hayes et al., 2002).

The task of an ACT therapist is to 'detect instances of psychological flexibility and inflexibility in their clients, and to use psychologically flexible responses to establish a therapeutic relationship that models, instigates, and reinforces client psychological flexibility' (Luoma et al., 2007: 223).

From this perspective, ACT therapists use self-disclosure to highlight processes as they are occurring. Self-disclosure of thoughts and feelings is used judiciously when it serves the client and can have the effect of modelling ACT processes; it also equalises the therapy relationship.

The therapeutic stance is based on a respect for the client's values and goals for therapy. ACT places the client's values at the centre of the clinical work but makes no assumptions about what these values are and how acting consistently with them may look. This stance stems from the model as the therapist is helping the client to flexibly work towards chosen values rather than rigidly trying to comply with external rules.

A key part of the therapy relationship is helping clients to come into contact with their direct experience and to separate this out from evaluations or judgements about this experience. This often means that the therapist will not automatically attempt to rescue a client from a painful psychological experience; rather, the stance is to model acceptance of the client's distress or pain through validation without avoiding, side-stepping or minimising.

Alongside this, ACT therapists seek to increase a client's tolerance of the contradictions and uncertainty related to their experience without trying to resolve the associated discomfort quickly. Often, when clients are trapped by language, the solution from an ACT perspective is not always intuitive or obvious. For example, a client who experiences social anxiety may rigidly hold a belief that they are an anxious person who must change before they can function socially. Rather than addressing whether this is accurate, an ACT therapist focuses more on the workability of such a belief in terms of valued action (e.g. being in social situations), and assists the client to hold this belief lightly and also to take valued action, even if this feels contradictory.

Strategies of Treatment

ACT is about helping clients take steps in their life that are consistent with their values. To do this, ACT works to assist clients in reducing unnecessary struggle with psychological content by developing a therapeutic context that enables them not be so excessively attached to the content of thoughts and conceptions of the self and world in a way that draws them out of the present moment and into the past or future. In doing this, ACT helps clients in choosing and committing to taking steps towards building actions that are in line with their values. To do this, six core processes are targeted, all of which are inter-related. The model does not specify a particular sequence in which these should be addressed, but rather emphasises the importance of the therapist skilfully addressing each process as needed, with the overall aim of promoting psychological flexibility.

Major Treatment Techniques

In this section we will discuss ACT's major treatment techniques.

Developing Acceptance and Willingness

The process of acceptance is to help the client let go of unnecessary or unworkable struggle with unwanted psychological content, such as distressing thoughts or emotions. This struggle often involves excessive avoidance or control of these experiences to the point where it does harm. Clients can become trapped as they unsuccessfully attempt to rid themselves of thoughts and feelings so that, paradoxically, this struggle becomes part of the problem itself. The ACT model is based on the premise that life will inevitably bring some level of pain, discomfort or distress as, for example, when we lose people close to us, decisions do not go as we wanted, or we experience traumatic events. Although it is theoretically possible to never have any of these experiences, this would come at a great cost. The notion of suffering is introduced to make the distinction between 'clean pain' (pain that is part of a rich and vital life) and 'dirty pain' (pain that results of excessive attempts to not experience discomfort, and the subsequent suffering that results from a life without valued action). Acceptance does not mean resignation or giving up, instead it is making space and turning towards discomfort and distress, and developing willingness to have those experiences that are there anyway.

A first step in developing willingness is to undermine the control agenda. Clients often come into therapy hoping the therapist will be able to help them to better avoid or eliminate the experience they have been struggling with. A key starting point is to examine the workability of the client's attempts to control their experience and, from the vantage point of their experience, to notice that this excessive control is often part of the problem. ACT has a number of metaphors that target workability and willingness, for example the 'tug-of-war with the monster' metaphor:

> Imagine you're in a tug-of-war with a monster and that monster is made up of all the things you've been struggling with – negative thoughts such as 'I'm worthless',

sadness, emptiness – all the things you've been trying to get rid of. Imagine that between you and the monster there is a bottomless pit and if you lose this battle, you'll fall in and die. So you pull and pull, trying not to fall in, but as you do so the monster pulls back too, and even harder. You notice yourself edging closer and closer to the edge. The hardest thing to see is that our job is not to win the tug-of-war. Our job is to drop the rope. (Adapted from Hayes et al., 1999)

Using this metaphor can bring the client into contact with different aspects of their experience, such as the unworkability of continuing with the struggle and that struggling (or pulling on the rope) actually seems to make the situation worse. The metaphor also points toward the next step, and although it is not clear what 'dropping the rope' actually means, it suggests qualities of stopping the struggle and coming into contact with unwanted psychological content. The 'tug-of-war with the monster' metaphor is one way to highlight these process; many other metaphors have been developed (see Hayes et al., 1999).

Promoting Defusion

Alongside developing willingness is the skill of defusion, as an alternative to cognitive fusion. Work on defusion is warranted when a client is fused with their thoughts in a way that prevents them from taking valued action. That is, they appear to be taking the content of their thoughts literally, are believing their thoughts or seem very 'close' to their thoughts so that they are not able to do things that are important to them.

The central aim of defusion work is to reduce the believability of or attachment to unhelpful thoughts, but without necessarily targeting the form or frequency of thoughts. Treatment strategies to promote defusion come from different angles to target various aspects of thinking. A starting point can be to discuss the limits of thinking and language, for example, how language can interfere with our ability to enjoy a sunset or learn a new skill such as playing an instrument.

A second set of techniques aims to create a distance between the thought and the person thinking the thought. A core ACT technique is to say the thought in a way that is very different to how it would normally be 'heard'. For example, a thought 'I'm worthless', which would normally have a low and heavy quality, could be sung out loud or said with a comical voice. The aim here is not to ridicule the thought but to help the client come into contact with different properties of the thought that may not be so evident as a result of fusion. Clients may be encouraged to 'thank their mind' for a thought or see thoughts as glasses they might wear or bubbles around their heads. A person could repeat a thought over and over, varying the speed, pitch or form of the thought. The aim of all of these strategies is to create contexts so that language can be experienced more directly and some of the unhelpful functions are reduced.

Finally, clients can be taught to recognise times when they are likely to be fused with their thinking. This could be when they notice excessively critical thoughts, when thoughts are very comparative or evaluative, when thoughts have a dry, familiar or old feel to them, or when thoughts have 'shoulds', 'oughts' and 'musts' attached.

Contacting the Present Moment

ACT aims to foster an increased contact with the present moment from an accepting, non-judgemental and defused stance. The model suggests that if people are able to more flexibly contact the present moment, then this promotes a willingness to experience internal events for the purpose of connecting with values. By doing this, key messages are communicated, including the notion that life in the present moment is already occurring and that problems do not need to be fixed before a valued life can be lived (Strosahl et al., 2004).

Contacting the present moment can be taught in a number of ways, one of which is the practice of mindfulness. Clients can engage in mindfulness exercises, as well as learn the underlying principals of mindfulness so that the skill of coming back to the present moment can be applied in any activity, for example, mindful walking or mindful showering. The therapist can also encourage present moment contact by asking the client in session to describe thoughts and feelings as they occur, or to bring sensory information to the fore (touch, smell, for example).

Distinguishing the Conceptualised Self from Self as Context

In ACT, the conceptualised self refers to the sense of self that is formed over a person's lifetime, made up of memories, thoughts, experiences and beliefs that produce an identity. For example, someone might have a conception of themselves as a 'good person' or as 'messed up'. If these conceptions are held too rigidly, destructive or unworkable behaviour can result with attempts to maintain a sense of consistency with an identity.

This can be contrasted with self-as-context, which refers to the transcendent sense of self in which memories, thought, experiences and beliefs occur. This self can be considered as the 'I' that observes all these events. Developing contact with this psychological space can assist the client to not so inflexibly hold on to an unhelpful sense of identity. The therapist helps the client contact this space and notice that they are not just made up of thoughts, images, memories or emotions: that there is a part of awareness that acts as a container to these experiences. The 'chessboard metaphor' (Hayes et al., 1999: 190) is used to illustrate this, where the client is asked to think of their thoughts and emotions as chess pieces, in which 'good' experiences (feeling confident, positive thoughts) fight against the 'bad' ones (anxiety, negative thoughts). The client is asked to notice the board, which is the container for these experiences, clinging neither to good nor bad, but always there, no matter what takes place between the pieces. The client can be asked whether they are at 'board' level or 'piece' level when it comes to their own psychological content.

Working on Values

Work on values is central to ACT and moving towards values provides the purpose and motivation for coming into contact with difficult emotions and thoughts. For example, an ACT therapist will not ask a client who is anxious about public speaking to talk in front of groups simply for the sake of it. However, if public speaking is part of the client's broader valued direction, the therapist will encourage the client toward concrete goals consistent with that value, which may involve the client coming into contact with the anxiety associated with this valued action.

Values clarification, the elucidation of what really matters to the client in their life, is often an ongoing process throughout therapy. Many clients find it difficult to articulate their values, with learning histories in which they have never been or only inconsistently reinforced for expressing their values (e.g. clients with borderline personality disorder), or those who have had early traumas or experiences that have interrupted their development (such as psychosis) and never have had the opportunity to consider what is important to them in their life, or express values more associated with social compliance.

Values clarification involves asking clients questions such as: 'What are the things that you really care about in life?', 'What kind of things do you stand for in life?', 'If you could lead a life that was rich and vital, what would you be doing?' Such questions help the client to consider not only what is important to them, but also what actions they want to take in order to live consistently with their values. The ACT approach involves shifting the goal of therapy from the control or elimination of unwanted experiences, to embracing experiences as part of taking action in valued directions; through this process, pain is dignified and can be accepted as part of a larger life canvas.

Developing Patterns of Committed Action

ACT applies the same principles as other behaviour therapies in helping the client to build patterns of committed action that are a reflection of the client's values. Key goals are identified that are consistent with identified values, and the therapist helps the client develop steps that are specific, measurable and practical. Metaphors, such as the 'swamp' metaphor, are introduced to illustrate that obstacles are a natural, expected part of moving toward values and that contacting these obstacles can be a valued action:

Suppose you are beginning a journey to a beautiful mountain you can clearly see in the distance. No sooner do you start the hike that you walk right into a swamp that extends as far as you can see in all directions. You say to yourself, 'Gee, I didn't realise that I was going to have to go through a swamp. It's all smelly, and the mud is all mushy in my shoes. It's hard to lift my feet out of the muck and put them forward. I'm wet and tired. Why didn't anyone tell me about this swamp?' When that happens you have a choice: abandon the journey or enter the swamp. We enter the swamp, not because we want to get muddy, but because it stands between us and where we are going. (Hayes et al., 1999: 248)

Overcoming Obstacles to Client Progress

A common obstacle to progress can occur when the client views current strategies as positive, in spite of long-term negative consequences (e.g. avoidance of anxiety provoking situations). It can be useful to contrast the short-term advantages of the current strategy (such as avoidance of anxiety) with the long-term consequences of not moving in a valued direction (e.g. not building fulfilling relationships, making meaningful career advances). It can also be useful to evaluate the overall workability of managing the problem by asking questions: 'Altogether, has this problem for you been getting less, or has it actually been getting worse over time?'

A lack of clarity in client values can often present significant obstacles to progress. Some clients find it very difficult to articulate their core values, either as a result of learning histories that have taught them not to, or family environments that have not allowed them to. Often values are described in a vague, general way, for example 'I want to be happy', or sound as if they are more associated with subjugation, for example 'I want to earn lots of money (so I can please my parents)'. It is often useful to start with defusion and acceptance work to target the processes that interfere with the client's ability to express their values. A key indicator that more meaningful values are being articulated is the presence of emotions, such as sadness, as the client talks about what is important to them.

At times, clients can become overly focused on cognitive content, such as evaluations and judgements or a strong need to 'find the answer', in such a way that prevents them from being in contact with more useful environmental contingencies, such as emotions or feedback from others. In these situations it can be useful to engage in present-moment focused exercises to help the client expand their awareness to incorporate other sources of information in addition to that provided by their mind.

Clients may have a rigidly held, content-focused self-identity that may act as barrier to making progress. Clients may view workable actions as a threat to this long-held view of themselves, and change can be associated with emotional pain. For example, a client who has long-held a belief about themselves as broken or incapable of being helped may find the prospect of progressing in therapy deeply distressing. Self-as-context exercises can help to reinforce the notion that this is a belief, probably one of many that are held, and that there is a sense of space and distance for the belief and the observer.

Case Example: Toni

Toni was a 38-year-old woman who was referred for psychological input during an informal admission to an acute psychiatric unit. She came to the unit following a period of significant low mood and a subsequent suicide attempt. Toni also reported experiencing high levels of anxiety associated with rumination and worry. Toni's low mood had started about four months before the admission and had coincided with her return to work after a holiday. Toni had experienced a number of similar episodes in her life, although she had never required hospitalisation before. She said the depressive episodes typically occurred 'out of the blue' and she struggled to identify any clear precipitants. Toni was married and had two teenage daughters. She reported that she was happily married and that her husband was very supportive. She did worry, however, about the burden her depression placed on the family and felt guilty about not being there for them. She described her suicide attempt, which had been her first, as largely driven by her belief that she was not going to get better and was a burden on her family.

Toni initially described her childhood as 'happy and normal', although noted that her parents were often distant and that the family was not emotionally warm. She reported that she had to work hard to earn her parents' praise and often felt her best was not enough. Toni stated that, as a result, she became a 'perfectionist' and would drive herself for excellence, or become very despondent and self-critical if she fell short of doing her best.

Whilst on the unit, Toni initially responded well to a period of respite, took part in the activities available and was socially active. However, after a few days, she became increasingly anxious about leaving the unit and returning to her family and work. She spent long periods worrying about the future and whether she would be well enough to return to work. Toni also reported being distressed about her worrying, stating 'If I don't stop worrying, I'll never get better', 'If I think too much about my problems, they'll come true' and 'It's my fault that I'm worrying so much'.

From the initial assessment it was evident that Toni was highly experientially avoidant of perceived negative emotions such as anxiety and would engage in frequent attempts to block or suppress such feelings. This was often either through distraction or avoidance of anxiety provoking situations, including being with her family, seeing friends or going to work. It was also apparent that she frequently applied such control strategies to her thinking in an attempt to avoid negative thoughts. This typically lead to extended periods of rumination and further self-criticism as she was unable to successfully stop such thinking patterns. One of the effects of this excessive rumination was that tended to take her out of the present moment and, as a result, she found it difficult to identify and label current emotional experiences.

Toni exhibited a high level of cognitive fusion, taking her thoughts very literally and in a manner that made it extremely difficult to act in accordance with her values. For example, Toni identified that her family were extremely important to her and, specifically, she wanted to be emotionally available for them. However, she was particularly fused with the thought 'I must feel better before I can be available for

(Continued)

(Continued)

my family'. She therefore felt unable to act on her values in the presence of any perceived negative emotions or thoughts, and this prevented her from committing actions that would lead her towards her value. This led to her often avoiding family situations, which tended to worsen her guilt. Overall, her broad set of avoidance strategies functioned to alleviate her anxiety in the short term, though severely restricted her ability to receive positive reinforcement from engaging in previously rewarding activities, such as spending time with family or friends.

Toni's initial goals for therapy were to decrease the worrying and improve her mood. She reported that if she were able to do this, she could return to work and be back with her family.

The Therapeutic Relationship

The therapeutic relationship with Toni was built by validating her feelings and attempts to solve her problems, while also encouraging her to notice her own experience of these problems. Sessions emphasised Toni noticing in the present moment her struggles with thoughts and feelings, and making room for these experiences through mindfulness. The 'two mountains' metaphor was introduced early in therapy in order to provide a model of the therapy relationship as collaborative rather directive.

Strategies of Treatment

To engage Toni in therapy, the strategies she had used to try to improve her situation were reviewed. Principally, her attempts to avoid negative emotions and thoughts were focused on. Toni acknowledged that while some of these strategies were helpful in the short term, she remained stuck. The 'tug-of-war with the monster' metaphor (see 'Developing acceptance and willingness' above) was introduced to illustrate some of the ways in which Toni was caught in an unhelpful struggle with her thoughts and feelings. Toni identified strongly with the metaphor and recognised that her approach to difficult thoughts and feelings, characterised by avoidance and attempts to control, had the tendency to increase her suffering. The metaphor also allowed for the introduction of the notion 'letting go of the rope' as an alternative to unhelpful struggle.

Major Treatment Techniques

Cognitive defusion techniques were introduced to help Toni develop a non-evaluative, observer stance towards unhelpful thoughts. The therapist deliberately used language to promote defusion, for example 'Notice when your mind says ...'. Toni was encouraged also to adopt this language to describe her thought processes, such as 'I notice my mind saying I'm never going to get better'.

The paradoxical effect of thought control attempts that lead to rebound effects was discussed using the 'white bear' thought suppression experiment (Wegner and Zanakos, 1994). Mindfulness was introduced as an alternative to engaging in thought suppression and Toni began to practice noticing thoughts as they occurred, making room for them without necessarily engaging with them. Brief mindfulness exercises were practised during sessions. Additionally, Toni was given a compact disc with recordings of different exercises that she used to practice in between sessions. In doing this, Toni noticed the habitual, repetitive nature of the unwanted thoughts, which enabled her to view the thoughts as less dangerous and more as 'boring and dull'. Using these approaches reduced Toni's tendency to ruminate on the occurrence of these unwanted thoughts, and subsequently the frequency of the thoughts reduced.

In ACT, symptom elimination is not a treatment target, although often symptoms tend to lessen as clients engage in more valued activity. Building on the 'tug-of-war with the monster' metaphor, consideration was given to how attempts to get rid of negative emotion had tended to amplify Toni's distress. Toni was encouraged to make space for these difficult emotions by developing a stance of willingness. Present-moment focused exercises were used to help Toni come into contact with difficult emotions in a non-judgemental, compassionate and accepting way, to track the natural ebbs and flows of emotion, whilst noticing and observing thoughts and judgements of this experience.

Overcoming Obstacles to Client Progress

The notion of willingness to experience unpleasant emotion in ACT is directly linked to taking valued action. Toni had a strong desire to not experience unwanted negative emotion, and this came at great cost as she would avoid situations where she felt likely to become anxious or depressed. This desire proved to be a significant obstacle to Toni moving forward, and her life had become very restricted, with limited opportunity to engage in valued activities.

Thus, the next stage of therapy was focused on values clarification. Toni had indentified from the outset of therapy that she wanted to be emotionally available for her family. She also wanted to be more open with family and friends. Toni identified a number of behaviours she could do that would reflect this value, which included, in the short term, leaving the unit, and in the longer term, looking after herself better so she could sustain valued action. Actions in this area included reconnecting with friends, reducing the amount of time she spent at work, and taking up exercise again. In considering taking steps towards these values, Toni identified a significant barrier in her unwillingness to experience anxiety.

Alongside this, an analysis of the workability of her avoidance of negative affect was carried out. Although Toni identified that avoidance typically reduced her distress, she recognised that over the longer term, her general strategy of avoidance had served to worsen her distress. This, in conjunction with the values work, helped Toni to choose to be more willing to experience distressing emotions so that she could do more of what was important to her.

Toni also reflected on the onset of her depression and recognised that she had been under considerable pressure at work, largely as a result of her inability to tolerate anxiety associated with not completing work to her very high standards. This had led Toni to work long hours and often not be satisfied with the results of her work. She was also able to recognise that she had experienced a significant increase in anxiety with the impending return to work after the holiday break. Toni

(Continued)

(Continued)

reflected that, due to her efforts to avoid and control feelings, she had not recognised that she was becoming so stressed, ignoring the warning signs. She also acknowledged that her suicide attempt was largely to escape a situation she believed she could not tolerate. Toni described feeling extremely guilty about this and the effect it had on her family.

The combination of defusion, willingness, mindfulness and values clarification work allowed Toni to develop greater flexibility in the face of these difficult and distressing thoughts and emotions. The therapy focused on assisting her to plan and commit to valued actions, reinforcing the notion that such actions can take place before the actual subsidence of distressing thoughts and emotions. As a result, Toni started to take steps toward leaving the unit, such as going on leave with her family and meeting close friends. She also decided to talk with her family and friends about her recent experiences, which although she found difficult, was part of her valued direction. Toni started making plans for a gradual return to work, which she had avoided considering for some time. She reported being initially very anxious about taking these steps and, although she remained anxious, was somewhat surprised not to be overwhelmed by anxiety. Alongside her feelings of anxiety, Toni also noticed a significant sense of pride and enjoyment in being able to do these activities, experiencing a concurrent lift in mood.

Outcome

Toni left the unit after a period of six weeks. She returned to work and negotiated a reduction in her hours so that she could spend more time with her family. During this time, Toni continued to experience relatively high levels of anxiety and ongoing worries about the presence of these feelings but noticed that they tended to be 'crowded out' by the rest of her life. She found her mood continued to improve, and started to notice a richer kaleidoscope of emotions, both positive and negative.

Research Status

Research into ACT has rapidly expanded over the last 10 years, as researchers have sought to determine the effectiveness of the treatment model and the mechanisms of change. Following the publication of the Hayes et al. (1999) treatment manual, there was scepticism regarding the ACT model and suggestions that initial enthusiasm was exceeding actual empirical support (e.g. Corrigan, 2001). Since this time, a significant number of randomised controlled trials have been published, demonstrating the effectiveness of ACT in a wide range of areas, including depression (Zettle and Hayes, 1986), work stress (Bond and Bunce, 2000), psychosis (Bach and Hayes, 2002; Gaudiano and Herbert, 2006), substance abuse (Hayes et al., 2004b), chronic pain (Dahl et al., 2004; Vowles and McCracken, 2008), borderline personality disorder (Gratz and Gunderson, 2006) and epilepsy (Lundgren et al., 2006).

In addition to studies investigating the efficacy and effectiveness of ACT, further research has employed mediational designs to determine if change resulting from the intervention occurs through the processes predicted by the ACT model. A number of studies have reported similar mediational effects, in that ACT variables have mediated the effect of the intervention on outcome, including experiential avoidance (Bond and Bunce, 2000), thought believability (Zettle and Hayes, 1986), acceptance of diabetes-related thoughts and feelings (Gregg et al., 2007) and believability of hallucinations (Gaudiano and Herbert, 2006).

Three meta-analytic reviews evaluating ACT outcome research have now been published (Hayes et al., 2006; Öst, 2008; Powers et al., 2009). Overall, these meta-analyses provide evidence that ACT is significantly better than wait list controls or treatment as usual. There is also modest evidence for ACT as superior to other treatments specifically designed for the problem examined. As Öst (2008) argues, there is a need for future ACT evaluation research to be more robust, particularly with the inclusion of empirically supported active comparison treatments such as CBT.

In summary, empirical support for the clinical utility of the ACT model is developing. ACT research has shown promising results across a broad range of areas, and furthermore, mediational, correlational and experimental studies that have investigated the underlying change processes have provided support for the ACT model.

Suggested Further Reading

Ciarrochi, J., and Bailey, A. (2008) *A CBT-Practitioner's Guide to ACT: How to Bridge the Gap Between Cognitive Behavioral Therapy and Acceptance and Commitment Therapy*. Oakland, CA: New Harbinger.

Harris, R. (2009) *ACT Made Simple: An Easy-to-read Primer on Acceptance and Commitment Therapy*. Oakland, CA: New Harbinger.

Hayes, S.C., Luoma, J., Bond, F., Masuda, A. and Lillis, J. (2006) 'Acceptance and commitment therapy: Model, processes, and outcomes', *Behaviour Research and Therapy*, 44: 1–25.

Hayes, S.C., Strosahl, K., and Wilson, K.G. (1999) *Acceptance and Commitment Therapy: An Experiential Approach to Behavior Change*. New York: Guilford Press.

Luoma, J.B., Hayes, S.C. and Walser, R.D. (2007) *Learning ACT: An Acceptance and Commitment Therapy Skills-training Manual for Therapists*. Oakland, CA: New Harbinger.

References

Bach, P. and Hayes, S.C. (2002) 'The use of acceptance and commitment therapy to prevent the rehospitalization of psychotic patients: A randomized controlled trial', *Journal of Consulting and Clinical Psychology*, 70: 1129–1139.

Bach, P.A.P. and Moran, D.J. (2008) *ACT in Practice: Case Conceptualization in Acceptance and Commitment Therapy*. Oakland, CA: New Harbinger.

Barnes-Holmes, Y., Barnes-Holmes, D., McHugh, L. and Hayes, S.C. (2004) 'Relational frame theory: Some implications for understanding and treating human psychopathology', *International Journal of Psychology and Psychological Therapy*, 4(2): 355–375.

Beck, J.S.B. (1995) *Cognitive Therapy: Basics and Beyond*. New York: Guilford Press.

Berens, N.M. and Hayes, S.C. (2007) 'Arbitrarily applicable comparative relations: Experimental evidence for a relational operant', *Journal of Applied Behavior Analysis*, 40(1): 45–71.

Bond, F.W. and Bunce, D. (2000) 'Mediators of change in emotion-focused and problem-focused worksite stress management interventions', *Journal of Occupational Health Psychology*, 5: 156–163.

Chomsky, N. (1959) 'A review of B.F. Skinner's verbal behavior', *Language*, 35, 26–58.

Corrigan, P. (2001) 'Getting ahead of the data: A threat to some behavior therapies', *The Behavior Therapist*, 24: 189–193.

Cullen, C. (2008) 'Acceptance and commitment therapy (ACT): A third wave behaviour Therapy', *Behavioural and Cognitive Psychotherapy*, 36 (Special Issue 06): 667–673.

Dahl, J.A., Wilson, K.G. and Nilsson, A. (2004) 'Acceptance and commitment therapy and the treatment of persons at risk for long-term disability resulting from stress and pain symptoms: A preliminary randomized trial', *Behavior Therapy*, 35(4): 785–801.

Devany, J.M., Hayes, S.C. and Nelson, R.O. (1986) 'Equivalence class formation in language-able and language-disabled children', *Journal of the Experimental Analysis of Behavior*, 46(3): 243.

Dymond, S. and Barnes, D. (1995) 'A transformation of self-discrimination response functions in accordance with the arbitrarily applicable relations of sameness, more than and less than', *Journal of the Experimental Analysis of Behavior*, 64(2): 163.

Gaudiano, B. and Herbert, J.D. (2006) 'Acute treatment of inpatients with psychotic symptoms using acceptance and commitment therapy: Pilot results', *Behaviour Research and Therapy*, 44: 415–437.

Gratz, K.L. and Gunderson, J.G. (2006) 'Preliminary data on an acceptance-based emotion regulation group intervention for deliberate self-harm among women with borderline personality disorder', *Behavior Therapy*, 37: 25–35.

Gregg, J.A., Callaghan, G.M., Hayes, S.C. and Glenn-Lawson, J.L. (2007) 'Improving diabetes self-management through acceptance, mindfulness and values: A randomized controlled trial', *Journal of Consulting and Clinical Psychology*, 75: 336–343.

Hayes, S.C. (1989) *Rule-governed Behavior: Cognition, Contingencies and Instructional Control*. New York: Plenum.

Hayes, S.C. (2004) 'Acceptance and commitment therapy, relational frame theory and the third wave of behavioral and cognitive therapies', *Behavior Therapy*, 35(4): 639–665.

Hayes, S.C. and Batten, S. (2000) 'A primer of acceptance and commitment therapy', *European Psychotherapy*, 1: 2–9.

Hayes, S.C. and Gifford, E.V. (1997) 'The trouble with language: Experiential avoidance, rules and the nature of verbal events', *Psychological Science*, 8(3): 170.

Hayes, S.C. and Wilson, K.G. (1994) 'Acceptance and commitment therapy: Altering the verbal support for experiential avoidance', *The Behavior Analyst*, 17(2): 289–303.

Hayes, S.C., Barnes-Holmes, D. and Roche, B. (2001) *Relational Frame Theory: A Post-Skinnerian Account of Human Language and Cognition.* New York: Springer.

Hayes, S.C., Luoma, J., Bond, F., Masuda, A. and Lillis, J. (2006) 'Acceptance and commitment therapy: Model, processes and outcomes'. *Behaviour Research and Therapy*, 44: 1–25.

Hayes, S.C., Masuda, A., Bissett, R., Luoma, J. and Guerrero, L.F. (2004a) 'DBT, FAP and ACT: How empirically oriented are the new behavior therapy technologies?', *Behavior Therapy*, 35(1): 35–54.

Hayes, S.C., Pankey, J., Gifford, E.V., Batten, S.V. and Quinones, R. (2002) 'Acceptance and commitment therapy in experiential avoidance disorders', in F.W. Kaslow and T. Patterson (Eds), *Comprehensive Handbook of Psychotherapy: Cognitive Behavioral Approaches.* New York: Wiley.

Hayes, S.C., Strosahl, K. and Wilson, K.G. (1999) *Acceptance and Commitment Therapy: An Experiential Approach to Behavior Change.* New York: Guilford Press.

Hayes, S.C., Wilson, K.G., Gifford, E.V., Bissett, R., Piasecki, M., Batten, S.V., Byrd, M. and Gregg, J. (2004b) 'A randomized controlled trial of twelve-step facilitation and acceptance and commitment therapy with polysubstance abusing methadone maintained opiate addicts', *Behavior Therapy*, 35: 667–688.

Hayes, S. C., Wilson, K.G., Gifford, E.V., Follette, V.M. and Strosahl, K. (1996) 'Experiential avoidance and behavioral disorders: A functional dimensional approach to diagnosis and treatment', *Journal of Consulting and Clinical Psychology*, 64(6): 1152–1168.

Lillis, J. and Luoma, J. (2005) 'Acceptance and commitment therapy initial case conceptualization form' sourced from www.contextualpsychology.org, 28 September 2005.

Lundgren, T., Dahl, J.C., Melin, L. and Kies, B. (2006) 'Evaluation of acceptance and commitment therapy for drug refractory epilepsy: A randomized controlled trial in South Africa: A pilot study', *Epilepsia*, 47: 2173–2179.

Luoma, J.B., Hayes, S.C. and Walser, R.D. (2007) *Learning ACT: An Acceptance and Commitment Therapy Skills-Training Manual for Therapists.* Oakland, CA: Context Press.

McHugh, L. Barnes-Holmes, Y., Barnes-Holmes, D. (2004) 'A relational frame account of the development of complex cognitive phenomena: Perspective-taking, false belief understanding and deception', *International Journal of Psychology and Psychological Therapy*, 4: 303–324.

Öst, L. (2008) 'Efficacy of the third wave of behavioral therapies: A systematic review and meta-analysis', *Behaviour Research and Therapy*, 46: 296–321.

Powers, M.B., Vörding, M. and Emmelkamp, P.M.G. (2009) 'Acceptance and commitment therapy: A meta-analytic review', *Psychotherapy and Psychosomatics*, 8: 73–80.

Strosahl, K., Hayes, S.C., Wilson, K.G. and Gifford, E.V. (2004) 'An ACT primer: Core therapy processes, intervention strategies and therapist competencies', in S.C. Hayes and K. Strosahl (Eds), *A Practical Guide to Acceptance and Commitment Therapy*. New York: Springer. pp. 31–58.

Vowles, K.E. and McCracken, L.M. (2008) 'Acceptance and values-based action in chronic pain: A study of treatment effectiveness and process', *Journal of Consulting and Clinical Psychology*, 76: 397–407.

Wegner, D.M. (1994) *White Bears and Other Unwanted Thoughts: Suppression, Obsession and the Psychology of Mental Control*. New York: Guilford.

Wegner, D.M. and Zanakos, S. (1994) 'Chronic thought suppression', *Journal of Personality*, 62: 615–640.

Zettle, R.D. and Hayes, S. (1986) 'Dysfunctional control by client verbal behavior: The context of reason giving', *The Analysis of Verbal Behavior*, 4: 30–38.

FIVE Dialectical Behaviour Therapy

MICHAELA SWALES,

Historical Development of DBT

Development of the Approach

In her seminal description of dialectical behaviour therapy (DBT), Linehan (1993a) articulates her early experiences in developing the treatment. She began with the application of behaviour therapy to chronically suicidal individuals, many of whom had a diagnosis of borderline personality disorder (BPD). She encountered several difficulties in these early treatment endeavours. First, clients frequently failed to complete homework tasks; second, the primary problems presented by the client at each session fluctuated dramatically; and third, clients frequently failed to attend sessions. Linehan conceptualised these problems as a result of the extreme challenge for clients with multiple and severe difficulties in a treatment exclusively focused on change. She hypothesised that the relentless focus on change invalidated clients who believed they were incapable of change or did not deserve to improve. In response, Linehan sought to incorporate a focus on acceptance into the treatment to balance the intense focus on change. She turned to Zen philosophy and in particular mindfulness to counterbalance behavioural theory. She adopted dialectics as a philosophical context that provides a framework for synthesising these two contrasting philosophies. The resulting treatment, DBT, is a principle-driven treatment that specialises in treating high-risk behaviours, particularly suicidal and self-harm behaviours, in the context of an identified diagnostic group, most commonly BPD.

DBT was first demonstrated as an efficacious treatment for suicidal behaviour in the context of BPD in a treatment trial published in 1991 (Linehan et al., 1991), with the treatment manuals being published shortly afterwards (Linehan, 1993a; 1993b). During the last 20 years, trials confirming the initial promise of the treatment have been conducted by research groups other than Linehan's and in countries outside the USA (see later). Linehan developed a training programme for learning DBT: DBT

Intensive Training. This is a 10-day programme consisting of two 5-week blocks of teaching separated by 6–8 months of development work. The first DBT Intensive Training course was conducted in Seattle in 1993. This training programme has seeded over 500 DBT programmes in the USA (Hibbs et al., 2010). DBT is also offered as a treatment in a number of European countries (Spain, Germany, Netherlands, UK) and in other parts of the English-speaking world (Australia and New Zealand).

DBT in the UK

The first DBT team from the UK trained in Seattle in 1994/95. In the ensuing years a small number of teams continued to train in the USA. In 1997, the first UK Intensive Training programme ran in the UK with the support of the Linehan Training Group, a group of specialist trainers in DBT trained by the treatment developer. Since 1997, the British Isles DBT Training Team, a team of UK practitioners trained both to adherence in the treatment and as trainers in the treatment, has trained most British teams. Recent research calculated that the British training programme has seeded 240 programmes (Swales et al., 2010). Treatment programmes report, despite positive experiences of treatment delivery, significant problems in implementation of the treatment which relate primarily to lack of organisational support for specialised treatment programmes that require significant investment of practitioner time (Taylor et al., Forthcoming).

Theoretical Underpinnings

Major Theoretical Concepts

DBT rests on three core theoretical pillars: behaviourism, Zen and dialectics. At its core, DBT is a behavioural treatment. Behaviourism influences the principles and practices of the treatment in several ways. DBT embraces a radical behaviourist philosophy in that anything an organism does – thinking, sensing, emoting, acting – constitutes behaviour. Conceptualising in this way, for example, transforms the understanding of diagnosis. From a behaviourist perspective, the diagnostic criteria are simply lists of overt and covert behaviours, more or less behaviourally defined. Thus, therapists can intervene with any behaviour engaged in by the client using principles of behaviour change. Following behaviour change, when the client no longer engages in the overt behaviours and no longer experiences the covert behaviours, the diagnosis has gone. This perspective often provides clients with a more hopeful perspective than hitherto. In addition to providing a theoretical conceptualisation of the difficulties of the client, the behavioural focus drives the central treatment strategies of DBT: problem solving. Regardless of the problem, DBT therapists spend the first part of each session conducting behavioural analyses of clients' behaviours targeted for change. These analyses form the basis for comprehensive solution analyses of clients' difficulties (see below).

For clients with serious and multiple problems, as discussed earlier, a relentless focus on change can be difficult to tolerate. Zen philosophy, emphasising acceptance of reality as it is, provides a counterpoint to this push for change. In embracing Zen, DBT therapists accept the client as he or she is in the moment, the client's current state of progress and the status of the therapeutic relationship. In so doing, therapists model for clients how to accept themselves and reality as it is in the moment. To promote an attitude of acceptance, DBT therapists practice mindfulness themselves and teach mindfulness to clients. In contrast to other psychological treatments utilising mindfulness that focus on clients engaging in extensive practices, DBT teaches mindfulness as a series of seven skills (Linehan, 1993b), each of which is rehearsed in shorter practices. These basics of mindfulness are taught in DBT skills groups. DBT therapists strengthen and generalise these skills by noticing when clients become unmindful and coaching in how to remain more focused in the present moment without judgement. In assisting clients to solve current problems DBT therapists balance solutions based on both acceptance-based skills and change-based skills.

Dialectical philosophy builds a bridge between acceptance and change within the treatment. As a world view, dialectics emphasises interconnectedness and wholeness, guarding against a unipolar perspective on reality. DBT therapists recognise and welcome multiple perspectives on problems. In endeavouring to synthesise data from more than one perspective, more effective solutions may be found.

How Client Problems are Conceptualised

Primacy of Affect

Linehan proposes that the primary difficulty for clients with a diagnosis of BPD is the experience and regulation of *affect*. The central difficulty of managing affect leads to the emotional lability that is at the heart of BPD. Emotional 'dysregulation', as Linehan refers to it, drives difficulties in other systems. Thus, clients experience interpersonal dysregulation (chaotic relationships and fears of abandonment), self-dysregulation (identity disturbances and sense of inner emptiness), cognitive dysregulation (paranoid ideation and dissociative thinking) and behavioural dysregulation (suicidal and impulsive behaviours). Conceptualising the diagnosis according to these systems of dysregulation articulates a central component of DBT conceptualisation that criterion behaviours of the BPD diagnosis are either a natural consequence of being emotionally dysregulated (chaotic relationships, identity and cognitive disturbances) or represent attempts to re-regulate (suicidal and impulsive behaviours). DBT therapists, therefore, in conceptualising client problems, place a strong emphasis on affect and understanding the relationship between the clients presenting problems and affect.

Capability and Motivational Deficits

DBT is based on a biosocial theory that explains the origins of the emotional vulnerability of BPD clients as a consequence of biological vulnerability transacting with invalidating environments. Linehan suggests that clients who develop BPD are biologically vulnerable to emotion regulation difficulties either as a result of genetic, intrauterine or neurobiological factors. Such biological predispositions will only lead to BPD in certain environmental contexts. Linehan described invalidating environments as the crucial type of environment that in concert with biological vulnerabilities transact over time, leading to the development of BPD. Invalidating environments have three major characteristics. First, these environments fail to recognise and validate the individual's own private experiences, frequently dismissing them as inaccurate, ill-judged or indicative of major character flaws. Second, in the face of emotional escalation, invalidating environments intermittently reinforce extreme emotional displays. Third, invalidating environments oversimplify the solution of social and emotional problems. These features of invalidating environments lead to several difficulties for clients with BPD. Frequently, clients are unable to recognise and label their emotional experiences in a manner normative to the wider community. As they have not received accurate feedback about their own emotional responses to situations and the validity of their responses, they learn to distrust or to ignore their own emotional responses. For significant periods of time, invalidating environments fail to attend to emotional communications or distress but then intermittently reinforce escalations. Thus, clients learn to oscillate between the inhibition of emotional responses and extreme behaviours, for example suicidal behaviours. As invalidating environments tend to imply that the solution to life's challenges lies in 'pulling yourself up by your own bootstraps', clients have not learnt how to solve complex problems by breaking them down into component parts and also tolerating the frustration of not having solved the problem yet. Whilst a degree of invalidation is common in all environments, development of BPD is more likely when invalidation is chronic or severe, or when the individual is highly biologically vulnerable. The transactional theory of the development of BPD, however, allows for the development of BPD in circumstances where there may be relatively minor biological vulnerability in the context of low levels of invalidation. In these circumstances, the poorness-of-fit between an individual and their environment may result in low levels of invalidation increasing the vulnerability in the child, resulting in subsequent, more intense levels of validation that further disrupt the child's capacity to emotionally regulate and, over years, lead to greater disturbance.

Consequent upon the invalidating environment that has failed to teach clients how to manage emotions, clients with BPD have significant

Table 5.1   Functions and modes of a DBT programme

Function of the DBT programme	Example modalities
Enhance client capabilities	Skills groups
Enhance client motivation	DBT individual psychotherapy
Ensure generalisation	Telephone consultation
Structure the environment:	a) Management of the DBT
a) Treatment	programme
b) Client	b) DBT family therapy
Enhance therapist capabilities and motivation	Consultation team

capability deficits in the management of emotions, relationships and behaviour and, in addition, clients have significant motivational deficits that impede effective resolution of their difficulties. Thus, DBT rests on a capability and motivational deficit model of BPD and recommends a comprehensive treatment programme to address these problems.

DBT treatment programmes possess five functions, each with corresponding modalities (see Table 5.1).

Enhancing client capabilities in the realm of affect regulation, interpersonal skills and crisis management represents a core component of a DBT programme. Most programmes address this function by running DBT skills groups, which follow a core curriculum (mindfulness, interpersonal effectiveness, emotion regulation and distress tolerance) described in detail in the *Skills Training Manual* (Linehan, 1993b). DBT individual psychotherapy focuses on identifying and resolving motivational impediments to behaviour change such as problematic affects, cognitions or reinforcement contingencies. To ensure generalisation of treatment gains outside of the treatment environment, DBT programmes contain specific modalities designed to both generalise skills and also reduce suicidal crises. Most commonly, DBT programmes provide telephone consultation between the DBT individual therapist and the client between sessions to fulfil this function. In recognition of the challenge of treating clients with BPD effectively and of the complexity of the problems presented by the clients, DBT programmes also attend to enhancing the capabilities and motivation of the therapists. DBT therapists meet weekly in consultation team, during which they receive consultation and supervision on their treatment of clients. Finally, DBT programmes require modalities to assist in maintaining the structure of the treatment programme and, in some cases, to promote treatment gains within the clients' natural environments.

Behavioural Conceptualisation

Following on from the behavioural approach to diagnosis, DBT conceptualises all of the problems of the client in behavioural terms. Thus, DBT therapists, in pre-treatment, discuss with clients the primary behavioural

Table 5.2   Hierarchy of behaviours in Stage 1 of DBT

Primary targets

Life-threatening behaviours, including:

- suicidal behaviours;
- non-suicidal self-injury;
- homicidal behaviours;
- serious aggressive acts;
- imminently life-threatening behaviours;
- threats and urges to engage in the above;
- significant changes in suicidal/homicidal ideation.

Therapy-interfering behaviours of the client and therapist.

Quality-of-life interfering behaviours, including:

- behaviours associated with other psychiatric diagnoses;
- seriously destabilising behaviours, e.g. frequent hospitalisations, violent behaviour, forensic behaviours.

Increase behavioural skills

targets for change. The specific behaviours of the client are then arranged hierarchically (see Table 5.2) according to the scheme utilised within DBT. During treatment itself, each week therapists select a specific example of one of the target behaviours that form the basis for the chain and solution analysis within the session.

DBT as a behavioural treatment is based on behavioural theory. Thus, DBT therapists apply learning theory to the problems of the client. In analysing client problems, DBT therapists seek to identify classical conditioning links in the sequence of events leading up to and operant conditioning links following target behaviours. For example, a client with a history of sexual abuse frequently dissociated at night on entering her bedroom when she saw her bed. As a child her father, just before bed, had frequently sexually abused her. For her, the bed was a cue that elicited anxiety and dissociation. This represented a classically conditioned link. Subsequent to dissociation, the client would cut herself to terminate the dissociative state which she experienced as aversive. Thus, cutting was negatively reinforced by the removal of the dissociative state. DBT therapists would then apply the appropriate intervention to treat each link. In this case, the therapist conducted an informal exposure programme to the cue of 'beds', helping the client to decrease dissociative behaviours when presented with the cue. Emotion regulation skills to manage anxiety as she approached bedtime and mindfulness enabled the client to tolerate and benefit from the exposure programme. To address the operant links, the therapist taught the client how to become 'reassociated' without cutting. Grounding skills were especially useful here, as were some cognitive restructuring of the client's beliefs that she deserved to suffer the distress of dissociation because she believed herself culpable in the abuse.

As indicated earlier, DBT applies the treatment to covert as well as overt behaviours. Thus, principles of learning theory can be applied to thoughts as well as actions. For example, many clients with a history of repeated suicidal behaviours when faced with an emotional difficulty find thinking about death soothing. Conceptually, then, the relief from distress negatively reinforces suicidal thinking. DBT therapists intervene both by providing alternative ways to experience relief other than thinking about suicide and also initiate a new learning history by challenging the client's belief that suicidal thinking is a solution to life's difficulties, that is, providing an aversive consequence to suicidal thinking.

Practical Applications

Therapeutic Relationship

DBT makes several assumptions about the therapeutic relationship: that the most caring thing a therapist can do is to help clients change in ways that bring them closer to their own goals; that principles of behaviour are universal affecting therapists as much as clients; and that therapists treating clients with BPD need support. At the start of the pre-treatment phase in DBT, therapists focus on identifying client goals and then explicitly link these to the goals of treatment. For example, a client who wants to develop better interpersonal relationships is helped to see that stopping suicidal behaviours will increase the likelihood of more mutually supportive relationships; or a client who wants to feel better is oriented to how the treatment teaches and helps to implement a range of longer-term solutions to emotional difficulties that whilst they lack the immediate affect regulatory capacity of cutting, they also lack the harmful effects on her body, her self-esteem and her family relationships. Occasionally, making these links explicit is more challenging; for example, the client who states that his or her goal in life is to be dead. In these circumstances, the DBT therapist explores what 'being dead' would do for the client. Frequently, clients will identify that being dead will relieve emotional suffering or escape intolerable life circumstances. The DBT therapist in these circumstances must build a case for the treatment to provide an alternative route to these same ends.

As principles of behaviour change are universal, the therapeutic process impacts therapists as well as clients. DBT recognises this process of reciprocal influence in the identification of therapy-interfering behaviours in the target hierarchy by explicitly stating that therapy-interfering behaviour is a 'two-way street' and that therapists may engage in behaviours that hinder client progress in therapy. DBT therapists need to practise openness in response to feedback from clients about their own behaviours and develop the capacity to scrutinise the impact of their behaviours with a willingness to modify their responses if necessary. Therapists also must remain awake to the impact of clients' responses on them. Just as therapists endeavour to shape client behaviour, clients' behaviours may shape therapists' behaviour out-of-awareness and sometimes in ways that ultimately are ineffective. For example, a client who was ashamed of her suicidal behaviour became either aggressive with the therapist or mute when it was discussed. Both behaviours the therapists found a challenge to respond to. He tried a number of different interventions without success and gradually decreased his focus on the client's suicidal behaviour. The client did become more comfortable in session, but her suicidal behaviour and high risk continued unchanged. The task of the DBT consultation team is to assist therapists in both identifying and changing these problematic patterns when they arise.

In DBT the therapeutic relationship is the major source of contingent relationships for client progress. Early in the process of behaviour change clients rarely receive any direct and immediate reinforcement for their early change efforts. New emotion regulation skills rarely work with the effectiveness of suicidal and self-harming behaviours, and small changes in interpersonal style often go unremarked by the chaotic environments in which clients live. The therapist, therefore, is often the only source of reinforcement to motivate the client to remain in what is often a painful process of change. DBT therapists attend to the impact of their behaviour on clients and use their own behaviour strategically to promote change. Just as the therapist will notice and reinforce any small effort that the client makes towards using non-harming methods to manage emotions, he or she will also refrain from reinforcing problematic behaviours. So, for example, DBT therapists will take care to eliminate any increase in warmth and validation in response to suicidal communications, tending to remain matter-of-fact and reserving increases in warmth and validation for clients' non-suicidal problem-solving efforts.

A significant component of the role of the DBT therapist is to be both a teacher and a consultant to the client. In skills training groups, therapists explicitly teach skills and indeed the format of the class is more that of an educational class than a therapy group. In individual therapy, therapists may help clients acquire new skills, but primarily they focus on assisting clients to strengthen new skills. DBT is entirely open with clients about its philosophy and its proposed methods of action. DBT therapists therefore orient clients to therapeutic strategies, especially to the four change procedures (skills training, cognitive modification, exposure and contingency management), to promote clients' capacity to mange their own behaviour. Whilst DBT therapists actively teach, model and demonstrate to clients and take an active problem-solving stance throughout therapy, their primary stance for solution implementation is consultation to the patient. Thus, rather than the therapist intervening to solve problems on behalf of the client with other professionals or other parts of the treatment system, the DBT therapist coaches the client on how to approach and solve whatever problems he or she is experiencing with others.

Strategies of Treatment

Within DBT all treatment techniques and strategies are arranged on the dialectic of acceptance and change. The core treatment strategies are *problem solving*, representing the change pole, and *validation*, representing the acceptance pole.

Problem Solving

Central to DBT is problem solving; standard CBT problem solving with a few novel twists. Each therapy session, the DBT therapist selects the most high-priority target behaviour that the client has engaged in the preceding week for analysis. First, the therapist obtains a precise definition of the topography and severity of the target behaviour before conducting a behavioural analysis of all the links in the sequence of events that led up to and followed the behaviour. In conducting the chain analysis the therapist seeks to identify and distinguish affective, cognitive and overt behavioural links and to clarify which of the links in the sequence of events are dysfunctional, and which of them are controlling variables with respect to the target behaviour.

The therapist uses the behavioural analysis as a basis for the solution analysis. If the therapist assesses that the problematic link occurred as a result of a skills deficit, then, if the client does not yet know the skill, the therapist teaches a new skill, or, if the client has acquired the basics of the skill in the skills training group, then the therapist strengthens the skill and assists the client to generalise the skill to the new context. If the problematic link is an unwarranted affect, or where the affect is warranted but the intensity of affect is unwarranted, the therapist may use exposure as a solution. When problematic cognitions interfere with skilful behaviour, then the therapist will use cognitive modification procedures. When more skilful behaviour is within the client's repertoire of behaviours but is low down in the response hierarchy, or where more dysfunctional behaviours are higher in the response hierarchy, then the therapist utilises contingency management procedures to modify client responses.

Once the therapist has selected a solution or range of solutions to address the target behaviour, the therapist rehearses the new behaviours with the client in session. Rehearsal provides the therapist with an opportunity to identify any problems in understanding or implementing the new behaviour and also to shape successive approximations to more skilful behaviour. Finally, the therapist considers with the client the detailed practicalities of implementing the new solutions outside the therapy session and troubleshoots any potential problems in generalising the new behaviours.

Validation

Balancing the problem-solving focus, DBT therapists distil from the myriad responses of their client – emotions, cognitions and behaviours – those which are valid, and feeds this back to them. The therapist thus provides a counterpoint to the invalidating environment by modelling and then teaching clients how to validate their own responses. Dialectically, therapists simultaneously validate the valid aspects of the client's responses whilst invalidating their invalid aspects. For example, a client may repeatedly cut herself in order to relieve anxiety. Cutting is, therefore, valid both because it relieves anxiety and because most people seek methods to reduce unpleasant levels of anxiety. The behaviour is invalid, however, in that it reduces the likelihood that the client will reach his or her ultimate goal of feeling better and enhancing his or her self-esteem.

Whilst many treatments more or less explicitly incorporate validation, DBT articulates a series of levels of validation, some of which are especially characteristic of the treatment. The lower levels of validation (staying awake to the client's responses moment-by-moment in the session; reflecting accurately the client's responses; mind-reading that which is unspoken; validating the client's behaviour in terms of their past learning history) are more typical of a wider range of therapies. The two higher levels, validation in terms of present context and radical genuineness, are particularly distinctive features of DBT. Validation in terms of present context requires the therapist to identify those aspects of a client's responses that are valid in the present context or are indicative of normative functioning. For example, a client with an abuse history agreed to work with a female therapist although she would have preferred a male therapist because female family members had persistently failed to rescue her from abusive situations. The client struggled to disclose matters of significance to the therapist. The therapist validated this in terms of normative functioning by saying 'It makes sense to me why you have difficulty trusting me as you've only just met me and don't know yet whether I can be trusted'. This was more effective with this client in promoting engagement with the therapist than a more traditional validation of her learning history, for example 'It makes sense why you don't trust me yet as women have often let you down.'

In using radical genuineness, the DBT therapist responds to the client in the way that he or she would to a family member or a colleague. In other words, the therapist 'tells it like it is', treating the client as another human being robust enough to hear the truth. For example, a client had broken a vase in the therapy room during an aggressive outburst and was immediately apologetic, saying 'I shouldn't have done that', hiding her face away from the therapist. The therapist responded 'You're right, it was totally inappropriate – how are you going to put it right?', validating the warranted shame, matter-of-factly. The client relaxed slightly in her posture, looked up at the therapist and was then able to discuss appropriate reparation. This example indicates a key characteristic of validation: it involves finding the validity or accuracy in the client's response and does not necessarily involve saying something positive.

Major Treatment Techniques

Stylistic Strategies

DBT therapists deliver problem solving and validation using two dialectically opposing styles: reciprocal and irreverent communication. Reciprocal communication is a fairly typical communication style in psychotherapy, consisting of warmth and genuineness. DBT therapists, in addition, use self-disclosure. In modelling self-disclosure, the therapist discloses personal examples of where they have encountered similar challenges to the client but have utilised skills or strategies from the treatment to solve the problem. Effective modelling self-disclosure uses a coping rather than a mastery model of skill use. Therapists also only disclose resolved or uncontentious problems from their own lives, ensuring that the focus of the session remains on the resolution of clients' difficulties. In self-involving self-disclosures, DBT therapists communicate directly to clients their own response to clients' behaviours, emotions and thoughts. For example, a client frequently said, without consideration, 'That won't work' to all of her therapist's suggestions, whilst demanding that her therapist provided her with help. The therapist responded to the client, 'When you demand my help and dismiss all my suggestions without detailed consideration, my motivation to help you decreases'. The client was surprised by this information as it had not been her intention to elicit this response in the therapist, rather her summary dismissals stemmed from an anxiety that she would be unable to change her behaviour. Disclosing her response to the client facilitated problem solving of how the therapist could more effectively make suggestions for change and what the client could do to manage her anxiety.

DBT therapists use irreverent communication when the client is entrenched or stuck with the aim of increasing engagement and shaking up established ways of thinking, feeling and acting. Irreverent strategies, however, just like reciprocal strategies, must also come from a position of compassion for the client. At its most basic, irreverence involves using a matter-of-fact or confrontational tone to discuss subjects that often are not discussed or skirted around. Most commonly, DBT therapists use this style in the discussion of suicidal behaviour. For example, in pre-treatment a client described her only goal in life was to die. The therapist said 'So what would dying do for you?' The client immediately looked up at the therapist and became more engaged in the discussion. The client then described that she thought that death would provide an escape from life's difficulties. The therapist then increased the intensity of irreverence using the strategy of 'plunging in where angels fear to tread' and asking what no-one else would ask. The therapist enquired 'So why not die now?' The client was surprised by the directness of the question and then listed a number of reasons, one of which was that she wanted to wait until her daughter had left home. The therapist was then able to explore why the client killing herself was likely to have an impact on the client's daughter whatever age and wherever she lived, facilitating negotiation of commitment to the treatment. Combined with these irreverent interventions, the therapist was simultaneously validating of the extreme difficulties in the client's life and the need to develop effective, alternative-to-death, solutions for them.

Dialectical Strategies

Dialectics permeates the whole of the treatment. Balancing acceptance of the client in the moment with a push for change, moving between validating the valid and invalidating the invalid, considering multiple perspectives on the same problem and how solutions for one problem impinge upon another, dialectics drives the movement and speed of the therapeutic interaction. The primary dialectical strategy is the continual movement and balancing of problem solving and validation, weaving the different styles seamlessly together.

In addition to the movement between different styles and strategies, DBT has a number of strategies (use of metaphor, devil's advocate, making lemonade out of lemons, extending, activating wise mind) that embrace aspects of change and acceptance within them. For example, DBT therapists frequently use metaphor to encapsulate aspects of the client's current situation yet also indicating how to change. With the client in the case example below, Renee, the therapist used metaphor to help her understand the treatment stance on reducing suicidal and self-harm behaviours prior to addressing past trauma. The therapist described therapy as akin to climbing a mountain, and that in climbing a mountain you need to be properly prepared with the appropriate equipment, provisions and skills, particularly as this particular mountain is challenging and experiences frequent adverse weather conditions. DBT treatment is the stage of developing mountain-climbing skills, acquiring all the necessary provisions and practising withstanding adverse weather conditions. Describing the task in this way not only validated the difficulty of the task and the client's desire to do it – the sense of achievement, the view from the top will transform how you see the future – but also indicated what the client needed to do to be successful.

Overcoming Obstacles to Client Progress

Two aspects of the treatment assist DBT therapists in solving obstacles to client progress: the first is the inclusion of therapy interfering behaviours on the target hierarchy, and the second is the team focus of the treatment. If during the week prior to the therapy session there have been no suicidal behaviours, then therapy-interfering behaviour takes priority for behavioural and solution analyses. Therapists use the same principles and strategies to analyse therapy interfering behaviours as they do for suicidal behaviours. Behaviours engaged in during the therapy session itself may also interfere with the conduct of therapy. In these circumstances, the therapist may do a brief 'detour' to analyse the links in the chain leading up to and following the in-session behaviour and rehearse solutions with the client before returning to the analysis of the out-of-session behaviour. This movement between in-session and out-of-session behaviour is also characteristic of DBT.

Clients with BPD experience multiple complex problems and frequently live in environments characterised by high levels of adversity. Consequently, progress is often slow and solving client problems a significant challenge. Therapists may become demotivated and risk burn-out in these circumstances. DBT assumes, therefore, that therapists delivering the treatment need support in order to maintain a therapeutic stance with clients who are in a lot of emotional pain and where progress is slow. Thus, DBT is a team treatment; an individual therapist alone cannot deliver DBT. The DBT team meets weekly to provide consultation and supervision to the therapists on the team. DBT consultation teams focus on enhancing therapists' capabilities and motivation to treat effectively. Therapists may seek to learn about how to more effectively implement strategies of the treatment from their colleagues and also ask for assistance in increasing motivation for treating the clients. Team members utilise the same treatment strategies and solutions on themselves that they are teaching to clients. So, for example, a team might teach a therapist the key principles of exposure therapy; have a therapist role-play an interaction from therapy that did not go well and provide feedback; validate the struggles of the therapists in helping a client experiencing a traumatic court case; generate new solutions for a therapist to try with a client for whom no solutions seem to have worked so far. Therapists on a DBT team need to be willing, therefore, to apply all skills and strategies that they use with clients to themselves.

Case Example: Renee

Renee is 25 years old, unemployed and lives alone in supported housing. She has a history of suicidal and self-harming behaviours that began when she was 10 years old. These behaviours have increased in intensity in recent years. Renee cuts herself three to four times per week, mainly with box cutters. Her wounds are frequently sutured, but she will also often treat them herself as she dislikes attending A&E. Renee has a history of taking overdoses, primarily with paracetemol, but also of fluoxetine that she takes for her depressed mood. She has taken five overdoses in the last 18 months. She has had frequent admissions to hospital, commencing with a 1-year stay in an adolescent unit at the age of 16. In the last year she has had two brief admissions. Her consultant psychiatrist is reluctant to admit her as she usually deteriorates during admission, becoming more suicidal during the admission and increasing the difficulty of discharging her. She has had one episode of attempted hanging on the inpatient unit. She frequently expresses the wish to die and to escape her unending emotional turmoil. In addition to her suicidal

(Continued)

(Continued)

behaviour, Renee meets criteria for BPD, post-traumatic stress disorder (PTSD) and substance abuse disorder (alcohol).

Renee was sexually abused by her biological father and one of her mother's subsequent partners. Neither man was successfully prosecuted. Her mother is dependent on alcohol and was dependent throughout Renee's childhood. Renee describes caring for her mother when she was drunk and that her own physical and emotional needs were not addressed. Current contact with her family remains fraught with tension.

Renee has had experience of psychological treatments before. She was treated for her PTSD during her adolescence with an exposure-based treatment that resulted in a worsening of her suicidal and self-injurious behaviours. She was referred for psychodynamic therapy but was judged too unstable to benefit and she dropped out of a course of CBT after five sessions. She intermittently attends scheduled appointments with her community psychiatric nurse (CPN) and consultant psychiatrist, but presents frequently in crisis at evenings and weekends.

Conceptualisation of Renee's problems

During pre-treatment, Renee described her primary goal for treatment as decreasing the extreme emotional distress in her life. Renee described frequent and intense symptoms of PTSD, especially flashbacks and dissociation, high levels of shame and avoidance of ordinary social situations that often triggered these symptoms. The therapist's initial conceptualisation of suicidal and self-harming behaviours as well as her alcohol misuse as attempted solutions to her problems resonated with Renee. Suicidal behaviours provided her with a sense of escape from her problems, whilst self-harm behaviours and alcohol misuse serve to release tension, stop flashbacks and dissociation and significantly reduced high levels of emotion. As treatment progressed, the therapist's behavioural conceptualisation about Renee's problems became more comprehensive (see Table 5.4).

Therapeutic Relationship

As is typical in DBT, Renee's therapist employed validation and reciprocal communication strategies balanced with challenge and confrontation (irreverent strategies) to build the relationship. Primarily, the therapist validated the wisdom of Renee's ultimate goal of reducing distress in her life. More irreverently, however, the therapist validated how effective suicidal and self-harm behaviours were in achieving this goal by suggesting that she (the therapist) could be in favour of them if it was not for their longer-term negative effects. This intervention caught Renee's attention, leading to a more thoughtful evaluation of the costs and benefits for Renee of retaining suicidal behaviours as a solution to her difficulties. Following this discussion, Renee made a provisional commitment to treatment. The therapist shaped this commitment by employing the 'devil's advocate' strategy, one of the dialectical strategies in the treatment. The therapist emphasised the difficulty of therapy and wondered why Renee would want to attempt something so challenging when she had dropped out of other therapies before. In response, Renee articulated some of

Table 5.3   Renee's preliminary target hierarchy

Life-threatening behaviours to decrease:

- hanging;
- overdoses;
- cutting;
- threats to self-harm;
- urges to self-harm.

Therapy-interfering behaviours to decrease:
- non-attendance;
- not phoning the therapist;
- saying 'I can't' repeatedly.

Quality-of-life interfering behaviours:

- PTSD:
  - decrease dissociation;
  - decrease flashbacks.
- Substance abuse:
  - decrease alcohol use to <10 units a week.
- Increase structured activity during the day.

Increase behavioural skills.

---

her own scepticism about therapy and with some problem solving from the therapist committed to working on those behaviours that might interfere with therapy. Renee reported that she found the therapist's directness about the likely difficulties refreshing and helpful. Following orientation to the treatment programme and to the telephone consultation modality in particular, Renee was willing to commit to relinquishing suicidal and self-harm behaviours for the year-long contract. Renee's target hierarchy, drawn up at the end of pre-treatment, is shown in Table 5.3.

Application of Treatment Strategies and Techniques

The early part of Renee's treatment focused on analysing and developing comprehensive solution analyses for her suicidal behaviour. During the first 10 weeks of treatment, the most frequent behaviour in the top category was cutting. An example of one of the chain analyses of cutting, is shown in Table 5.4. The left-hand column describes Renee's therapist's conceptualisation of the chain, where affective, cognitive and behavioural links and reinforcing and punishing consequences are clearly distinguished. Identification of links in this way facilitates a more accurate and comprehensive solution analysis. The central column describes the links in the chain. The right-hand column outlines potential solutions to each of the links.

The solution analysis demonstrates several hallmarks of DBT. First, the therapist used solutions from more than one set of change procedures (skills, exposure, contingency management and cognitive restructuring) and recommends a balance of acceptance-based (mindfulness and distress tolerance skills) and change-based skills (acting opposite to emotion and interpersonal skills).

(Continued)

(Continued)

Table 5.4 Chain and solution analysis of cutting behaviour

Conceptualisation	Links in the chain	Potential solutions
Vulnerability factors	Low mood. Poor sleep.	
Prompting event	Argument with sister when Renee refuses to attend family event.	Interpersonal effectiveness skills: how to say 'No' more effectively.
Affective link	Anger.	Emotion regulation skills: unclench hands, sit down calmly, do not stomp about, validate why her sister may want her to attend the event.
Cognitive links	'She's never understood.' 'It was different for her.' 'She doesn't really believe what happened.'	Mindfulness. Self-validation.
Behavioural link	Tears up a drawing she was doing.	Emotion regulation: acting opposite to the emotion; continue to be creative. Distress tolerance: self-soothe.
Affective link	Anger decreases.	
Behavioural link	Curls up on sofa.	Acting opposite: go for a walk, remain seated upright, distraction.
Affective link	Sadness. Urge to withdraw.	Behavioural activation: text friend. Exposure to sadness as a cue that frequently elicits shame.
Cognitive link	'I shouldn't destroy things.'	Cognitive restructuring of the judgement. 'Destroying things doesn't help me.' Mindfulness of the judgement 'I'm just noticing that I am judging myself for tearing the drawing'.
Affective link	Sadness increases.	
Cognitive link	'It's all my fault.' 'I damage things and people.'	Mindfulness. Cognitive restructuring: 'I have hurt people in the past, I'm working on changing that.' 'I've been hurt in the past too.' 'I'm not totally responsible for all the difficulties in my family.'
Affective link	Shame	Act opposite to urge to hide away: reach out – call therapist or friend.
Cognitive link	Flashback to past emotional abuse by Mum.	Grounding skills: mindfully describe room and current context.

Conceptualisation	Links in the chain	Potential solutions
Behavioural link	Rocking to and fro with hands over her ears.	Sit in upright posture in the chair and …
Affective link	Shame increases.	… mindfully follow the breathing. Practice self-soothe.
Behavioural link	Goes to kitchen. Picks up box cutters from draw.	Avoid kitchen – go for walk. Remove box cutters from the house or lock away so harder to access. Crisis survival skills: review cons of self-harm behaviours as a solution.
Behavioural link	Cuts herself four times with box cutters on upper thigh.	
Negative reinforcement	Shame decreases.	
Positive reinforcement	'I've punished myself.'	Psychoeducation that cutting is reinforced by the consequences, not punished.
Behavioural link	Steri-strips on cut	
Positive reinforcement	Soothed.	Use alternative strategies to soothe self earlier in the chain.
Positive reinforcement	Texts friend who is sympathetic and comes over.	Contingency management: text friend before cutting, not after. Write out own chain and solution analysis (positive punishment).

Second, in approaching cognitive links, the therapist used mindfulness, in particular noticing and letting go of judgements, as well as traditional cognitive restructuring. One of the challenges for the therapist in working with Renee was that many of her most distressing cognitions were not inaccurate, that is, she frequently destroyed things and had often caused distress and upset to others. In DBT, the therapist, in a radically genuine way, will not avoid confirming the validity of some of these thoughts, although the therapist will ensure that the client sticks with the facts of the situation without adding interpretations or judgements. For example, in this chain the therapist did validate that many of Renee's friends had been hurt by her at various times but challenged the belief that her friends had been 'damaged' as there was no evidence that this was the case. The therapist also validated that Renee had at times damaged property. The movement between 'validating the valid' and promoting restructuring of the invalid components demonstrates dialectics in action.

Third, the therapist observed over a number of behavioural analyses that when Renee experienced sadness, this frequently elicited shame and thoughts that she was to blame for her sadness. This sequence was, in part, related to her history of

(Continued)

(Continued)

her mother berating her when anything went wrong in the family. Thus, the link between sadness and shame was classically conditioned. In DBT, when faced either with affects that are unwarranted by the situation or where the affect may be warranted but the intensity is not, as in this case, DBT therapists will use exposure as a solution. The therapist, therefore, asked Renee to imagine tearing up the drawing and the experience of sadness elicited by her actions. As Renee did this, her sense of shame began to rise. The therapist encouraged Renee to re-focus mindfully on her sadness, without judging herself or the behaviour, coaching her to say 'I have torn up my drawing. I notice my sadness that I did that. I notice the thought that I wish I hadn't done that'. The therapist also blocked any of Renee's typical shame behaviours, for example curling up and saying 'Everything is my fault'. By remaining more mindful of the sadness, less judgemental and more upright, Renee experienced a gradual reduction in shame, and sadness was less likely to trigger shame.

Fourth, the therapist developed contingency management strategies. For Renee, cutting primarily functioned to decrease shame. Blocking this immediately negatively reinforcing effect of self-harming behaviours is almost impossible, so the task of the therapist was to identify the function of the self-harm and find alternative behaviours to fulfil this same function. So in addition to decreasing the likelihood that she would experience shame, the therapist worked on decreasing shame when it arose, using skills, primarily acting opposite and reaching out to others, and countering cognitions associated with shame, such as Renee reminding herself that she was not solely responsible for the problems in her family. The therapist noticed, again over several chains, that Renee was more likely to call her one good friend after she had harmed herself. As the friend was very supportive and validating at these times and often justified Renee's self-harm behaviour, the therapist and Renee agreed that she, Renee, would approach her friend prior to but not after harming herself. The therapist also introduced a positive punishment for self-harm behaviours: if Renee did self-harm, she was to complete her own chain and solution analysis. In keeping with the stance of the treatment that teaches clients to know as much about the principles of behaviour change as therapists, the therapist explained the principles of contingency management to Renee and together they negotiated how to implement the solutions.

Learning to do chain analyses and developing the attentional and memory capacities to recall relevant events is a skill in itself and takes time to learn. Early chains from Renee were sketchy but still provided sufficient material to work on. Renee's very first chain consisted of Renee saying 'I felt crap and I cut myself – what else do you need to know?' The therapist expanded this to the following sequence: 'I was at home, felt lonely, sad I'm alone. Thought "it's all my fault", cut self, sadness decreased'. The therapist in this session chose skills to reduce sadness and reviewing the pros and cons of cutting as a solution to emotional problems.

Sixteen weeks into treatment, Renee's suicidal behaviour was significantly reduced. Therapy sessions were then directed at Renee's quality-of-life interfering behaviours. As a direct consequence of working on links leading to self-harm, Renee had already acquired some basic skills in re-grounding herself and the reduction of shame. Once flashbacks became a target in their own right, Renee and the therapist developed a hierarchy of cues that elicited flashbacks, for example any contact with men, visiting cafés, shopping, and implemented an exposure programme based on this. Gradually Renee's confidence increased and she began attending an evening class. Working on managing cues that elicited flashbacks helped to further decrease suicidal thinking, but also impacted on Renee's alcohol use as the primary function of drinking was to decrease painful memories from the past. Additional links addressed in reducing Renee's alcohol use involved her reducing the frequency of contact with her mother and also cognitively restructuring her self-blame beliefs about the abusive events of her childhood. As Renee made progress in managing her PTSD and alcohol misuse she reported that she no longer felt the earnest desire to discuss her past trauma that she had experienced at the start of therapy. She decided instead to join the graduate DBT skills training group, which focused on more autonomous problem solving, and to gradually increase her time in education.

Overcoming Obstacles in Therapy: Solving Therapy-Interfering Behaviours

In the early phase of therapy Renee frequently missed group skills training. Analysing Renee's decision not to attend group sessions revealed two important links. First, she felt ashamed of her self-harm behaviours and believed that other group members were judging her for this; these thoughts increased her urges not to attend. Second, she had often spent her bus fare on alcohol so that even when she was more motivated to come she lacked the financial wherewithal to travel to the group. For the first link the therapist helped Renee practise mindfulness of her judgements and cognitive restructuring focussing on Renee reminding herself of the primary focus of the skills group – to learn new skills. For the second link, the therapist devised a plan with Renee for keeping 'emergency' bus fare in a locked tin which had alternative strategies to alcohol use taped to the lid, but also worked out a walking route to the group if this failed. The therapist was clear in her expectation that Renee should attend the group even if she had to walk. This changed the contingencies for Renee sufficiently to motivate her not to raid her emergency bus money for alcohol.

Three months into therapy, Renee experienced a significant suicidal crisis. At this time her collaboration in therapy diminished and she frequently demanded hospital admission. The therapist was adamantly opposed to this course of action given Renee's previously unsuccessful hospital admissions. The therapist's frequent outlining of her reasons why she believed this would be unhelpful rapidly escalated a therapeutic impasse. The therapist's DBT consultation team recognised that the therapist had lost her capacity to remain dialectical and worked with the therapist to help her decrease negative value judgements about hospitalisation, to help her analyse the function of Renee's requests for hospitalisation and to promote her ability to validate Renee's requests. Implementing these changes increased the therapist's effectiveness in developing solutions that honoured both Renee's sense that she was at the limit of her capacity to cope and the therapist's view that hospital admission may have some deleterious effects. Renee and her therapist, therefore, arranged more frequent contact during the difficult period and discussed the possibility of a short time-limited admission with clear goals with Renee's psychiatrist.

Research Status

Since the first RCT published in 1991 (Linehan et al., 1991), DBT has become one of the most evaluated treatments for BPD. There are now five further treatment trials on the efficacy of the treatment for clients with the original diagnostic profile (Linehan et al, 2006; Koons et al., 2001; Verheul et al., 2003; Clarkin et al., 2007; McMain et al., 2009). Generally, these studies demonstrate that DBT is efficacious in decreasing suicidal behaviours, medical seriousness of suicidal and non-suicidal self-injurious behaviours, inpatient days and increasing global and social functioning. Strength of findings was greatest in studies with less robust control procedures. On the basis of this evidence, the National Institute of Health and Clinical Excellence recommends that clinicians consider using DBT for women with BPD and chronic suicidal behaviour where reduction in self-harm is a clinical priority (NICE, 2009).

DBT has been applied to diagnostic groups other than clients with BPD and suicidal behaviour and to clients in different settings. Two small trials of DBT for substance-dependent, BPD women indicated benefits in decreasing the use of psychoactive substances and demonstrated higher rates of treatment retention than is typical in most treatments for this client group (Linehan et al., 1999; Linehan et al., 2002). RCT data is also available to support the use of DBT in for the treatment of older adults with co-morbid depression and personality disorder (Lynch et al., 2003; Lynch et al., 2007) and the treatment of adult women with a diagnosis of binge-eating disorder (Telch et al., 2001). Controlled trial data also supports using DBT in inpatient settings for adults with a BPD diagnosis (Bohus et al., 2004).

Suggested Further Reading

Dimeff, L. and Koerner, K. (2007) *Clinical Applications of Dialectical Behaviour Therapy*. New York: Guilford.

Linehan, M.M.L. (1993a) *Cognitive-behavioural Treatment for Borderline Personality Disorder*. New York: Guilford.

Linehan, M.M.L. (1993b) *Skills Training Manual for Borderline Personality Disorder*. New York: Guilford.

Lynch, T.R., Chapma, A.L., Rosenthal, M.Z., Kuo, J.R. and Linehan, M. (2006) 'Mechanisms of change in dialectical behavior therapy: Theoretical and empirical observations', *Journal of Clinical Psychology*, 62: 459–80.

Swales, M.A. and Heard, H.L. (2008) *Dialectical Behaviour Therapy: Distinctive Features*. London: Routledge.

References

Bohus, M., Haaf, B., Simms, T., Limberger, M.F., Schmahl, C., Unckel, C., Lieb, K. and Linehan, M.M. (2004) 'Effectiveness of inpatient dialectical behavioral therapy for borderline personality disorder: A controlled trial', *Behaviour Research and Therapy*, 42: 487–499.

Clarkin, J.F., Levy, K.N., Lenzenweger, M.F. and Kernberg, O.F. (2007) 'Evaluating three treatments for borderline personality disorder: A multiwave study', *American Journal of Psychiatry*, 164: 922–928.

Hibbs, R.A.B., Swales, M.A. and Taylor, B.H. (2010) 'Disseminating DBT: Comparative rates of dissemination in the USA, UK and Germany', paper presented at the 1st International Congress on Borderline Personality Disorder, Berlin, 1–3 July.

Koons, C.R., Robins, C.J., Tweed, J., Lynch, T.R., Gonzalez, A.M., Morse, J.Q., Bishop, G.K., Butterfield, M.I. and Bastian, L.A. (2001) 'Efficacy of dialectical behavior therapy in women veterans with borderline personality disorder', *Behavior Therapy*, 32: 371–390.

Linehan, M.M.L. (1993a) *Cognitive-behavioural Treatment for Borderline Personality Disorder*. New York: Guilford.

Linehan, M.M.L. (1993b) *Skills Training Manual for Borderline Personality Disorder*. New York: Guilford.

Linehan, M.M., Armstrong, H.E., Suarez, A., Allmon, D. and Heard, H.L. (1991) 'Cognitive-behavioral treatment of chronically parasuicidal borderline patients', *Archives of General Psychiatry*, 48: 1060–1064.

Linehan, M.M., Comtois, K.A., Murray, A.M., Brown, M.Z., Gallop, R.J., Heard, H.H., Korslund, K.E., Tutek, D.A., Rynolds, S.K. and Lindenboim, N. (2006) 'Two-year randomized controlled trial and follow-up of dialectical behavior therapy vs therapy by experts for suicidal behaviors and borderline personality disorder', *Archives of General Psychiatry*, 63: 757–766.

Linehan, M.M., Dimeff, L.A., Reynolds, S.K., Comtois, K.A., Shaw-Welch, S., Heagerty, P. and Kivlahan, D.R. (2002) 'Dialectical behavior therapy versus comprehensive validation plus 12-step for the treatment of opioid dependent women meeting criteria for borderline personality disorder', *Drug and Alcohol Dependence*, 67: 13–26.

Linehan, M.M., Schmidt, H., Dimeff, L.A., Craft, J.C., Kanter, J. and Comtois, K.A. (1999) 'Dialectical behavior therapy for patients with borderline personality disorder and drug-dependence', *The American Journal on Addictions*, 8(4): 279–292.

Lynch, T.R., Cheavens, J.S., Cukrowicz, K.C. and Linehan, M.M. (2007) 'Treatment of older adults with co-morbid personality disorder and depression: A dialectical behavior therapy approach', *International Journal of Geriatric Psychiatry*, 22: 131–143.

Lynch, T.R., Morse, J.O., Mendelson, T. and Robins, C.J. (2003) 'Dialectical behavior therapy for depressed older adults: A randomized pilot study', *American Journal of Geriatric Psychiatry*, 11(1): 33–45.

McMain, S.F., Links, P.S., Gnam, W.H., Guimond, T., Cardish, R.J., Korman, L. and Streiner, D.L. (2009) 'A randomized trial of dialectical behavior therapy versus general psychiatric management for borderline personality disorder', *American Journal of Psychiatry*, 166(12): 1365–1374.

McMain, S., Sayrs, J.H.R., Dimeff, L.A. and Linehan, M.M. (2007) 'Dialectical behavior therapy for individuals with borderline personality disorder and substance dependence', in L.A. Dimeff and K. Koerner (Eds), *Dialectical Behavior Therapy in Clinical Practise: Applications Across Disorders and Settings*. New York: Guilford.

National Institute for Health and Clinical Excellence (2009) *Borderline Personality Disorder: Treatment and Management, Clinical Guideline 78*; M.A. Swales (Ed.). London: NICE.

Swales, M.A., Hibbs, R.A.B. and Taylor, B.H. (2010) 'Disseminating DBT: Factors in sustainable implementation of DBT programmes in the UK', paper presented at the 1st International Congress on Borderline Personality Disorder, Berlin, 1–3 July.

Taylor, B.H., Swales, M.A. and Hibbs, R.A.B. (In press) 'Implementation of DBT in the UK: Results of a retrospective survey'.

Telch, C.F., Agras, W.S. and Linehan, M.M. (2001) 'Dialectical behavior therapy for binge eating disorder', *Journal of Consulting and Clinical Psychology*, 69(6): 1061–1065.

Verheul, R., Van Den Bosch, L.M.C., Koeter, M.W.J., De Ridder, M.A.J., Stijnen, T. and Van den Brink, W. (2003) 'Dialectical behaviour therapy for women with borderline personality disorder: 12-month, randomised clinical trial in The Netherlands', *British Journal of Psychiatry*, 182(2): 135–140.

SIX   Metacognitive Therapy

PETER L. FISHER

Metacognitive therapy (MCT) is predicated on the idea that persistent emotional distress is a consequence of a particular way of responding to negative thoughts and emotions. Although feelings and thoughts associated with anxiety and depression are ubiquitous, these are generally transient experiences. The metacognitive model of psychopathology (Wells and Matthews, 1994) proposes that these transitory mental events and feelings become clinical problems through the activation of three processes:

- perseveration, in the form of worry and/or rumination;
- threat monitoring;
- coping strategies that disrupt cognitive-emotional regulation.

This constellation of responses to triggering stimuli (thoughts and feelings) is termed the 'cognitive attentional syndrome' (CAS).

The next question is why do people activate or use the CAS in response to negative thoughts and feelings? The answer is metacognition. People hold positive metacognitive beliefs about the usefulness or value of the CAS. For example, in generalised anxiety disorder (GAD), a worry episode is typically triggered by a brief negative thought in the form of a 'What if?' question. The trigger activates positive metacognitive beliefs about the benefits of worry, for example 'Worry helps me cope', and therefore worry is strategically selected and an extended bout of worrying ensues. During the worry episode, negative beliefs about the uncontrollability and danger of worry are activated, changing the content of worry into concerns about worry itself, such as 'Worrying will make me lose control of my mind'. Holding uncontrollability beliefs about worry means attempts to stop the worry process occur infrequently, thus maintaining negative metacognitive beliefs and worry. From this cursory description of the role of positive and negative metacognitive beliefs, it can be seen how metacognitive beliefs orchestrate the CAS. These issues will be elaborated upon during the course of the chapter. In essence, MCT ameliorates emotional distress by removing the CAS and by modifying erroneous metacognitive beliefs.

Historical Development of MCT

Advances in psychological therapies invariably develop from careful clinical observation. MCT is no different in this regard. Adrian Wells noted that during cognitive therapy, patients were describing a collection of strategies aimed at alleviating their distress. These strategies included self-focused attention, vigilance for external threat, worry and rumination. Thus, Wells and colleagues began to empirically investigate the relationships between these psychological processes. Early studies demonstrated that self-focused attention was positively correlated with worry and anxiety (Wells, 1985), and adversely affected coping abilities under stressful conditions (Matthews and Wells, 1988). Findings from both experimental studies and clinical observations were beginning to tell a coherent story and the scene was set for the development of MCT. Before this work is discussed in more detail, it is important to place the development of MCT in its historical context.

Several key innovations in understanding and treating psychological disorders served as foundation stones for the evolution of MCT. Two of the most significant developments were the advent of cognitive therapy based on schema theory (Beck, 1967, 1976), and clinical psychology's adoption of the information processing paradigm. Schema theory and cognitive therapy has directly and indirectly influenced the development of MCT. The basic structure of treatment sessions in MCT would be highly familiar to cognitive therapists, as it includes agenda setting, case formulations, Socratic dialogue, verbal and behavioural reattribution methods, homework setting and relapse prevention strategies. However, the actual content and focus of MCT represents a radical departure from the practice of cognitive therapy. Wells (2000) outlined that schema theory contained several important tenets, and possibly the most relevant to MCT was the idea that information stored in long-term memory can influence how an individual interprets and responds to incoming stimuli. However, it is not readily apparent how schemas guide information processing and result in persistent emotional distress. In order for psychological therapy to progress, a conceptual framework was required that specified how self-knowledge regulates cognitive-emotional processing. From a MCT perspective, the answer lay in a multi-level model of psychopathology termed the 'self-regulatory executive function model' (S-REF) (Wells and Matthews, 1994), which is described in more detail later.

Research conducted under the information processing paradigm blossomed during the 1970s and 1980s, and exploration of cognitive variables associated with psychopathological states was producing some intriguing results. Of direct relevance to the development of MCT was the finding, from several independent research groups, that heightened self-focused attention occurred in a wide array of clinical disorders (cf. Ingram, 1990). There was some debate about the utility of the self-focused attention construct and it was assumed to be a nonspecific component of psychopathology. However,

Wells (1990) proposed that modifying excessive self-focused attention would result in amelioration of anxiety, and conducted a single case study on a panic disorder patient to explore this hypothesis. A treatment strategy, the 'attention training technique (ATT; Wells, 1990), was developed specifically to reduce self-focused attention and to enable execution of greater control over perseverative thinking. The first study of ATT resulted in amelioration of panic attacks, and the treatment effects were maintained over a 12-month follow-up period.

A related line of research, falling under the information processing rubric, explored the role of attentional biases in anxiety disorders. At that time, it was generally accepted that attentional biases were primarily an automatic process (e.g. Williams et al., 1988). Wells and Matthews (1994) proposed an alternative hypothesis: that attentional biases (i.e. the preferential allocation of attention towards threatening stimuli compared to neutral stimuli observed in experimental paradigms) were the product of strategic or controlled processing rather than automatic processes. In support of their theoretical position they drew on earlier work on attention in non-clinical populations, which distinguished between levels of control in the form of automatic and controlled processing (e.g. Shiffrin and Schneider, 1977), or indeed between fully automatic and partially automatic processes (e.g. Norman and Shallice, 1980). In addition, research on the role of metacognition in learning and memory supported the primacy of strategic control relative to automatic processes (e.g. Nelson and Narens, 1990) and informed the development of the S-REF model.

The resultant outcome was the S-REF model; a transdiagnostic theory of psychopathology that has been the keystone for the development of many disorder specific models and treatments. The model that first came to prominence was the metacognitive model of 'generalised anxiety disorder' (GAD) (Wells, 1995). This was followed by a range of disorder-specific models and associated metacognitive treatment protocols for post-traumatic stress disorder (PTSD), obsessive compulsive disorder (OCD), depression and bulimia nervosa, amongst others. As the metacognitive approach is a transdiagnostic model, it offers the opportunity to develop a single treatment that can be effective across disorders in diverse populations. Wells (2008) has outlined the main components of a universal treatment for psychological disorder/persistent emotional distress. This is an intriguing possibility, and could prove to be the beginning of a new journey in the history of MCT.

Theoretical Underpinnings

The theoretical basis for MCT is the S-REF model (Wells and Matthews, 1994; Wells, 2000, 2008). The S-REF model is illustrated in Figure 6.1 and consists of three interacting levels of cognition: a level of reflexive or

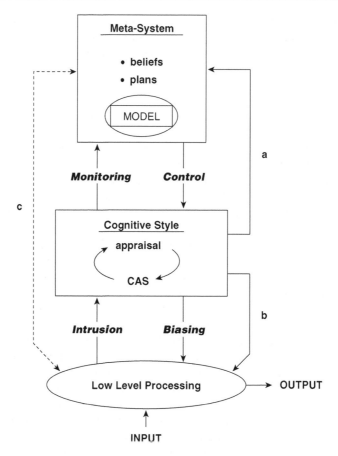

Figure 6.1 The S-REF model of psychological disorder with metacognitions revealed (reproduced with permission)

low-level processing, which runs with minimal conscious awareness, effort or intention. The next level is online processing, which is conscious and capacity limited, responsible for regulating and implementing appraisal and action. In the model, the online conscious processing is represented as cognitive style and involves activation of the CAS. The final level is the meta-system containing metacognitive knowledge in long-term memory.

Online processing or the CAS is controlled and guided by the meta-system towards a particular goal or goals. For example, in OCD, an intrusion enters into consciousness, activating a plan for processing as to how to respond to that unwanted thought. One goal might be to remove the intrusion from consciousness and therefore the person will engage in coping strategies such as forming an alternative image or using a thought suppression strategy. Some of the core theoretical components of the metacognitive model of psychological disorder are now described.

Major Theoretical Concepts

Cognitive Attentional Syndrome (CAS)

The CAS is a specific style of thinking that perpetuates psychological disorders. The first major component is perseveration (worry and rumination). Worry and rumination consist of extended chains of verbal thinking, although memories and images can occur at any point in the chain of thinking. Although there are some differences between worry and rumination (e.g. worry is more future oriented than rumination), both are forms of maladaptive coping. In worry, the main goal is to generate ways of anticipating, avoiding and coping with potential threats, whereas rumination primarily focuses on attempting to understand and comprehend past events and emotional states. In MCT, these perseverative processes are viewed as a form of coping, but instead they interfere and disrupt self-regulation. Although these processes occasionally are successful in achieving their objectives, generally they result in impaired control over distressing thoughts and emotions and prevent the acquisition of new knowledge required for alleviation of distress.

Threat monitoring is the second major component of the CAS and involves allocating attention towards possible threat, which can be internal signs such as thoughts, sensations and emotions. This includes monitoring one's mind for the presence of unwanted thoughts or scanning one's body for associated symptoms. Alternatively, threat monitoring, especially in PTSD and some sub types of OCD, is focused on external signs of danger. In MCT, threat monitoring is problematic as it maintains and sometimes increases the person-subjective sense of danger, thereby resulting in persistent or even escalating anxiety. Second, threat monitoring may increase the frequency of intrusive thoughts by biasing the lower-level fear networks. Third, continued threat monitoring consolidates counterproductive plans for processing. In other words, the patient develops and improves their ability to detect threat. Finally, in the metacognitive model of PTSD (Wells, 2000; Wells and Sembi, 2004), cognitive processes require time to return to their pre-trauma status and threat monitoring interferes with that natural adaptation process, leading to persistent distress.

Counterproductive coping strategies represent the final component of the CAS. Coping strategies are guided by metacognitive beliefs with the goal of regulating cognitive-emotional states. As with the other components of the CAS, maladaptive coping strategies maintain disorders by preventing acquisition of appropriate metacognitive knowledge and by disrupting self-regulatory processes. Fallacious metacognitive beliefs initiate and select coping strategies. In OCD, rituals are used to remove intrusive thoughts and to control worry, for example a person with contamination fears washes their hands whilst forming an image of cleanliness to achieve peace of mind. Metacognitive beliefs such as 'Rituals are the only way I can stop myself from worrying' or 'I must perform my rituals or I will lose control of my mind' determine and guide rituals. Coping strategies can be deleterious in several ways depending upon the specific coping strategy adopted. In the above example, the patient has used thought control strategies, which are typically unreliable and therefore serve to reinforce negative metacognitive beliefs about uncontrollability. Handwashing is used to regulate cognition and emotion, which prevents the person from learning that their fear of losing mental control is incorrect.

Metacognition
Metacognition is a level of cognition that monitors and executes control over all forms of cognitive processing including thinking, allocation of attention and memory (Flavell, 1979). Metacognition is often considered from a tripartite theoretical framework consisting of knowledge, experiences and strategies or skills. Each facet of metacognition is briefly described.

Metacognitive Knowledge
Metacognitive knowledge (MK) refers to the understanding people have about their own cognition. Significant inter-individual variation exists in nature of the theories and models held about cognition. MK also includes knowledge about strategies and tasks and how and when to implement those tasks. For example, the various revision strategies adopted by students depend upon MK. They have beliefs about the way in which their memory works, and which strategies are most likely to result in effective encoding.

In metacognitive theory of psychological disorder (Wells and Matthews, 1994) there are two forms of knowledge. First, there is explicit knowledge or declarative beliefs that people are able to report, for example 'Rumination will lead to a mental breakdown' or 'Worrying will prevent me from making mistakes'. The other form of knowledge is implicit knowledge, which cannot be verbally reported, although it can be inferred through questioning. This type of knowledge represents the plans or programmes that control and run cognitive processes such as memory and attention. Further fundamental aspects of metacognitive knowledge are positive and negative metacognitive beliefs.

Positive Metacognitive Beliefs
The question arises as to why people engage in the sustained thinking, threat monitoring or coping responses that have deleterious effects. Positive metacognitive beliefs (PMB) concern the benefit or value of engaging in each aspect of the CAS, for example 'Worry and/or rumination will help me to cope', 'Focusing on possible signs of threat keeps me safe', 'I must try to control my thoughts otherwise I will lose control of my mind'. Some PMB are common to all disorders, whereas others are most closely associated with specific disorders. For example, PMB in OCD concern the need to control thoughts and remove thoughts from consciousness, and these may support different forms of coping such as forming a positive image to replace an obsessional thought. A common PMB in PTSD is 'I must fill any gaps in my trauma memory before I can move on'. In depression, PMBs

focus on the benefits of understanding the causes and meaning of symptoms through rumination, such as 'Rumination will help me discover the root cause of my depression' with the goal of overcoming depression.

Negative Metacognitive Beliefs

Negative metacognitive beliefs (NMB) focus on the significance and importance of cognition, including intrusions, negative automatic thoughts, memories, impulses and perseverative thinking. In general, negative metacognitive beliefs can be conceptually divided into beliefs about the uncontrollable nature of worry and rumination, for example 'My worry is out of control', and beliefs about the danger/significance of thoughts and mental events and consequences of thinking in a particular manner. As with PMBs, some NMB are most closely tied to specific disorders. For example, obsessive compulsive disorder is characterised by negative metacognitive fusion beliefs about intrusions. These take three forms:

- thought event fusion, which is the belief that thoughts can influence events (e.g. thinking about a crime means it happened);
- though action fusion refers to the belief that thoughts will lead to commission of action (e.g. If I think of hurting my child, it will make me do it);
- thought object fusion, in which people believe that thoughts, feelings, memories can be transferred into objects (e.g. my guilty thoughts can infect my books).

Also, OCD patients sometimes express uncontrollability beliefs regarding their rituals. The NMBs in depression primarily focus on the uncontrollable nature of rumination, although some patients hold NMB about the interpersonal implications of excessive rumination. The same types of uncontrollability beliefs about rumination/worry is seen in PTSD and GAD, together with beliefs about the dangers of worrying, for example 'Worrying could make me lose control of my mind.' Recent work on emotional distress in adolescent survivors of cancer (Fisher et al., forthcoming) has illustrated that very similar metacognitive beliefs are held by people with physical health problems experiencing persistent emotional distress. Holding beliefs about the uncontrollable nature of perseverative thinking means that patients make infrequent attempts to bring worry and rumination under control. Also, if an individual believes certain types of thought are highly significant or dangerous, it is understandable that people engage in thought monitoring and thought control. However, the counterproductive nature of such strategies is readily evident; searching or monitoring for signs of threat generates more unwanted thoughts.

Metacognitive Experiences

This facet of metacognition is concerned with awareness, appraisals and feelings about cognitive events and processes. In MCT, metacognitive experiences primarily refer to appraisals about thinking, for example about the significance of intrusive thoughts in OCD and PTSD or about the dangerousness of worry (Wells, 2008). Metacognitive experiences also extend to the feelings that people have on becoming aware of a task and during performance of that task. An array of metacognitive feelings have been described, including judgements of learning, feelings of certainty or feelings of knowing, in which a person is able to judge whether particular knowledge exists in memory (Efklides, 2008). However, these metacognitive experiences are not always accurate and can variously contribute to persistence of disorders. Patients tend to accept metacognitive experiences as accurate readouts of reality, which in turn keeps their subjective sense of threat alive and are used as a signal to continue with maladaptive coping efforts.

Metacognitive Strategies

Critically, in MCT it is assumed that the strategies chosen in response to unwanted thoughts and emotions are under volitional control. An individual can choose from a wide array of strategies in order to achieve self-regulation. For example, a patient may choose to respond to an intrusive thought with worry, thought suppression, distraction or more helpful responses. Strategy selection is key to effective regulation, and in emotional disorders, selection of strategy is guided by erroneous metacognitive beliefs. In PTSD, the patient may believe that allocating their attention towards possible threat will keep them safe and better prepared to cope with dangerous situations. However, the consequence of the strategy is that it keeps the person focused on threat and often increases the perception of danger.

Modes of Processing

The metacognitive model proposes that information processing operates within and across cognitive and metacognitive subsystems, with the possibility that an individual can experience cognitive and emotional events in different ways. The two modes of experiencing mental events have been termed the 'object model and the metacognitive mode' (Wells, 2000). In object mode, thoughts are experienced as undifferentiated from external events, whereas in metacognitive mode thoughts can be experienced as mental events separate from oneself. For example, when in object mode, an individual with doubting obsessions in the form of 'I have left the door unlocked' experiences it as an accurate reflection of reality. In MCT, the aim is to enable the person to experience the intrusion in the metacognitive mode, in which the person would be aware of the doubt but be able to see it as just an event in the mind and not fuse it with reality. Enabling patients to adopt a metacognitive model of processing changes the way that intrusions are related to, and the person comes to see that the problem is not that the door is unlocked or that they are responsible for preventing harm form occurring, but that the problem is attributing too much meaning and significance to mental events. The same is true in other disorders, for example in depression; the person has a negative thought such as 'I am a failure' and if experienced in object mode, the person relates to this thought as if it is a fact. Consequently, further conceptual analysis will occur as the person searches for evidence, and counterevidence against the thought, or simply ruminates on all the evidence in support of the thoughts. In metacognitive mode the person is able to view the thought as merely an event in the mind which does not require any analysis. In MCT, an early treatment goal is to help patients switch from an object to a metacognitive mode of processing. This enables the person to execute flexibility in their response to typical triggers, in turn leading to minimal activation of the CAS. Patients should have extended experiential practice of experiencing thoughts in the metacognitive mode as this helps to consolidate and modify the metacognitive plans that oversee cognitive processing.

Conceptualisation of Client Problems

Optimal practice of MCT requires that client problems are conceptualised according to disorder specific models. However, as the foregoing account of the theoretical components of MCT has illustrated, commonalities exist across disorders. The two essential components in all metacognitive conceptualisations are metacognitive beliefs and the CAS. The aim of the conceptualisation is to provide a meaningful account of the clinical disorder, which also resonates with the clients' experience. In addition, the conceptualisation needs to be an effective vehicle for promoting change and to highlight which psychological processes require modification.

The manner in which clients problems are conceptualised in MCT can be illustrated with reference to the metacognitive model of PTSD (Wells, 2000; Wells and Sembi, 2004). In PTSD, when intrusive thoughts or emotions related to the traumatic event occur, metacognitive beliefs are activated. These beliefs determine that the patient responds to the triggers with the CAS. Common responses include worry about the future and symptoms, and rumination about the traumatic event, which may involve attempts to fill any memory gaps of the event. Additional strategies might include threat monitoring and attempts to control thoughts. Each strategy is guided by positive metacognitive beliefs, for example 'Worrying about future threats keeps me safe', 'I must monitor for signs of danger so I can react quickly', 'Controlling my thoughts helps me to get rid of the bad memories'. Further adding to distress and preventing adoption of more appropriate responses to symptoms were negative metacognitive beliefs about the uncontrollability of worry ('When I start to worry about the future I can't stop it') and about threat monitoring ('I've tried not to focus on possible signs of threat, but it just happens'). The patient is helped to see that the strategies encapsulated by the CAS are guided by metacognitive beliefs, and in turn the strategies exacerbate and maintain symptoms of

PTSD. Therefore the goal of MCT is to remove the counterproductive coping strategies (CAS) with more adaptive responses, and in order to achieve this it is necessary to modify the beliefs that determine strategy selection.

Practical Applications

Therapeutic Relationship

Theoretical work on the relative importance of the therapeutic relationship on the efficacy of MCT has yet to be conducted. Currently, the development of a good working relationship is not heavily emphasised in MCT, as the structure and process of therapy itself is designed to facilitate an effective working alliance, overcome resistance and increase motivation with the therapeutic goals of MCT. A core component of MCT is the development of disorder specific case formulations followed by socialisation to the model. These aspects of treatment facilitate the development of an effective working relationship even if this is not the explicit goal of the therapist. The case formulation helps patients to understand how metacognitive beliefs and the CAS lead to problem maintenance, providing the basis for a shared understanding and effective working relationship. Providing a coherent framework for patients can be a normalising and validating process (Kuyken et al., 2009) and MCT achieves these aims by clearly delineating the psychological processes underpinning clinical disorders, but at the same time highlights that worry, rumination, obsession and trauma symptoms are natural and normal processes.

Socialisation to the case formulation plays a pivotal role in developing a good therapeutic relationship in MCT and the use of verbal and behavioural strategies to help the patient view their problem from a metacognitive perspective rapidly develops a collaborative relationship. Perhaps most importantly, evidence from cognitive therapy indicates that effective interventions lead to a better therapeutic alliance (DeRubeis et al., 2005), and in MCT the goal is to achieve a degree of symptomatic improvement in the first two to three treatment sessions. Although not yet evaluated, it is reasonable to assume that early treatment gains promote a positive therapeutic alliance.

Strategy of Treatment

The S-REF model specifies that psychological disorders occur as a result of responding to intrusive thoughts and feelings with a high level of perseverative thinking, self-focused attention and coping styles, which is guided by metacognition. This translates into two overarching treatment strategies: the removal or reduction of all components of the CAS; and modification of erroneous positive and negative metacognitive beliefs. These two broad treatment strategies are achieved by following specific treatment protocols (Wells, 2008) that outline a particular sequence of treatment. Regardless of disorder, MCT begins with a case formulation, which incorporates the relevant metacognitive beliefs and the CAS and patients are socialised to the model. Early targets of treatment are to help patients develop metacognitive awareness and to shift from object to a metacognitive mode of processing. Patients are helped to recognise that the problem does not lie in the occurrence of negative thoughts, but how the person relates and responds to their mental activity. The case formulation and socialisation strategies help patients to adopt a metacognitive mode of processing. Specific treatment techniques including detached mindfulness and the attention training technique facilitate the shift towards a new ways of experiencing mental events. As previously mentioned, the CAS is driven by metacognitive beliefs, so a fundamental strategy is to challenge and reduce the conviction with which positive and negative metacognitive beliefs are held. Through Socratic questioning and experiential exercises patients are helped to abandon perseverative thinking, threat monitoring and attempts at coping, before completing therapy with a relapse prevention package.

Major Treatment Techniques

Although, there are a broad range of treatment techniques within the MCT armoury, it is essential to recognise that MCT is not simply a collection of techniques. Each treatment technique has multiple goals and should be used in a manner which maximises metacognitive change. A technique can be deployed by the therapist to modify positive and negative metacognitive beliefs, whist at the same time promoting lower levels of conceptual processing, and enhancing cognitive flexibility and control of attention. A few of the most often utilised treatment techniques are outlined below.

Detached Mindfulness and Worry/Rumination Postponement

Detached mindfulness (DM) is the antithesis to the CAS. DM was developed by Wells and Matthews (1994) to ameliorate the CAS and promote a metacognitive mode of processing. DM has two components: mindfulness and detachment. In MCT, mindfulness simply refers to being aware of thoughts or beliefs when they intrude into consciousness. Detachment is the second component and involves (a) the suspension of any conceptual or coping activity in response to the thought, and (b) the separation of sense of self from the thought. Patients are provided with a range of in-session experiential exercises (see Wells, 2005, 2008 for a detailed account) to develop metacognitive awareness and to facilitate detachment in response to triggering thoughts. Patients are instructed that whenever they notice a trigger thought (a worry, obsession, negative thought, memory) they should apply detached mindfulness and postpone any response till later in the day. Rumination or worry postponement is used in conjunction with

DM as an experiment to challenge uncontrollability beliefs. Specifically, patients are asked to allocate a 15-minute worry/rumination period during which they can worry or dwell on whatever the topic was for the 15-minute period. However, they are also instructed that it is not necessary to use the worry time; most people never use the postponed rumination/worry periods as (a) they have forgotten about the worry/rumination issue, (b) the issues seems unimportant, (c) the person does not want to engage in a process which will have aversive emotional consequences. It is important for patients to recognise that detached mindfulness should not be used as a method to manage symptoms, or as a form of avoidance or coping.

Attention Training Technique (ATT)

ATT was developed in order to modify the CAS and the supporting metacognitive beliefs. It aims to increase executive control and to interrupt perseverative self-focused attention. Although ATT is most often used as a component of MCT, it has been used as a stand-alone treatment for a variety of disorders including depression (Papageorgiou and Wells, 2000), health anxiety (Papageorgiou and Wells, 1998), panic disorder and social phobia (Wells et al., 1997). Recently, the potential of ATT in modifying auditory hallucinations was explored with promising results (Valmaggia et al., 2007). Wells (2008) reports that ATT began life as a visual attention task, but it appeared to have limited impact upon the processes it was designed to modify, and so it became an auditory task. Before describing the basic task, it is important to note that ATT is designed to be attentionally demanding in order to strengthen regulatory processes and that the auditory stimuli should not be self-relevant material, thereby enabling patients to interrupt self-focused and self-relevant processing. When patients complete the task, it is imperative that they do not use the task as a symptom management strategy because this will prevent modification of metacognitive beliefs and the development of executive control.

ATT consists of three components: selective attention, attention switching, and divided attention. All three components are practiced in a single session lasting approximately 12 minutes. ATT begins with selective attention, which lasts for 5 minutes. In this phase, the patient is instructed to allocate their attention to different sounds in different locations in the immediate environment. The patient is encouraged to focus strongly on only one sound at a time and to allocate all of their attention to that sound. In the second 5-minute phase, attention switching, the patient is instructed to switch their attention from one sound to another as instructed. Switching speed increases over the task. The final phase is a brief divided attention task lasting 1–2 minutes, which requires that the patient attempts to broaden and deepen their attention by simultaneously processing multiple sounds across distinct spatial locations. This task is usually practiced in session and set as a daily homework task. Full details on implementation of ATT can be found in Wells (2008).

Modification of Negative Metacognitive Beliefs

A broad range of verbal and behavioural reattribution methods can be used to modify negative metacognitive beliefs. DM and worry/rumination postponement is one of the most effective strategies to modify uncontrollability beliefs. Additional strategies include loss of control experiments in which patients are instructed to try and lose control of their worry. This can be introduced as an in-session experiment or coupled with DM and worry postponement, in which patients use the worry postponement periods as a time in which they worry as much as they possibly can in order to lose control. These experiments demonstrate that worry is under the person's control as (a) loss of control does not occur, and (b) the person becomes aware that they are guiding and directing the worry. A similar strategy is the worry/rumination modulation experiment in which the person is asked to induce rumination and then suspend rumination. This can be repeated a few times to illustrate that rumination can be easily initiated and terminated at the person's will, thereby confirming that rumination is not uncontrollable.

Modification of Positive Metacognitive Beliefs

A similar array of strategies can be used to modify positive metacognitive beliefs (PMB) about (a) usefulness of perseverative thinking, (b) benefits of threat monitoring and (c) the helpful nature of coping strategies. The therapist can explore the duality of beliefs held by patients and heighten the existing cognitive dissonance between positive and negative beliefs, for example 'Rumination will help me find answers to depression' versus the belief 'Rumination will lead to a breakdown'. Other verbal reattribution methods include reviewing the evidence for and against each belief, for example 'Worry helps me cope', 'Worry prevents disasters from occurring'. A basic verbal strategy involves questioning the mechanisms, for example in OCD thought object fusion may be questioned such as 'How can memories be transfered into objects?', or in GAD such as 'How does worry lead to loss of control of your mental abilities?'.

Behavioural reattribution strategies include worry/rumination modulation experiments, which ask the person to increase their level of perseverative thinking on one day and ban it on the subsequent day. The goal is to challenge predictions about the usefulness of specific positive beliefs, such as 'I will make more mistakes if I do not worry'. Careful specification of the prediction is required to ensure success of the experiments. Worry mismatch strategies (Wells, 1997) are used to correct faulty beliefs about the content of worry.

Case Example: Metacognitive Therapy for Depression

Maggie was a 37-year-old woman with a long history of depression beginning when she moved away from home, aged 21, to take up a training post in Southern England. Her first episode of depression lasted approximately nine months and she was treated with a low dose of antidepressant medication. Maggie subsequently experienced a further five discrete episodes of depression, each lasting for at least one year. She was referred by her GP for psychological therapy as pharmacological approaches were having minimal impact on her symptoms. Her main goals for therapy were to improve her mood to reverse avoidance and feel less tense. She said that she would really like have a period of not crying and that she is aware that her career and interpersonal situation has suffered as a result of her depression. Maggie met DSM-IV criteria for recurrent major depressive disorder and scored in the moderately severe range on the Beck Depression Inventory-II (BDI-II) (Beck et al., 1996).

Theoretical Underpinnings

The metacognitive model of depression (Wells, 2008) is presented as a case formulation in Figure 6.2. In line with all disorder specific models derived from the S-REF model, depression is maintained by activation of the CAS, which is guided by metacognitive beliefs. Specifically, the model highlights that following a negative thought or feeling associated with depression (e.g. tiredness, sadness), positive metacognitive beliefs are activated about the need to ruminate as a means of understanding and overcoming depression. Patients may have additional positive beliefs about the benefits of threat monitoring to cope more effectively with their low mood or to prevent relapse. Consequently, patients engage in high levels of rumination, counterproductive attentional and coping strategies, with the effect of exacerbating depressive affect and thinking. Engaging the CAS leads to activation of negative metacognitive beliefs concerning the uncontrollability of rumination and, in some cases, the dangerous nature of depressogenic thinking and emotions. These beliefs result in limited attempts to suspend rumination and/or to alter their counterproductive attentional and coping strategies, thereby maintaining depression. A more detailed exposition of the theory underpinning the metacognitive model of depression can be found in Wells (2008).

Case Conceptualisation and Therapeutic Relationship

In the first treatment session, the MCT therapist constructed a case formulation based on the metacognitive model of depression (Wells, 2008). Construction of the case formulation began by asking Maggie to think back to a recent time when she had noticed a decrease in her mood. Maggie was immediately able to identify such a time and the context. She had been asked out for a drink by two of her colleagues, and whilst driving home from work she started to cry and had to stop driving. The therapist helped Maggie to identify the triggering thought 'No-one really likes me'. This negative thought activated positive metacognitive beliefs about using rumination as a strategy to determine whether her negative thoughts were valid and also to understand why she always looked at situations in a negative

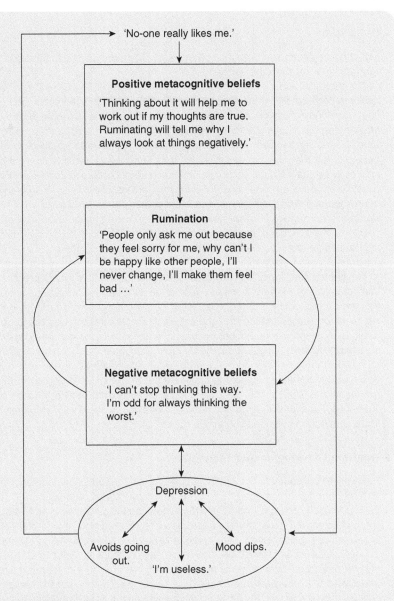

'No-one really likes me.'

Positive metacognitive beliefs

'Thinking about it will help me to work out if my thoughts are true. Ruminating will tell me why I always look at things negatively.'

Rumination

'People only ask me out because they feel sorry for me, why can't I be happy like other people, I'll never change, I'll make them feel bad ...'

Negative metacognitive beliefs

'I can't stop thinking this way. I'm odd for always thinking the worst.'

Depression

Avoids going out.

Mood dips.

'I'm useless.'

Figure 6.2 Metacognitive case formulation

manner. As her mood deteriorated, negative metacognitive beliefs about the uncontrollable nature of her depressive thinking were activated, which led to further rumination about the underlying causes of the rumination, as well as exacerbating her negative feelings as she started to think about how she was always going to be depressed and could never see the positive side of life, which included

(Continued)

(Continued)

self-critical evaluations for thinking that way. A diagrammatic representation of the formulation is illustrated in Figure 6.2.

The therapist shared the formulation with Maggie and highlighted that her tendency to dwell on and think about her depressed mood and feelings was a significant contributory factor in maintaining her low mood. It was further highlighted that Maggie held some positive metacognitive beliefs about the usefulness of rumination in enabling her to overcome her persistent low mood. Specifically, Maggie believed that analysing her negative thoughts and feelings would shed light on the causes of her depression, and once she could identify the cause it would then be possible to move on. She also believed that unless she analysed why she was depressed she would be giving in to the depression, and if she did this her life would deteriorate even further as she would stop caring, make even less effort to overcome her low mood and become 'nothing'. The therapist also highlighted that she had some negative beliefs about rumination, including 'Rumination is uncontrollable' and 'Not being able to control my thinking must mean I'm odd or ill'.

Maggie felt that formulation was a reasonable account of her depression, but immediately stated that it wasn't just a belief that she couldn't control her thoughts, it was a fact. The therapist asked her whether she was currently ruminating, to which Maggie replied that she wasn't. A simple question was then posed, 'If rumination is completely uncontrollable, how does it ever stop?' Maggie was not sure how to answer the question; the therapist explained that her belief was a common belief in depression and that therapy would examine this belief in more detail. Socialisation continued by asking Maggie a set of questions designed to develop her comprehension of the negative impact of rumination and attendant coping strategies. For example, 'Has rumination helped you to solve your problems?' and 'Does rumination ever lead you to feel happy?'.

Treatment Strategies and Techniques

Following socialisation to the metacognitive model of depression, session 1 ended with the introduction and practice of the attention training technique (ATT) (Wells, 1990). Maggie reported finding it difficult to concentrate at work and frequently spent considerable time thinking about how she felt and how her life had resulted in always feeling depressed. The therapist introduced ATT as a method to counteract her excessive self-focus and ruminative style of thinking. Prior to starting ATT, Maggie had rated herself as being moderately self-focused; following in-session practice of ATT, she had rated herself as mildly externally focused. Maggie was encouraged to practice ATT at least once each day. It was emphasised that ATT should not be used as a symptom management strategy. Maggie continued with ATT for the duration of treatment, at every treatment session and for homework.

The main focus of session 2 was modification of her belief about the uncontrollability of rumination, which involved the introduction and practice of detached mindfulness (DM) and rumination postponement exercise. Maggie was helped to recognise that there is a substantial difference between a negative thought and rumination that typically follows such a thought. Furthermore, that it was possible to respond to negative thoughts without rumination or indeed any form of response.

Experiential exercises were used to give Maggie the opportunity to experience DM. A free-association task was used for this purpose; specifically, Maggie was asked to passively observe any thoughts that came into her mind whilst the therapist named 10 objects aloud. Maggie noticed that for most of the words, an image appeared in her mind, which appeared and disappeared from her mind without her influence. The therapist suggested that exactly the same response could be adopted in response to negative thoughts. To consolidate learning and to increase her awareness of the distinction between DM, thought suppression and rumination, the three strategies were contrasted. Maggie was asked to bring a negative thought to mind and deliberately ruminate, then suppress the thought, and finally apply DM. Upon completing the task, the therapist also highlighted that Maggie was able to select three strategies in response to a typical trigger for rumination. Maggie recognised that this must mean she can exercise control over how and what she thinks.

By the fourth treatment session, Maggie's belief that rumination is uncontrollable had reduced from 75 per cent to 45 per cent, with a similar magnitude of change in her positive beliefs. Maggie reported using DM in response to negative thoughts about 40 per cent of the time over the course of the week. The postponed rumination time was never used because she didn't want to make herself feel low and was unable to see any merit in using the scheduled rumination time. Over the next two sessions, Maggie was helped to systematically apply DM to more instances of intrusive thoughts, and by session 6, she reported postponing rumination in response to approximately 90 per cent of triggering thoughts. The times in which she did engage in rumination were very brief, lasting approximately 5 minutes. At this point, the therapist strongly reinforced the idea of continuing to ban rumination and focused on modifying her positive metacognitive beliefs about rumination. As Maggie had suspended rumination, conviction in her positive beliefs about the function of rumination had dropped substantially. She explained that her mood had improved, she was able to concentrate at work and that time spent trying to work out the causes of her depression was a futile exercise. However, Maggie expressed the positive belief 'I need to check my mind for depressive thoughts to make sure I'm well' and the related belief 'I must keep an eye out for any symptoms of depression so I can act quickly prevent the low moods returning'.

The final two sessions of therapy concentrated on developing a relapse prevention plan, which consisted of the diagrammatic case formulation accompanied by a brief explanatory notes. In addition, the therapist and Maggie worked together to generate a list of evidence against the positive and negative metacognitive beliefs identified and modified during therapy. Finally, the relapse prevention included a summary of the old and new plans for dealing with the most typical triggers for sustained rumination, in particular negative thoughts and memories and sad feelings. Following nine sessions of MCT, Maggie no longer met diagnostic criteria for major depressive disorder; her scores on the BAI and BDI were within the asymptomatic range. With regard to the metacognitive beliefs and processes, Maggie did not endorse any positive beliefs about rumination and the majority of scores on her negative metacognitive beliefs were zero and none of the components of the CAS were being used in response to fleeting negative thoughts and feelings.

(Continued)

(Continued)

Obstacles to Client Progress

Several pitfalls can befall the unwary MCT therapist. A fundamental error is to work at the object level rather than the meta level. MCT requires that therapy focuses on beliefs about cognition and seeks to identify and modify each aspect of the CAS, rather than attempting to modify the content of cognition. For example, Maggie often experienced the negative thought 'No-one likes me', and in MCT there would be no attempt to modify or logically dispute this cognition by looking at evidence for and against this thought, or by helping her to recognise the cognitive errors. In MCT, the negative thought is viewed as a trigger for perseveration, and it is this style of extending thinking and the supporting metacognitive beliefs which need to be modified. It is relatively easy to mix working at the cognitive and metacognitive levels; however, this provides the patient with very contradictory messages – there is a need to examine the content of negative automatic thoughts, versus the idea that these thoughts are merely events in the mind which require no further attention or conceptual processing. Conflating MCT methods and cognitive methods has the potential to hinder the progress of therapy.

A related obstacle to progress occurs when the therapist has not fully socialised the patient to the metacognitive model. More specifically, this frequently means that the therapist has not enabled the patient to become aware of each aspect of the CAS. For example, Maggie may not have been helped to become aware of the pervasive nature of rumination or how her attentional strategies were maintaining her preoccupation with her negative thoughts and feelings. Patients tend to engage in each aspect of the CAS in the early stages of therapy, and it is necessary for the therapist to help the patient to recognise these processes both within and between sessions. If this is done insufficiently, it is likely that therapeutic change will be delayed.

In summary, the successful implementation of MCT requires that the therapist works consistently at the meta level throughout each stage of treatment. This includes socialising patients to the metacognitive model and highlighting how metacognitive beliefs and processes are contributing to problem maintenance. Treatment strategies have be delivered in a manner which is theoretically consistent, so the use of behavioural and verbal reattribution strategies must focus on metacognitive beliefs (e.g. rumination is uncontrollable) and not on cognitive belief domains.

Research Status

Over two decades of research evidence supporting the theoretical basis of MCT has been accumulated and therefore the following review is necessarily selective. For more details of the research basis underpinning the metacognitive model of psychopathology, see Wells (2008, 2011). The metacognitive model of psychopathology and disorder specific models are supported by a large number of empirical studies which used a broad range of methodologies.

The role of each component of the CAS is robustly linked to psychopathology. Perseverative thinking (worry and rumination) has a broad range of adverse effects. Worry results in more intrusive thoughts and images, for example Borkovec et al., 1983). Wells and Papageorgiou (1998) replicated and extended this effect. Rumination tends to exacerbate and prolong depressive episodes as well as interfering with effective problem solving and reducing motivation (see Nolen-Hoeksema and Morrow, 1991; Lyubomirsky and Nolen-Hoeksema, 1993; Nolen-Hoeksema, 2000). Selective attention towards threat is a fundamental component of the CAS and there is a vast literature demonstrating that people with elevated levels of anxiety demonstrate an attentional bias towards threatening stimuli compared to neutral stimuli (Bar-Haim et al., 2007). Evidence is now steadily accumulating that selective attention biases occur in depressive disorders, with recent studies on depressed adolescents showing a preferential bias for self-relevant material (Hankin et al., 2010) and adults with suicidal ideation (Cha et al., 2010). Furthermore, recent studies exploring whether attentional biases in anxiety disorders are attributable to early or late stages of processing; the answer appears to be that most of the effect is carried by later stages of processing (e.g. Cisler and Koster, 2010; Phaf and Kan, 2007), specifically, difficulty disengaging from threatening stimuli. These findings are entirely consistent with the hypotheses proposed by the S-REF model (Wells and Matthews, 1994).

One of the strengths of the evidence base supporting the metacognitive theory is the use of studies which test rival predictions derived from different theoretical accounts. In OCD, the role of cognitive beliefs versus metacognitive beliefs have been tested in numerous studies (e.g. Gwilliam et al., 2004; Myers, and Wells, 2005; Myers et al., 2008, 2009). Across these studies, metacognitive beliefs were more predictive of the severity of OCD symptoms than cognitive beliefs (e.g. inflated responsibility and intolerance of uncertainty), both cross-sectionally and prospectively. To cite one example from the PTSD literature, many cognitive models argue that memory disorganisation plays an important role in the persistence of symptoms. However, the metacognitive model of PTSD (Wells, 2000; Wells and Sembi, 2004) argues that metacognitive beliefs about trauma memories are more predictive of trauma symptoms than and memory disorganisation, a hypothesis supported in a recent study (Bennett and Wells, 2010).

Efficacy of MCT

Empirical support for the efficacy of MCT is steadily growing. The efficacy of MCT for generalised anxiety disorder is beginning to be established through a series of small-scale studies including an open trial (Wells and King, 2006) and in an RCT comparing MCT against applied relaxation (Wells et al., 2010). Using standardised outcome criteria across both trials, 80 per cent of patients were recovered, which compares very favourably with existing cognitive behavioural approaches that produce recovery rates of approximately 55 per cent (Fisher, 2006). In an independent study, Van der Heiden et al. (Submitted) compared MCT with a CBT approach based on the intolerance of uncertainty (IU) model of GAD (Dugas et al., 1998). Patients receiving MCT had 10–15 per cent higher recovery rates than IUT on the cardinal feature of GAD, worry and on trait anxiety at post-treatment and at six months' follow-up.

In PTSD, a series of treatment studies have been conducted. A case series (Wells and Sembi, 2004) and an uncontrolled trial (Wells et al., 2008) demonstrated that MCT could be effective. Subsequent small-scale control-led trials demonstrated the superiority of MCT over wait list (Colbear and Wells, 2009) and imaginal exposure (Proctor et al., 2009). Recovery rates across participants in the MCT conditions are similar to those in the GAD studies, namely 75–90 per cent. This level of recovery is extremely high, and represents a highly promising treatment development. The results require independent replication in larger-scale controlled trials.

Evaluation of treatment efficacy in OCD indicates that MCT could be an effective treatment for this often chronic disorder. The first study (Fisher and Wells, 2008) was a direct replication case series across four adult outpa-tients with a range of OCD sub-types. Standardised recovery criteria for OCD (see Fisher and Wells, 2005) were applied to each patient, all four patients achieved recovery at post-treatment, maintained at three months' follow-up. Rees and van Koesveld (2008) evaluated MCT delivered in a small group format and obtained very promising results in a small open trial, where seven of the eight (88 per cent) treated patients were recovered at the three months' follow-up. The third study compared the effects of MCT in combination with CBT against ERP for children and adolescents (Simons et al., 2006), with results indicative of a potentially effective treatment (MCT plus CBT) for this younger age group. Further studies are required in adoles-cent samples in order to test the efficacy of 'pure' MCT. Studies examining the role of metacognitive mechanisms in OCD have produced results con-sistent with the metacognitive model (e.g. Fisher and Wells, 2005). In an intriguing study, Solem et al. (2009) illustrated that changes in metacognitive beliefs over the course of exposure and response prevention for OCD pre-dicted recovery, whereas changes in cognitive belief domains did not. This suggests that the mechanism of change in psychological therapies may be attributable to changes in metacognitive beliefs and/or processes.

The first evaluations of MCT for depression, a case series (Wells et al., 2009) and a small open trial (Wells et al., Forthcoming) have demonstrated the potential efficacy of this approach, with over 70 per cent of patients achieving recovery at post-treatment. These gains were maintained over a 12-month follow-up period. MCT for depression also appears potentially very cost-effective as the treatment was delivered in six to eight 1-hour sessions, which compares favourably with the 12–20 hours of therapy seen in the cognitive behavioural approaches (e.g. Dimidjian et al., 2006).

Overall, the preliminary results from a range of small-scale studies are very encouraging, and strongly point towards MCT being a highly effective and cost-effective psychological treatment for a broad range of clinical problems. However, treatment efficacy research on MCT is in its infancy and there is a pressing need for large-scale randomised controlled evaluations conducted in a manner which overcomes the limitations of small-scale studies. Larger-scale trials would also permit assessment of the mediating mechanisms of change. The S-REF model predicts that psychological therapies exert treatment change through modification of metacognitive processes; this is an intriguing hypothesis which requires empirical testing.

Suggested Further Reading

Fisher, P.L. (2009) 'Obsessive compulsive disorder: A comparison of CBT and the metacognitive approach', *International Journal of Cognitive Therapy*, 2(2): 107–122.

Fisher, P.L. and Wells, A. (2009) *Metacognitive Therapy*. London: Routledge.

Wells, A. (2000) *Emotional Disorders and Metacognition: Innovative Cognitive Therapy*. Chichester: Wiley.

Wells, A. (2008) *Metacognitive Therapy for Anxiety and Depression*. New York: Guilford Press.

Wells, A. and Matthews, G. (1996) 'Modelling cognition in emotional disorder: The S-REF model', *Behaviour Research and Therapy*, 34: 881–888.

References

Bar-Haim, Y., Lamy, D., Pergamin, L., Bakermans-Kranenberg, M. and van Ijzendoorn, M. (2007) 'Threat-related attentional bias in anxious and nonanxious individuals: A meta-analytic study', *Psychological Bulletin*, 133: 1–24.

Beck, A.T. (1967) *Depression: Clinical, Experimental, and Theoretical Aspects*. New York, Hoeber Medical Division: Harper & Row.

Beck, A.T. (1976) *Cognitive Therapy and the Emotional Disorders*. New York: International Universities Press.

Beck, A.T., Epstein, N., Brown, G. and Steer, R.A. (1988) 'An inventory for measuring depression', *Archives of General Psychiatry*, 4: 561–571.

Beck, A.T., Steer, R.A. and Brown, G. (1996) *Beck Depression Inventory-II*. San Antonio, CA: Psychological Corporation.

Bennett, H. and Wells, A. (2010) 'Metacognition, memory disorganization and rumination in posttraumatic stress symptoms', *Journal of Anxiety Disorders*, 24: 318–325.

Borkovec, T.D., Robinson, E., Pruzinsky, T. and DePree, J.A. (1983) 'Preliminary explorations of worry: some characteristics and processes', *Behaviour Research and Therapy*, 21: 9–16.

Cha, C.B., Najmi, S., Park, J.M., Finn, C.T. and Knock, M.K. (2010) 'Attentional bias towards suicide related stimuli predicts suicidal behavior', *Journal of Abnormal Psychology*, 119: 616–622.

Cisler, J. and Koster, E. (2010) Mechanisms of attentional bias towards threat in anxiety disorders: An integrative review', *Clinical Psychology Review*, 30: 203–216.

Colbear, J. and Wells, A. (2009) 'Randomised controlled trial of metacognitive therapy for post-traumatic stress disorder'. Manuscript submitted for publication.

DeRubeis, R.J., Brotman, M.A. and Gibbons, C.J. (2005) 'A conceptual and methodological analysis of the nonspecifics argument', *Clinical Psychology: Science and Practice*, 12: 174–183.

Dimidjian, S., Hollon, S.D., Dobson, K.S., Schmaling, K.B., Kohlenberg, R.J., Addis, M.E., Gallop, R., McGlinchey, J.B., Markely, D.K., Gollan, J.K., Atkins, D.C., Dunner, D.L. and Jacobsen, N.S. (2006) 'Randomized trial of behavioural activation, cognitive therapy, and antidepressant medication in the acute treatment of adults with major depression', *Journal of Consulting and Clinical Psychology*, 74: 658–670.

Dugas, M.J., Gagnon, F., Ladouceur, R. and Freeston, M. H. (1998) 'Generalized anxiety disorder: A preliminary test of a conceptual model', *Behaviour Research and Therapy*, 36(2): 215–226.

Efklides, A. (2008) 'Metacognition: Defining its facets and levels of functioning in relation to self-regulation and co-regulation', *European Psychologist*, 13: 277–287.

Fisher, P.L. (2006) 'The effectiveness of psychological treatments for generalized anxiety disorder' in G. Davey and A. Wells (Eds), *Worry and Psychological Disorders, Assessment and Treatment*. Chichester: Wiley.

Fisher, P.L. and Wells, A. (2005) 'Experimental modification of beliefs in obsessive-compulsive disorder: A test of the metacognitive model', *Behaviour Research and Therapy*, 43: 821–829.

Fisher, P.L. and Wells, A. (2008) Metacognitive therapy for obsessive-compulsive disorder: A case series', *Journal of Behavior Therapy and Experimental Psychiatry*, 39: 117–132.

Fisher, P.L., McNicol, K., Young, B. and Salmon, P. (In press) 'The AEDA study: Metacognitive beliefs and processes in persistent distress in adolescent survivors of cancer'.

Flavell, J.H. (1979) 'Metacognition and metacognitive monitoring: A new area of cognitive-developmental inquiry', *American Psychologist*, 34: 906–911.

Gwilliam, P., Wells, A. and Cartwright-Hatton, S. (2004) 'Does meta-cognition or responsibility predict obsessive-compulsive symptoms: A test of the meta-cognitive model', *Clinical Psychology and Psychotherapy*, 11: 137–144.

Hankin, B.L., Abela, J., Gibb, B.E. and Flory, K. (2010) 'Selective attention to affective stimuli and clinical depression among youths : Role of anxiety and specificity of emotion', *Journal of Abnormal Psychology*, 119: 491–501.

Ingram, R.E. (1990) 'Self-focused attention in clinical disorders: Review and conceptual model', *Psychological Bulletin*, 107: 156–176.

Kuyken, W., Padesky, C.A. and Dudley, R. (2009) *Collaborative Case Conceptualization: Working Effectively with Clients in Cognitive Behavioral Therapy*. New York: Guilford Press.

Lyubomirsky, S. and Nolen-Hoeksema, S. (1993) 'Self-perpetuating properties of dysphoric rumination', *Journal of Personality and Social Psychology*, 65: 339–349.

Matthews, G. and Wells, A. (1988) 'Relationships between anxiety, self-consciousness and cognitive failure', *Cognition and Emotion*, 2: 123–132.

Myers, S. and Wells, A. (2005) 'Obsessive-compulsive symptoms: The contribution of metacognitions and responsibility', *Journal of Anxiety Disorders*, 19: 806–817.

Myers, S.G., Fisher, P.L. and Wells, A. (2008) 'Belief domains of the obsessive beliefs questionnaire-44 (OBQ-44) and their specific relationship with obsessive-compulsive symptoms', *Journal of Anxiety Disorders*, 22(3): 475–484.

Myers, S., Fisher, P.L. and Wells, A. (2009) 'An empirical test of the metacognitive model of obsessive-compulsive symptoms: Fusion beliefs, beliefs about rituals and stop signals', *Journal of Anxiety Disorders*, 23: 436–442.

Nelson, T.O. and Narens, L. (1990) 'Metamemory: A theoretical framework and some new findings', in G.H. Bower (Ed.), *The Psychology of Learning and Motivation*. New York: Academic Press. pp. 125–173.

Nolen-Hoeksema, S. (2000) 'The role of rumination in depressive disorders and mixed anxiety/depressive symptoms', *Journal of Abnormal Psychology*, 109: 504–511.

Nolen-Hoeksema, S. and Morrow, J. (1991) 'A prospective study of depression and post-traumatic stress symptoms after a natural disaster: The 1989 Loma Prieta earthquake', *Journal of Personality and Social Psychology*, 61: 115–121.

Norman, D.A. and Shallice, T. (1980) *Attention to Action: Willed and Automatic Control of Behavior* (CHIP Report 99). San Diego, CA: University of California.

Papageorgiou, C. and Wells, A. (1998) 'Effects of attention training in hypochondriasis: An experimental case series', *Psychological Medicine*, 28: 193–200.

Papageorgiou, C. and Wells, A. (2000) 'Treatment of recurrent major depression with attention training', *Cognitive and Behavioural Practice*, 7: 407–413.

Phaf, R.H. and Kan, K. (2007) 'The automaticity of emotional Stroop: A meta-analysis', *Journal of Behavior Therapy and Experimental Psychiatry*, 38: 184–199.

Proctor, D., Walton, D.L., Lovell, K. and Wells, A. (2009) 'A randomised trial of metacognitive therapy versus exposure therapy for post-traumatic stress disorder', Submitted for publication.

Rees, C.S. and van Koesveld, K.E. (2008) 'An open trial of group metacognitive therapy for obsessive-compulsive disorder', *Journal of Behavior Therapy and Experimental Psychiatry*, 39: 451–458

Shiffrin, R.M. and Schneider, W. (1977) 'Controlled and automatic human information processing: II Perceptual learning, automatic attending, and a general theory', *Psychological Review*, 84: 127–190.

Simons, M., Schneider, S. and Herpertz-Dahlmann, B. (2006) 'Metacognitive therapy versus exposure and response prevention for pediatric obsessive-compulsive disorder', *Psychotherapy and Psychosomatics*, 75: 257–264.

Solem, S., Haland, A.T., Vogel, P.A., Hansen, B. and Wells, A. (2009) 'Change in metacognitions predicts outcome in obsessive-compulsive disorder patients undergoing treatment with exposure and response prevention', *Behaviour Research and Therapy*, 47: 301–307.

Valmaggia, L.R., Bouman, T.K. and Schuurman, L. (2007) 'Attention training with auditory hallucinations: a case study', *Cognitive and Behavioral Practice*, 14(2): 127–133.

Van der Heiden, C., Muris, P., Van der Molen, H.T. (Submitted) 'Randomized controlled trial of the effectiveness of metacognitive therapy and intolerance-of-uncertainty therapy for generalized anxiety disorder'. Submitted for publication.

Wells, A. (1985) 'Relationship between private self-consciousness and anxiety scores in threatening situations', *Psychological Reports*, 57: 1063–1066.

Wells, A. (1990) 'Panic disorder in association with relaxation induced anxiety: An attention training approach to treatment', *Behaviour Therapy*, 21: 273–280.

Wells, A. (1995) 'Meta-cognition and worry: a cognitive model of generalized anxiety disorder', *Behavioural and Cognitive Psychotherapy*, 23: 310–320.

Wells, A. (1997) *Cognitive Therapy of Anxiety Disorders: A Practice Manual and Conceptual Guide.* Chichester: Wiley.

Wells, A. (2000) *Emotional Disorders and Metacognition: Innovative Cognitive Therapy.* Chichester: Wiley.

Wells, A. (2005) 'Detached mindfulness in cognitive therapy: A metacognitive analysis and ten techniques', *Journal of Rational-Emotive and Cognitive-Behavior Therapy*, 23: 337–355.

Wells, A. (2008) *Metacognitive Therapy for Anxiety and Depression.* New York: Guilford Press.

Wells, A. (2011) 'Metacognitive therapy', in J. Herbert and E. Forman (Eds), *Acceptance and Mindfulness in Cognitive Behavior Therapy: Understanding and Applying the New Therapies.* Chichester: Wiley.

Wells, A. and King, P. (2006) 'Metacognitive therapy for generalized anxiety disorder: An open trial', *Journal of Behavior Therapy and Experimental Psychiatry*, 37: 206–212.

Wells, A. and Matthews, G. (1994) *Attention and Emotion: A Clinical Perspective.* Hove: Erlbaum.

Wells, A. and Papageorgiou, C. (1998) 'Relationships between worry, obsessive-compulsive symptoms, and meta-cognitive beliefs', *Behaviour Research and Therapy*, 39: 899–913.

Wells, A. and Sembi, S. (2004) 'Metacognitive therapy for PTSD: A preliminary investigation of a new brief treatment', *Journal of Behavior Therapy and Experimental Psychiatry*, 35: 307–318.

Wells, A., Fisher, P.L., Myers, S., Wheatley, J., Patel, T. and Brewin, C. (2009) 'Metacognitive therapy in recurrent and persistent depression: A multiple-baseline study of a new treatment', *Cognitive Therapy and Research*, 33: 291–300.

Wells, A., Fisher, P.L., Myers, S., Wheatley, J., Patel, T. and Brewin, C. (Forthcoming) 'Metacognitive therapy in recurrent and persistent depression: An open trial'. Submitted for publication.

Wells, A., Welford, M., Fraser, J., King, P., Mendel, E., Wisely, J., Knight, A. and Rees, D. (2008) 'Chronic PTSD treated with metacognitive therapy: An open trial', *Cognitive and Behavioral Practice*, 15: 85–92.

Wells, A., Welford, M., King, P., Papageorgiou, C., Wisely, J. and Mendel, E. (2010) 'A pilot randomized trial of metacognitive therapy vs. applied relaxation in the treatment of adults with generalized anxiety disorder', *Behaviour Research and Therapy*, 48(5): 429–434.

Wells, A., White, J. and Carter, K. (1997) 'Attention training: Effects on anxiety and beliefs in panic and social phobia', *Clinical Psychology and Psychotherapy*, 4: 226–232.

Williams, J.M.G., Watts, F.N., MacLeod, C. and Mathews, A. (1988) *Cognitive Psychology and Emotional Disorders*. Chichester: Wiley.

SEVEN Compassion-Focused Therapy

PAUL GILBERT

Historical Development of the Approach

An interest in using a compassion focus for therapy grew out of working with people with complex mental health difficulties who often came from neglectful, abusive and/or emotionally insecure backgrounds. Working within a CBT model, some clients would say they could understand the logic of 'alternative' thinking and could become very good at generating alternative thoughts, but then say: 'I know logically I am not a failure but I still *feel* like a failure; I know logically I am not to blame for the abuse but I *feel* blameworthy and bad'. This is a well-known cognition emotion mismatch (Stott, 2007). When I explored the *feeling* in people's alternative thoughts themselves, they were either cold or slightly aggressive. The counteracting thought to 'being a failure' of 'well, actually I have achieved good things today' will have a very different emotional impact if delivered in a kind, encouraging, warm tone, rather than a detached, clinical dismissive or aggressive tone, such as 'Look at the evidence, you shouldn't feel like this' or even 'Stop being stupid'. This raised the question of how we come to *feel* reassured and have a sense of relief (emotion change) from our 'helpful' thoughts (Haidt, 2001). This led to consideration of the emotional sources and regulators of reassurance, the importance of attachment and affiliation in the experience of reassurance, and more recently the neuroscience of reassurance and soothing. By the time of the second edition of *Counselling for Depression* (Gilbert, 2000a), the importance of developing capacities for inner self-directed warmth, and ideas for developing a compassionate approach to self-help were being developed (Gilbert, 1997).

A second historical influence was a long interest in evolutionary psychology and the way our goal focusing and processing are underpinned by evolved, motivational systems, for example for close attachments, group belonging, finding sexual relationships, advancing our status and so forth (Gilbert, 1984, 1989, 1992). While cognitive therapy focused on schemas and core beliefs, the reality of our psychology is that we are riddled with *conflicts* between our different motives and emotions – due partly to the 'piecemeal' way our brains have evolved over millions of years (Gilbert, 1989, 1992, 2007a; Ornstein, 1986). Although a variety of psychodynamic theories addressed issues of implicit affect processing and internal conflict, I was interested in the conflict of emotions and motives as indicated from mainstream psychological research, especially theories of emotion regulation and classical conditioning (Gilbert, 1992, 2007a).

A third historical influence was my interest in competitive behaviour and 'shame', and in particular the link between self-criticism and shame (Gilbert, 1989, 1998, 2002; Zuroff et al., 2005). Space does not allow a detailed exposition into the nature of shame (see Gilbert, 1998, 2002, 2007a, In press), but we can distinguish between external and internal shame. In external shame, our attention is focused *outwards* on what other people are thinking and feeling about us, and for this we may use both projection and mentalizing (Bateman and Fonagy, 2003). We sense that in other people's minds we are viewed as an undesired and unwanted self; this can activate a variety of defensive safety behaviours such as aggression appeasement or avoidance (Gilbert, 2002, 2007a). In internal shame, our attention is focused inward. The internal self-evaluating and critical processes are textured with self-directed emotions such as anger, contempt and even hatred (Gilbert et al., 2004; Whelton and Greenberg, 2005). These emotions are crucial to the self-critical experience and can activate a variety of defensive safety strategies such as emotional avoidance, drug taking and self-harm (Gilbert and Irons, 2005).

To illustrate how our internal images (of how we exist for others and our own self-judgements) are physiologically powerful, we use a very simple behavioural principle: that internal stimuli can operate like external stimuli. For example, suppose one is hungry and sees a delicious meal, this will stimulate the hypothalamus, increasing saliva and stomach acids, but equally if we have no money and simply fantasise a delicious meal, such imagery can produce the same physiological effects. Similarly, with a sexual stimulus, fantasies can produce high arousal in the absence of any external object. If we bring to mind a happy memory of (say) being with friends or winning other people's approval and dwell for a while in that memory, we might have a warm glow again. However, if we bring to mind an unhappy or a frightening time where (say) we were criticised, we can re-experience more unpleasant emotions. Internal stimuli based on memory, imagery and thinking are physiologically powerful, and positive and negative self-evaluations can act on similar brain systems as positive and negative evaluations from others. Longe et al. (2010) found that 'bringing to mind' self-criticism stimulated different brain systems to those of self-reassurance. Higher levels of self-criticism were associated with a threat response when trying to be self-reassuring.

From these historical themes a number of questions arose, such as: What is self-reassurance and self-compassion? Do they have therapeutic properties? How do they work in our brains? Could we teach people to focus on these elements in their relationships with themselves and others? Could we get any data on how useful that would be? It was from efforts to answer these questions that Compassion Focused Therapy (CFT) began to develop.

Theoretical Underpinnings

Major Theoretical Concepts 1: The Nature and Functions of Compassion and the Compassionate Mind

All psychotherapies believe that psychotherapy should be conducted compassionately, although some disagree on exactly what that entails. Rogers (1957) suggested that therapy should involve compassion-type qualities of positive regard, genuineness and empathy. Recently, the specific qualities, forms and focus of compassion (for and from others, and self-compassion) have become areas of study in their own right with slightly different concepts and definitions (Fehr et al., 2009; Gilbert, 2005). The word 'compassion' comes from the Latin word *compati*, which means 'to suffer with'. A well-known definition is that of the Dalai Lama, who defines compassion as 'a *sensitivity* to the suffering of self and others, with a deep *commitment* to try to relieve it', that is sensitive attention-awareness plus motivation. Kristin Neff (2003, 2011; see www.self-compassion.org) derived her model of self-compassion and measures from Theravada Buddhism with three main components: 1. Being mindful and open to one's suffering, 2. Being kind and non-self-condemning, and 3. An awareness of sharing experiences of suffering with others, not feeling ashamed and alone – an openness to our common humanity. In this approach the motivational aspects are given less prominence in comparison to more cognitive elements.

The model of compassion used in compassion-focused therapy (CFT) is based on an evolutionary approach to psychological functioning, which argues that compassionate motives and competencies are linked to evolved brain systems that underpin altruism, attachment and affiliative behaviours (Gilbert, 1989, 2005). Compassion will (normally) function in a similar way to affiliative behaviours, providing opportunities for experiencing connectedness, safeness, soothing, sharing, encouragement and support. Humans are a highly social species, and being the recipient of affection, affiliation and compassion from others (especially early in life) has major impacts on a whole range of physiological, psychological and social processes that are conducive to good affect regulation and wellbeing (Cozolino, 2007). Hence, these processes should be a key focus for psychological therapies.

The Compassionate Mind

The evolutionary model of compassion developed for therapy was first considered in *Human Nature and Suffering* (Gilbert, 1989). I was particularly influenced by work on the qualities of nurturing and caring behaviours as outlined by Fogel et al. (1986). They defined the core element of care-nurturance as 'the provision of guidance, protection and care for the purpose of fostering developmental change congruent with the expected potential for change of the object of nurturance' (1986: 55). They also suggested that nurturance involves *awareness* of the need to be nurturing, *motivation* to nurture, *expression* of

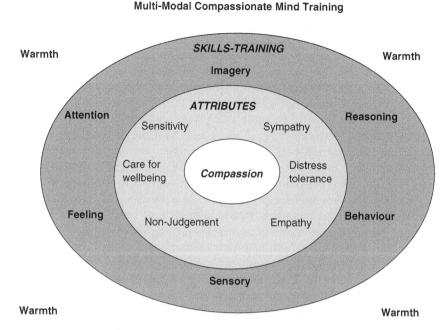

Figure 7.1 The compassion circle

nurturing feelings, *understanding* what is needed to nurture and an ability to match nurturing with the *feedback* on the effects of being nurtured from the nurtured other. Only later was I to discover that some of these qualities mapped to a degree on to what the Buddha called the 'eightfold path' (e.g. developing compassionate motivation, attention, thinking and behaviour). (For an accessible outline of these concepts, see Landaw and Bodian 2003). Although some Buddhist concepts of compassion also include ones of generosity, patience and effort, integrating Buddhist concepts with more recent psychological research led to the development of the compassion circle, the basis of our compassionate mind (Gilbert, 2005) (see Figure 7.1). We call it a compassionate *mind* to indicate that compassion is not a simple concept but an integration of a number of different attributes, skills and competencies.

CFT distinguishes compassion attributes (things that are necessary for compassion) and compassion skills. Compassion attributes start with motivation and the desire to be caring and helpful to the self and others. Importantly, that in itself can be problematic for some people (Gilbert et al., In press). Second is an attentional sensitivity and openness to suffering in self and others. This attentional sensitivity allows us to have an emotional connection and sympathy with those feelings. Third, sympathy (sometimes called emotional empathy) is an automatic emotional reaction and connection linked to mirror neurones. For example, you see a young child playing happily, then she falls and painfully hits her head – the emotional feelings arise spontaneously (Eisenberg, 2002). A fourth quality is being able to tolerate feelings of distress or painful and unpleasant feelings, both in ourselves and others. This links into other therapies which focus on experiential avoidance and developing acceptance and mindfulness (Hayes et al., 2004). It also links to concepts in rational emotive behaviour therapy, regarding the way some people tell themselves certain feelings or things are 'unbearable' rather than difficult (Dryden, 2009). Fifth is the ability to be empathic, which requires cognitive elements of imagining what it is like to be the other person. In empathic connectedness we have to imagine ourselves 'walking in their shoes', and being confronted with the types of life events that they have (Wispe, 1986). This is basic to Rogerian person-centred therapies, but is now seen as being underpinned by important qualities such as mentalizing (Bateman and Fonagy, 2003). Sixth is holding positive regard and neutrality which is non-judgemental and non-condemning. It is not a position of 'anything goes' because it is clear that some behaviours, such as drug taking or causing harm to others, are undesirable and counteract the compassion focus.

In regard to the *skills* which help *develop* compassion attributes, these are traditional, multi-modal therapeutic targeted qualities. So we teach people to develop compassion in their attention, thinking, reasoning, feeling and behaviour, and how to use and develop compassion awareness with imagery and compassionate sensory (re)focusing. As with all such models, these are just guidelines and not to be taken too rigidly. Both the attributes and skills of compassion are contextualised within an emotional climate of warmth – a term that is difficult to describe but conveyed through verbal and non-verbal communication styles (Gilbert, 2007a, 2007b). Importantly, then the inner circle and outer circle relate to two very different psychologies. The inner circle relates to the process of engagement and the outer to the process of alleviation. So for example attention sensitivity on the inner circle is awareness of the triggers and nature of distress whereas attention in the outer circle is focusing on what is helpful.

Major Theoretical Concepts 2: The Neurophysiological Model

In CFT, the nature and functions of compassion are linked to kindness, altruism and affiliation. The evolution of affiliative behaviour required significant changes in the organisation of basic fight-or-flight behaviours; affiliation cannot take place if individuals are frightened of each other, avoid each other, or are constantly fighting – as occurs with some species (Porges, 2007). Affiliative behaviour evolved with capacities to tone down threat processing, whilst at the same time stimulating positive affect and approach behaviour.

A model derived from neurophysiological research has revealed that our brains contain at least three *types* of major emotion regulation systems (Depue and Morrone-Strupinsky, 2005; LeDoux, 1998; Panksepp, 1998). These are:

- *Threat and self-protection focused systems* – designed to attract attention to, detect, process and respond to threats. There is a menu of threat-based emotions such as anger, anxiety and disgust, and a menu of defensive behaviours such as fight, flight, submission, freeze.

Figure 7.2 **Three types of affect regulation system**

From Gilbert, *The Compassionate Mind* (2009), reprinted with permission from Constable & Robinson Ltd.

- *Drive, seeking and acquisition focused system* – designed to pay attention to advantageous resources and experience 'activation' to try to acquire them; pleasure in pursuing and securing them.
- *Contentment, soothing and affiliative focused system* – designed to enable a state of peacefulness and openness when individuals are no longer threat-focused or focused on seeking resources. Over evolutionary time this system of calming has been adapted for many functions of attachment and affiliative behaviour.

These three interacting systems are depicted in Figure 7.2.

Understanding the importance of the interaction between positive and negative affect regulation systems has been central to a range of different affect regulation theories. Prominent to the development of CFT was Gray's (1987) outline of the behavioural inhibition system (BIS) and behavioural approach system (BAS), to which I (Gilbert, 1989, 1992, 1993) suggested a third system based on creating feelings of safeness and calm, linked to Bowlby's attachment theory (Bowlby, 1969, 1973). The concept of a safe place, feelings of peaceful wellbeing and contentment, are important in CFT, especially because they regulate threat and drive.

Distinguishing different types of *positive* affect (drive and excitement and BAS focused vs soothing and safeness focused) is crucial to CFT. Positive drive and excitement-based emotions may be particularly linked to the neurotransmitter *dopamine*. If one gets good marks in an examination or wins the lottery, the consequent energised positive feelings may be linked to dopamine. In contrast, feelings of *peaceful* wellbeing and contentment may be linked to the *endorphins* (Depue and Morrone-Strupinsky, 2005; Panksepp, 1998), and these feelings often arise from feeling safe, as conferred in affiliative relationships, but also from extended practice in various meditations.

In addition, research has shown that a major hormone called *oxytocin* is very important in the formation of attachment bonds and affiliative behaviour, and has 'soothing' qualities. For example, when a baby or child is distressed, the love of the parent soothes and calms the infant. Affection and kindness from others helps soothe stressed adults too. Oxytocin is linked to feelings of social safeness and (along with the endorphins) gives feelings of wellbeing that flow from feeling loved, wanted and safe with others (Carter, 1998; Depue and Morrone-Strupinsky, 2005). CFT seeks to develop a 'compassionate mind' that recruits these neurophsyiological systems and *builds capacities* to engage with 'the difficult work' of the therapy, and facilitate experiences of reassurance, safeness and wellbeing. The (mammalian) threat-regulating properties of affiliation have been evolving for 120 million years, and so it seems sensible that therapies should try to recruit this system for therapeutic purposes (Gilbert 2005).

How Client Problems are Conceptualised

The CFT formulation is typical of a CBT formulation. The therapist understands the emergence of the client's difficulties in terms of life experiences, (problem maintaining) safety strategies and unintended consequences (Salkovskis, 1996; Thwaites and Freeston, 2005). We are interested in the experiences that have shaped the threat, the drive/achievement and the soothing/affiliative systems (see Welford, 2010 for examples). In particular, we are interested in how peoples' experiences relating to threat give rise to a range of safety strategies that become part of the person's sense of self (Gilbert, 2007a, 2010a, 2010b; Gumley et al., 2010). In CFT we distinguish between internal and external fears, and internally and externally directed safety strategies. Internal fears are linked to emergence of things within oneself, such as overwhelming feelings or traumatic memories. Safety strategies are focused on controlling these inner states of mind and could include drug-taking, self-harm or other forms of experiential avoidance (Hayes et al., 2004). They may be enacted when alone. External fears focus on things in the outside world. Externally directed safety strategies are often linked to avoiding certain things or people in the outside world. People who are frightened of those in authority may routinely engage in submissive behaviours but feel resentful in doing so. Externally directed safety strategies usually require some external trigger whereas internal ones require internal triggers.

As in other therapies, one aspect of the formulation explores the ways people process emotions and, in particular, emotions that are feared, avoided or unacknowledged. Sometimes different emotions are 'embedded' within other emotions. For example, a client lost her mother some years before but always found grief overwhelming and tried to avoid thoughts and things that could spark it. When exploring 'What other emotions do you feel when you begin to feel grief?', we discovered much anger, self-blaming, shame, guilt, regret and fear. These were all embedded in her grief 'feeling' which she had difficulties recognising or articulating, but also made grief feel 'overwhelming'. Working on these specific emotions, especially (mostly) unrecognised anger and shame provided relief and freed up the grief process.

Basic to the formulation is also to help people recognise the unintended consequences that go with their safety strategies. So, for example, people who use experiential avoidance never learn how to tolerate problematic emotions and cope in new ways. People who usually behave submissively don't learn assertiveness, how to deal adaptively with anger or conflicts, or may avoid positions of authority out of fear of failing and being criticised. Another unintended consequence is in becoming self-critical of one's difficulties and safety strategies and their consequences. Individuals who have lacked validation of their feelings often 'battle' with feelings and can become very self-critical (e.g. 'I get so frustrated with myself when I can't do ...; I hate myself when I feel like this; I think there's something wrong with me to feel like this; I feel I'm bad at the core for having these fantasies; I am weak to behave like this'). As another example, an avoidant socially anxious person feels lonely and isolated and then contemptuous for their 'weakness and anxiety'; a person who overeats to regulate their emotions comes to 'hate themselves for poor control'. Self-criticism undermines the sense of self and increases the disposition towards the overuse of unhelpful safety strategies.

So it can be difficult to create 'a safe space and place' within their minds to work with these feelings. It is therefore important to explore the sources and origins (including evolutionary ones) of these difficulties, validate them, and begin to compassionately work with them. These themes are explored in more detail in the case example of Catherine below.

Practical Applications

The Therapeutic Relationship

All therapies believe the therapeutic relationship plays an important role in outcomes, although there is debate on exactly how (Zuroff and Blatt, 2006). Creating a safe and containing therapeutic relationship is key in working with high shame and self-critical clients, for which CFT was originally developed. The therapist tries to enact the compassion circle in mindful, attentive ways (Gilbert, 2007a, 2007b) and has a keen eye on the role of shame (Gilbert, 1998, 2002, In press). The mirco-skills, Socratic dialogues, guided discovery, monitoring of thoughts, feelings and behaviours, 'balanced view', behavioural experiments, in vivo and imagery exposure, and practising interventions (e.g., compassion focused imagery meditations) are all facilitated in a good therapeutic relationship. A major emphasis in the relationship is on de-shaming and de-pathologising (see Gilbert, 2007a: ch. 7, 2007b).

Strategies of Treatment

CFT refers to all aspects of the therapy, from the relationship though to the range of interventions that facilitate the development and access of affiliative and soothing systems to help balance threat and drive. Compassionate mind training (CMT) refers to specific compassion-focused exercises. Much of the work in CFT is focused on *building compassionate capacity* by:

- developing an internal capacity to engage with (unhelpful) threat and drive processes. Taking a compassionate position to the frightening aspects of our minds such as trauma memories, or powerful emotions helps engagement and coping rather than being avoidant, shaming or self-blaming.
- building capacity to experience positive emotions, particularly affiliation and contentment. Many clients are fearful of these positive feelings (Gilbert et al., In press).
- using multimodal interventions that focus on (for example) soothing rhythm breathing, attention (e.g. mindfulness) training, exploring cognitive and emotional biases, behavioural avoidance, using imagery and sensorimotor focusing.

Major Treatment Techniques: Compassionate Imagery

Imagery can have very powerful physiological effects, and more so than verbal efforts to change (see Stopa, 2009 for reviews). In CFT imagery can be a major intervention focusing on a number of different domains. All these require mindful practice and are 'done' mindfully (Allen and Knight, 2005; Germer, 2009).

- *Developing the inner compassionate self* – These exercises focus on creating a sense of a compassionate self, just like 'method actors' do if they are trying to get into a role (see http://en.wikipedia.org/wiki/Method_acting). The individual engages in slowing their breathing and taking up a relaxed but alert state and posture. Suggest relaxing the facial muscles, starting at the forehead and cheeks, and letting the jaw drop slightly. Then create a compassionate smile by curving the mouth, stopping at the point at which one feels comfortable, with sense of a compassionate facial expression and a focus on feelings of kindness and a genuine desire to be helpful and caring. People then imagine themselves to be a deeply compassionate person with the qualities of wisdom (able to reflect and see things from different perspectives with an understanding of the nature of difficulties), a sense of authority, confidence and calmness, a sense of kindness and warmth and a sense of responsibility of genuinely being motivated to be helpful and supportive. So the person is invited to imagine themselves being at their very best, as their ideal confident, assertive and compassionate self.

- *Compassion flowing out from the client to others* – These exercises focus on bringing to mind a person (or animal) one cares about and wishes to see happy and free of suffering. Through the feelings and eyes of the compassionate self one imagines directing compassionate feelings towards that person (or animal). This type of exercise is common for loving-kindness (*metta*) practice (Kabat-Zinn, 2005; Germer, 2009).
- *Compassion flowing into the self* – Here the focus is on being open to the kindness of others. This may involve memory and recalling specific episodes or events when other people were kind. In other exercises the client works on imagining an ideal compassionate being and relating to that being in specific ways.
- *Compassion to self* – This is linked to developing feelings, thoughts and experiences that are focused on compassion to the self (Gilbert 2009; Germer, 2009; Neff, 2011). In this exercise we engage with compassion-ate self or compassionate image and then imagine 'seeing ourselves'. This exercise requires the individual to explore compassion for the self they are imagining; wishing themselves to be happy, flourish and free from suffering. Many clients find this difficult and it takes some practice and gradual engagement and exposure to these feelings and processes. Clients can then imagine a future self, of actually being happy, noticing how that would feel, how they'd look and sound, how they would get there. Research suggests that helping people create positive imagery can have positive effects on mood (Holmes et al., 2009; Tarrrier, 2010).
- *Compassionate images at work* – In CFT these images aid the work of engaging with and tolerating different emotions and experiences within the self and 'courageously' changing behaviour. For example, one might engage with the compassionate self and then 'see in one's mind's eye' a specific aspect of that self which is troublesome. One can imagine oneself when anxious, and practise imagining looking at one's facial expressions – how we look when anxious – the thoughts and feelings going through our minds. We then just imagine having compassion for that anxious self we see in our mind; how we would like to help, what we like to say. There are similar processes with many aspects of the self, including the angry self, lonely self and self-critical self. If people feel a little overwhelmed by this you simply bring them back to their breathing and refocus on the compassionate self and, when ready, start again. In some ways this fol-lows standard de-sensitisation practice. There is a 1,000-year-old practice that is very similar to this called 'Feeding Your Demons' (Allione, 2008). Here the person imagines *feeding* the troublesome part of the self so that it gets what it wants, and they see how it changes.

Developing Compassionate Skills

Figure 7.1 outlined some compassion skills. It is well known that humans tend to be biased towards threat. For example, if you go shopping and nine out of ten assistants are kind and helpful but one is rude, which one do you talk about when you get home? We forget about the nine who were helpful and ruminate on the rude one. Thus, we 'normally' over-focus on negative events at the expense of positive events – partly because our brains have evolved that way (Baumeister et al., 2001) and are set up to detect threats in a 'better safe than sorry' way (Gilbert, 1998). So, compassionate attention training can be learning to focus on the nine helpful people; recognising the helpful things people do. A set exercise might be to look out for acts of kindness, no matter how small (e.g. a smiling shop assistant), for say a week.

Compassionate thinking is about recognising how our behaviours, thoughts, worries and ruminations can be threat focused, concerned with safety seeking or damage limitation. Genuinely looking at what is *helpful* thinking is important. This might be taking an objective stance, looking at the evidence, or thinking about what one would say to a friend. However, the key quality is to *compassionately feel* these as helpful and supportive. Therefore, once a person has generated (say) an alternative or coping thought we spend some moments in silence, compassionately engaging with this thought with a genuine sense of caring and encouragement. Or we might first engage with the compassionate self or image and then generate the alternatives, for example 'What would the compassionate self say to this or about this? How could you bring your compassionate self to this situation?'. It is enabling the *emotional experience* of the thought that is important. We suggest that people practice compassionate imagery and attention as many times during the day as possible (even when relaxing in the bath), and to address as many of life's problems with it as they can.

Compassionate Letter Writing

An aide to compassionate thinking and reflection is compassionate letter writing (Leary et al., 2007). The CFT approach is derived from the work of Pennebaker (e.g. 1997), and Neff (2003, 2011) where clients write letters about their own difficulties. Some are burnt or thrown away, others shared. The shared letter should be validating, understanding and supportive. Sometimes clients write letters (believing them to be compassionate) which are quite authoritarian and just offer a lot of advice and 'you shoulds'. Training clients in compassionate writing can be very helpful and revealing. It can be helpful if the therapist leaves the room for five minutes while the client attempts to write a compassionate letter.

Three Chairs

Lesley Greenberg and colleagues pioneered the development of the two-chair technique, where different parts of the self can engage in dialogue and further exploration (Greenberg et al., 1993). This can be especially powerful when there is a dialogue between the self-critical and criticised side of self (Whelton and Greenberg, 2005). In CFT we use three (or more) chairs; the third chair becomes the compassionate self chair (Gilbert and Irons, 2005). It is useful to help the client detach from the 'critical exchange' of the other two chairs and reflect on it in a compassionate way. When using a third chair the client focuses on their breathing, then on engaging in a compassionate self-image, with some degree of compassionate feeling. This is why *building inner compassionate capacity* first is so important because it facilitates a strengthening of that part of self. Without building compassionate capacity some clients, particularly very self-critical people, struggle to deal with their self-critical side.

Working with Memories

Emotional memories work in many complex ways, including in conscious and unconscious domains, and can have major impacts on physiological systems (e.g. Ogden et al., 2006). CFT takes a similar view because of its central focus on classical conditioning (Gilbert, 1989, 1992, 2000b, 2007a). In addition, new research suggests that change can arise from working directly with changing emotional memories and facilitating activation of (competing) emotional memory in different situations (Brewin, 2006; Lee, 2005). In CFT the aim is to create an alternative emotional experience, utilising the brain's own natural affect regulation systems (i.e. the affilia-tive system) via compassion focusing. Hence, generating compassion-focused affects imagery and refocusing, and re-scripting has been very successfully used with trauma (Lee, 2005; Wheatley et al., 2007).

Working with Emotions and Emotional Conflicts – the Multiple Selves Appraoch

CFT notes that that many motives and emotions can conflict (Gilbert, 2000b), which can cause major problems in the organisation of responses (Dixon, 1998). To help clients understand how compassion can help, we explain that in many situations we can have *different inner parts of ourselves or voices* and different reactions to the same event. To demonstrate this, ask the client to imagine an argument (or any appropriate event) with someone close to them that caused distress – but nothing too heavy to start with. Draw a circle in the centre of a page with the word 'argument' in it, with (say) four smaller circles around it. Then ask them to focus on different parts of themselves.

First, using Socratic questions and guided discovery you ask, 'What does/did your angry part think? How does/did your angry part feel in your body? What would happen if these feelings mounted; what would your fear be? If you didn't try to contain your anger, what might happen; what would your anger have you do?' Here it is helpful to explore fantasies of anger. These can vary, such as becoming violent, saying (or screaming) damaging or offensive things or simply walking out on a relationship (a good example of this can be seen in the film *Good Will Hunting*). Then ask if any memories come to mind. Only go to the depth the client feels able to. Don't rush – give plenty of time for exploration. The idea is not to over-whelm people, but to start a process of guided discovery and de-sensitisa-tion. You can also ask 'What is the greatest hope of this part of yourself; what would be a good outcome for it?'

Then ask the client to focus on slowing the breath and let that inner 'anger voice' go and refocus on their anxious part – ask the same questions for the anxious part focusing on thoughts, bodily feelings, what would happen if those feelings mounted and fantasies of what one would do if anxiety was in control. One might then look at sad self. Anger, anxiety and sad self are common 'parts' to explore but one can do the same for any part of the self, including sadness or self-criticism (see example of Catherine in the case example below).

CFT then encourages the person to stand back and *think about the relationships between these different parts or selves* – how they think and *feel* about each other. You can ask 'what does angry self feel about anxious self; what does anxious self feel (and fear) about angry self?' – and so on. So they discover that anxious self can be frightened of angry self, that the anxious self can feel angry self could damage or shame it. In contrast, angry self can be hostile to and contemptuous of anxious self and feels caged and trapped by anxious self. The point is to show this conflict between different 'selves' and feelings and also how individuals can be quite frightened of allowing their emotions to become too powerful, and how they can engage in monitoring, restraint and safety strategies (repression-like). Now, while it is clear that CFT does not encourage the acting out of strong emotion, the process of exploring rather than avoiding emotion, emotional education, de-shaming and desensitisation, is similar to that of CBT with, say, panic or trauma – although only go with what the person is able to work with and build from there. By asking 'What is the greatest hope' of each part of the self, sometimes people recognise that the hopes are similar – each part really wants to be recognised, validated, respected, cared for and so on – they are just different strategies and tactics in our minds for feeling and acting when we don't receive these things.

Compassion Shifting

We then shift to the compassionate self by taking a few deeper, slower breaths to focus on a feeling of slowing down, then imagining becoming a wise, confident, calm, caring, compassionate person. It's 'you at your very best; you as you would like to be when at your most confidently compassionate'. You will have practiced this a few times before doing 'multiple selves' work so that they will have some sense of the self they are seeking to become. Then gently explore the compassionate self's feelings, thought and desired behaviour about the (in this case) argument. We then explore the compassionate mind's thoughts and feelings to angry, anxious and sad selves. The compassionate mind will often have very different feelings and thoughts about the argument than their (angry, anxious and sad) reactions. It can sometimes see the similar fears and hopes underlying the different aspects of the self. The compassionate self is also more likely to be able to 'mentalize' and understand the argument (or whatever situation) in a more empathic way.

This exercise demonstrates some important aspects of how our minds work. First, that threat reactions (e.g. anger, anxiety) are typically the first reactions to some events. Second, demonstrating the emotions of the threat system often 'fight' and conflict with each other. So, people can feel angry at their anxiousness or submissiveness, or anxious at the level of their anger or violent fantasies, or guilty about their anger and so on. CFT helps people understand this 'normal' conflict of emotions (Gilbert, 2000b, 2007a, 2007b). Third, clients can learn that one 'voice/part' can block out another. For example, angry reactors may not pay attention to their anxious, more cautious or sad voices/selves. Anxious people may be hardly aware of their anger, and are frightened of certain fantasies. One client did not want to think about his angry part because it brought back memories of him watching his father beat his mother. When he started to feel angry he would become very anxious (he felt terrified, relating to a complex emotional memory of being frightened of his father but also wanting to attack him). This would emerge with difficulty in breathing and feeling overwhelmed. This undermined his assertiveness, and his lack of assertiveness made him angry with himself.

A compassionate approach helps people recognise that compassion can incorporate and understand the nature and origins of the threat-based responses, understand how they conflict and how secondary emotions occur (e.g. fear of anger, fear of fear, or anger of fear). Guilt is also common to these threat emotions (Gilbert and Irons 2005). For example, Kath wanted to talk about her abusive father and her anger but when she did she felt overwhelmed by guilt of 'betraying him, letting him down and being bad and unlovable' with feelings of loss and aloneness. This was partly because she also loved him and had wanted him to be kinder. So there can be guilt over conflicts to feelings linked to 'the wanted but feared/hated other' (e.g. parent). Compassion can take an overview of many different voices, sense of selves and conflicts in our minds. In compassion we understand that it is only natural to have different voices, sense of selves and feelings for the same situation (or another person), but we can also pull back from them and think about what the compassionate position is to this situation – being clear to distinguish compassion from submissiveness or non-assertiveness (Hackmann, 2005). However, developing this compassionate overview of the situation requires us to build a compassionate capacity using interventions noted above.

Compassion and Courage

Perhaps one of the biggest misunderstandings about CFT is that the concept of soothing means 'soothing away' rather than 'soothing in order to engage'. For example, if you suffer from agoraphobia the compassionate thing to do is to kindly but firmly go out and confront your anxiety. It is not taking soothing relaxing baths. If you have a weight problem, then resisting eating unhealthy foods to improve one's health is the compassionate thing to do. Staying in an aversive relationship is not helpful; developing the courage to leave may be. Saying 'no' to some of the things our children want is compassionate; just giving in to them is not (Gilbert, 2009). We become compassionate to and learn about our anger, anxiety, guilt, depression, shame and so on because these are part of the human mind and it is via compassion that they can soften and we may transform them. Compassion is about understanding the nature of our suffering and being motivated to *skilfully* do something about it. Compassion helps to normalise, validate, understand and tolerate. Compassion operates as a balancing mechanism, and it provides a 'grounding' and return point.

Case Example: Catherine

Formulation: How Client Problems are Conceptualised

Catherine (partially invented case) was a 42-year-old divorced mother of two who came from a chaotic and emotion-avoidant family. Like her mother, she had suffered depression on and off for most of her life. The first steps to formulation begin with an opening question such as 'What has brought you here today?', leading into a standard symptomatic and problem focused assessment. For Catherine the symptoms were typical depression and anxiety ones. She felt stuck in a low-paid job, and would like to make, but fears making, an intimate relationship. CFT works on practical problems in standard ways, if appropriate. When asked 'Do you find your mind going over and over things that upset you?', 'To what extent would you say you are a self-critical person?' and 'How do you criticise yourself; what *feelings* do you have about you?' we discoverd that Catherine ruminates and is highly self-critical, including being critical about being depressed and does 'not like herself much'.

Catherine's practical problems are addressed where appropriate, but the more basic ones are contextualised within her history. We looked at how some key fears and safety strategies developed from childhood. We explored relationships in detail (see Gilbert, 2007a: ch. 8). From this emerged a story of a depressed mother who was not affectionate and a rather hard-working but absent father. She acknowledged a mixture of confusing feelings of yearning, guilt, anger and sadness towards her mother. She recalled times when she was angry with mother and then her mother wouldn't speak to her for days on end. Catherine said she just had this awful sense of emotional isolation associated with a feeling that she been bad in some way. In CFT experiences associated with loneliness and emotional isolation are important to explore and work with, and are viewed as conditioned emotion memories (Gilbert 1992: 416; Gilbert and Irons, 2005). She had wanted her father to be more present but he 'had more important things to do than be with me'. Children in these situations can feel anger towards the wanted but ultimately absent parent, yet also have fear and guilt about their anger towards the person they want to be loved by – very familiar ideas in both psychoanalytic and behavioural approaches (Gilbert, 1992: Part III) . For those following the cognitive formulation, one can see that her experiences of others are linked to disconnection and feelings that others are preoccupied with their own issues. In CFT we would focus

Table 7.1   Example of the key themes in CFT formulation

Background experiences	Key fears	Safety/defensive strategies	Unintended and unhelpful consequences
The case of Catherine: Mother was depressed, emotionally 'unavailable' and critical. Father working away and absent a lot.	External: Being criticised by others. Being ignored – put into emotional isolation Trying to develop a relationship but others always having (more important) other things to do. Internal: Never feeling close and loved. Feeling inadequate, and not worth bothering with. Being overwhelmed by loneliness and anger.	External: Trying to please people, working out what they want; hiding feelings that could upset people. Internal: Trying to avoid difficult feelings. When feels particularly bad has strong sense of emotional isolation which is difficult to overcome. Wanting medication to control feelings.	Keeping distance, not sharing thoughts and feelings. Often having confused or mixed feelings and frightened of some feelings; not realising other people can feel the same way. Staying lonely and unable to learn from others. Becoming very easily upset and then self-critical. Becoming more angry and self-critical and feeling inadequate – sometimes to the point of wanting to self-harm. Stuck in a cycle of feeling inadequate and self-critical.

on the conflicts of feelings that these experiences can create. When asked how she thinks she coped (e.g. her safety strategies) we learned that she is not assertive because she feels her views are unimportant, she is frightened of anger and conflicts, and she can be overly caring (to be liked). She rarely discussed feelings in any depth with her husband and may have married somebody who was equally emotionally avoidant. She saw herself as weak, inadequate, boring and easily made anxious. Table 7.1 offers an overview.

The Therapeutic Relationship

As for most therapies, compassion begins in the first moments of meeting the client by ensuring that one's manner is open and friendly. People make judgements about how safe and approachable people are within seconds, based on facial expression and demeanour. Catherine appeared to engage but often spoke at me rather than to me. Her ability to be open to others' helpfulness, or even think about what I was saying, was not well developed and she had a tendency to do things in therapy from her submissive orientation, to please me rather than to experience, by guided discovery, her own ways to recovery. This was openly explored. 'I wonder if you are doing this to try to please me rather than because you really understand

(Continued)

(Continued)

the value of it for you?', 'What would be your greatest fear if you felt you were displeasing or annoying *me*?', 'Suppose I really annoyed *you* how would you express that? What might be your greatest fear?', 'What would be your greatest hope?' The therapeutic relationship is an opportunity to revisit a whole range of feelings to do with being cared for, about relating to authority and so on. CFT therapists are very mindful of these aspects of the transference and countertransference and facilitating opportunities for working on these themes, without being overwhelming or becoming a rescuer as such. The relationship therefore is a source of many things, such as encouragement, inspiring, mentoring, supporting, containing, setting boundaries and working through relational conflicts (Gilbert, 2007b)

Strategies of Treatment

CFT offers evolutionary explanations for the source of depression with an understanding that we are biologically orientated for certain emotions and mental states (such as depression), and experiencing them is *absolutely not our fault*. However, there are things that can make those unpleasant mental states more or less likely and intense. This is a powerful insight that begins the process of de-shaming, because many shame-prone clients have a basic belief and 'felt sense' that there is something bad about them. We contextualised the history in terms of the basic model and introduced her to the three circle model (see Figure 7.2). Catherine instantly saw that she lived a lot of her life in the threat system, trying to defend herself from rejection. She found it very difficult to be kind or compassionate to herself. She felt that she didn't deserve compassion; that she should really just 'pull herself together and get on with life and stop wallowing in self-pity'. As for many people there was a misunderstanding of compassion, with much unaddressed anger and fear of conflict.

We introduced Catherine to the basic exercises for compassion, beginning with soothing breathing rhythm. She found this difficult at first but gradually got the hang of practising 'slowing down' in her breathing. She was also given some basic mindfulness training. We then discussed whether compassionate self or compassionate image might be the preferable first imagery task. She chose compassionate self.

Major Treatment Strategies

The overarcing strategy is to help clients experience compassion (activation of soothing affiliative system) and to understand what compassion really means. While imagery is an important part of that process, it's how that imagery is used that is key. Hence, I will outline one particular major strategy that helped her understand that compassion is not about a weakness, self-indulgence or 'soothing things away'.

Once capacity has been built to slow the breathing and create a sense of 'inner space' and a 'compassionate self' we can then put this imagery to work. Because emotions seemed to be problematic for Catherine we decided to explore these in detail, using the techniques outlined in 'Working with emotions and emotional conflicts' above. Catherine's angry thoughts related to ideas that people were ignoring her, treating her as unworthy of attention. This is a feeling she had with her mother, husband and commonly at work. When she focused on the anger feelings in her body they were located in her chest, arms and going 'into my head'. If she let those feelings build, she felt she would start choking or explode. If she acted on her anger, she felt that she could become aggressive, irrational and 'make a fool of myself'. In the extreme her aggressive behaviour would be to smash things, shout obscenities at people or 'shake and hit them'. While exploring these feelings Catherine was clearly very tense. When asked what memories came to mind, she recalled that occasionally her mother could 'lose it' and she was frightened of her and of being like her. She also recalled that a few times she had been very angry at home and her mother hadn't talked to her for days: 'It was just an unbearable atmosphere. I felt she didn't want me to exist' (see also Table 7.1). So we now had a lot of information about the thoughts associated with anger, the triggers, the bodily experiences, feelings and fantasises, the action tendencies and the fears of anger, the linked memories that were acting partly as inhibitors, and the safety strategies (suppression, submissiveness and avoidance).

I then asked Catherine to engage in a few breaths, to slow down, and to imagine the anxious self. Thoughts were 'I shouldn't be angry, no one really likes me and they will like me less now.' The bodily feelings of anxiety were tightening in the stomach and a sense of impending disaster. Her action tendencies were submissive and apologetic – or to simply run. Memories associated were linked to both family and experiences at school where she felt bullied and unable to defend herself. Those memories caused her to become tearful. We noted this and asked her to take a breath but asked if it 'would be OK just to stay with anxious self' until the exploration was finished but that we would be talking to sad self shortly. This helps people see that they can hold their attention and notice the blending in and out of different parts of self – in this case, how quickly anxiety gives way to sadness. Anxious self wanted to close down angry self and just 'run away'.

The sad self had thoughts about being alone, no-one coming, feeling very empty. Catherine was able to note that the body feelings of sadness were very different to the body feelings of anger or anxiety. Sad self had a slumped, heavy feeling. When she focused on these feelings she wanted to curl up. In terms of the action tendencies, she felt that if she became 'too sad' things would become so empty that she might even contemplate killing herself – that frightened her so much that she wanted to stay away from the feelings of sad self. She hadn't fully realised this before. Sometimes angry folk notice that 'maybe underneath my anger is deep sadness'.

I then asked Catherine to think about *the relationships between these different aspects of herself*. Catherine recognised that her angry self was very critical and contemptuous of the anxious self and saw it as a 'wimp'. In contrast, anxious self was very frightened of angry self and was constantly trying to keep it under wraps. She felt that if the angry self got the upper hand it would be very damaging. Interestingly, both angry self and anxious self were rather frightened of sad self. The reason for this was that sad self tended to collapse and then wanted to hide away with thoughts of suicide. This exercise helped Catherine realise that she had complex emotions that came with their own thoughts and bodily experiences, their own action tendencies, memories, and had their own hopes, yet most importantly were often in conflict with each other. She hadn't been aware of this complexity before.

(Continued)

(Continued)

Compassion Shifting

Catherine then spent a few moments focusing on her soothing breathing and, when ready, brought to mind the compassionate self with facial expression and imagining her kind, compassionate voice. After 3–4 minutes I asked her, 'How does this part of you see the argument?' Catherine recognised that arguments come and go, that both parties have a point of view (in other words, when in compassionate self she was able to mentalise in a way that she couldn't when in the angry, anxious or sad self). She felt calmer. Importantly, she was able to acknowledge angry, anxious and sad self – to have an overview of these different parts of herself, and be accepting and understanding of them, noting they had similar hopes and wants. We highlighted (positively connoted) how she has her own inner wisdom, strength and kindness which will help her if she practices bringing it to mind and 'building on it'.

This approach helps people recognise what compassion is and is not – compassion is the ability to stand back, with wisdom to take a wider view, being able to mentalise and focus on (motivation to/for) being kind and supportive. You can then use 'cognitive alternatives' in very different ways. It helps counteract views that compassion is about being soft or weak. It helps understanding of what we mean when we talk about the wisdom of compassion, the authority/strength/confidence of compassion, and the motivated kindness and support of compassion.

As therapy unfolded we did some empty chair work with feared emotions to others (e.g. mother and father), and then engaged in compassionate reflections. We also worked with her inner critic. Importantly though, we created a third chair where Catherine could sit for a few minutes, with eyes closed, focusing on her breathing and imagining the compassionate self, and then thinking about (say) the interactions between the critical and criticised self – their hopes and fears. In fact any combinations of self (e.g. angry self in relationship to anxious or sad self, etc.) can be enacted in chair work with compassionate reflections following. Sometimes it's useful if you ask the client to take up the body postures of the anxious or angry self when they move to different chairs.

By providing a third or fourth chair for the compassionate self, giving space to become mindful, slowing down the breathing and focusing on the key qualities of compassion, one is *building capacity to do their own therapeutic work*. So, as a behavioural intervention of engaging the emotion (Greenberg et al., 1993), it is important to facilitate acting them out and experiencing them – and *building compassionate capacity* to work with them. As therapy unfolds more focus is given to specific problems as they emerge. For some clients this could be traumatic memories, and the therapist works on re-scripting in relatively standard ways but with a compassionate focus. Catherine learned how to monitor depressing thoughts and how to generate mindful compassionate attention, thinking and behaviour (such as going out with friends more). Compassionate imagery was useful as the therapy progressed, but Catherine never had a clear image of a compassionate figure, although she did have a 'sense of presence' and could imagine a kind, caring voice.

Overcoming Obstacles: The Fear of Compassion

Shame and self-critical people from complex, neglectful and abusive back-grounds can find compassion difficult and be very resistant to it in the first instance (Gilbert, 2010a). Self-criticism is associated with a threat response to compassionate imagery (Longe et al., 2010) and a range of fears about giving and receiving compassion (Gilbert et al., In press). Moreover, open-ing the affiliative system can reveal unprocessed trauma memories and feelings of grief (Gilbert, 2007a; Lee, 2005). Gilbert and Irons (2005) sug-gested that although people can be resistent and avoidant of working on their sadness grief, the grief process is important and facilitates emotional change – as borne out by the client's testimony of the effectiveness of CFT (Gilbert and Procter, 2006; see also Lecours and Bouchard, 2011). A helpful way of working with resistance to compassion is with careful functional analysis, illuminating the beliefs and emotional memories that maintain it. We then focus on compassion as enabling us to develop courage and capac-ity to work with our emotional difficulties, to experience cognitive change as wisdom rather than 'just logic', and begin to build the kind of self one would actually like to become.

Research Status of Value of Compassion

There is now good evidence that caring about others, showing appreciation and gratitude, and having empathic and metalizing skills, builds positive relationships, which significantly influence wellbeing, mental and physical health. There is also increasing evidence that the kind of 'self' we try to become will influence our wellbeing and social relationships, with compas-sionate (rather than self-focused) self-identities, being associated with bet-ter outcomes (Crocker and Canevello, 2008).

In terms of specific training, Fredrickson et al. (2008) found that six 60-minute weekly group sessions with home practice of loving-kindness meditations (compassion directed to self, then others, then strangers) increased positive emotions, mindfulness, feelings of purpose in life and social support and decreased illness symptoms. In a small uncontrolled study of people with chronic mental health problems CFT significantly reduced shame, self-criticism, depression and anxiety (Gilbert and Procter, 2006). In a study of group-based CFT for 19 clients in a high-security psy-chiatric setting, Laithwaite et al. (2009) found 'a large magnitude of change for levels of depression and self-esteem ... moderate magnitude of change was found for the social comparison scale and general psychopathology, with a small magnitude of change for shame ... These changes were main-tained at 6-week follow-up' (p. 521). Compassionate mind training has also been found to be helpful for psychotic voice hearers (Mayhew and Gilbert,

2008). In a study of 99 clients with eating disorders, where CFT has been gradually introduced into the eating disorders service, highly clinical and statistically significant changes were found on all of the subscales of the Eating Disorder Examination Questionnaire and Stirling Eating Disorder Scale (Gale et al., 2011, submitted). The gradual accumulation of evidence for compassion-focused therapy lends itself to the next stage of research, which is randomised controlled trials.

Conclusion

CFT has evolved through working with high shame and self-critical people. It is based on an evolutionary and neuroscience model, and suggests that whatever intervention we use (cognitive, behavioural, emotional or imagery), the client benefits if they can *experience* the intervention as genuinely helpful, validating and encouraging. In addition learning to tolerate and understand the nature of strong emotions, and the conflicts between emotions, is important. In the absence of a 'compassionate capacity' and some kind of safe base as Bowlby (1973) would call it, this can be difficult. Key also is helping people use the evolution model to gain 'deep' insight that facilitates shifting from shaming and blaming to taking responsibility.

In CFT, emotions and their functions cannot be reduced to single cognitive, behavioural or bodily processes but represent complex multimodal systems, underpinned by complex neurophysiological processes, operating in both conscious and unconscious domains. Moreover, the evolved mind is riddled with many potentially competing systems that operate through excitation and inhibition. CFT integrates practices from other traditions that have focused on building compassionate capacities, such as Buddhism, but has also developed specific exercises with clients. Current research is exploring the value of bringing compassionate mind concepts to a range of therapies.

Further reading

Gilbert, P. (Ed.) (2005) *Compassion: Conceptualisations, Research and Use in Psychotherapy*. London: Routledge.

Gilbert, P. (2007) *Psychotherapy and Counselling for Depression*, 3rd Edn. London: Sage.

Gilbert, P. (2009) *The Compassionate Mind*. London: Constable Robinson.

Gilbert, P. (2010) *Compassion Focused Therapy: The CBT Distinctive Features Series*. London: Routledge.

Gilbert, P. (2010) 'Compassion focused therapy: Special issue', *International Journal of Cognitive Therapy*, 3: 95–201.

References

Allen, N.B. and Knight, W.E.J. (2005) 'Mindfulness, compassion for self and compassion for others: Implications for understanding the psychopathology and treatment of depression', in P. Gilbert (Ed.), *Compassion: Conceptualisations, Research and Use in Psychotherapy.* London: Routledge. pp. 239–262.

Allione, T. (2008) *Feeding Your Demons.* New York: Little, Brown.

Bateman, A. and Fonagy, P. (2003) *Psychotherapy for Borderline Personality Disorder: Mentalization Based Treatment.* Oxford: Oxford University Press.

Baumeister, R.F., Bratslavsky, E., Finkenauer, C. and Vohs, K.D. (2001) 'Bad is stronger than good', *Review of General Psychology,* 5: 323–370.

Bowlby, J. (1969) *Attachment: Attachment and Loss,* Vol. 1. London: Hogarth Press.

Bowlby, J. (1973) *Separation, Anxiety and Anger: Attachment and Loss,* Vol. 2. London: Hogarth Press.

Brewin, C.R. (2006) 'Understanding cognitive behaviour therapy: A retrieval competition account', *Behaviour Research and Therapy,* 44: 765–784.

Carter, C.S. (1998) 'Neuroendocrine perspectives on social attachment and love', *Psychoneuroendorinlogy,* 23: 779–818.

Cozolino, L. (2007) *The Neuroscience of Human Relationships: Attachment and the Developing Brain.* New York: Norton.

Crocker, J. and Canevello, A. (2008) 'Creating and undermining social support in communal relationships: The role of compassionate and self-image goals', *Journal of Personality and Social Psychology,* 95: 555–575.

Depue, R.A. and Morrone-Strupinsky, J.V. (2005) 'A neurobehavioral model of affiliative bonding', *Behavioral and Brain Sciences,* 28: 313–395.

Dixon, A.K. (1998) 'Ethological strategies for defence in animals and humans: Their role in some psychiatric disorders', *British Journal of Medical Psychology,* 71: 417–445.

Dryden, W. (2009) *Rational Emotive Behaviour Therapy: Distinctive Features.* London: Routledge.

Eisenberg, N. (2002) 'Empathy-related emotional responses, altruism, and their socialization', in R. Davidson and A. Harrington (Eds), *Visions of Compassion: Western Scientists and Tibetan Buddhists Examine Human Nature.* New York: Oxford University Press. pp. 31–164.

Fehr, C., Sprecher, S. and Underwood, L.G. (2009) *The Science of Compassionate Love: Theory Research and Application.* Chichester: Wiley.

Fogel, A., Melson, G.F. and Mistry, J. (1986) 'Conceptualising the determinants of nurturance: A reassessment of sex differences', in A. Fogel and G.F. Melson (Eds), *Origins of Nurturance: Developmental, Biological and Cultural Perspectives on Caregiving.* Hillsdale, NJ: Lawrence Erlbaum. pp. 53–67.

Fredrickson, B.L., Cohn, M.A., Coffey, K.A., Pek, J. and Finkel, S.A. (2008) 'Open hearts build lives: Positive emotions, induced through loving-kindness meditation, build consequential personal resources', *Journal of Personality and Social Psychology*, 95: 1045–1062.

Gale, C., Gilbert, P. and Goss K. (2011, submitted) 'An evaluation of a compassion focused therapy treatment programme for people with eating disorders', *British Journal of Clincial Psychology*.

Germer, C. (2009) *The Mindful Path to Self-Compassion: Freeing Yourself from Destructive Thoughts and Emotions*. New York: Guilford.

Gilbert, P. (1984) *Depression: From Psychology to Brain State*. London: Lawrence Erlbaum.

Gilbert, P. (1989) *Human Nature and Suffering*. Hove: Lawrence Erlbaum.

Gilbert, P. (1992) *Depression: The Evolution of Powerlessness*. New York: Guilford Press.

Gilbert, P. (1993) 'Defence and safety: Their function in social behaviour and psychopathology', *British Journal of Clinical Psychology*, 32: 131–153.

Gilbert, P. (1997) 'The evolution of social attractiveness and its role in shame, humiliation, guilt and therapy', *British Journal of Medical Psychology*, 70: 113–47.

Gilbert, P. (1998) 'What is shame? Some core issues and controversies', in P. Gilbert and B. Andrews (Eds), *Shame: Interpersonal Behavior, Psychopathology and Culture*. New York: Oxford University Press. pp. 3–36.

Gilbert, P. (2000a) *Counselling for Depression*, 2nd Edn. London: Sage.

Gilbert, P. (2000b) 'Social mentalities: Internal "social" conflicts and the role of inner warmth and compassion in cognitive therapy', in P. Gilbert and K.G. Bailey (Eds), *Genes on the Couch: Explorations in Evolutionary Psychotherapy*. Hove: Psychology Press. pp. 118–150.

Gilbert, P. (2002) 'Evolutionary approaches to psychopathology and cognitive therapy', *Cognitive Psychotherapy: An International Quarterly (Special Edition: Evolutionary Psychology and Cognitive Therapy)*, 16: 263–294.

Gilbert, P. (Ed.) (2005) *Compassion: Conceptualisations, Research and Use in Psychotherapy*. London: Routledge.

Gilbert, P. (2007a) *Psychotherapy and Counselling for Depression*, 3rd Edn. London: Sage.

Gilbert, P. (2007b) 'Evolved minds and compassion in the therapeutic relationship', in P. Gilbert and R. Leahy (Eds), *The Therapeutic Relationship in the Cognitive Behavioural Psychotherapies*. London: Routledge. pp.106–142.

Gilbert, P. (2009) *The Compassionate Mind*. London: Constable Robinson.

Gilbert, P. (2010a) *Compassion Focused Therapy: The CBT Distinctive Features Series*. London: Routledge.

Gilbert, P. (2010b) 'Compassion focused therapy: Special issue', *International Journal of Cognitive Therapy*, 3: 95–201.

Gilbert, P. (In press) 'Shame in psychotherapy and the role of compassion focused therapy', in R.L. Dearing and J.P. Tangney (Eds), *Shame in the Therapy Hour*. Washington: American Psychological Society.

Gilbert, P. and Irons, C. (2005) 'Focused therapies and compassionate mind training for shame and self-attacking', in P. Gilbert (Ed.), *Compassion: Conceptualisations, Research and Use in Psychotherapy*. London: Routledge. pp. 263–325.

Gilbert, P. and Procter, S. (2006) 'Compassionate mind training for people with high shame and self-criticism: A pilot study of a group therapy approach', *Clinical Psychology and Psychotherapy*, 13: 353–379.

Gilbert, P., Clarke, M., Kempel, S. Miles, J.N.V. and Irons, C. (2004) 'Criticizing and reassuring oneself: An exploration of forms style and reasons in female students', *British Journal of Clinical Psychology*, 43: 31–50.

Gilbert, P., McEwan, K., Matos, M. and Rivis, A. (In press) 'Fears of compassion: Development of three self-report measures', *Psychology and Psychotherapy*.

Gray, J.A. (1987) *The Psychology of Fear and Stress*, 2nd Edn. Cambridge: Cambridge University Press.

Greenberg, L.S., Rice, L.N. and Elliott, R. (1993) *Facilitating Emotional Change: The Moment-by-Moment Process*. New York: Guilford Press.

Gumley, A., Braehler, C., Laithwaite, H., MacBeth, A. and Gilbert, P. (2010) 'A compassion focused model of recovery after psychosis', *International Journal of Cognitive Therapy*, 3: 186–201.

Hackmann, A. (2005) 'Compassionate imagery in the treatment of early memories in axis: I Anxiety disorders', in P. Gilbert (Ed.), *Compassion: Conceptualisations, Research and Use in Psychotherapy*. London: Brunner-Routledge. pp. 352–368.

Haidt, J. (2001) 'The emotional dog and its rational tail: A social intuitionist approach to moral judgment', *Psychological Review*, 108: 814–834.

Hayes, S.C., Follette, V.M. and Linehan, M.N. (2004) *Mindfulness and Acceptance: Expanding the Cognitive Behavioral Tradition*. New York: Guilford Press.

Holmes, E.A., Lang, T.J. and Shah, D.M. (2009) 'Developing interpretation bias modification as a cognitive vaccine for depressed mood: Imagining positive events makes you feel better than thinking about them verbally', *Journal of Abnormal Psychology*, 118: 76–88.

Kabat-Zinn, J. (2005) *Coming to our Senses: Healing Ourselves and the World through Mindfulness*. New York: Piatkus.

Laithwaite, H., Gumley, A., O'Hanlon, M., Collins, P., Doyle, P., Abraham, L. and Porter, S. (2009) 'Recovery after psychosis (RAP): A compassion focused programme for individuals residing in high-security settings', *Behavioural and Cognitive Psychotherapy*, 37: 511–526.

Landaw, J. and Bodian, S. (2003) *Buddhism for Dummies*. Chichester: Wiley.

Leary, M.R., Tate, E.B., Adams, C.E., Allen, A.B. and Hancock, J. (2007) 'Self-compassion and reactions to unpleasant self-relevant events: The implications of treating oneself kindly', *Journal of Personality and Social Psychology*, 92: 887–904.

Lecours, S. and Bouchard, M.A. (2011) 'Verbal elaboration of distinct affect categories and BPD symptoms', *Psychology and Psychotherapy: Theory Research and Practice*, 84: 28–41.

LeDoux, J. (1998) *The Emotional Brain*. London: Weidenfeld and Nicolson.

Lee, D.A. (2005) 'The perfect nurturer: A model to develop a compassionate mind within the context of cognitive therapy', in P. Gilbert (Ed.), *Compassion: Conceptualisations, Research and Use in Psychotherapy*. London: Brunner-Routledge. pp. 326–351.

Longe, O., Maratos, F.A., Gilbert, P., Evans, G., Volker, F., Rockliff, H. and Rippon, G. (2010) 'Having a word with yourself: Neural correlates of self-criticism and self-reassurance', *NeuroImage*, 49: 1849–1856.

Mayhew, S. and Gilbert, P. (2008) 'Compassionate mind training with people who hear malevolent voices: A case series report', *Clinical Psychology and Psychotherapy*, 15: 113–138.

Neff, K.D. (2003) 'Self-compassion: An alternative conceptualization of a healthy attitude toward oneself', *Self and Identity*, 2: 85–102.

Neff, K. (2011) *Self-Compassion. Stop Beating Yourslef Up and Leave Insecurity Behind*. New York: Morrow.

Ogden, P., Minton, K. and Pain, C. (2006) *Trauma and the Body: A Sensorimotor Approach to Psychotherapy*. New York: Norton.

Ornstein, R. (1986) *Multimind: A New Way of Looking at Human Beings*. London: Macmillan.

Panksepp, J. (1998) *Affective Neuroscience*. New York: Oxford University Press.

Pennebaker, J.W. (1997) *Opening Up: The Healing Power of Expressing Emotions*. New York: Guilford.

Porges, S.W. (2007) 'The polyvagal perspective', *Biological Psychology*, 74: 116–143.

Rogers, C. (1957) 'The necessary and sufficient conditions of therapeutic change', *Journal of Consulting Psychology*, 21: 95–103.

Salkovskis, P.M. (1996) 'The cognitive approach to anxiety: Threat beliefs, safety-seeking behavior, and the special case of health anxiety and obsessions', in P.M. Salkovskis (Ed.), *Frontiers of Cognitive Therapy*. New York: Guilford. pp. 48–74.

Stopa, L. (2009) *Imagery and the Threatened Self: Perspective on Mental Imagery and the Self in Cognitive Therapy*. London: Routledge.

Stott, R. (2007) 'When the head and heart do not agree: A theoretical and clinical analysis of rational-emotional dissociation (RED) in cognitive therapy', *Journal of Cognitive Psychotherapy: An International Quarterly*, 21: 37–50.

Tarrier, N. (2010) 'Broad-minded effective coping (BMAC): A "positive" CBT approach to facilitating positive emotions', *Journal of Cognitive Therapy*, 3: 65–78.

Thwaites, R. and Freeston, M.H. (2005) 'Safety-seeking behaviours: Fact or fiction: How can we clinically differentiate between safety behaviours and additive coping strategies across anxiety disorders?', *Behavioural and Cognitive Psychotherapy*, 33: 177–188.

Welford, M. (2010) 'A compassion focused approach to anxiety disorders', *International Journal of Cognitive Therapy*, 3: 124–140.

Wheatley, J., Brewin, C.R., Patel, T., Hackmann, A., Wells, A., Fischer, P. and Myers, S. (2007) '"I'll believe it when I see it": Imagery re-scripting of intrusive sensory memories', *Journal of Behavior Therapy and Experimental Psychiatry*, 39: 371–385.

Whelton, W.J. and Greenberg, L.S. (2005) 'Emotion in self-criticism', *Personality and Individual Differences*, 38: 1583–1595.

Wispe, L. (1986) 'The distinction between sympathy and empathy', *Journal of Personality and Social Psychology*, 50: 314–321.

Zuroff, D.C. and Blatt, S.J. (2006) 'The therapeutic relationship in the brief treatment of depression: Contributions to clinical improvement and enhanced capacities', *Journal of Consulting and Clinical Psychology*, 74: 130–140.

Zuroff, D.C., Santor, D. and Mongrain, M. (2005) 'Dependency, self-criticism, and maladjustment', in J.S. Auerbach, K.N. Levy and C.E. Schaffer (Eds), *Relatedness, Self-Definition and Mental Representation: Essays in Honour of Sidney J. Blatt*. London: New York. pp. 75–90.

EIGHT   Schema Therapy

VARTOUHI OHANIAN AND RANA RASHED

Historical Development of the Approach

'Schema therapy is an innovative, integrative therapy developed by Young and colleagues that significantly expands on traditional cognitive behavioural treatments and concepts' (Young et al., 2003a: 1). Schema therapy has been found to be effective in the treatment of personality disorders, chronic depression and other Axis I disorders (APA, 2000) as well as couples problems.

Jeffrey Young, PhD, founder of Schema Therapy, trained and worked in cognitive therapy with Dr Aaron T. Beck in Philadelphia. He became interested in the 'treatment failures', that is, those clients who did not respond to or frequently relapsed with traditional cognitive behavioural therapy (CBT). Young noted that these cases had many characteristics in common, such as: presenting problems which were chronic, often vague yet pervasive; very rigid thinking and behaviour patterns; a high level of avoidance and/or entitlement; difficulties in following standard cognitive behavioural techniques such as keeping diaries and doing home-based tasks; long-term interpersonal difficulties; a significant gap between their intellectual understanding of their problems and emotional change. He further noted that these entrenched emotional and psychological problems had significant origins in negative or abusive childhood and adolescent development. This led Young to consider and integrate attachment theories (Ainsworth and Bowlby, 1991) and some elements of psychodynamic theory, in particular object relations, into schema therapy. Finally, acknowledging the role of highly intense emotions in the reactions of these clients, Young incorporated emotion-focused techniques such as imagery as well as role plays and dialogues from Gestalt therapy (Kellogg, 2004).

Thus, whilst maintaining the structured, systematic, collaborative and empirical approach of CBT, exploration of childhood origins and developmental processes necessitated schema therapy to be longer than standard CBT. Young also placed a much greater emphasis on the therapy relationship as pivotal for change to occur, suggesting that 'limited reparenting' and 'empathic confrontation' are key ingredients. In addition, greater focus was directed at entrenched belief systems ('schemas') and negative life patterns ('coping styles') than changing negative automatic thoughts and specific behaviours. Young (1990) named the core psychological themes that are typical of clients with personality disorders 'early maladaptive schemas' (EMS).

A model of 18 EMS, grouped under five domains and three main coping styles, was developed together with specific assessment tools and treatment strategies for each schema and coping style.

While the schema model proved very valuable in treating many clients, the challenge posed by individuals with borderline personality disorder (BPD), and to a lesser extent narcissistic personality disorder (NPD), led Young to expand on his schema model and develop the schema mode concept. Clients with BPD not only scored very highly on almost all of the schemas and had many maladaptive coping responses but also exhibited rapid shifts in affect and behaviour, referred to as 'mode flipping'. This made working with individual schemas overwhelming.

Young et al. (2003a) proposed that a schema mode comprises a set of schemas or coping responses which can be activated by internal and external stimuli. Ten schema modes were identified and grouped into four broad categories. Young proposed specific interventions in schema mode work that enable the therapist to work with the frequent 'flipping' of these clients. The model was subsequently adapted to treat NPD. Bernstein et al. (2007) expanded Young's mode model to incorporate four additional schema modes that were commonly observed in forensic clients.

Young's first book, *Cognitive Therapy for Personality Disorders: A Schema-Focused Approach*, was published three times (1990, 1994, 1999). 'Schema-focused therapy' was later renamed 'schema therapy'.

Dr Young established the first Schema Therapy Institute in New York in the mid-1990s. *Schema Therapy: A Pratitioner's Guide* (Young et al., 2003a), *Reinventing Your Life* (Young and Klosko, 1994) and the schema inventories are now translated into several languages. Schema therapy is also widely taught in Europe, the Middle East, the Far East, Australia and the USA.

In the UK, Dr Young delivered the first workshop on schema therapy in Oxford in 1989, followed by others in 1993 and 1994. Unaware of these workshops, the first author of this chapter was introduced to schema therapy in 1990 by Dr Mary Anne Layden, a colleague of Dr Young's in Philadelphia, during the time she was on a sabbatical in London. Dr Layden delivered the early schema therapy workshops in the UK. Momentum gathered after that, with many more schema therapy workshops being given mostly by Dr Young primarily under the auspices of Schema Therapy UK, organised by Vartouhi Ohanian, its Director. Indeed, the first author has been instrumental in introducing and disseminating schema therapy in the UK. More recently, similar workshops were organised by other organisations with presenters including Dr Young, Vartouhi Ohanian, Professor Arnoud Arntz and colleagues. In addition, Vartouhi Ohanian has been regularly invited to teach schema therapy on clinical psychology training courses and CBT diploma courses in London. In 2009, following the establishment of guidelines and minimum criteria for certification, several approved training programmes in schema therapy[1] in the UK were provided by the first author.

Theoretical Underpinnings

Major Theoretical Concepts

The significant influence of Beck's original model of cognitive therapy (Beck et al., 1979) and Young's training and background in CBT is evidenced by the systematic and empirical approach to assessment and treatment adopted by schema therapy. Other fundamental concepts shared with CBT include: the collaborative nature of the therapeutic relationship and case conceptualisation; the directive role of the therapist; psycho-education; the emphasis on cognitive and behavioural change; goal setting; structured home-based tasks; teaching skills such as assertiveness, relaxation and social skills to name but a few. Similarly, some aspects of Beck's (1967) early definition of schemas and subsequent description of schemas and modes in the revised model of cognitive therapy (Alford and Beck, 1997) are included in the concept of EMS.

However, as mentioned above, recognising the limitations of cognitive therapy in the treatment of personality disorders, Young turned to other psychotherapy models to find other ways of conceptualising problems for this client group and to develop more effective interventions. Thus, exploration of childhood origins of current problems, the presence of unconscious processes, the focus on the therapy relationship in terms of transference and countertransference (in schema terms, therapists and clients triggering each other's schemas) and the necessity to process trauma on an emotional level, was influenced by psychodynamic models. More specifically, object relations school of thought directed the focus to interpersonal relations primarily in the family, and the concept of internalization of significant others in the child's early life as shaping the child's view of self and the world. Schema therapy incorporated the notion that patterns learnt during early interactions with primary caregivers often persisted and significantly influenced the life of the adult.

Schema therapy was also strongly informed by attachment theory and Bowlby's work (Ainsworth and Bowlby, 1991), particularly in the development of the abandonment schema and the schema conceptualisation of BPD. Bowlby's concept of dysfunctional 'internal working models' is similar to that of EMS, as

---

[1]Approved by the International Society of Schema Therapy (ISST).

is the principle that the internal working models guide how the individual attends to and processes information. Schema therapy also acknowledges the presence of basic emotional needs in children and regards the gratification thereof through healthy interactions within a stable early attachment to the mother, or other significant caregiver, as the basis for autonomy and individuation. Both theories suggest that the failure to form successful early attachments leads to later interpersonal difficulties, including in the therapy relationship.

Finally, the power of experiential strategies in bringing about emotional change was recognised, and many Gestalt techniques were incorporated and utilised in schema therapy. However, it is important to emphasise that this is not done in a random fashion or that schema therapy is an eclectic therapy. On the contrary, it is based on a theory which is tightly woven with cognitive, behavioural, emotional and experiential strategies to form a unifying conceptual framework. In addition, the therapeutic relationship is considered an equally important component.

Schema Theory

As mentioned earlier, schema theory comprises four main concepts of early maladaptive schemas, schema domains, coping styles and schema modes.

Young et al. (2003a) defined EMS as:

- a broad, pervasive theme or pattern;
- comprised of memories, emotions, cognitions and bodily sensations;
- regarding oneself and one's relationships with others;
- developed during childhood or adolescence;
- elaborated throughout one's lifetime;
- dysfunctional to a significant degree.

Young proposed that these schemas serve as templates for the processing of later experience and have certain characteristics.

They are unconditional rigid beliefs and feelings about oneself and the world that the individual never challenges. They form the core of an individual's sense of self. They are self-perpetuating and are very resistant to change. They usually operate in subtle ways outside of the individual's conscious awareness. EMS are usually triggered by events relevant to that particular schema and are associated with extreme negative emotions. Behaviours do not form part of the schema; instead the schema 'drives the behaviour' (Young et al., 2003a). Young did not include the individual's behaviour in the concept of schema but theorised that the coping styles and responses are also developed early in life as a way of surviving negative childhood experiences and dealing with schemas.

According to Young and colleagues, schemas can be positive or negative, can develop early or later in life and can be of varying degrees of severity.

Late onset schemas are generally not as entrenched and powerful as EMS. Schema therapy focuses mostly on EMS as they are considered to form the core of personality disorder pathology.

Origins of Schemas

Young et al. (2003a) theorise that EMS develop when children's core emotional needs are consistently not met. They hypothesise the existence of five core emotional needs which they consider universal:

1 Secure attachment to others (includes safety, stability, nurturance and acceptance).
2 Autonomy, competence and sense of identity.
3 Freedom to express valid needs and emotions.
4 Spontaneity and play.
5 Realistic limits and self-control.

Four mechanisms through which schemas can be acquired are proposed (Young et al., 2003a: 10–11):

- *Toxic frustration of needs* – refers to an absence of healthy experiences.
- *Traumatisation or victimisation* – consists of specific traumatic and abusive experiences.
- *Too much of a good thing* – where the parents do not set realistic limits, are overprotective or overinvolved.
- *Selective internalisation or identification with significant others* – for example, some aspect(s) of the parent's thinking and behaviour.

Young and colleagues (2003a) postulate that the development of schemas is also influenced by a child's emotional temperament interacting with negative childhood experiences. They cite research by Kagan et al. (1988), which showed that temperamental traits in infancy remained unchanged over time. However, they add that a very positive or negative childhood environment can significantly outweigh emotional temperament.

Moreover, a neurobiological perspective regarding the formation and modification of schemas is hypothesised, based on Le Doux's research (1996), on emotion and the brain, as well as developments in interpersonal neurobiology (Siegel, 2007).

Eighteen EMS were identified and grouped under five domains, reflecting the above-mentioned five areas of core emotional needs which have been thwarted. For a description of the five domains and their associated schemas, see Table 8.1.

Young et al. (2003a) state that EMS are dimensional, varying in severity and pervasiveness. They also differentiate between unconditional schemas formed earliest in life and conditional schemas which are said to develop later.

Two primary schema operations named 'schema perpetuation' and 'schema healing' are proposed. Schema perpetuation refers to all thoughts, feelings

Table 8.1   Early maladaptive schemas (adapted from
Young et al., 2003a)

DISCONNECTION and REJECTION

1. **Abandonment/Instability**
   The perceived *instability* or *unreliability* of those available for support and connection.
2. **Mistrust/Abuse**
   The expectation that others will hurt, abuse, humiliate, cheat, lie, manipulate, or take advantage.
3. **Emotional Deprivation**
   Expectation that one's desire for a normal degree of emotional support will not be adequately met by others.
4. **Defectiveness/Shame**
   The feeling that one is defective, bad, unwanted, inferior, or invalid in important respects; or that one would be unlovable to significant others if exposed.
5. **Social isolation/Alienation**
   The feeling that one is isolated from the rest of the world, different from other people, and/or not part of any group or community.

IMPAIRED AUTONOMY and PERFORMANCE

6. **Dependence/Incompetence**
   Belief that one is unable to handle one's *everyday responsibilities* in a competent manner, without considerable help from others.
7. **Vulnerability to harm or illness**
   Exaggerated fear that *imminent* catastrophe will strike at any time and that one will be unable to prevent it.
8. **Enmeshment/Undeveloped self**
   Excessive emotional involvement and closeness with one or more significant others (often parents), at the expense of full individuation or normal social development.
9. **Failure**
   The belief that one has failed, will inevitably fail, or is fundamentally inadequate relative to one's peers, in areas of *achievement*.

IMPAIRED LIMITS

10. **Entitlement/Grandiosity**
    The belief that one is superior to other people; entitled to special rights and privileges; not bound by the rules of reciprocity that guide normal social interaction.
11. **Insufficient self-control/Self-discipline**
    Pervasive difficulty or refusal to exercise sufficient self-control and frustration tolerance to achieve one's personal goals, or to restrain the excessive expression of one's emotions and impulses.

OTHER-DIRECTEDNESS

12. **Subjugation**
    Excessive surrendering of control to others because one feels *coerced* – usually to avoid anger, retaliation or abandonment.
13. **Self-sacrifice**
    Excessive focus on *voluntarily* meeting the needs of others in daily situations, at the expense of one's own gratification.
14. **Approval-seeking/Recognition-seeking**
    Excessive emphasis on gaining approval, recognition or attention from other people, or fitting in, at the expense of developing a secure and true sense of self.

(Continued)

Table 8.1 (Continued)

OVERVIGILANCE and INHIBITION

15. **Negativity/Pessimism**
    A pervasive, life-long focus on the negative aspects of life while minimizing or neglecting the positive or optimistic aspects.
16. **Emotional inhibition**
    The excessive inhibition of spontaneous action, feeling or communication – usually to avoid disapproval by others, feelings of shame or losing control of one's impulses.
17. **Unrelenting standards/Hypercriticalness**
    The underlying belief that one must strive to meet very high *internalized standards* of behaviour and performance, usually to avoid criticism.
18. **Punitiveness**
    The belief that people should be harshly punished for making mistakes. Involves the tendency to be angry, intolerant, punitive and impatient with those people (including oneself) who do not meet one's expectations or standards.

and behaviours which reinforce and therefore perpetuate the schema. Schema healing is achieved in therapy when the intensity of the memories, affect, bodily sensations and dysfunctional cognitions associated with the schema is significantly decreased and the maladaptive behaviour patterns are modified. When this happens, EMS become more difficult to trigger.

Schema Coping Styles

Three maladaptive schema coping styles are identified:

1 *Schema surrender* refers to ways clients give in to a schema and therefore confirm it both at a cognitive level through cognitive distortions and behaviourally through self-defeating behaviour patterns. Thus, they experience the painful emotions of the schema directly.
2 *Schema avoidance* refers to ways in which clients avoid activation of the schema or avoid experiencing the extreme negative affect associated with the schema.
3 *Schema overcompensation* refers to cognitive and behavioural styles utilised by clients which appear to be the opposite of what their schema suggest and is a means of avoiding the activation of the schema. On the surface, individuals who overcompensate may appear healthy. However, they 'overshoot the mark' and alienate others, thus perpetuating the schema.

Clients may utilise different coping styles in different situations at different stages of their lives to cope with the same schema. Moreover, different clients use widely varying, even opposite behaviours to cope with the same schema.

Schema Modes

A mode has been defined as 'those schemas or schema operations – adaptive or maladaptive – that are currently active for an individual ... An individual may shift from one dysfunctional schema mode into another; as that shift occurs, different schemas or coping responses, previously dormant, become active' (Young et al., 2003a: 37, 40). This shifting, also referred to as 'flipping', is a reaction to external and internal stimuli and can be very rapid.

Modes are viewed as parts of the self that have not been fully integrated and seen along a continuum of dissociation, depending on the level of awareness and ability to moderate and integrate them.

A mode can be distinguished from a schema in that it is a mindset or state that an individual is in at a given time, whereas a schema is more of a trait or an enduring aspect of the person.

Young et al. (2003a) have proposed ten schema modes grouped into four categories:

1 Child modes are believed to be innate and universal. They include Vulnerable Child, Angry Child, Impulsive/Undisciplined Child and Happy Child. Like schemas, these modes develop when specific core emotional needs are not met in childhood.
2 Maladaptive coping modes include Compliant Surrenderer, Detached Protector and Overcompensator. These are dysfunctional because they represent an overuse of surrender, avoidance and overcompensation coping styles.
3 Maladaptive parent modes include Punitive Parent and Demanding/Critical Parent. These represent the internalised parental opinions and behaviours towards the client as a child and which have become entrenched.
4 Healthy adult mode is the functional part of the self. The goal of schema therapy is to help clients achieve and remain in this mode.

The advantages of a mode perspective is that it allows the therapist to track the responses in affect, cognition and behaviour as they occur during the session. Specific treatment strategies for each dysfunctional mode can be developed. Furthermore, educating clients about modes provides them with an understanding about their varied reactions to different life situations, helps them learn to monitor their modes and gradually to heal the maladaptive modes.

The mode concept is now seen as the essence of schema therapy with severe personality disorders such as BPD and, following the work of Bernstein et al. (2007), with antisocial personality disorder. It is also an effective way of treating NPD. In addition, the mode approach has proved valuable in working with higher functioning clients who are extremely rigid and avoidant. For a full discussion of the mode model, see Young et al. (2003a).

How Client Problems are Conceptualised

In schema therapy, EMS determine how an individual feels, thinks, acts and relates to others. They are therefore ego-syntonic and try to survive by driving the person to re-enact negative childhood situations in their adult life without realising it. Thus, accurate identification of EMS, coping styles and their links to negative childhood experiences is essential for constructing a case conceptualisation.

Schema therapy is not usually indicated or should be postponed if the client is presenting with a severe untreated Axis I disorder, psychotic experiences, current and primary substance misuse problem or a major crisis. Once a client's suitability for schema therapy is determined, the therapist begins by assessing the client's presenting problems clearly and in specific terms to enable both therapist and client to stay focused on them.

The therapist then takes a focused life history to establish whether the client's current difficulties represent dysfunctional life patterns in the client's relationships and work. To achieve this, the therapist pays particular attention to schema eruption in the past, schema triggers and coping styles and responses used by the client. The therapist gives an explanation of the schema model and assigns the following schema inventories:

- Young Schema Questionnaire – YSQ-L3 (Young, 2005).
- The Young Parenting Inventory – YPI (Young, 2003b).
- Young-Rygh Avoidance Inventory (Young and Rygh, 2003).
- Young Compensation Inventory (Young, 2003c).

Imagery Assessment

Imagery is the most commonly used experiential method for assessing schemas. After the client is provided with a rationale for imagery work, s/he is asked to close their eyes and imagine themselves as a child in an upsetting situation with each parent or significant caregiver from their childhood and adolescence. The client is then encouraged to express their thoughts, feelings and what they needed to get from the other person. The same process is repeated with a current situation which feels the same as the childhood one. This procedure can be carried out in reverse order, that is, with an image of an upsetting event in the client's current life and tracking back to an event from childhood when the same feelings and meanings were experienced. Imagery exercises need to begin and end with safe-place imagery.

Using imagery as an assessment tool helps identify and activate schemas and connect them to their origins in childhood. This technique also enables clients who are schema avoiders to feel the schemas and link them to their current difficulties. In such cases and where there is severe trauma in the client's history, it is necessary to build a trusting relationship with the client before undertaking imagery work.

The use of self-report measures, experiential and behavioural methods for assessment and observing and addressing schemas triggered in the therapy relationship, maximises the accuracy of schema identification and of coping styles and responses in a client.

Modes are assessed by administering the schema mode inventory (SMI) (Young et al., 2007). The therapist also pays close attention to environmental triggers of different modes and to the cognitive, affective and behavioural components of each mode as they are activated in and out of the therapy sessions.

Educating Clients about Schema Therapy

As mentioned above, the therapist would have explained the schema model to the client during the assessment phase to help them understand their schemas, the triggers and origins of schemas and the specific ways they have learnt to cope with schematic activation. This process is a collaborative one where the client contributes at each stage towards their case conceptualisation.

Reinventing Your Life (Young and Klosko, 1994) is recommended to the client as homework. The book covers 11 schemas, referred to as 'lifetraps', and explains the three coping styles. As the client understands the schema model and learns about their schemas, they become better able to observe their schemas and the predominant coping styles they use in their current life.

Finally, the material obtained from the various assessment modalities[2] is integrated using the comprehensive schema therapy case conceptualisation form. This initial formulation is revised and refined in collaboration with the client as therapy progresses.

Practical Applications

In schema therapy, the phase that follows 'assessment and education' is referred to as the 'change phase'. During this phase, the therapist would employ cognitive, experiential and behavioural strategies to challenge and modify early maladaptive schemas as well as coping styles and modes. As well as utilizing specific techniques, a schema therapist would also make use of the therapy relationship as a platform for assessment and treatment.

The Therapeutic Relationship

The therapeutic relationship is an important component of schema therapy. In the assessment phase the therapist notes any schema activation in the therapy relationship, as this provides additional material to identify schemas, triggers and coping styles. Furthermore, Young et al. (2003a) discuss the use of the therapeutic relationship during the assessment phase of the therapy to establish rapport, conceptualise the client's difficulties, assess the client's reparenting needs and to educate the client about the therapy. During the assessment phase, the schema therapist would also look at their own schemas and how they may interfere with the therapeutic process. This would involve the therapist assessing their own emotional reactions towards

---

[2]The forms and questionnaires mentioned above can be purchased as a package from the Schema Therapy Institute (www.schematherapy.com).

the client as a person as well as the client's presenting difficulties. Young et al. identify different therapist/client interactions that can prove problematic, such as therapist and client schemas clashing or the client triggering the therapist's schemas or dysfunctional modes. Therefore the therapist needs to be aware of their own schemas as well as be flexible about adapting their style to provide interventions that are specific to the client's schemas. In all phases of therapy, valuable information can be obtained by discussing any similarities between schema activation in the therapy session with situations in the current and past life of the client that share the same feeling.

Although the focus on the therapy relationship is not unique to schema therapy (e.g. Beck et al., 1990), schema therapy during the 'change phase' focuses on two specific features referred to as 'empathic confrontation' and 'limited reparenting'. Empathic confrontation describes a therapist stance which incorporates an understanding and validation of the client's experiences (empathy) at the same time as highlighting a need for change (confrontation). It is mainly used to encourage a client to challenge their schemas and break dysfunctional behavioural patterns. Empathic confrontation typically starts with an acknowledgement of a client's reality or truth, followed by reality testing to correct any misinterpretations or schema-driven distortions. The confrontation is always directed at the schemas and not at the client's experience.

Limited reparenting refers to the therapist using the therapeutic relationship to partially meet a client's core childhood emotional needs (as mentioned above) which were not met by the primary caregivers during childhood. This has to happen within clear limits and boundaries of the therapy as well as in accordance with professional codes of conduct. The therapist would also do this within a therapeutic relationship that emulates a 'parent–child' relationship but which is done in such a way that neither the therapist tries to 'be a parent' nor is the client regressed to a 'child role'. Thus the schema therapist is viewed as a 'good parent' who can, within limits, meet a client's basic emotional needs and model a 'Healthy Adult' that can be internalised by the client. The same principles are used when working with the different modes; accessing and healing the Vulnerable Child, setting limits on the avoidant and compensatory modes that block access to the Vulnerable Child, allowing the Angry Child to verbalise its frustration but to express it through healthy behaviours and helping the client fight the punitive and/or demanding parent modes. These steps are usually facilitated and enhanced by the use of experiential techniques, which will be expanded on later.

Strategies of Treatment

Schema therapy has evolved since its inception. The original model focused on schema change. The last few years saw the introduction of the mode model, which will be mentioned briefly in this section. Both models make use of similar strategies consisting of cognitive, behavioural and experiential work. As the therapeutic relationship is also considered to be an active element of treatment, all treatment strategies happen within a framework of empathic confrontation.

Cognitive Strategies

The main aim of cognitive work in schema therapy is to introduce doubt about the veracity of schemas. As discussed earlier, schemas are experienced as facts and are rarely challenged or doubted by the person who holds them. The task of a schema therapist would be to collaborate with the client and encourage a 'healthy' voice that can question and counter the schemas. Cognitive strategies help clients look at their schemas in an empirical way in order to identify evidence to dispute their veracity. Cognitive strategies used in schema therapy are similar to those used in CBT and involve a range of techniques that can help therapist and client promote a healthier voice or message that can be internalised by the client to use in and outside of therapy to challenge schemas.

Young et al. (2003a) describe various cognitive techniques, usually used in the following order:

1   *Testing the validity of a schema*: This is done collaboratively by generating lists of evidence supporting and negating schemas. In view of the long-standing nature of Axis II difficulties, the client is invited to draw evidence from their whole life, including early childhood, rather than just from their current circumstances.
2   *Reframing the evidence supporting a schema*: The evidence generated in the list supporting a schema is then scrutinised. The therapist helps the client to objectively look at the evidence and to consider alternative explanations for it. For instance, evidence from the client's childhood is often reframed as indicative of poor or inadequate parenting rather than reflecting the qualities or actions of the child. Evidence from later life is reframed in the context of early experiences and schema perpetuation. The therapist suggests that early maladaptive schemas influence choices that a client makes later on in life which lead to schemas being reinforced rather than tested and discounted.
3   *Evaluating the advantages and disadvantages of the client's coping styles*: Maladaptive coping styles are formulated as adaptive strategies in childhood which become redundant or problematic later on in life. They are also regarded as the client's best way of coping in the absence of healthier strategies. Each coping style is then scrutinised, generating advantages and disadvantages of the client's typical responses and behaviours. The aim of this strategy is to demonstrate how the maladaptive coping styles prevent the client from having their needs met. Alternative, more adaptive ways of coping are explored and the client is encouraged to test them out. This usually is a challenging part of the treatment as the schemas strongly attempt to undermine the healthier behaviours and discredit adaptive interpretations. The therapist works closely with the client supporting them in this process.

4 *Conducting dialogues between the 'schema' side and 'healthy' side*: As the client continues to develop healthier, more adaptive schemas and coping styles, the therapist encourages the client to engage in a dialogue between their 'schema' side and their 'healthy' side. This is often done through the use of chairwork (Kellogg, 2004), inviting the client to take turns to 'be' either side, often by using different chairs and moving back and forth between them. It is usual for the therapist to be more involved in the early stages of this work, stepping in to role-play the healthier side while the client is still developing and strengthening their 'healthy' side and learning to express it more freely.

5 *Schema flashcards* (Young et al., 2003b): In acknowledging the strength of schemas and their tendency to self-perpetuate, clients are encouraged to actively fight them at every opportunity. Flashcards are used as reminders of the client's 'healthy' side, listing the evidence for and against schemas and maladaptive coping styles, preferably in the client's own words. Flashcards can be prepared in advance for the client to use in forthcoming situations they anticipate will trigger their schemas.

6 *Schema diaries* (Young, 2003a): Schema diaries are ideally used at a later stage in therapy, once the client feels more confident at challenging their schemas through practising healthier responses both in and out of sessions. With a schema diary, the therapist asks the client to generate healthier views and responses as their schemas are being triggered between sessions. Clients are asked to look at their schema-driven reactions in terms of thoughts, feelings and behaviours, and to identify the underlying schemas for the situation and to generate healthy perspectives and behaviours.

Experiential Strategies

Experiential strategies are used in all phases of schema therapy. During the assessment phase, they are utilized to elicit emotions and assess EMS. In the treatment phase, they are used to meet clients' emotional needs and heal their EMS. Young et al. (2003a) refer to experiential strategies as a means to help clients in their transition from 'knowing intellectually that the schemas are false' to 'believing it emotionally' (p. 110). The most commonly used experiential strategies in schema therapy are imagery, chairwork and letters to parents (Kellogg, 2004).

Imagery

This is the main experiential strategy used in schema therapy. Young et al. (2003a) provide a step-by-step guide to using imagery in the different stages of therapy. They make suggestions about allocating time specifically in sessions for the imagery exercise, taking into consideration the need to discuss and reflect on the exercise afterwards. The importance of providing a clear rationale for imagery work and refraining from giving too many instructions is noted. The latter is to allow for the true experiences of the client to come to the surface and to safeguard against the therapist inadvertently imposing their own ideas or interpretations. Furthermore, they describe the role of 'safe-place' imagery to help a client feel safe, calm and centred, and suggest that every imagery session starts and ends with this.

The aim of imagery involving childhood experiences would be to challenge and heal schemas on an emotional level. This can be done through imagery dialogues, where clients are encouraged to express their anger towards a parent or significant figure from childhood, asserting their right to have had their childhood emotional needs met. Expressing such feelings can also have the added effect of helping clients distance themselves from their schemas by externalising them as childhood messages they received from caregivers as opposed to being a truth about themselves; for example, 'I am unlovable' vs. 'My father often told me I was unlovable'.

Limited reparenting is also used in imagery. Young et al. (2003a) suggest this is done in three stages: first, the therapist enters an image to speak to the client's child self; then the therapist reparents the child as a healthy parent would have done; and finally the client, having internalised the 'healthy' side, is empowered to nurture their child self in the image. This process is similar to mode work, which will be discussed later.

Chairwork
Chairwork is a Gestalt therapy technique that can be used in two main ways. The 'empty-chair' technique involves clients engaging in a dialogue with a significant person from their life who they imagine is sitting in an empty chair in the therapy room. The purpose of this technique is for clients to express their needs as well as their anger towards the significant person who did not meet them. The 'two-chair' technique involves the client using two chairs, representing the schema side and healthy side, in order to conduct the schema dialogues mentioned above. Chairwork is also used in the same way in mode work, where different chairs are reserved for different modes.

Letters to Parents
Another technique used in schema therapy involves the client writing a letter to their parent(s) or significant figure(s) from their childhood who has caused them harm. The letter is used as a tool to help clients express their feelings and assert their needs and rights. The client is encouraged to incorporate within it their newly acquired knowledge and understanding from the therapy. Such a letter is typically not sent, but is rather read in and out of sessions to consolidate learning. A discussion of the pros and cons of sending the letter takes place, and possible repercussions for the client, the person the letter is addressed to and the wider family are considered.

Behavioural Strategies
Behavioural pattern-breaking is usually addressed in the latter stages of therapy and is considered to contribute the most to long-term change and to help prevent relapse. This intervention addresses clients' maladaptive

coping styles/responses as the focus of change. This is accomplished by defining the problem behaviours, proposing adaptive ones and examining the pros and cons of each one of those. Clients deal with one problem behaviour at a time. Flashcards, practising the healthy behaviour in roleplay and imagery as well as outside sessions, form an essential part of this strategy.

The therapist looks for signs of readiness in the client for this stage of therapy. Such signs include the client being able to identify and name their schemas, understand their childhood origins, and defeat schemas through strengthening their healthy side. Additional interventions during this stage may be considered appropriate, for example assertiveness training, anxiety and anger management.

Schema Mode Work

As mentioned above, Young et al. (2003a) advocate for schema mode work for more complex presentations such as BPD and NPD, and they suggest seven main stages of mode work with the overarching goal of developing the client's Healthy Adult mode so that in time it is able to meet the needs of the other modes. These steps are as follows (Young et al., 2003a: 281–304):

1 Identify and label the client's modes.
2 Explore the origin of the modes.
3 Make links between modes and the client's current presenting problems.
4 Evaluate the advantages and disadvantages of each maladaptive mode.
5 Use imagery to gain access to the Vulnerable Child.
6 Conduct dialogues between the different modes (often through roleplay, chairwork and imagery).
7 Facilitate generalisation from therapy to everyday life situations.

In the early stages, the therapist acts as the Healthy Adult until the client has sufficiently internalised the therapist's healthy role and strengthens their own Healthy Adult mode.

Overcoming Obstacles to Client Progress

Therapists can face obstacles during different stages of schema therapy. These can present as resistance to experiential and behavioural work as well as ruptures in the therapeutic relationship.

With regard to experiential work, schema avoidance and schema over-compensation are common obstacles that come up in imagery work as clients who typically use these coping styles have great difficulty tolerating negative affect. In such cases and where there is severe trauma in the client's history, it is necessary to build a trusting relationship with the client before undertaking imagery work. In addition, Young et al. (2003a) propose the following strategies to overcome such resistance:

- Revisiting the rationale for imagery work.
- Listing advantages and disadvantages of doing imagery.
- Constructing a hierarchy of images and starting with the one that is least anxiety provoking.
- Using relaxation or mindfulness techniques.
- Allowing the client time to produce an image.
- Carrying out a dialogue with the avoidant part of the client.
- Considering the appropriateness of medication.

Obstacles to behavioural change can be addressed through the following strategies:

- Assessing the client's motivation for change and understanding the nature of the difficulty in changing schema driven behaviours.
- Using imagery to assist the client verbalise where the obstacle is as well as using it to rehearse the desired or adaptive behaviour.
- Carry out dialogues between the avoidant part of the client and the healthy part.
- Writing flashcards that specifically address the obstacles identified above.

Ruptures in the therapeutic relationship are common in the course of any therapy. A rupture in the therapy relationship can vary from a simple misunderstanding to a more complex problem reflecting the entrenched nature of EMS and associated coping styles. Different EMS, when triggered in the session, can interfere with the therapy alliance in different ways. For instance, the abandonment schema may drive a client to either be excessively compliant to prevent a perceived abandonment or to terminate therapy prematurely to avoid painful feelings of abandonment. On the other hand, the defectiveness schema can interfere with the alliance when a client withholds information about themselves through shame and fear of being judged negatively. Alternatively, they may overcompensate for this schema by being dismissive and critical of the therapist/therapy rather than focusing on change.

These obstacles can provide the therapist with an opportunity to use the schema model to demonstrate to clients the pervasive and repetitive pattern of their problems and how to overcome them.

The therapist schemas and responses should also be taken into consideration when ruptures occur. For example, if the therapist schemas match those of the clients, over-identification can occur with the therapist losing objectivity. Similarly, a mismatch in schemas (e.g. emotional deprivation in client and emotional inhibition in therapist) can lead to the therapist being unable to meet the client's needs through limited reparenting.

Case Example: Bob

Background Information

Bob is a 35-year-old Caucasian male referred by his general practitioner (GP) for psychological therapy after presenting with relationship difficulties and anger problems. Bob's relationship with his wife was at the point of breakdown. His wife was threatening to leave him due to his anger outbursts. His anger was also affecting his work and at the time he entered therapy he was on sick leave from his job.

Bob was mainly brought up by his paternal grandparents from the age of 8 as his father left before he was born and his mother was absent a lot of the time. When around, his mother was cold and rejecting, blaming him for anything that went wrong in her life, including the father leaving. Between the ages of 4 and 8, Bob was sexually and emotionally abused by a maternal uncle, but did not disclose this until much later when he returned to live with his mother at the age of 17. His mother did not believe him and accused him of being a troublemaker.

At school, Bob struggled academically partly due to truanting and substance misuse, mainly cannabis and alcohol. His early attachment to his grandfather was interrupted at the age of 14 when his grandfather died. This loss was significant in Bob's life as the grandfather represented a strong figure that provided safety and stability. He had a good relationship with his grandmother, but she was frail and became increasingly unwell after her husband's death. She died when Bob was 17.

Assessment

A focused life history established that Bob's current difficulties represented dysfunctional life patterns in his relationship and work. On the YSQ-L3, he scored highly on Emotional Deprivation, Abandonment, Mistrust/Abuse and Defectiveness schemas. The YPI confirmed the family origins of the identified schemas. Further assessment suggested that Bob's main coping style over the years has been one of surrendering, leading him not to assert himself when criticised unfairly or when having unrealistic demands put on him. Three years prior to presenting to mental health services, Bob's abuser made contact with Bob's mother because he was terminally ill. This prompted renewed regular contact between Bob's mother and the uncle, and a pressure was exerted on Bob to attend frequent family events. Despite many attempts to resist this situation, Bob felt unable to assert himself with his mother. It was around the same that he began to react with angry outbursts when difficult situations arose at home and work. This was identified as Bob's overcompensation coping style. Early on in sessions, Bob initially did not seem forthcoming with personal information. This was addressed within the therapy relationship, and his reticence improved in later sessions.

Formulation

The therapist and client developed a schema conceptualisation of Bob's difficulties by identifying links between his early experiences of sexual and emotional abuse, rejection by his mother, and later academic difficulties and the development of specific EMS and coping styles. Abandonment and emotional deprivation schemas were directly linked to the cold and rejecting parenting style of his mother. The mistrust/abuse schema was directly related to the emotional and sexual abuse his uncle subjected him to and later reinforced by his mother not believing him. The defectiveness schema was explained by the critical, rejecting and later invalidating parenting style as well as the emotional abuse by the uncle. This was later reinforced by his academic difficulties. Repetitive life patterns such as mostly choosing and staying in relationships where the other person seemed either emotionally cold or critical and rejecting were identified. His surrender coping style was also evident in his overly apologetic and self-denigrating manner of communication and difficulty in asserting his needs for fear of being judged negatively, criticised and rejected. Similarly, his overcompensation coping style meant he reacted inappropriately with angry outbursts.

Bob's schemas and coping style demonstrated themselves in therapy through his suspicion of the therapist's questions and anxiety about who would access the information collected about him and how it would be used (mistrust/abuse schema). Similarly, his reluctance to disclose personal information was partly explained by his fear of the therapist's negative judgement and possible criticism (defectiveness schema).

Bob identified and agreed with the formulation and expressed the wish to work on the following therapy goals:

1 To address the early abuse by his uncle.
2 To feel better about himself.
3 To learn to assert his needs without resorting to destructive anger.

Practical Applications

The Therapeutic Relationship

The therapist's stance throughout Bob's therapy was characterised by empathy, validation and limited reparenting. Overall, Bob and the therapist established a good rapport that facilitated the intervention. It the early stages of therapy, Bob seemed to agree with all of the therapist's suggestions. This was formulated within the schema model as Bob's attempt to prevent or avoid 'expected' criticism by being compliant. As Bob began trusting the therapist, the relationship became more collaborative and Bob was able to assert his needs and views. In doing so, Bob was sometimes more aggressive than assertive in the way he expressed himself, a communication style that was evident in his later life and which brought him to therapy. On such occasions, the therapist used limit setting and empathic confrontation.

Strategies of Treatment

Following an initial phase of formulation and psychoeducation, Bob was ready to address his EMS. The first phase of treatment focused on cognitive interventions, including identifying evidence for and against his EMS, testing the validity of the schemas and looking for more adaptive alternatives. Bob gradually reframed the evidence supporting his schemas as dysfunctional parenting and sequelae of abuse and not as proof of his EMS. A list of the advantages and disadvantages of his surrender and overcompensation coping styles was constructed to help Bob recognise their self-defeating nature and the need to replace them with healthier behaviours. Flashcards summarising the most powerful evidence against each

(Continued)

(Continued)

schema and its coping style were written to help Bob practice the healthy responses. Later on in his therapy, Bob carried out dialogues between his healthy side and the schema side to further strengthen the healthy part.

Experiential strategies included imagery involving childhood experiences of abuse. Initially, Bob chose to have his core childhood needs met by his grandfather, who was able to stand up to the abuser and give him the corrective information that the abuse was not his fault, he was not bad and he should not blame himself. In later images, Bob, the healthy adult, was able to enter the image and further reinforce his grandfather's healthy messages. Further imagery work facilitated Bob's healthy expression of anger towards his mother for failing to nurture and protect him as a child and invalidating his experiences later on.

As Bob was able to name and challenge his schemas successfully. He was encouraged to substitute maladaptive behaviours with healthier ones and empathic confrontation was used to overcome any resistance to implement more functional behaviours. Teaching Bob anger management techniques and using role plays in sessions helped Bob assert his needs and rights at work and at home more effectively. Bob was ready to leave therapy after 18 months. He had already returned to work and acknowledged the need for couple therapy to enhance the progress that had been achieved in the marital relationship.

Overcoming Obstacles to Client Progress

Bob's mistrust of others was one of the main obstacles to his progress in therapy. This was evident in his reluctance to share information early on in therapy despite being compliant and eager to please the therapist. Most of his answers and account of his childhood experiences were vague. Consequently, developing an early formulation became difficult. This challenge prompted discussion about other situations outside therapy where Bob felt and reacted in a similar way. The therapist used limited reparenting specific to this EMS by being honest and genuine with Bob, asking him about trust issues and any negative feelings in relation to the therapist. In order to build trust, the therapist also delayed imagery work relating to the abuse and proceeded slowly through the negative memories, allowing Bob to set the pace. These discussions, together with limited reparenting appropriate to his mistrust schema, were instrumental in building trust and an emotional connection between Bob and the therapist. As Bob felt safe and empowered, he learnt not to misinterpret the therapist's and other people's intentions, and to distinguish between the individuals from his past who deserved the anger and those in his current life who did not.

Research Status

There is a wealth of research on Young's schema theory and its applications. Carine (1997) confirmed Young's theory that emotion is integral to schemas. Freeman's work (1999) also offered empirical support to Young's model of EMS. Further studies investigated Young's schemas in populations presenting with depression, eating disorders, personality disorders, substance misuse and offending behaviour (Young et al., 1993; Riso et al., 2006; Waller et al., 2001b; Gude and Hoffart, 2008; Brotchie et al., 2006; Bernstein et al., 2007).

The psychometric properties of both the long- and short-forms of the Young schema questionnaires have also been subjected to rigorous research and were shown to have good psychometric properties (e.g. Schmidt et al., 1995; Lee et al., 1999; Waller et al., 2001a).

Stallard and Rayner (2005) have developed and carried out an initial evaluation of a schema questionnaire for children and the initial results suggest that the SQC is a valid and developmentally appropriate way of assessing EMS in children.

There is no research on the original schema mode inventory (SMI) (Young et al., 2007), but Lobbestael et al. (2010) constructed a short version (118 items) of the SMI and investigated its psychometric properties. They concluded that the short SMI could be used reliably in the assessment of modes in schema therapy.

The mode model in schema therapy has also been subjected to research. Lobbestael and Arntz (2010), as well as others before them, carried out empirical tests of schema mode presence in samples of clients with a diagnosis of personality disorder. Recent years have seen the publication of outcome studies on Young's schema mode model. The Giesen-Bloo et al. (2006) multicentre randomised control trial of schema-focused therapy versus transference-focused psychotherapy (TFP) demonstrated that schema therapy led to recovery in almost half the clients with BPD, and to clinically significant improvement in BPD symptoms in two-thirds of the clients. Spinhoven et al. (2007) reported much higher ratings by both therapists and clients for the therapeutic alliance in ST than in TFP. Therapist frustration decreased significantly over time in ST but increased in TFP. Nordahl and Nysaeter (2005) reported similar results in a series of case studies.

An implementation study of outpatient ST for BPD by Nadort et al (2009) showed recovery from BPD in 42 per cent of clients after 18 months.

Group schema therapy is a new area of research looking mainly at clients with a BPD diagnosis. Farrel et al. (2009) showed that at the end of eight months of group ST, 94 per cent of ST plus TAU ('treatment as usual') clients no longer met diagnostic criteria for BPD, versus 16 per cent in TAU alone. There are currently pilot studies being carried out on schema therapy with inpatients and in forensic settings and we await publication of the data.

Suggested Further Reading

Arntz, A. and Van Genderen, H. (2009) *Schema Therapy for Borderline Personality Disorder*. Chichester: Wiley.

Rafaeli, E., Bernstein, D.P. and Young, J.E. (2010) *Schema Therapy: The CBT Distinctive Features Series*. London: Routledge.

Riso, L.P., du Toit, P.L., Stein, D.J. and Young, J.E. (2007) *Cognitive Schemas and Core Beliefs in Psychological Problems: A Scientist-Practitioner Guide*. New York: American Psychological Association.

Young, J.E. and Klosko, J.S. (1994) *Reinventing Your Life*. New York: Plume.

Young, J.E., Klosko, J.S. and Weishaar, M. (2003) *Schema Therapy: A Practitioner's Guide*. New York: Guilford Press.

References

Ainsworth, M.D.S. and Bowlby, J. (1991) 'An ethological approach to personality development', *American Psychologists*, 46: 331–341.

Alford, B.A. and Beck, A.T. (1997) *The Integrative Power of Cognitive Therapy*. New York: Guildford Press.

APA (American Psychiatric Association) (2000) *Diagnostic and Statistical Manual of Mental Disorders – Text Revison* (DSM-IV-TR), 4th Edn. Washington, DC: APA.

Beck, A.T. (1967) *Depression: Causes and Treatment*. Philadelphia, PA: University of Pennsylvania.

Beck, A.T., Freeman, A. and Associates (1990) *Cognitive Therapy of Personality Disorders*. New York: Guilford Press.

Beck, A.T., Rush, A.J., Shaw, B.F. and Emery, G. (1979) *Cognitive Therapy of Depression*. New York: Guilford Press.

Bernstein, D., Artz, A. and De Vos, M. (2007) 'Schema-focused therapy in forensic settings: Theoretical model and recommendations for best clinical practice', *International Journal of Forensic Mental Health*, 6(2): 169–183.

Brotchie, J., Hanes, J., Wendon, P. and Waller, G. (2006) 'Emotional avoidance among alcohol and opiate abusers: The role of schema-level cognitive processes', *Behavioural and Cognitive Psychotherapy*, 35: 231–236.

Carine, B.E. (1997) 'Assessing personal and interpersonal schemata associated with Axis II Cluster B personality disorders: An integral perspective', *Dissertations Abstracts International*, 58: 1B.

Farrell, M.M., Shew, I.A. and Webber, M.A. (2009) 'A schema-focused approach to group psychotherapy for outpatients with borderline personality disorder: A randomised controlled trial', *Journal of Behaviour Therapy and Experimental Psychiatry*, 40(2): 317–328.

Freeman, N. (1999) 'Constructive thinking and early maladaptive schemas as predictors of interpersonal adjustment and marital satisfaction', *Dissertation Abstracts International*, 59, 9B.

Giesen-Bloo, J., Van Dyck, R., Spinhoven, P., Van Tilburg, W., Dirksem, C., Van Asselt, T., Kremers, I., Nadort, M. and Arntz, A. (2006) 'Outpatient psychotherapy for borderline personality disorder: Randomized controlled trial of schema-focused therapy vs transference-focused psychotherapy', *Archives of General Psychiatry*, 63: 649–658.

Gude, T. and Hoffart, A. (2008) 'Change in interpersonal problems after cognitive therapy and schema-focused therapy versus psychodynamic treatment as usual of inpatients with agoraphobia and Cluster C personality disorders', *Scandinavian Journal of Psychology*, 49(2): 195–199.

Kagan, J., Reznick, J.S. and Snidman, N. (1988) 'Biological bases of childhood shyness', *Science*, 240: 167–171.

Kellogg, S.H. (2004) 'Dialogical encounters: Contemporary perspectives on 'chairwork' in psychotherapy', *Psychotherapy: Theory, Research and Practice*, 41: 310–320.

Le Doux, J. (1996) *The Emotional Brain*. New York: Simon and Schuster.

Lee, C.W., Taylor, G. and Dunn, J. (1999) 'Factor structure of the schema questionnaire in a large clinical sample', *Cognitive Therapy and Research*, 23: 441–451.

Lobbestael, J. and Arntz, A. (2010) 'Emotional, cognitive and physiological correlates of abuse-related stress in borderline and antisocial personality disorder', *Behaviour Research and Therapy*, 48(2): 116–124.

Lobbestael, J., Van Vreeswijk, M., Spinhoven, P., Schouten, E. and Arntz, A. (2010) 'Reliability and validity of the short schema mode inventory (SMI)', *Behavioural and Cognitive Psychotherapy*, 38: 437–458.

Nadort, M., Van Dyck, R., Smit, J.H., Giensen-Bloo, J., Eikelenboom, M., Wensing, M., Spinhoven, P., Dirksen, C., Bleecke, J., Van Milligan, B., Van Vreeswijk, M. and Arntz, A. (2009) 'Preparatory studies for promoting implementation of outpatient schema therapy for borderline personality disorder in general mental health care', *Behaviour Research and Therapy*, 47: 938–945.

Nordahl H.M. and Nysaeter, T.E. (2005) 'Schema therapy for patients with borderline personality disorder: A single case series', *Journal of Behaviour Therapy and Experimental Psychiatry*, 36(3): 254–264.

Riso, L.P., du Toit, P.L., Stein, D.J. and Young, J.E. (2007) *Cognitive Schemas and Core Beliefs in Psychological Problems: A Scientist-Practitioner guide*. New York: American Psychological Association.

Schmidt, N.B., Joiner, T.E., Young. J.E. and Talch, M.J. (1995) 'The schema questionnaire: Investigation of psychometric properties as to the hierarchical structure of a measure of maladaptive schemas', *Cognitive Therapy and Research*, 19(3): 295–321.

Siegel, D.J. (2007) *The Mindful Brain: Reflection and Attunement in the Cultivation of Well-being*. New York: Norton.

Spinhoven, P., Van Dyck, R., Giesen-Bloo, J., Kooiman, K.A. and Arntz, A. (2007) 'The therapeutic alliance in schema-focused therapy and transference-focused psychotherapy for borderline personality disorder', *Journal of Consulting and Clinical Psychology*, 75(1): 104–115.

Stallard, P. and Rayner, H. (2005) 'The development and preliminary evaluation of a schema questionnaire for children (SQC)', *Behavioural and Cognitive Psychotherapy*, 33: 217–224.

Waller, G., Meyer, C. and Ohanian, V. (2001a) 'Psychometric properties of the long and short versions of the Young schema questionnaire: Core beliefs among bulimic and comparison women', *Cognitive Therapy and Research*, 25: 137–147.

Waller, G., Shah, R., Ohanian, V. and Elliot, P. (2001b) 'Core beliefs in bulimia nervosa and depression: The discriminant validity of Young's schema questionnaire', *Behaviour Therapy*, 32(1): 139–153.

Young, J.E. (1990) *Cognitive Therapy for Personality Disorders*. Sarasota, FL: Professional Resources Press.

Young, J.E. (1999) *Cognitive Therapy for Personality Disorders: A Schema-focused Approach*, Rev. Edn. Sarasota, FL: Professional Resources Press.

Young, J.E. (2003a) *The Schema Diary*. New York: Schema Therapy Institute.

Young, J.E. (2003b) *Young Parenting Inventory*. New York: Cognitive Therapy Center of New York.

Young J.E. (2003c) *Young Compensation Inventory*. New York: Schema Therapy Institute.

Young, J.E. (2005) *Young Schema Questionnaire*. New York: Schema Therapy Institute.

Young, J.E. and Klosko, J. (1994) *Reinventing Your Life*. New York: Plume.

Young, J.E. and Rygh, J. (2003) *Young-Rygh Avoidance Inventory*. New York: Schema Therapy Institute.

Young, J.E., Arntz, A., Atkinson, T., Lobbastael, J., Weishear, M.E., van Voleeswijk, M.F. and Klokman, J. (2007) *The Schema Mode Inventory*. New York: Schema Therapy Institute.

Young, J.E., Beck, A.T. and Weinberger, A. (1993) 'Depression', in D.H. Barlow (Ed.), *Clinical Handbook of Psychological Disorders*, 2nd Edn. New York: Guilford Press. pp. 240–277.

Young, J.E., Klosko, J.S. and Weishaar, M.E. (2003a) *Schema Therapy: A Practitioner's Guide*. New York: Guilford Press.

Young, J.E., Wattenmaker, D. and Wattenmaker, R. (2003b) *Schema Therapy Flashcard*. New York: Schema Therapy Institute.

NINE   Rational Emotive Behaviour Therapy (REBT)

WINDY DRYDEN

Historical Development of REBT

Rational emotive behaviour therapy (REBT) was founded in 1955 by Albert Ellis, a New York clinical psychologist. Having acquired a PhD in clinical psychology, he trained in psychoanalysis, which he considered the most effective form of psychotherapy available. Ellis's experiences as a sex-marital counsellor had taught him that disturbed relationships were really a product of disturbed persons, and he became increasingly dissatisfied with psychoanalysis as an effective form of treatment. In the early 1950s, he began experimenting with different forms of therapy, including psychoanalytic-orientated psychotherapy and eclectic-analytic therapy. Although becoming more effective with his clients, he remained dissatisfied about the efficiency of these methods and was at this time influenced by the Stoic philosophers (e.g. Epictetus and Marcus Aurelius) who emphasised the primacy of philosophic causation of psychological disturbances. The Stoic view, that people are disturbed not by things but by their view of things, became the foundation of REBT in particular and remains at the heart of present-day cognitive-behavioural approaches to psychotherapy.

Major Philosophical Influences

Apart from Stoicism, REBT owes a philosophical debt to a number of other sources that have influenced its development:

1 Immanuel Kant's writings on the power (and limitations) of cognition and ideation strongly impressed Ellis (1981).
2 Philosophers of science, for example Karl Popper and Bertrand Russell, influenced Ellis's view that all humans develop hypotheses about the nature of the world. They stressed the importance of testing out the validity of such hypotheses rather than assuming that they are correct. Ellis frequently argued that the practice of REBT is synonymous, in

many respects, with the logico-empirical methods of science (Ellis, 1962). Ellis (1994) also stressed the flexibility of the scientific method, holding that REBT opposes all dogmas, just as science does, and that rigid absolutism is the very core of human disturbance.

3   Although REBT's philosophy, as found in Ellis's writings, differs from devout religiosity, REBT's theory of human value is similar to the Christian viewpoint of condemning the sin but forgiving the sinner (Nielsen et al., 2001).

4   Due to its stand on self-acceptance and bias against all forms of human rating, REBT allies itself with ethical humanism which opposes the deification and devilification of humans. Since REBT places humans at the centre of *their* universe (but not of *the* universe) with the power of choice (but not of unlimited choice) with regard to their emotional realm, it has roots in the existential philosophies of Martin Heidegger and Paul Tillich. Ellis (1973) often portrayed REBT as having a pronounced humanistic-existential outlook.

5   Ellis was influenced, particularly in the 1960s, by the general semanticists who outlined the powerful effect language has on thought and the fact that our emotional processes depend on how we, as humans, structure our thought by the language we employ.

Major Psychological Influences

Ellis, in developing REBT, was influenced by the work of a number of psychologists:

1   Ellis received training analysis from a practitioner of the Karen Horney school, and Horney's (1950) concept of the 'tyranny of the shoulds' was an early influence on his emphasis on the primacy of rigid beliefs in developing and maintaining psychological disturbance.

2   Adler's work was important to REBT's development in several respects. Adler (1927) was the first to emphasise inferiority feelings while REBT similarly stresses self-rating and the ego anxiety to which it leads. Like Adler and his individual psychology, REBT also emphasises people's goals, purposes, values and meanings, and follows Adler regarding the use of active-directive teaching, the stress placed on social interest, the use of a holistic and humanistic outlook, and in employing a highly cognitive-persuasive form of psychological treatment (Ellis, 1994).

3   Although REBT was originally termed 'rational psychotherapy', it has always advocated the use of behavioural methods as well as cognitive and emotive techniques in the practice of therapy. Indeed, Ellis utilized methods advocated by the earliest pioneers in behaviour therapy in overcoming his own early fears of speaking in public and of approaching women, and in the active-directive form of sex therapy which he

practised in the early 1950s. This behavioural active-directive emphasis remains prominent in present-day REBT.

In its 50 years' existence, REBT has been practised in various therapeutic modalities (individual, group, marital and family) by many kinds of helping professionals (e.g. psychologists, psychiatrists, social workers) with a variety of client populations (e.g. adults, children, the elderly) suffering from a wide range of psychological problems and disorders. Apart from its use in counselling and psychotherapy, rational-emotive principles have been applied in educational, industrial and commercial settings. A recent development has been the application of REBT to public education in the form of nine-hour intensive workshops. In this respect, it is playing a significant role in the field of preventative psychology through its use of intensive workshops to the general public. Finally, it is contributing to the development of coaching (e.g. Dryden, 2011). REBT is practised throughout the world: there are REBT Institutes in the USA, Italy, Germany, Holland, Israel, Australia, England and Mexico. It is thus a well-established form of CBT.

Theoretical Underpinnings

Major Theoretical Concepts

REBT is based on a set of assumptions stressing the complexity and fluidity of human beings. Given this fundamental view of human nature, REBT rests on the following theoretical concepts.

Goals, Purposes and Rationality
According to REBT theory, humans are happiest when they establish important life goals and purposes and actively strive to attain these. Ellis argued that human beings, in establishing and pursuing these goals and purposes, should consider the fact that they live in a social world and that a philosophy of self-interest, where a person places him or herself first, also involves putting others a close second. This contrasts with a philosophy of selfishness where others' desires are neither respected nor regarded. Given that humans tend to be goal-directed, 'rational' in REBT theory means whatever helps people to achieve their basic goals and purposes, whereas 'irrational' means whatever prevents them from achieving these goals and purposes. Thus, rationality is not defined in any absolute sense but is relative in nature.

The Interaction of Psychological Processes and the Place of Cognition
REBT theory has always stressed an interactive view of human psychological processes. Cognitions, emotions and behaviours are not experienced in

isolation and often, particularly in the realm of psychological disturbance, overlap significantly. Ellis (1994) stressed the inferential nature of activating events and showed how events (or more correctly, how we perceive events) interact with our beliefs, emotions and behaviours. This point will be amplified in the section below entitled 'The ABC assessment framework'.

Given this interactional view, REBT is most noted for the special place it has accorded cognition in human psychological processes, particularly the role that beliefs play in psychological health and disturbance. One of REBT's unique contributions to the field of CBT lies in its distinction between rational beliefs (RBs) and irrational beliefs (IBs). RBs are flexible, expressing what we want to happen while acknowledging that we don't have to get what we want. Positive feelings of pleasure and satisfaction are experienced when we get what we want, whereas healthy negative feelings of displeasure and dissatisfaction (e.g. sadness, concern, regret, healthy anger) are experienced when we don't get what we want, but do not demand that we have to get it. These negative feelings are regarded as constructive responses to negative events and do not significantly interfere with the pursuit of established or new goals and purposes. These beliefs, then, are 'rational' in that they are flexible and do not impede the attainment of basic goals and purposes.

IBs, on the other hand, differ in two respects from RBs: (a) they are rigid in nature and are expressed in the form of 'musts', 'shoulds', 'oughts', 'have-tos' and so on, and as such (b) they lead to unhealthy negative emotions (UNEs) which largely interfere with goal pursuit and attainment (e.g. depression, anxiety, guilt, unhealthy anger). Ellis (1994) noted that RBs tend to underlie functional behaviours, whereas IBs underpin dysfunctional behaviours such as withdrawal, procrastination, alcoholism, substance abuse and so forth.

Two Basic Biological Tendencies

Unlike most theories of therapy which stress the impact of significant life events on the development of psychological disturbance, REBT theory, mainly through Ellis's writings (1976), hypothesises that the biological tendency of humans to think irrationally has a notable impact on such disturbance. This hypothesis (always interacting with influential environmental conditions) rests on the apparent ease with which humans think crookedly and the prevalence of such thinking even among people who have been rationally raised (Ellis, 1976). Ellis (1984) noted that 'even if we had the most rational upbringing, virtually all humans would often take their individual and social preferences and irrationally escalate them into absolutistic demands on (a) themselves, (b) other people, and (c) the universe around them'.

However, Ellis argued that humans have a second basic biological tendency: to exercise the power of human choice and work towards changing their irrational thinking. Thus, they are able to (a) see that they make themselves disturbed by the irrational views they bring to situations, (b) see that they can change their thinking and, most importantly, (c) work actively and continually towards changing this thinking by applying cognitive, emotive and behavioural methods. While REBT theory asserts that humans have a strong biological tendency to think both irrationally and rationally, it holds that they are not enslaved by this tendency and can transcend its effects, although not fully. Ultimately, the REBT image of the person is optimistic.

Two Fundamental Human Disturbances

Ellis (1994) argued that humans can make absolute demands on self, other people and the world. If these demands are more closely investigated they can be seen to fall into two major categories of psychological disturbance: ego disturbance and discomfort disturbance.

In ego disturbance, a person makes demands on self, others and the world; if these demands are not met in the past, present or future, the person becomes disturbed by depreciating himself. Self-depreciation involves (a) giving one's 'self' a global negative rating and (b) 'devil-ifying' oneself as being bad or less worthy. The rational, healthy alternative to self-depreciation is unconditional self-acceptance which involves (a) refusing to give one's 'self' a single rating (because it is an impossible task, due to one's complexity and fluidity; and because it normally interferes with attaining one's basic goals and purposes), and (b) acknowledging one's fallibility.

In discomfort disturbance, the person again makes demands on self, others and the world which are related to dogmatic commands that comfort and comfortable life conditions must exist. When these demands are not met in the past, present or future, then the person disturbs himself. Tolerating discomfort in order to aid goal attainment and long-range happiness is the healthy and rational alternative to demands for immediate gratification.

Unconditional self-acceptance and discomfort tolerance are thus the two main cornerstones of the REBT image of the psychologically healthy human being (Ellis, 1994).

How Client Problems are Conceptualised

In this section, I will discuss REBT's 'ABC' assessment model, the importance of assessing meta-disturbance and REBT's position on case formulation.

The 'ABC' Assessment Framework

REBT puts forward an 'ABC' framework to conceptualise clients' problems. Other CBT approaches use an 'ABC' framework, but REBT's model is distinctive. Let me deal with these components one at a time.

'A' = Adversity

'A' stands for adversity which is a negative event. An 'A' can be an actual negative event or may be inferential, representing an aspect of the situation about which the person is most disturbed. When carrying out an assessment the REBT therapist is particularly focused on the idiosyncratic nature of the person's 'A'.

REBT also notes that each of the eight disturbed emotions for which people seek help (to be discussed below) are associated with identifiable inferential themes at 'A'. Thus, when depressed the person infers (1) that he has lost something important to him, (2) that he has failed at an important task or (3) that he or others have experienced an undeserved plight and when anxious he infers the presence of a threat to some important aspect of his personal domain. (See Dryden (2009a) for a full discussion of the inferential themes related to each of the eight disturbed emotions.)

'B' = Irrational Beliefs

As mentioned above, REBT distinguishes between RBs and IBs. When conceptualising clients' problems, REBT therapists hypothesise the existence of a set of IBs deemed to underpin these problems. IBs are seen in REBT theory to be false, illogical and largely unhelpful to the person holding them. They are either rigid or extreme. Ellis (1994) argued that rigid beliefs are at the very core of psychological disturbance and one or more extreme beliefs are derived from this core. These are:

- an 'awfulising' belief, where the person makes an extreme negative evaluation when his demand (i.e. rigid belief) is not met (e.g. 'It's awful that ...'; 'It's the end of the world that ...');
- a discomfort intolerance belief, where the person believes he cannot tolerate the discomfort associated with his unmet demand ('I can't bear it that ...');
- a depreciation belief, where the person depreciates whoever or whatever he deems responsible for his demand not being met ('I am no good for ...').

In ego disturbance the person primarily holds a rigid belief and a self-depreciation belief, while in discomfort disturbance the person typically holds a rigid belief and either an awfulising belief or a discomfort intolerance belief or both.

'C' = Consequences of Irrational Beliefs

REBT theory holds that there are three major consequences of IBs.

- *Emotional consequences* – People seek help for a number of unhealthy negative emotions (UNEs). These tend to be anxiety, depression, shame, guilt, hurt, unhealthy anger, unhealthy jealousy and unhealthy envy, all stemming from IBs about inferential themes that are specific to the UNE in question (Dryden, 2009a).
- *Behavioural consequences* – When a person experiences an unhealthy negative emotion, she acts or experiences a tendency to behave in certain ways. These behaviours tend to prevent the person dealing with the adversity at 'A' and thus serve unwittingly to perpetuate the person's emotional problem.

- *Cognitive consequences* – In addition, when a person experiences an unhealthy negative emotion, she tends to think in ways that exaggerate the nature and consequences of the adversity. As with behavioural consequences, these thinking consequences of IBs tend to prevent the person from dealing with the adversity at 'A' and thus serve unwittingly to perpetuate that person's emotional problem.

Meta-Disturbance

REBT recognises that once a person disturbs herself, it often happens that she disturbs herself about this original disturbance. This is known as meta-disturbance (literally disturbance about disturbance). REBT also distinguishes between different types of meta-disturbance, arguing that a person can disturb herself about:

- *her disturbed emotions at 'C'* – a person may disturb herself either because of the pain of the emotional experience (e.g. 'I can't stand the pain of feeling depressed') or because of the meaning the disturbed emotion has for the person (e.g. 'Feeling depressed is a weakness and proves that I am a weak person');
- *her dysfunctional behaviour or action tendencies* – here the person focuses on what she did or what she felt like doing but did not do and disturbs herself about one or the other, largely because of the meaning the behaviour or action tendency has for the person (e.g. 'I felt like punching her lights out which is really nasty and proves that I am a nasty person');
- *her distorted cognitions at 'C'* – here a person may focus on a distorted cognition, which becomes her new 'A' and disturbs herself about the meaning that such a thought has for her. Thus, suppose the person disturbs himself about finding a young girl attractive and thinks that he may abuse her (his distorted cognitive consequence at 'C'). He may then disturb himself about this thought because he infers that it is shameful and that he is a disgusting person for having it.

REBT's position on case formulation in conceptualising clients' problems

Currently, most CBT therapists carry out a formulation of a 'case' before embarking on treatment unless the need is pressing to treat a client before such a formulation is undertaken. Case formulation in CBT is done collaboratively. REBT therapists tend to intervene more quickly on a client's target problem and build up a formulation of the 'case' as we go rather than structuring therapy into formulation–intervention stages. As with many other issues, Ellis is the driving force here. When he started his career he became dissatisfied with an approach to therapy that saw therapeutic intervention being dependent upon a thorough assessment of clients' psychopathology and personality based on the completion and analysis of a large number of questionnaires, inventories and other assessment tools.

Ellis (1962) regarded this process as inefficient, noting that a significant number of clients tended to drop out of this process before treatment had commenced. Ellis noted the waste of the therapist's, client's and organisation's time when many person-hours were spent preparing the client for an intervention based on the accumulation and analysis of these data which was subsequently not effected because the client had dropped out before treatment proper had commenced. Ellis therefore considered starting treatment as quickly as possible as the best use of everyone's time and resources. He tended to eschew a case formulation approach to REBT where a formal formulation routinely precedes treatment.

Of course, Ellis was a highly skilled formulator of 'cases', as anyone who had received clinical supervision from him will testify, but tended to do this in his head rather than on paper and made his formulations during rather than before therapy. Indeed, Ellis argued that a client's response to therapy tells the therapist a great deal about the client and their problems, and for this to become manifest, therapy must be initiated.

I have perhaps put forward the most developed approach to using case formulation in REBT (Dryden, 1998), which I call UPCP ('Understanding the Person in the Context of his or her Problems') because I dislike referring to a person as a 'case'. I argue that there are several factors that need to be identified when conducting a UPCP:

1 Basic information on the client and any striking initial impressions.
2 A list of the client's problems.
3 The client's goals for change.
4 A list of the client's problem emotions (UNEs).
5 A list of the client's problem critical 'A's (e.g. disapproval, uncertainty, failure, injustice).
6 The client's core irrational (rigid and extreme) beliefs.
7 A list of the client's dysfunctional behaviours.
8 The purposive nature of dysfunctional behaviours.
9 A list of the ways in which the client prevents or cuts short the experience of their problems.
10 A list of the ways in which the client compensates for problems.
11 A list of meta-emotional problems.
12 A list of the cognitive consequences of core IBs.
13 How the client expresses problems and the interpersonal responses to these expressions.
14 The client's health and medication status.
15 A list of relevant predisposing factors.
16 Predicting the client's likely responses to therapy.

As the above shows, developing a UPCP takes time, which may be better spent helping the client to address their problems. Thus, I do not recommend that REBT therapists carry out a full UPCP with every client. But it should be conducted:

- when it is clear that the person has many complex problems;
- when resistance occurs in clients who have at first sight non-complex problems and where usual ways of addressing such resistance have proven unsuccessful;
- when clients have had several unsuccessful previous attempts at therapy, particularly REBT.

Practical Applications

The Therapeutic Relationship

REBT is an active-directive form of psychotherapy: therapists are active in directing their clients to identify the philosophical source of their psychological problems, and in showing them they can challenge and change their IBs. Ellis (1994) has conceptualised the role of the effective REBT therapist as that of an authoritative (but not authoritarian!), encouraging teacher striving to teach his or her clients how to be their own therapists once formal therapy sessions have ended.

Therapeutic Conditions
Unconditional acceptance
REBT therapists strive to accept unconditionally their clients as fallible human beings who often act self-defeatingly but are never essentially good or bad. No matter how badly clients behave in therapy, the REBT therapist attempts to accept them as people but will frequently, if appropriate, let them know his or her reactions to the client's negative behaviour (Ellis, 1973).

Therapeutic Genuineness
In the therapeutic relationship Ellis (1977a) strived to be as open as therapeutically feasible and was prepared to give highly personal information about himself if his clients asked for it, except when he judged that they might use such information against themselves. REBT therapists often disclose examples from their own lives concerning how they experienced similar problems and, more importantly, how they have gone about solving these problems. Thus, they strive to be *therapeutically genuine* in conducting sessions.

Humour
REBT therapists tend to be *appropriately humorous* with most clients since they think that much emotional disturbance stems from clients' taking themselves, their problems, other people and the world *too* seriously. They thus strive to model for their clients the therapeutic advantages of taking a serious but humorously ironic attitude to life. They endeavour, however, not to poke fun at clients themselves but rather at the clients' self-defeating thoughts, feelings and actions (Ellis, 1994). Similarly, REBT therapists tend to be informal

and easygoing with most of their clients. However, REBT opposes therapists' unethically indulging themselves at their clients' expense (Ellis, 2002).

Empathy

REBT therapists show their clients a special kind of empathy, offering them not only 'affective' empathy (communicating that they understand how their clients feel), but also 'philosophic' empathy (showing them that they understand the philosophies underlying these feelings).

Warmth

Thus, with certain modifications, REBT therapists agree with person-centred views concerning therapist empathy, genuineness and unconditional positive regard. However, REBT therapists are very wary of showing the vast majority of their clients *undue warmth*. Ellis (in Dryden, 1997) has argued that if REBT therapists get really close to their clients and give them considerable warmth, attention, caring and support, as well as unconditional acceptance, these therapists run two major risks:

1 REBT therapists may unwittingly reinforce their clients' dire needs for love and approval: two IBs which are at the core of much human disturbance. When this happens, clients appear to improve because their therapists are giving them what they believe they must have. They begin to 'feel better' but do not necessarily 'get better' (Ellis, 1972). Their 'improvement' is illusory because their irrational philosophies are being reinforced. Since they seem to improve, their therapists have restricted opportunities to identify these ideas, show them how they relate to their problems, and help them challenge and change them. Consequently, while clients are helped by their therapists, they are not shown how to help themselves and are thus vulnerable to future upset.

2 REBT therapists may unwittingly reinforce their clients' philosophies of discomfort intolerance, leading them to seek interminable help from others instead of coping with life's difficulties themselves. Any therapy that does not specifically encourage clients to accept responsibility for their own happiness tends to confirm their IB that others must help them. Ellis (1977a) held that close relationship therapy is frequently the worst offender in this respect and thereby can do considerable harm. However, since REBT is relative in nature and is against the formulation of absolute, dogmatic therapeutic rules, it does recognise that under certain conditions (e.g. where a client is extremely depressed, accompanied by powerful suicidal ideation), distinct therapist warmth may be positively indicated for a restricted period of time.

Therapeutic Style

While Ellis (1994) recommended that REBT therapists adopt an active-directive style with most clients and a particularly forceful version of that

style with some very disturbed and resistant clients, not all REBT therapists concur with this view. Some recommend a more passive, gentle
approach under specific, or even most conditions with clients (e.g. Garcia,
1977). Eschenroeder (1979: 5) notes that it is important to ask in REBT
'Which therapeutic style is most effective with which kind of client?' In
this vein, it may be best for REBT therapists to avoid (a) an overly friendly,
emotionally charged style of interaction with 'histrionic' clients, (b) an
overly intellectual style with 'obsessive-compulsive' clients, (c) an overly
directive style with clients whose sense of autonomy is easily threatened
(Beutler, 1983), and (d) an overly active style with clients who easily retreat
into passivity. This line of reasoning fits well with the notion of flexibility
that REBT advocates as a desirable therapeutic quality.

Strategies of Treatment

Ellis (1980) pointed out that there are two forms of REBT: specific and general.
General REBT is synonymous with other approaches within CBT tradition,
while specific REBT is unique in a number of important respects. Since a
major aim of this book is to present the distinctive features of different forms
of CBT, the emphasis here will be on specific REBT (although REBT therapists
routinely use strategies derived from both forms of REBT). The major goal of
specific REBT is an ambitious one: to encourage clients to make a profound
philosophic change in the two main areas of ego disturbance and discomfort
disturbance. This involves helping clients, as far as humanly possible, to give
up their irrational (i.e. rigid, extreme) beliefs and replace them with rational
(i.e. flexible, non-extreme) beliefs when they face adversities at 'A'.

Rational Beliefs

When clients do this they hold the following RBs about adversity, which
are seen in REBT theory as true, logical and largely helpful to the person
holding them. Ellis (1994) argued that flexible beliefs are at the very core
of psychological health and one or more extreme beliefs are derived from
this core. These are:

- a non-awfulising belief, where the person makes a non-extreme negative evaluation when his non-dogmatic desire (i.e. flexible belief) is not
  met (e.g. 'It's bad, but not awful that ...', 'It's unfortunate, but not the
  end of the world that ...');
- a discomfort tolerance belief, where the person believes he can tolerate
  the discomfort associated with his non-dogmatic desire not being met
  and it's worthwhile doing so, even though it is a struggle ('It's hard to
  bear it that ..., but I can do so and it's worth it to me to do so');
- an acceptance belief, where the person accepts whoever or whatever he
  deems responsible for his non-dogmatic desire being met ('I am a fallible human being for ...').

In ego health, the person primarily holds a flexible belief and uncondi-tional self-acceptance belief, while in discomfort health, the person typi-cally holds a flexible belief and either a non-awfulising belief or a discomfort tolerance belief or both.

'C' = Consequences of Rational Beliefs
REBT theory holds that there are three major consequences of RBs:

- *Emotional consequences* – When they hold RBs about theme-based adversities, people will experience a number of healthy negative emo-tions (HNEs). These tend to be: concern (rather than anxiety), sadness (rather than depression), disappointment (rather than shame), remorse (rather than guilt), sorrow (rather than hurt), healthy anger (rather than unhealthy anger), healthy jealousy (rather than unhealthy jealousy) and healthy envy (rather than unhealthy envy).
- *Behavioural consequences* – When a person experiences an HNE, she acts or experiences a tendency to act in certain ways. These behav-iours tend to help the person to deal with the adversity at 'A' and then move on.
- *Cognitive consequences* – In addition, when a person experiences an HNE, she tends to think about the nature and consequences of the adversity in ways that are realistic and balanced. As with behavioural consequences, these thinking consequences of RBs tend to help the person to deal with the adversity at 'A' and move on.

In specific REBT, then, the major goals help clients pursue their long-range basic goals and purposes and help them do so as effectively as possible by fully accepting themselves and tolerating unchangeable uncomfortable life conditions. Practitioners of specific REBT further strive to help clients obtain the skills which they can use to prevent the development of future disturbance. In encouraging clients to achieve and maintain this profound philosophic change, REBT therapists implement the following strategies. They help their clients to see that:

- emotional and behavioural disturbances have cognitive antecedents tak-ing the form of IBs; REBT practitioners train their clients to observe their own psychological disturbances and trace these back to these beliefs;
- people have a distinct measure of self-determination and can thus choose to work at undisturbing themselves; thus, clients are shown that they are not slaves to their biologically-based IBs;
- people can implement their choices and maximise their freedom by actively working at changing their IBs; this is best achieved by employ-ing cognitive, emotive and behavioural methods often in quite a deter-mined manner (Ellis, 1994).

With the majority of clients, from the first session onwards, REBT thera-pists are likely to use strategies designed to effect profound philosophic change. The therapist begins therapy with the hypothesis that this particu-lar client may be able to achieve such change and thus begins specific REBT, which he or she will abandon when and if he or she collects suffi-cient data to reject the initial hypothesis. Ellis regularly implemented this viewpoint, based on the notion that the client's response to therapy is the best indicator of his or her prognosis. What proportion of REBT therapists share and regularly implement this position is unknown.

When it is clear that the client is unable or doesn't wish to achieve philo-sophic change, whether on a particular issue or in general, the therapist often switches to general REBT, using methods to effect inferential and behavioural-based change. For instance, a therapist was working with a middle-aged married woman who reported feeling furious every time her ageing father would telephone her and enquire 'What's doing?'; she con-sidered this a gross invasion of her privacy, insisting that he had no right to do so. The therapist initially intervened with a specific REBT strategy by attempting to dispute this client's rigid belief and help her see that there was no law in the universe which stated that he *must* not do such a thing. Meeting initial resistance, the therapist persisted with different variations of this theme, all to no avail.

Changing tack, he initiated a general REBT strategy designed to help the client question her inference that her father was actually invading her privacy. Given her father's age, the therapist enquired, wasn't it more likely that his question represented his usual manner of beginning tele-phone conversations rather than an intense desire to pry into her affairs? This enquiry proved successful: the client's rage subsided because she began to reinterpret her father's motives. Interestingly enough, although he returned to the specific REBT strategy later, the therapist never suc-ceeded in helping this client to give up her IB. However, some clients are more receptive to re-evaluating their IBs having been helped to correct distorted inferences.

It is important to note that REBT therapists, if they follow Ellis's lead, show REBT's distinctiveness in helping clients question their IBs much earlier in the therapeutic process than do other CBT therapists (Dryden, 2009b).

Major Treatment Techniques

REBT represents 'theoretically consistent eclecticism' in that techniques are liberally borrowed from other therapeutic systems, but employed for purposes usually consistent with REBT's underlying theory. In particular, REBT therapists are mindful of the short- and long-term effects of particu-lar therapeutic techniques and will rarely employ a technique that has beneficial immediate but harmful long-range consequences. While REBT employs many cognitive, emotive and behavioural techniques, only the major ones will be discussed here. Probably all the following techniques have cognitive, emotive and behavioural elements to them and 'pure' techniques (e.g. purely cognitive) probably do not exist. Techniques are grouped below to show which psychological process predominates.

Cognitive Techniques

Probably the most common technique employed by REBT therapists with the majority of clients involves the *disputing of IBs*.

Disputing Irrational Beliefs

There are four sub-categories of disputing (Ellis, 1977b):

- *Detecting* – Looking for IBs, both rigid beliefs (particularly musts, shoulds, oughts and have-to's) and the extreme beliefs derived from these rigid beliefs that, together, lead to self-defeating emotions and behaviours.
- *Defining* – Therapist helps client to make increasingly accurate definitions in the language employed when referring to their beliefs.
- *Discriminating* – Therapist helps client to distinguish clearly between their IBs and RBs.
- *Debating* – Therapist asks a number of questions designed to help client give up IBs. In particular, the therapist questions the client on the empirical status (e.g. 'Where is the evidence ...?'), logical status (e.g. 'Does it make sense to believe ...') and pragmatic status (e.g. 'Does it help or hinder you to believe that ...?) of both his IBs and RBs. The therapist proceeds with such questioning until the client acknowledges the falseness of his IB and, in addition, acknowledges the truth of its rational alternative.

Rational-emotive therapists are often very creative in their use of disputing sequences (cf. Dryden (1989) on the work of Howard Young) and sometimes employ such methods in a highly dramatic fashion. They also encourage clients to use a variety of cognitive homework forms, the purpose of which is to provide a clear framework for clients to learn disputing for themselves.

Other Cognitive Techniques

Clients who do not have the intellectual skills necessary to perform cognitive disputing are usually helped to develop *rational self-statements* which they memorise or write out on 7 x 12 cm (3 x 5 in) cards and repeat at various times between session. Two cognitive methods often employed by REBT therapists to help clients reinforce their new rational philosophy are *bibliotherapy*, where clients are assigned self-help books to read (e.g. Ellis, 2000; Dryden, 1994), and *the use of REBT with others*, a technique which gives clients an opportunity to practise thinking through rational arguments with friends and relatives.

Emotive Techniques

REBT, as a therapeutic system, has often been falsely accused of being too intellectual and insufficiently emotive. However, this is far from being true, and REBT sessions are frequently charged with emotion.

Humorous Techniques

The practice of effective REBT is based upon the therapist offering the client the emotional attitude of unconditional acceptance (as discussed in the section on the therapeutic relationship). From this foundation, REBT therapists frequently and judiciously employ humorous techniques to reduce the client's IBs to absurd, amusing conclusions, for example amusing anecdotes encourage the client to think rationally by not taking him or herself, others and the world *too* seriously.

Other Emotive Techniques

REBT therapists strive to serve as good *rational role models* both in their interactions with their clients and in their disclosures concerning how they handle their own psychological problems. In doing so, they employ a good measure of *therapist self-disclosure*. They encourage the use of role-playing and, in particular, *rational role reversal* where the therapist may adopt the irrational side of the client and encourage the client to dispute IBs from his or her rational side, a technique particularly employed with clients who have gained some mastery of the 'ABC' framework and disputing methods.

Another frequently used emotive technique is that of *rational-emotive imagery* (Ellis, 1979; Maultsby and Ellis, 1974). Here clients gain practice at changing their UNEs to healthy ones while keenly imagining the negative event. What they are in fact doing is learning to change their self-defeating emotions by changing their underlying philosophy.

Finally, clients are encouraged to act and think in forceful but rational ways (Ellis, 1994). For example, they are urged to act in ways consistent with their goals, but which they find difficult to do. Repeating rational self-statements in a *passionate, forceful* manner is often used in conjunction with such behaviours and at other times.

Behavioural Techniques

The use of a wide variety of behavioural techniques is advocated wherever possible, since cognitive change is often facilitated by behavioural change (Ellis, 1994).

In-vivo Exposure

However, some behavioural techniques are favoured over others. Thus, in vivo rather than imaginal techniques are preferred because 'live' exposure presents clients with more opportunities for philosophic change than 'imagined' exposure (Ellis, 1983a). For the same reason, REBT therapists often encourage clients *to expose themselves fully* to, say, feared events, although in practice compromises often have to be reached concerning how fully clients are prepared to expose themselves (Dryden, 1985). Whatever rate of change clients opt for, they are actively discouraged from using safety-seeking measures designed to keep them safe in the moment but which prevent them from facing up to and dealing constructively with adversity (Salkovskis, 1996).

Other Behavioural Methods
Other behavioural methods often used in REBT include: (a) *'stay-in-there' activities* (Grieger and Boyd, 1980) which give clients an opportunity to raise their level of discomfort tolerance by encouraging them to remain in uncomfortable (but not harmful or traumatic) situations for a period of time while tolerating their feelings of chronic discomfort; (b) *anti-procrastination* exercises where clients are encouraged to push themselves to start tasks earlier rather than later, thus disputing their dire need for comfort-of-the moment; (c) *skill training methods* which equip clients with key skills (e.g. assertion and social skills training), and which are usually employed after cognitive disputing methods have been used and some philosophic change has been encouraged (Ellis, 1994); and (d) *rewards and penalties* to encourage clients to implement self-change programmes.[1]

Overcoming Obstacles to Client Progress

Effective REBT practice can achieve remarkable results, but obstacles to client progress may be encountered in REBT and other forms of therapy. Three major types occur in REBT:

1 *Relationship obstacles*: These may be due to poor therapist–client matching or because therapist and client may get on 'too well' and become distracted from more mundane therapy tasks. This can be resolved by the therapist helping himself and then the client to overcome the philosophy of discomfort intolerance implicit in this collusive short-range hedonism.
2 *Therapist obstacles*: These can be:

   • *skill-orientated* – these may appear in a variety of forms, for example improperly inducting clients into therapy and failing to correct unrealistic expectations; incorrectly assessing clients' problems and thus working on 'problems' that clients do not have; failing to show clients that their emotional problems are largely determined by IBs at 'B' and not by adversities at 'A'; and so on.

---

[1]For a full discussion of techniques and methods avoided or used minimally in REBT, see Ellis (2002).

- *disturbance-orientated* – client progress can be hindered because therapists may bring their own disturbance to the therapeutic process. In such cases, REBT therapists should apply REBT principles and methods to dispute their own self- and client-defeating IBs which may (a) impede them from confronting their clients; (b) distract them and their clients from getting the therapeutic job done; (c) foster undue therapist anxiety and anger; and (d) encourage inappropriate behaviour antithetical to the practice of effective and ethical therapy.

3 *Client obstacles* (Dryden and Neenan 2004): To benefit from REBT, clients must achieve three forms of insight:

- psychological disturbance is mainly determined by the rigid and extreme beliefs that they hold about themselves, others and the world;
- though people may acquire IBs in their early lives, they perpetuate their disturbance by re-indoctrinating themselves in the present with these beliefs and acting and thinking in ways that are consistent with them;
- only if they constantly work and practise in the present and future to think, feel and act against these IBs are clients likely to surrender their irrationalities and make themselves significantly less disturbed.

Clients' own extreme level of disturbance is a significant obstacle to their own progress. Therapists can adopt a number of strategies to enhance therapeutic effectiveness with these clients:

1 Be consistently and forcefully encouraging in their therapeutic interactions with these clients, showing them that they can do better if they try.
2 Keep vigorously showing these resistant clients that they (the therapists) unconditionally accept them with all their psychological difficulties and that they can accept themselves in the same way.
3 Consistently show clients that their refusal to work on their problems will generally lead to bad consequences and needless suffering.
4 Be flexible in experimenting with a wide range of therapeutic techniques (including some unusual ones) in their persistent efforts to help their 'difficult' clients.

REBT therapists had better be good representatives of their therapeutic system and accept themselves and tolerate the discomfort of working with difficult clients while sticking to the therapeutic task!

Case Example: Dinah

Dinah, a married 34-year-old, running her own business from home, had wide-ranging anxiety problems. When she first saw me she could only leave home within her 'safe area'. One of the reasons she contacted me was because my consulting room was in that area.

The Conceptualisation of the Client's Problems

On assessment, I discovered that Dinah's anxiety problems were about three different kinds of threats – 'A's' in the 'ABC' framework – anxiety about the prospect of:

- losing self-control;
- not being the best at what she does;
- being judged negatively if others see her losing self-control and not being the best at what she does.

We agreed to target her anxiety about losing self-control first because her anxiety-based self-imposed restrictions were having a negative impact on her business: she could not travel outside her 'safe area' to win new contracts. I proceeded to assess this problem using REBT's 'ABC' framework (see Table 9.1 for a sample of this assessment).[2]

In this assessment, I distinguished between two types of thinking consequences of Dinah's IBs that underpinned her anxiety about losing self-control: safety-seeking thinking and threat-exaggerating thinking, both of which are particular features of anxiety. I used the 'ABC' framework to assess Dinah's two other problems, but did this only after Dinah had made progress on dealing effectively with her anxiety about losing self-control.

Practical Applications

The Therapeutic Relationship

I developed a collaborative relationship with Dinah, who was very motivated to help herself. I was initially mindful that her motivation might be a double-edged sword as she would probably bring her need to be in self-control to therapy which would paradoxically serve to maintain her problems rather than deal with them effectively. My explicit approach to outlining the REBT view of her problems, and how she could use it to help herself, resonated with her preference for a clear understanding of what therapy could and couldn't offer her. She had a good sense of humour and I was able to use humorous interventions to good effect. Dinah also appreciated it when I used therapist self-disclosure to show her I used similar techniques to deal with my own need to be able to control my stammer, a rigid belief that hindered rather than helped me deal with my anxiety about stammering. She remarked on several occasions that being a man, I didn't fully appreciate the stresses and

---

[2]Space restrictions prevent me from providing full details of all elements of Dinah's problems.

Table 9.1   A sample of Dinah's anxiety about losing self-control

'A' = Threat	Irrational beliefs ('B')	Behavioural consequences at 'C'	Thinking consequences at 'C'
The prospect of losing self-control.	I must not lose self-control and it will be terrible if I do.	• Avoidance of places that I deem to be 'unsafe'. • Taking valium with me wherever I go in case I begin to lose self-control. • Ensuring that I have my mobile phone with me so that I can call my husband if I need help. • Spending long periods of time practising relaxation and breathing techniques so I can use them if I need to. • Reading self-help books on self-control and overcoming anxiety.	Safety-seeking thinking: • Reassuring myself that I am in control and am expert on relaxation and breathing exercises. • Reminding myself that I am a strong and capable woman. Threat exaggerating thinking: • If I begin to lose control of myself, I will quickly lose complete self-control and will go mad.

strains of being a woman trying to thrive in the business world, but this didn't seem to threaten our therapeutic alliance.

Strategies of Treatment

My main strategies focused on helping Dinah gain a different type of self-control than she was used to and, indeed, continued to seek. I did this indirectly by adopting a flexible, non-extreme approach to not being in self-control and to set goals based on this concept (Table 9.2 gives an example of these goals). She wanted to gain self-control by applying techniques and eliminating not being in self-control immediately. I helped her see that this direct, rigid approach would actually perpetuate her problems.

This was difficult for Dinah to accept but I convinced her with two arguments:

• I encouraged her to add to her self-control repertoire rather than suggest she gave up her direct approach to self-control entirely.
• She resonated with the pragmatic approach which invited her to use the indirect approach and compare it to the direct approach with respect to its effects.
• I encouraged her to use similar strategies later in therapy with her other two forms of anxiety:

   – To deal with the prospect of not being the best at what she does rather than to eliminate this form of what she regarded as failure.
   – To deal with the prospect of being judged negatively if others see her lose self-control and not be the best at what she does rather than ensure this doesn't happen.

(Continued)

(Continued)

Table 9.2   Dinah's concern-based goals about dealing with
losing self-control

'A' = Threat	Rational beliefs ('B')	Behavioural consequences at 'C'	Thinking consequences at 'C'
The prospect of losing self-control.	I really don't want to lose self-control, but that does not mean that I must not do so. If I do, it would be bad, but not terrible.	• Being tempted to avoid places that I deem to be 'unsafe', but not doing so. • Being tempted to take valium with me wherever I go in case I begin to lose self-control, but not doing so. • Feeling the urge to ensure that I have my mobile phone with me so that I can call my husband if I need help, but leaving it at home. • Being tempted to spend long periods of time practising relaxation and breathing techniques so I can use them if I need to, but not doing so. • Feeling the urge to read self-help books on self-control and overcoming anxiety, but not doing so.	Safety-seeking thinking: • Feeling the urge to reassure myself that I am in control and am expert on relaxation and breathing exercises, but not engaging with this thought. • Feeling the urge to remind myself that I am a strong and capable woman, but not engaging with this thought. Threat exaggerating thinking: • If I begin to lose control of myself, I may quickly lose complete self-control and will go mad, but it's more likely that I won't.

Once Dinah accepted these strategies, she saw that she could implement them by developing RBs about these threats and by acting and thinking accordingly.

Major Treatment Techniques

Because Dinah was oriented to self-help, I taught her how to use REBT's self-help techniques such as *disputing IBs*, using *rational-emotive imagery* to rehearse her RBs while facing her threats in her mind's eye and directly in vivo without engaging in behavioural and thinking safety-seeking measures. This was particularly important when she dealt with her anxiety about losing self-control. To guard against possible overuse of these techniques (to which Dinah was particularly vulnerable), I encouraged her to use an incremental approach to developing a rational approach to losing self control. Just as she would not expect to get fit by exercising non-stop until she achieved a state of fitness, she should practise techniques in short bursts and allow herself to experience urges to engage in behavioural and thinking safety-seeking measures without actually doing so. Similarly, she should expect to retain threat-exaggerating thoughts, which she should accept without either engaging in or trying to eliminate. This incremental approach was key to her improvement. Additionally, she agreed to stop reading self-help books and practising relaxation and breathing techniques, both of which served to perpetuate her anxiety.

Overcoming Obstacles to Client Progress

Initially, Dinah found it difficult to refrain from trying to eliminate her urges to engage in behavioural and thinking safety-seeking measures and threat-exaggerating thinking. She readily understood that engaging in these processes served to perpetuate her anxiety, but her conclusion that she needed to eliminate these urges was based on her direct rigid approach to self-control (if it's bad, eliminate it).

I helped Dinah understand that there's a world of difference between experiencing an urge and engaging with it. Once she had learned this experientially she made greater strides towards her goals. At the end of therapy, she could travel freely around London and bid for work outside her comfort zone. We agreed to terminate therapy with an understanding that she would contact me when she next had to fly so that we could tackle her fear of flying.

The Research Status of REBT

I will consider the evidence-based status of REBT in terms of REBT theory and clinical strategies derived from the theory. For a discussion on what we still don't know, see Dryden et al. (2009).

The Evidence-Based Status of REBT Theory

As a specific type of cognitive appraisal, whether primary and/or secondary (see Lazarus, 1991), IBs are regarded as key causal mechanisms in a number of clinical conditions such as discomfort intolerance (involved in anger), awfulising (involved in anxiety and pain) and self-depreciation, a basic element of depressed mood (e.g. David et al., 2002, 2005; Solomon et al., 2003).

1 A major irrational cognitive process is 'demandingness', in which the impact of an activating event, such as a traumatic episode, on the affective and/or behavioural consequences is mediated by *rigid beliefs* as a *primary irrational appraisal mechanism*, and 'awfulising beliefs, discomfort intolerance beliefs and depreciation beliefs as *secondary irrational appraisal mechanisms* (see David et al., 2002). In 2007 DiLorenzo et al. published a study in pursuance of this view. They researched the inter-relations between IBs in engendering distress among students, at the start of term and before a mid-term exam. Ninety-nine students completed the Attitudes and Beliefs Scale II (measuring IBs) and the Profile of Mood States-Short Version (measuring distress) at the start of term (Time 1) and prior to the exam (Time 2). The four IBs above were

directly related to distress levels at both times ($p < .05$). However, mediation analyses revealed that the effect of rigid beliefs on distress was mediated by awfulising beliefs, discomfort intolerance beliefs and depreciation beliefs. Rigid beliefs might, of course, follow the other three IBs, in being endemic to the process of re-appraisal (see Lazarus, 1991). For instance, rigid beliefs can be endemic to the re-appraisal process (i.e. metacognition); as described above, the other three IBs can be secondary appraisal mechanisms involved in appraisal process (Lazarus, 1991).

2   IBs are regarded as cognitive vulnerability factors, that is, they will only engender a clinical condition in conjunction with specific stressful activating events. One can therefore hold IBs, but unless activated by stressful activating events, one will experience no distress or maladaptive behaviours.

3   IBs about particular activating events generate distorted inferences and descriptions (e.g. automatic thoughts, intermediate and core beliefs) about that event. Szentagotai and Freeman (2007), for instance, showed that IBs influence the automatic thoughts which exacerbate the depressed mood of patients with major depression. They studied the relationship between IBs and automatic thoughts in predicting distress (i.e. depression in 170 patients with major depressive disorder). Although both constructs have been hypothesised before and found to engender emotional distress in stressful situations, the relationships between these two types of cognitions in predicting distress have not been properly considered in empirical studies. Results indicate that IBs and automatic thoughts both relate to distress (specifically depressed mood/depression), and that automatic thoughts partially mediate IBs' impact on distress.

4   IBs have a particular pattern in relation to a number of clinical mood states: rigid beliefs and discomfort intolerance beliefs for unhealthy anger; rigid beliefs and awfulising beliefs for anxiety; rigid beliefs and depreciation beliefs (especially self-depreciation or depressed mood – see e.g. David et al., 2002).

The Empirical Status of REBT Clinical Strategies

REBT empirical outcome research has developed over three periods (based on David et al., 2005): before 1970; 1970–1990; and 1990s to present. There was little rigorous empirical research before 1970 on REBT efficacy (i.e. how REBT functions in controlled conditions) and effectiveness (i.e. how REBT functions in real-life clinical conditions), based on experimental or quasi-experimental designs. Since 1970, a number of outcome studies have been published which formed the basis for a more rigorous quantitative approach to examining REBT's efficacy.

A number of qualitative reviews to date (for example, David et al., 2005; DiGiuseppe et al., 1977; Ellis, 1973; Haaga and Davison, 1989a, 1989b; Zettle and Hayes, 1980) have explored REBT's effectiveness and efficacy.

These qualitative reviews, although mainly positive, have also highlighted various methodological problems that need to be corrected to strengthen the conclusion that REBT is an effective treatment.

Outcome research has become the foundation for a quantitative approach in examining REBT's efficacy, and for enabling meta-analyses to address a majority of the criticisms advanced in previous REBT qualitative reviews (Engels et al., 1993; Lyons and Woods, 1991). Regarding outcome research, there are two types of quantitative reviews: general – concerned with cognitive behavioural psychotherapy in general; and specific – concerned specifically with REBT efficacy.

General Quantitative Reviews

REBT has generally rated highly in quantitative reviews of psychotherapy. For instance, Smith and Glass (1977), one of the first psychotherapy meta-analyses, cited REBT as establishing the second highest average effect size among ten major forms of psychotherapy. The proportion of REBT outcome studies included in psychotherapy meta-analyses is, however, small, and authors tend to consign all forms of cognitive-behavioural therapy into a single category (e.g. Wampold et al., 1997). While psychotherapy meta-analyses usually indicate that cognitive-behavioural therapy has the highest overall effect size, as REBT is included in the general CBT category, the extent to which REBT independently contributes to these results is unclear.

Specific Quantitative Reviews

REBT's efficacy and effectiveness have been evaluated by two significant meta-analyses (Engels et al., 1993; Lyons and Woods, 1991), which form the basis for the following summary:

1 REBT is effective in a broad spectrum of clinical diagnoses and outcomes. Interestingly, REBT appears to have a much stronger impact on 'untargeted variables' which do not seem to relate to the treatment directly (e.g. physiological measures like blood pressure), than on 'targeted variables' which have a direct relationship with the treatment (e.g. IBs). This implies that REBT's effect is not due to compliance or task-demand characteristics.
2 Individual and group REBT are broadly similar in efficacy.
3 REBT is as useful for clinical populations as for non-clinical, for males and females and for a broad age range (9–70 years).
4 More REBT sessions produce better results.
5 The higher the level of training of the therapist generally, the better the results of the REBT intervention. This is interesting, as most psychotherapy meta-analyses find no relationship between treatment outcome and therapist training, and requires further study.
6 Greater REBT effectiveness is indicated by higher quality outcome studies.

NB: As one of REBT's strengths is that it is equally effective for clinical and sub-clinical problems, the outcome research was conducted on people with sub-clinical problems. For example, while it is important for REBT to help those with major depressive disorder, it can equally benefit people with less severe, perhaps more temporary, dysphoric conditions. REBT is not just a clinical theory for clinical populations, but an educational system with implications for non-clinical and sub-clinical populations such as those with depressed mood, lack of assertiveness and anxiety, who are interested in self-help materials and personal development.

Suggested Further Reading

Dryden, W. (2009) *Understanding Emotional Problems: The REBT Perspective*. Hove: Routledge.

Dryden, W. (2009) *Rational Emotive Behaviour Therapy: Distinctive Features*. Hove: Routledge.

Dryden, W. (2009) *Skills in Rational Emotive Behaviour Counselling and Psychotherapy*. London: Sage.

Dryden, W., DiGiuseppe, R. and Neenan, M. (2010) *A Primer on Rational Emotive Behavior Therapy*, 3rd Edn. Champaign, IL: Research Press.

Ellis, A. (1994) *Reason and Emotion in Psychotherapy*, Rev. Edn. New York: Birch Lane Press.

References

Adler, A. (1927) *Understanding Human Nature*. New York: Garden City.

Beutler, L.E. (1983) *Eclectic Psychotherapy: A Systematic Approach*. New York: Pergamon.

David, D., Schnur, J. and Belloiu, A. (2002) 'Another search for the "hot" cognition: Appraisal irrational beliefs, attribution and their relation to emotion', *Journal of Rational-Emotive and Cognitive-Behavior Therapy*, 20: 93–131.

David, D., Szentagotai, A., Kallay, E. and Macavei, B. (2005) 'A synopsis of rational-emotive behavior therapy (REBT): Fundamental and applied research', *Journal of Rational-Emotive and Cognitive-Behavior Therapy*, 23: 175–221.

DiGiuseppe, R., Miller, N.J. and Trexler, L.D. (1977) 'A review of rational-emotive psychotherapy studies', *The Counseling Psychologist*, 7: 64–72.

DiLorenzo, T.A., David, D. and Montgomery, G. (2007) 'The interrelations between irrational cognitive processes and distress in stressful academic settings', *Personality and Individual Differences*, 42: 765, 776.

Dryden, W. (1985) 'Challenging but not overwhelming: A compromise in negotiating homework assignments', *British Journal of Cognitive Psychotherapy*, 3(1): 77–80.

Dryden, W. (Ed.) (1989) *Howard Young – Rational Therapist: Seminal Papers in Rational-Emotive Therapy*. London: Gale Centre Publications.

Dryden, W. (1994) *Ten Steps to Positive Living*. London: Sheldon.

Dryden, W. (1997) *Therapists' Dilemmas*, Rev. Edn. London: Sage.

Dryden, W. (1998) 'Understanding persons in the context of their problems: A rational emotive behaviour therapy perspective', in M. Bruch and F.W. Bond (Eds), *Beyond Diagnosis: Case Formulation Approaches in CBT*. Chichester: Wiley. pp. 43–64.

Dryden, W. (2009a) *Understanding Emotional Problems: The REBT Perspective*. Hove: Routledge.

Dryden, W. (2009b) *Rational Emotive Behaviour Therapy: Distinctive Features*. Hove: Routledge.

Dryden, W. (2011) *Dealing with Emotional Problems in Life Coaching*. Hove: Routledge.

Dryden, W. and Neenan, M. (2004) *The Rational Emotive Behavioural Approach to Therapeutic Change*. London: Sage.

Dryden, W., David, D. and Ellis, A. (2009) 'Rational emotive behavior therapy', in K.S. Dobson (Ed.), *Handbook of Cognitive-Behavioral Therapies*, 3rd edn. New York: Guilford. pp. 226–276.

Ellis, A. (1962) *Reason and Emotion in Psychotherapy*. Secaucus, NJ: Lyle Stuart.

Ellis, A. (1972) 'Helping people get better; Rather than merely feel better', *Rational Living*, 7(2): 2–9.

Ellis, A. (1973) *Humanistic Psychotherapy: The Rational-Emotive Approach*. New York: McGraw-Hill.

Ellis, A. (1976) 'The biological basis of human irrationality', *Journal of Individual Psychology*, 32: 145–168.

Ellis, A. (1977a) 'Intimacy in psychotherapy', *Rational Living*, 12(1): 13–19.

Ellis, A (1977b) 'The basic clinical theory of rational-emotive therapy', in A. Ellis and R. Grieger (Eds), *Handbook of Rational-Emotive Therapy*. New York: Springer.

Ellis, A. (1979) 'The practice of rational-emotive therapy', in A. Ellis and J.M. Whiteley (Eds), *Theoretical and Empirical Foundations of Rational-Emotive Therapy*. Monterey, CA: Brooks/Cole.

Ellis, A. (1980) 'Rational-emotive therapy and cognitive behaviour therapy: Similarities and differences', *Cognitive Therapy and Research*, 4(4): 325–340.

Ellis, A. (1981) 'The place of Immanuel Kant in cognitive psychotherapy', *Rational Living*, 16(2): 13–16.

Ellis, A. (1983a) 'The philosophic implications and dangers of some popular behavior therapy techniques', in M. Rosenbaum, C.M. Franks and Y. Jaffe (Eds), *Perspectives in Behaviour Therapy in the Eighties*. New. York: Springer.

Ellis, A. (1983b) 'Failures in rational-emotive therapy', in E.B. Foa and P.M.G. Emmelkamp (Eds), *Failures in Behavior Therapy*. New York: Wiley.

Ellis, A. (1984) 'Foreword', in W. Dryden (Ed.), *Rational-Emotive Therapy: Fundamentals and Innovations*. Beckenham: Croom Helm.

Ellis, A. (1994) *Reason and Emotion in Psychotherapy*, Rev. Edn. Secaucus, NJ: Birch Lane.

Ellis, A. (2000) *How to Control Your Anxiety Before it Controls You*. New York: Citadel.

Ellis, A. (2002) *Overcoming Resistance: A Rational Rmotive Behavior Therapy Intergrated Approach*, 2nd Edn. New York: Springer.

Engels, G.I., Garnefsky, N. and Diekstra, F.W. (1993) 'Efficacy of rational-emotive therapy: A quantitative analysis', *Journal of Consulting and Clinical Psychology*, 6: 1083–1090.

Eschenroeder, C. (1979) 'Different therapeutic styles in rational-emotive therapy', *Rational Living*, 14(1): 3–7.

Garcia, E.J. (1977) 'Working on the E in REBT', in J.L. Wolfe and E. Brand (Eds), *Twenty Years of Rational Therapy: Proceedings of the First National Conference on Rational Psychotherapy*. New York: Institute for Rational Emotive Therapy.

Grieger, R. and Boyd, J. (1980) *Rational-Emotive Therapy: A Skills-based Approach*. New York: Van Nostrand Reinhold.

Haaga, D.A.F. and Davison, G.C. (1989a) 'Slow progress in rational-emotive therapy outcome research: Etiology and treatment', *Cognitive Therapy and Research*, 13: 493–508.

Haaga, D.A.F. and Davison, G.C. (1989b) 'Outcome studies of rational-emotive therapy', in M.E. Bernard and R. DiGiuseppe (Eds), *Inside Rational-Emotive Therapy: A Critical Appraisal of the Theory and Therapy of Albert Ellis*. New York: Academic Press.

Horney, K. (1950) *Neurosis and Human Growth*. New York: Norton.

Lazarus, R.S. (1991) *Emotion and Adaptation*. New York: Oxford University Press.

Lyons, L.C. and Woods, P.J. (1991) 'The efficacy of rational-emotive therapy: A quantitative review of the outcome research', *Clinical Psychology Review*, 11: 357–369.

Maultsby, M.C., Jr and Ellis, A. (1974) *Technique for Using Rational-Emotive Imagery*. New York: Institute for Rational-Emotive Therapy.

Nielsen, S., Johnson, W.B. and Ellis, A. (2001) *Counseling and Psychotherapy with Religious Persons: A Rational Emotive Behavior Therapy Approach*. Florence, KY: Erlbaum.

Salkovskis, P.M. (1996) 'The cognitive approach to anxiety: Threat beliefs, safety-seeking behaviour and the special case of health anxiety and obsession', in P.M. Salkovskis (Ed.), *Frontiers of Cognitive Therapy*. New York: Guilford Press. pp. 48–74.

Smith, M.L. and Glass, G.V. (1977) 'Meta-analysis of psychotherapy outcome studies', *American Psychologist*, 32: 752–760.

Solomon, A., Bruce, A., Gotlib, I.H. and Wind, B. (2003) 'Individualized measurement of irrational beliefs in remitted depressives', *Journal of Clinical Psychology*, 59: 439–455.

Szentagotai, A. and Freeman, A. (2007) 'An analysis of the relationship between irrational beliefs and automatic thoughts in predicting distress', *Journal of Cognitive and Behavioral Psychotherapies*, 7: 1–11.

Wampold, B.E., Mondin, G.W., Moody, M., Stich, F., Benson, K. and Ahn, H. (1997) 'A meta-analysis of outcome studies comparing bona fide psychotherapies: Empirically, "all must have prizes"', *Psychological Bulletin*, 122: 203–215.

Zettle, R.D. and Hayes, S.C. (1980) 'Conceptual and empirical status of rational-emotive therapy', *Progress in Behavior Modification*, 9: 125–166.

TEN   Narrative CBT

JOHN RHODES

Historical Development of the Approach

Narrative CBT is an integration, in practice and theory, of ideas taken from CBT and from narrative solution focused therapies (NSFT), the latter being a series of developments in the field of systemic therapy, lead principally by de Shazer and associates (de Shazer, 1985, 1988; Lipchick, 2002), and by White and Epston (1990; White, 2007). There are three strands of thought that particularly contribute to and characterise NSFT that can be summarised as follows (these are discussed in detail later). First, that change can be generated by building on what is going well or working in the life of a person. This can be thought of as a 'constructional' emphasis. Second, NSFT is strongly influenced by those ideas in psychology and the humanities that emphasise what Sarbin (1986) termed the 'narratary principle', namely that it is the actual nature of the mind to think, perceive and experience in narrative and related forms, such as metaphor (Bruner, 1986). Third, NSFT is influenced by theories generally described as constructivist: the latter is a broad term, but tends to be a perspective which emphasises how people actively produce and construct meaning as they develop and experience their lives. The therapeutic idea of being constructional was developed specifically in the practice of NSFT, whilst the other two strands were developed from more general theories in the social sciences.

Ideas of narrative and constructivism have also influenced developments in CBT. Guidano and Liotti (1983) were perhaps the first to develop a fusion of cognitive therapy with ideas taken from constructivism. Their approach emphasised understanding psychopathology by the re-examination of early experience in its developmental context of attachment relationships: they wished to examine how taken-for-granted meanings and ideas of identity were constructed, and then continued to influence a person's active construing over the lifespan. Mahoney (1991, 2003) was likewise interested in fundamental 'ordering' principles of experience and how these influenced subsequent adult meaning systems. In this therapy he suggested, using basic CBT approaches for dealing with specific problems, but drew on a very wide range of approaches for working with long-term, usually interpersonal difficulties. To explore meaning he used a wide range of methods including journal writing, artistic expression of any type, role play, borrowed fixed-role therapy from Kelly (1955), and suggested various types of life story exploration. The breadth of these methods originated from his constructivist ideas of meaning, in that meaning is regarded as more diverse than simple explicit thoughts.

Russell (1991), Meichenbaum (1993), and Gonçalves (1994) noted deep similarities in the way that meaning is central in CBT and narrative therapy. They all suggested that the idea of narrative was more inspirational and useful than a model of the mind based on computers and information processing. Ramsay (1998) thought likewise, but also suggested the use of constructional ideas from NSFT. In Padesky's (1994) article on working with core ideas of the self, she suggested the use of a positive data log: that is, the person is asked to list and look out for any positive features of the self. This is clearly a constructional approach. Different in detail, but similar in spirit, de Shazer (1985) would give clients the task of listing anything they valued about themselves, their relationships, and life.

Hallam and O'Connor (2002) described a dialogical approach to working with OCD, influenced by narrative ideas: they suggested identifying and working with the negative 'voices' of a person, that is, the way a person might argue for and against an action, and hypothesised that such voices derive from dialogue experienced in the context of difficult childhood interactions. O'Connor et al. (2009) also described how adult clients with OCD generate 'bridging' narratives between what they actually see (the door is shut) and elaborate hypothetical possibilities ('Did I open it again and forget just now?').

In recent years, there have been several accounts of therapists finding it useful to combine CBT and aspects of NSFT, in particular constructional ones. Griffin (2003) described work with childhood OCD: this involved combining 'externalisation' (i.e. a sort of personalisation of OCD characters) and basic cognitive challenging of negative ideas. Postma and Rao (2006) described first giving a CBT formulation to a client with food phobia, but due to him rejecting the suggested CBT techniques, then turning to solution focused approaches, which the client was able to implement. Guterman and Rudes (2005) outlined a theoretical integration of solution focused therapy and rational emotive therapy.

With colleagues I have published a series of articles (see Research section) outlining how NSFT approaches can be combined with CBT for working with various aspects of psychosis, and related emotional and social difficulties. The flexibility of this combined approach has been shown to help in complex and challenging situations. Our approach is constructional, narrative and constructivist, but is also open to the central ideas of CBT, and is the topic of this chapter.

Theoretical Underpinnings

Major Concepts

NCBT aims for the integration of techniques that have been proven to be useful, and a selective but critical openness to a range of theories from the traditions of CBT and NSFT. To carry out this integration, some common but also specific ideas are emphasised from the two traditions, whilst others are considered less relevant. The key guiding ideas and theories are as follows.

How Therapy Works

Brewin (2006) argued that the theories used to explain how patients actually change in successful CBT are not yet persuasive. Considerable evidence suggests that negative behaviours and cognitions often return under later stressful conditions: if that is the case, then it is difficult to see how traditional behaviourist explanations of changes in 'associations' or cognitive explanations of restructuring 'content' are complete and accurate. As an alternative, Brewin argues that in successful CBT a patient either builds, or has more ready access to, positive representations such as 'I can cope with the fear' or 'Some people like me'. In exposure therapy for phobia it is possible that what changes after successful therapy is a person's capacity to generate memories such as 'I was able to copy'. He suggests there is a competition between positive and negative representations, and successful therapy improves access to the former by making these representations more elaborate, memorable and vivid. Teasdale (1997) made a different but related point, that the most important aspect of CBT for depression might not be direct rational challenge of negative content, but building by the client of an alternative model, namely that negative thoughts are reactions to be dealt with, rather than the truth of a person's nature.

Though the constructional stance of NSFT long pre-dates Brewin's theory, the latter does throw an interesting light on solution-building activities and, in a sense, brings constructional ideas within a more general cognitive framework. Brewin himself notes how his theory might illuminate White's approach.

Meaning

CBT and NSFT share a claim that meaning is central to understanding difficulties and that most clients suffer the effects of negative meanings, beliefs, metaphors and stories. White spoke of clients with problem-saturated stories, and Beck et al. (1979) of negative thoughts, assumptions and core beliefs. These two sets of ideas are different yet compatible. Brewin and Power (1999) emphasised a common thread across therapies in that they all involve a transformation of meaning.

It is also emphasised in NCBT that 'meaning' as such is not reducible to explicit thinking, but is manifest in many different forms such as emotion (Greenberg, 2002) and interactions (MacIntyre, 1981). Consciousness is a fundamental phenomena, utterly imbued with meaning and interconnected in multiple and complex ways (Searle, 1992). Simple linear models using stimulus and response concepts cannot capture the reality of the mind and self. Beck himself has also abandoned his earlier theory that emotions could all be explained by thoughts (Beck, 1995), something long argued for by constructivists such as Greenberg.

Making Sense

Ideas and practices generated by the client tend to be ones that make the most sense and are ones clients are more likely to put into practice. These claims are part of the constructional emphasis of de Shazer and White, but are also very much in line with the constructivist stance (Kelly, 1955). Even a simple technique such as calm breathing will only be acceptable to a client if it fits the meaning making or 'ordering' processes of the person (Mahoney, 2003). The practice of NSFT demonstrates that one can ask clients for ways forward, for solutions, and so forth, and that often these prove to be the most useful ideas discussed in therapy.

The constructivist approach to 'making sense' of phenomena is carried out in diverse ways; it often involves helping clients find new words for experiences. The therapy of White is particularly concerned with 'naming' the problem in client-centred ways.

Client-Generated Solutions

Clients can generate ideas and discuss possible 'exceptions', that is, times the problem does not occur when it might be expected to do so. This is central to NSFT and perhaps its most distinctive claim. In therapy one can explore these, and sometimes, if appropriate, it can be suggested that the client does more of 'what works'. Of course, the detail is everything and there may be good reasons why the person has not already done this – most of the art of NSFT revolves around how and when to make such suggestions or refrain from doing so.

NCBT also uses a focus on exceptions, particularly in the first phases of therapy; however, it is accepted that one might need to borrow techniques or suggest ready-made ones if the client is not making progress. The issue then is, do these therapist-led ideas and techniques make sense? Does the client feel empowered to choose? Can they be adapted by the client and thus made their 'own'?

The Narrative Mind

The mind, as Turner (1996) argued, is intrinsically 'literate' and we think and experience in these ways from earliest childhood. Narrations, metaphor, dialogue and so on are used spontaneously: when things make sense to a person it is likely that this involves the building of narrative and elaboration of metaphoric and other conceptually complex models (Lakoff and Johnson, 1980; Lakoff, 1987; Fauconnier and Turner, 2002). Therapeutic exploration and interventions are therefore aided by the use of narration and metaphor; this has been recognised by many writers from diverse therapeutic traditions, and it has always been central to NSFT.

Resources

It is clearly useful in the generation of positive representations if there are actual resources of various sorts in the life of the person. Narrative CBT is compatible with critical realism (Bhaskar, 1989), the claim that there is a social and material reality external to any one person's perspective, even if our perception is structured by our own history and culture. The nature of this external reality is crucial in the life of the person. The potential for well being is not just dependent on how we 'interpret' things. Where possible, it is therapeutically useful to help the person, particularly those with psychosis, to access resources and change environments, for example through work and education (Rhodes and Jakes, 2009). Several strands of research have also indicated a buffering effect of resources (MacLeod and Moore, 2000), that is, those with at least some areas of life going well will better survive negative events than those with very little or no areas going well.

Intentionality

Finally, it is claimed that the most persuasive model of mind, self, consciousness and of meaning is found in the conceptual analysis of philosophers such as Searle (1992), Nagel (1979), MacIntyre (1981) and Goldie (2000). They argue in diverse ways that mental phenomena such as beliefs and desires need to be understood as non-reducible; that is, that we do not get a better understanding of these by attempting to reduce them to explanations using just the concepts of behaviour, brain activity or so-called information processing. Rather, we need to grasp the subjective realities of a person and work with everyday concepts such as intentions to act, beliefs and desires.

How Problems are Conceptualised

To conceptualise problems, NCBT draws upon the two traditions of theorising in CBT and NSFT. The critical integration of these leads to a conceptualisation of problems as due to various unwanted, destructive effects of meaning and behaviour such that fundamental needs of the person are frustrated. Needs range from security to the capacity to function in the everyday world (Rhodes and Gipps, 2008).

Drawing particularly upon the systemic tradition of NSFT, problems are also assumed to be created and maintained within a specific 'system' and/or concrete living cultural context. Meaning, or sometimes the absence of useful meaning, is context-dependent and may be created and maintained by this wider context. Persons within a context articulate and construe many 'representations' and other forms of explicit meaning, but they also engage in 'repetitions' of meaningful behaviours (i.e. both automatic responses and more deliberate actions). While behaviourism has always underlined the importance of context, the systemic emphasis is more fluid, dynamic and points to the multiplicity of mutual influences over time. Consistent with the concept of intentionality, it is assumed that meaning as such is implicit in all aspects of a person's conscious experience, that is, in ideas, emotion, motivation, actions, perceptions. There areas are both separate yet deeply interconnected.

Brewin and Power (1999) suggested that the suffering of clients often involves common themes such as believing oneself to be inferior, bad, or others as abandoning. In addition to speaking of themes, as most cognitive therapists do, theories drawing on narrative ideas also emphasis how any specific thought or belief occurs in a complex context of shifting narrations of the self over time. To really understand a theme, one needs to grasp the present and past contexts. For example, one client stated that if anything good happened, she would be punished. One needs to understand how this claim links with many other thoughts and, in fact, to an attempt to explain difficult events that have occurred over the life span. The client in question was preoccupied by two memories: one of feeling happy when visiting a hospital as a teemager, only to find her brother dead, and a second memory of feeling happy to be in love, only to find that the man was violent and abusive. She ended up believing that the occurrence of the bad was typical for her, part of her very identity and life story.

In addition to negative meanings, NSFT suggests that another common difficulty is that many clients do not possess positive, benign, useful meanings. Over the life span of the person positive things and events might have occurred, or are presently occurring, but for whatever reason the client may not 'see' this. There is a silence, or as some argue these things remain 'pre-narrative' (Talvitie and Tiitinen, 2006). The 'exception', the times of coping are not seen at all, or ignored, or construed as having no relevance to initiating change.

NCBT, drawing on the tradition of CBT, and in contrast with NSFT, does use clinical and research-based knowledge about specific symptoms and hypotheses about possible causation providing this knowledge helps to understand difficulties or design appropriate interventions. For example, in depression it is well known that there can be rumination about a range of topics and several ways of ending rumination (Pearson et al., 2008). Using this knowledge with NCBT one could ask: 'What have you found that works to stop rumination?'

PRACTICAL APPLICATIONS

The Therapeutic Relationship

Narrative CBT incorporates the usual practices of CBT toward clients; however, NSFT adds something distinctive, that one really needs to learn from the client, and in the end the client will be the best person to articulate what is needed, where to go and how one might get there. It is a stance that relies upon and actively encourages a client's potential for creating problem solving. The client is an active participant in the construction of interventions. It is not the stance: 'I will conduct my scientific assessment and then tell you the cause and cure.' When asked what a client could do to survive the feared visit of the 'demons' that weekend, he eventually gave a list of activities such as turning on the radio and leaving the door ajar (Rhodes and Jakes, 2002). These solutions do not appear to make sense from an outside perspective. If there were demons, how could a radio help to stop them? Yet that was the best that could be generated, and suggestions by others were of no use.

It may seem odd to make the above claims given that clients come to therapy precisely because they are 'stuck', often seeming not to know how to move forward. However, a central task of therapy is to unblock this stuckness, to open dialogues and thinking such that dormant problem solving and the very motivation to solve problems is encouraged.

In NCBT the general movement is to start with an in-depth investigation of possible solutions generated by the client, and only later to bring in ideas or practices for the client from other areas of expertise. By repeated solution-orientated questions, clients often construct their own versions of CBT, that is, they see the importance of taking behavioural steps such as telephoning a relative and practising the saying of new ideas to themselves ('I will tell myself I can do it').

Taking its fundamental attitude to therapeutic alliance from NSFT, NCBT involves learning from the client, showing curiosity, respect and being tentative. There is a real interest in what the client says about problems, ways of coping, exceptions and the client's actual language. The therapist adopts a cautious tentativeness when suggesting ideas (Bliss and Bray, 2009).When a client has managed something difficult, the therapist explores this: How did you do this? How did you prepare yourself? What went through your mind? How could you do this again? Was it something new for you? Time and interest is dedicated to this.

This therapeutic stance characterises the first phase of NCBT, and in fact might be the only 'method' used (Bliss and Bray, 2009), yet it is also manifested when suggesting well-known techniques such as the use of headphones for coping with voices. Here the stance is: 'Some people have found this useful, it's something you could try.' And for something as risky to therapeutic rapport as questioning a delusion, a much better stance than direct challenging is: 'What has made you puzzled over the idea of being secretly monitored by your relatives as you flew on the plane?' That is, one that works within the frame of the client's meaning system and attempts to recruit the client's own curiosity and active questioning.

Strategies

Aims

There are three very broad, overarching strategic aims: the building of the therapeutic working relationship (already discussed); the construction of problems; and the construction of solutions. The second aim therefore is to explore and put into words the 'problem' as experienced and perceived by the client. It is not assumed that the client will automatically be able to describe the problem, nor that any descriptions are fixed. It is certainly not assumed that technical words such as 'psychosis' or 'depression' should be used or are appropriate. The attention to clients' 'constructions', their idiosyncratic meaning systems, is central to the NSFT traditions and carries over into NCBT.

A simple description of difficulties, before proceeding to ideas of change, may be enough for some clients. For others, it may be necessary to return to talk of difficulties several times and construct with the client some sort of conceptualisation, a 'formulation'. The latter, however, should not be a simple 'formula' handed over to the client: rather, a good 'formulation' develops from a dialogue with the client in which diverse and distressing features are accounted for and begin to make sense. A good conceptualisation is also one that points to a way forward and brings together the person's resources and potential strengths within a coherent narrative account.

The aim of the assessment is above all to construct a shared rich description of difficulties and aims. It is not a necessary requirement that a full causal formulation is developed and presented. The stance of narrative CBT is similar to the cautious and critical ideas expressed by Harper and Spellman (2006). Good therapy can occur without an explicit formulation, and for some clients there are good reasons to believe that the presentation of a technical formulation is potentially negative and distressing, and serves no actual use (Pain et al, 2008). However, for some clients, at some stage of therapy, a formulation in the form of a narrative that connects themes in a person's life and yields new understanding can be highly enriching.

The third broad strategy is the exploration and construction of 'solutions', 'ways forward'. In essence, these are things to do more of (that work), things to do differently, and sometimes drawing on specific techniques from CBT and/or client expertise, new ideas to try out. It is useful to present the latter as 'things that have worked for others, and might work for you'.

Pathways
Given these broad aims, it is useful to think of therapy as a potential 'pathway' and perhaps the most common pathway, at least for clients with psychosis, is as follows.

- Explore the client's presenting difficulties, and simultaneously, the client's motivational attitudes towards doing therapy. The latter are highly variable and can range from full commitment, through hesitancy, to attendance due to politeness or demands by the psychiatric system. Such issues need to be addressed.

- At this point, given the presentation, different approaches to therapy can be chosen, in particular, whether to work with the individual or rather to use consultation (Rhodes and Ajmal, 1995; Rhodes, 2000) to family or staff who live and work with the client. One can also decide to work on different issues in different phases.
- Next, to investigate naturally occurring exceptions to the problem, what the client can do differently, how the client copes, to build a picture of the future, and possible areas of strength or resources that might be relevant for constructing solutions. For some there can be extended work on self-esteem issues and narrative explorations of difficult past events.
- If the above yields no results, or not sufficient, then to move on to the re-investigation of the nature of the problem and open dialogue with the client about possible techniques borrowed from CBT or ideas suggested by other clients who have had similar experiences. Direct work on delusions and voices might be done at this stage.
- To end therapy by building commitment to long term changes in areas such as relationships, interests and work.

The movement is essentially one from problem to solution and oscillates between the two as needed. In planning therapy one needs to consider the severity and number of problematic areas. Some clients come with a specific focus, and only require a small number of sessions: others with many difficulties may require extended work, or sometimes intermittent therapy, that is, work over years but with many gaps.

For work with depression (in the context of psychosis or not) it might be appropriate that solution-orientated questions focus not only on the goals clients suggest, but also on typical features of depression such as rumination, lack of activities, and self care (For example, you said that sometimes you talk to others, how do you manage that?). As emphasised earlier, this should be a dialogue and led by what is relevant to the client. The specific details of what might be done for different clients and other presenting difficulties cannot be specified here (see the history section for examples).

Major Treatment Techniques

Goals and Scaling Question

After sufficient and appropriate assessment of difficulties, ranging from just a simple problem description in some cases to a complex narrative for others, it is crucial to explore the client's goals with regard to the specific problems: that is, those things the client wants to achieve by doing therapy. A particular emphasis is to ask clients how they will know what the completed goal will look like and how they will know the first steps have begun. While some clients arrive with clear ideas, many need assistance in constructing pictures of these goals.

A useful technique taken from de Shazer is the scaling question: where 10 equals your goal achieved, the number one the worst things have ever been, where are you now? Given a number four, what will take you to a five or even less? This can be a very useful question to ask at each session as a way of mapping progress.

Exceptions, Initiatives, Resources

Exception questions focus on times the problem is less or when the problem is not occurring: are there times when you are not afraid of the voices? What is different at such times? What do you do when you manage not to give in to its demands? Such questions can be used near the beginning of therapy and returned to as required at any stage.

If a client does something new or differently between sessions, one can ask: did this surprise you? Was this a welcome development? How did you prepare for this step? What would help you to take such a step again? What effects did this action have on other areas of your life? How did others react?

The tone of exploration should be one of curiosity, not one of trying to be persuasive. Exploration can lead to many possible routes: as the client comes to better articulate how these actions were achieved it might be decided to do more of these. If the exception was long ago, the decision might be to start this behaviour again. However, it should not be assumed that taking what seems a positive step is 'obvious': this is something the client must decide.

Future Focused Questions

The client is asked to construct a picture of life without the problem and, given that this has occurred, how the client will 'know' the problem is past. Usually this leads to a series of questions: can you describe life without these problems? What will first tell you the problem is over? How long does this need to happen before you are confident the problem is over? What will you be doing differently? Who will be the first to notice? What will they notice? Is any of this happening now in your life? Has this happened at all in the past? What would I see if watching this on a video?

For some clients it can be useful to reintroduce some aspect of the problem and then ask how this will be dealt with in the future better life: so, if someone has described life without drugs, one could ask: but, given the problem is over, how would you handle the urge to take cocaine if it returned one day? What would you do differently in this better life you want, how would you cope?

Metaphor and Images,

In exploration of difficulties or goals it is useful to consider both naturally occurring images and metaphors, or to explicitly ask the client to think of examples of these. For the latter, the clients can be given questions to consider over the week such as 'I feel like ... in a difficult situation' or 'others seem like ... when things are difficult'. Most clients very quickly grasp what a metaphor is when given examples from songs. The information from the metaphors can be used in a variety of ways, for example, to understand aspects of the problem not well expressed in literal terms, to give a 'feel' of the problem for the client. Metaphors are not just vivid ways of communicating, but sometimes the very way clients experience their suffering in that during the most painful moments it is a malign metaphor that comes to dominate a person's introspection and feelings, for example 'I'm a freak' (Rhodes and Jakes, 2004).

Identities

White has outlined how one might help a person construct a benign narrative of self as opposed to a narrative in which the person sees him- or herself as being utterly negative. A distinct feature of White's approach is to move back and forth between levels of description, from concrete episodes to ideas or values, purposes, intentions. Times when the problem doesn't occur are called 'unique outcomes' by White (2007). His approach is distinctive in that he suggests the following steps:

- Try to give the experience a name or phrase that makes idiosyncratic sense to the person. On being asked how to characterise an occasion when a client had been able to say no to someone, this might be named 'the new independent me'.
- Next, one asks about the effects of this action: a client might report feeling good and experiencing no negative consequences.
- The above effects are evaluated: How did you feel about this? Is this change welcome?
- Finally, how does the client 'justify' this evaluation? For example, a client might say 'I value being independent and want to move in that direction.'

Asking a client to explore a reaction like this often induces a client to think about their personal value system and its relevance; for some clients this seems to help tap into former motivations, or motivations not put into words. By such questions White builds connections across 'episodes', often involving the whole life span, to help the person articulate a picture of a preferred life and identity.

One client was utterly negative about his past and future and self, yet I noticed his anger and walking away from a part-time job when he had been asked to cheat. He was asked to name the action taken, he thought and said: 'being honest'. One can then explore why this is important: Are there other examples which contribute to this sense of honesty? Is this something you want to uphold in spite of all the negatives in your life? How have you kept this up? Who did you learn this from?

Life Narrative Overview

For some clients there are strong indicators that taking an 'overview' of the person's life can be beneficial: often the purpose is to 'make sense' of some trauma; sometimes it is to identify a lost or hidden story of resistance. There are in fact many approaches to a broad life narration. Mahoney (1991, 2003), Guidano (1991), Gonçalves, (1994), Roberts (1999) and others have all illustrated interesting and different ways of exploring and structuring narratives.

The approach for clients with psychosis (Rhodes and Jakes, 2009) took specific ideas from Neuner and colleagues (2002), who had worked with refugees suffering from the effects of multiple traumas. We observed that many psychotic clients had also suffered many traumas, and hence were more like refugees than persons who have suffered one-off traumas. Within a limited timeframe of 4–8 weeks (this being after and before other therapeutic work), clients were asked to describe major difficult life events. Neuner et al. (2002) suggests writing these out and in the following session presenting this to the client. The method can be varied by presenting a letter written toward the end of the whole phase of work, and then spending time discussing the narration. In addition to this, and after finishing the investigation of the worst memories, we deliberately looked at periods of success or initiatives or at least periods of calm, here borrowing from the approach of White and Epston (1990).

Life narration can be a piece of work in itself, particularly where the client wants to make sense of a breakdown; however, details from this exploration can also be used in other types of work with the client, such as preferred identity construction as outlined earlier.

Another important use of life narrative can be to examine the indirect and sometimes direct effects of the sociological and historical context of the person, that is, effects that might emerge due to a family or individual being different from those around due to race, class, religion, sexuality and so on. Extended narrative work can also be the occasion for work concerned with a person's direction in life and evaluation of meaning and purpose. These concerns can often arise after trauma, and for those clients with long-term psychosis who often find it difficult to pursue conventional aims such as work and relationships.

Key Techniques from CBT

Any standard CBT technique could in principle be used in NCBT, but some are more compatible, particularly if they are constructional. Padesky's (1994) approach has an emphasis on helping the client to build a positive picture of self and others through questions such as 'I prefer that I am ...' and 'I prefer others to be ...' This approach was found to work well with many psychotic patients (Rhodes and Jakes, 2009). Compassion-based approaches (Gilbert, 2005) are also highly compatible.

After one life review, I was able to characterise with a client how she was often hard on herself, and wondered if this derived from the man who had been violent and abusive to her (we had discussed this topic as part of the life narrative): this frame allowed a way of looking at specific thoughts and actions that occurred over the week, and to consider alternatives. In one subsequent session, after a discussion of taking an initiative of taking her daughter to visit a new school, the client mentioned that on one occasion that week she had forgotten her watch, and instead of attacking herself as usual, she had just repeated to herself 'I forgot the watch, I forgot the watch ...'. We wondered how she could continue to use this self-invented technique in the coming week to keep away the self-attack monologue. We also spend time considering what this initiative could be named (she settled for 'not telling myself off'). This is an example of how CBT-type ideas can be applied and made concrete using solution-orientated questions.

Overcoming Obstacles

A theory of overcoming obstacles requires general ideas as well as ideas on how to work with specific difficult conditions such as chronic depression. A general approach to obstacles is in fact one of the very key features of NCBT in that the fundamental attitude of the therapist to the client is, as stated earlier, one of being willing to learn (Bliss and Bray, 2009) Therefore, if one assumes that one can craft an intervention based on this learning, one should make as few 'impositions' of any kind on the client as possible. It is not essential or demanded in NCBT that a client accept any diagnosis, any particular view on the problem, and there is not even the requirement to talk about a problem. One might do such activities if the client wants these or sees the necessity of doing these (the vast majority of clients do in fact want to describe their difficulties for at least a limited time, and this is the usual way of proceeding, but in some circumstances even problem talk can be avoided and useful therapeutic work can take place).

For avoiding obstacles one needs to carefully note the client's motivation for therapy, something discussed by de Shazer (1988). Many obstacles and blocks are due to the therapist and client straying from a close fit in this area. When obstacles do occur, one needs to ask question such as:

- Is there a misunderstanding concerning the problem and how to get to a goal?
- What are the client's ideas concerning change?
- Is the therapist too far 'ahead' of the client in any area? For example, too enthusiastic about a new initiative or exception?
- Has the therapist really misunderstood the nature of the problem? Are certain aspects of it more important than so far realised? Can it be described in new and more useful ways? Has the client omitted to mention essential aspects?

Given this general approach of revisiting the client's motivations and constructions, then ideas for overcoming obstacles can also be taken from CBT, in particular those developed for specific areas. Butler et al. (2008) have listed common difficulties and obstacles in challenging anxiety disorders; Moore and Garland (2003) have considered the role of severe hopelessness in persistent depression. Some clients with extreme difficulties appear disengaged or seem reluctant to communicate at all. In such cases, it is useful to think of the wider system surrounding the person and to consider who the client really is; if appropriate, it can be more useful to see the 'referrer' as the client and to work in a solution-orientated consultative fashion (Rhodes, 2000; Rhodes and Ajmal, 1995).

Case Example: James – Rebuilding Life After a Breakdown

Conceptualisation

James had been diagnosed with paranoid schizophrenia when beginning his first employment: he had broken down with overwhelming delusional ideas of persecution, voices and other psychotic features such as ideas of reference. When I met him at age 23 he stated that he had a range of difficulties including anger, no motivation to do activities, no work and no partner, feeling depressed and was engaging in self-harm several times a week. This was a difficult and chaotic presentation. From the beginning he was reluctant to discuss any events in the past, near or distant, and particularly events concerning his parents. The clinical notes told me of a dramatic breakdown at work, serious problems in his childhood, plus a recent bereavement. At this stage, he also seemed disinclined to discuss any symptoms, stating that the voices were not relevant anymore and barely audible. In the second meeting, I found out that his self-harming was done in moments of low mood in the evenings. I enquired about any constructive activities he was doing and it was striking that he had done many interesting hobbies over his life, though he had stopped all of these. The issue of anger related to many topics: the relationship to his family, what had happened at work, and attitudes of others toward him in social situations.

Therapeutic Relationship

A crucial point in the therapeutic relation occurred a few sessions in; he told me how his family was controlling him, and the psychiatric system was telling him what to do. I asked directly about my role and did he think I was telling him what to do? He said my approach was OK, not a problem, and it was left at that. (This was a deliberate decision on my part. Sometimes it is better to leave a topic unresolved. It seemed quite possible that he was in two minds about my potential to be controlling or not.) I noted these attitudes and always checked that all interventions were tentative, things to try if he liked. I explored with him what he could do to get the system 'off his back' (this idea is taken from de Shazer). He clearly enjoyed this

(Continued)

(Continued)

irreverent idea. A few sessions later we also discussed the positives and negatives of medication, all the while emphasising his choice.

Strategy

Given the multitude of problems and a certain 'confusion' in words and descriptions of 'what is happening', I thought a NCBT approach would be appropriate with an emphasis on maintaining a good working relationship, moving to difficulties only as they emerged, to not challenging certain occasional strange statements, and to go with James's motivation for 'doing' and getting back his life. A decision was made to shorten the assessment and avoid discussing an explicit 'formulation' with James in the early stage if at all (since to do so would have risked breaking the emerging rapport). Instead, emphasis was placed on potential ways forward and exceptions in his immediate context. Explanatory simple formulations were discussed much later, but tended to be simple ones focussing on stress and vulnerability, for example discussing how excess use of street drugs might have affected him. This can be seen as an attempt at normalisation (Kingdon and Turkington, 2004).

Techniques

The first phase of work used the techniques of asking what is working now in his life, to imagine a good future, and to use a scaling question. The future-focused question extended over two sessions: he described doing many activities such as working, exercise, hobbies, but an emphasis was on an improved relationship with his family. What would we see on a 'video'? He suggested more talk, hugs and open affection. Had any of this happened in his life? Once after the breakdown when leaving the hospital, and recently he had walked away from an argument. On the scaling question he scored a 6. When we looked at initiatives he undertook and what values they implied, he emphasised being honest and having 'self-pride'.

Over two years of intermittent therapy (that is, about 31 sessions with gaps of several months) new problems emerged at different periods. In the eleventh session he became preoccupied by a complex delusional idea: there had been transmitted a negative TV programme about him whilst at his work, though he had not seen it. I did not know if this had always been an active problem for him and not mentioned, or had re-emerged just recently.

Given his clear interest in discussing this, I first explored the positives and negatives of continuing to believe as opposed to discovering these ideas to be true or otherwise (Rhodes and Jakes, 2009). To discover the ideas to be false was a better option but 'scary', whilst no advantages were found for continuing to believe them. Over two or three sessions, we simply thought together about the 'evidence' and explored why his father had said it was not true. What did not fit the idea of TV programme about him in his view? The therapeutic stance was essentially non-committal, not trying to prove any idea true or false. The percentage conviction dropped from 98 per cent to 43 per cent to where he said he wasn't thinking about it, and conviction was just 5 per cent. The therapy here used a version of challenging meaning, but with a very explicit solution-orientated stance of allowing James to discover and invent his own doubts (an approach well described in de Shazer (1988) for work with delusions). It is very easy to slip into an everyday style of 'proving' a point. Even if 'obvious' to the therapist, it is best to make a conscious choice of stepping back, waiting, just being curious, and allowing discoveries to be made by the client within their own meaning system.

After a year James was much less depressed and anxious: residual symptoms were moderate, and he was doing a lot of activities. At this time I started a group for coping with emotions using a selection of specific skills as described by Berking et al. (2008), but modified for this client group. Of these skills James chose to frequently practice deep breathing and muscle relaxation, and to take up the attitudes of resilience (accepting the emotion is occurring and stating that one can survive) and compassion. These were very useful when he was almost overwhelmed by anxiety just before starting a work placement. I was also able to use compassion at this time in that he was vehemently insulting himself ('waste of space' being a typical insult): we explored how this was simply destructive, and how a kinder attitude could help him to do more things.

Obstacles

The four greatest obstacles in this case were: 1) a shifting unstable presentation of diverse difficulties and symptoms; 2) a powerful sense of hopelessness at some points; 3) James's feelings that others were controlling him; 4) the real lack of resources in the community for helping with recovery activities, for example, supported work placements. These obstacles were approached with a flexible attitude as to which problems to focus on; by early pursuit of small steps; by asking others to help with finding education or work; and careful attention to not 'impose' ideas or practice. It was important to maintain James's autonomy throughout while adopting an attitude of 'learning' from the client. This included searching deeply into James's experiences for ways of moving forward, while exploring techniques from CBT that James could chose to use or not.

Outcome

James filled in a questionnaire several times examining levels of anxiety and depression: the scores suggested moving out of clinical levels of depression and anxiety by the sixteenth session and remaining so until the end of therapy. Likewise, there was no recurrence of the delusional preoccupations. He argued less with his family and reported neither drugs nor alcohol use, something he had decided for himself. He engaged in a work-related course. His difficulties were not over and his condition certainly seemed to vary with life activities and events, yet we had made, I believe, significant steps.

Research Status of NCBT

There is some early stage research supporting NCBT for psychosis. In Jakes et al. (1999), our evidence suggested that the solution-orientated phase could have a significant impact on a range of mainly social and emotional difficulties. In Rhodes and Jakes (2002) we presented a single case using time series data suggesting that a solution-focused phase could be used for a crisis involving delusions; here conventional CBT could not have been used, at least for the first few months, given the client's desperate and rejecting attitudes and behaviours. In Jakes and Rhodes (2003), five single cases demonstrated that NCBT had specific effects upon delusions: that is, for some clients the most change in their delusions occurred in the explicit phase of discussing solutions, whilst for others the change tended to occur later when the delusion was discussed directly. Eakes et al. (1997) demonstrated positive effects using SFT for families of patients with psychosis.

There is, of course, separate evidence for CBT and for SFNT therapies in general (Gingerich and Eisengart, 2000 discuss NSFT): we are not making the claim that NCBT would be superior to basic CBT in randomised trials, rather, the evidence above suggests that NCBT offers a flexible way of adapting work to unique individuals in unique situations.

Concluding Comments

The ideas and techniques of NCBT make a very useful addition to and transformation of basic CBT. It possesses new methods to use in early stage work, before in fact most CBT techniques could be used; it provides many ideas which could be used in creative conjunction with CBT; it opens up the possibility of including systemic thinking and practices where appropriate; and it provides an articulation of a way of doing client-centred therapy at all stages with an emphasis on client creativity.

Suggested Further Reading

Lipchik, E. (2002) *Beyond Technique in Solution Focused Therapy.* New York: Guilford Press.

Mahoney, M.J. (2003) *Constructive Psychotherapy: A Practical Guide.* New York: Guilford Press.

Rhodes, J.E. and Jakes, S. (2002) 'Using solution focused therapy during a psychotic crisis: A case study', *Clinical Psychology and Psychotherapy*, 9: 139–148.

Rhodes, J.E. and Jakes, S. (2009) *Narrative CBT for Psychosis.* London: Routledge.

White, M. (2007) *Maps of Narrative Practice.* New York: Norton.

References

Beck, A.T. (1995) 'Beyond belief: A theory of modes, personality and psychopatholgy', in P.M. Salvoskis (Ed.), *Frontiers of Cognitive Therapy.* New York: Guilford.

Beck, A.T., Rush, A.J., Shaw, B.F. and Emery, G. (1979) *Cognitive Therapy of Depression*. Chichester: Wiley.

Berking, M., Wupperman,P., Reichardt, A., Pejic, T., Dippel, A. and Znoj, H. (2008) 'Emotion-regulation skills as a treatment target in psychotherapy', *Behaviour Research and Therapy*, 46: 1230–1237.

Bhaskar, R. (1989) *Reclaiming Reality*. London: Verso.

Bliss, E.V. and Bray, D. (2009) 'The smallest solution focused particles: Towards a minimalist definition of when therapy is solution focused', *Journal of Systemic Therpies*, 28: 62–74.

Brewin, C.R. (2006) 'Understanding cognitive behaviour therapy: A retrieval competition account', *Behaviour Research and Therapy*, 44(6): 765–784.

Brewin, C.R. and Power, M.J. (1999) 'Integrating psychological therapies: Processes of meaning transformation', *British Journal of Medical Psychology*, 72: 143–157.

Bruner, J. (1986) *Actual Minds, Possible Worlds*. Cambridge: Harvard University Press.

Butler, G., Fennell, M. and Hackmann, A. (2008) *Cognitive Behavioural Therapy for Anxiety Disorders*. New York: Guilford.

de Shazer, S. (1985) *Keys to Solution in Brief Therapy*. New York: Norton.

de Shazer, S. (1988) *Clues: Investigating Solutions in Brief Therapy*. New York: Norton.

Eakes, G., Walsh, S., Markowski, M., Cain, H. and Swanson, M. (1997) 'Family centred brief solution-focused therapy with chronic schizophrenia: A pilot study', *Journal o f Family Therapy*, 19: 145–158.

Fauconnier, G. and Turner, M. (2002) *The Way We Think: Conceptual Blending and the Mind's Hidden Complexities*. New York: Basic Books.

Gilbert, P. (Ed.) (2005) *Compassion: Conceptualisation, Research and Use in Psychotherapy*. Hove: Routledge.

Gingerich, W.J. and Eisengart, S. (2000) 'Solution-focused brief therapy: A review of the outcome research', *Family Process*, 39: 477–498.

Goldie, P. (2000) *The Emotions: A Philosophical Exploration*. Oxford: Oxford University Press.

Gonçalves, O.F. (1994) 'Cognitve narrative psychotherapy: The hermeneutic construction of alternative meanings', *Journal of Cognitive Psychotherapy: An International Quarterly*, 8(2): 105–123.

Greenberg, L.S. (2002) *Emotion-Focused Therapy*. Washington: APA.

Griffin, M. (2003) 'Narrative Behaviour Therapy?', *Australian and New Zealand Journal of Family Therapy*, 24(1): 33–37.

Guidano, V.F. (1991) *The Self in Process*. New York: Guilford Press.

Guidano,V.F. and Liotti, G. (1983) *Cognitive Processes and Emotional Disorders*. New York: Guilford Press.

Guterman, T. and Rudes, J. (2005) 'A solution-focused approach to rational-emotive behaviour therapy: Toward a theoretical integration', *Journal of Rational-Emotive and Cognitive-Behaviour Therapy*, 23(3): 223–244.

Hallam, R.S. and O'Connor, K.P. (2002) 'A dialogical approach to obsessions', *Psychology and Psychotherapy: Theory, Research and Practice*, 75: 333–348.

Harper, D. and Spellman, D. (2006) 'Social constructionist formulation', in L. Johnstone and R. Dallos (Eds), *Formulation in Psychology and Psychotherapy*. Hove: Routledge.

Jakes, S. and Rhodes, J. (2003) 'The effect of different components of psychological therapy on people with delusions: Five experimental single case', *Clinical Psychology and Psychotherapy*, 10: 302–315.

Jakes, S., Rhodes, J. and Turner, T. (1999) 'Effectiveness of cognitive therapy for delusions in routine practice', *British Journal of Psychiatry*, 175: 331–335.

Kelly, G. A. (1955) *The Psychology of Personal Constructs, Vol. 1 and 2*. New York: Norton.

Kingdon, D.G. and Turkington, D. (2004) *Cognitive Therapy of Schizophrenia*. Guildford Press.

Lakoff, G. (1987) *Women, Fire and Dangerous Thing:. What Categories Reveal about the Mind*. Chigaco, IL: University of Chicago Press.

Lakoff, G. and Johnson, M. (1980) *Metaphors We Live By*. Chicago, IL: University of Chicago Press.

Lipchik, E. (2002) *Beyond Technique in Solution Focused Therapy*. New York: Guilford Press.

MacIntyre, A. (1981) *After Virtue: A Study in Moral Theory*. London: Duckworth.

MacLeod, A.K. and Moore, R. (2000) 'Positive thinking revisited: Positive cognitions, well-being and mental health', *Clinical Psychology and Psychotherapy*, 7: 1–10.

Mahoney, M.J. (1991) *Human Change Processes*. New York: Basic Books.

Mahoney, M.J. (2003) *Constructive Psychotherapy: A Practical Guide*. New York: Guilford Press.

Meichenbaum, D. (1993) 'Changing conceptions of cognitive behaviour modification: Retrospect and prospect', *Journal of Consulting and Clinical Psychology*, 61(2): 202–204.

Moore, R. and Garland, A. (2003) *Cognitive Therapy for Chronic and Persistent Depression*. Chichester: Wiley.

Nagel, T. (1979) *Mortal Questions*. Cambridge: Cambridge University Press.

Neuner, F., Schauer, M., Roth, W.T. and Elbert, T. (2002) 'A narrative exposure treatment as intervention in a refugee camp: A case report', *Behavioural and Cognitive Psychotherapy*, 30: 205–209.

O'Connor, K., Koszegi, N., Aardema, F., van Niekerk, J. and Taillon, A. (2009) 'An inference-based approach to treating obsessive-compulsive disorders', *Cognitive and Behavioural Practice*, 16: 420–429.

Padesky, C.A. (1994) 'Schema change processes in cognitive therapy', *Clinical Psychology and Psychotherapy*, 1(5): 267–278.

Pain, M., Chadwick, P. and Abba, N. (2008) 'Clients' experience of case formulation in cognitive behaviour therapy for psychosis', *British Journal of Clinical Psychology*, 47(2): 127–134.

Pearson, M., Brewin, C.R., Rhodes, J. and McCarron, G. (2008) 'Frequency and nature of rumination in chronic depression', *Cognitive Behavior Therapy*, 37(3):160–168.

Postma, K. and Rao, N. (2006) 'Using solution-focused questioning to facilitate the process of change in cognitive behavioural therapy for food neophobia in adults', *Behavioural and Cognitive Psychotherapy*, 34(3): 371–375.

Ramsay, J.R. (1998) 'Postmodern cognitive therapy: Cognitions, narratives and personal meaning-making', *Journal of Cognitive Psychotherapy: An International Quarterly*, 12(1): 39–55.

Rhodes, J. (2000) 'Solution-focused consultation in a residential setting', *Clinical Psychology Forum*, 141: 29–33.

Rhodes, J. and Ajmal, Y. (1995) *Solution Focused Thinking in Schools*. London: BT Press.

Rhodes, J. and Gipps, R. (2008) 'Delusions, certainty and the background', *Philosophy, Psychiatry and Psychology*, 15(4): 295–310.

Rhodes, J.E. and Jakes, S. (2002) 'Using solution focused therapy during a psychotic crisis: A case study', *Clinical Psychology and Psychotherapy*, 9: 139–148.

Rhodes, J. E. and Jakes, S. (2004) 'The contribution of metaphor and metonymy to delusions', *Psychology and Psychotherapy: Theory, Research and Practice*, 73: 211–225.

Rhodes, J. and Jakes, S. (2009) *Narrative CBT for Psychosis*. Hove: Routledge.

Roberts, G. (1999) 'Healing stories', in G. Roberts and J. Holmes (Eds), *Narrative in Psychiatry and Psychotherapy*. Oxford: Oxford University Press.

Russell, R.L. (1991) 'Narrative in views of humanity, science and action: Lessons for cognitive therapy', *Journal of Cognitive Psychotherapy: International Quaterly*, 5(4): 241–256.

Sarbin, T. (1986) 'The narrative as a root metaphor for psychology', in T.R. Sarbin (Ed.), *Narrative Psychology: The Storied Nature of Human Conduct*. New York: Praeger.

Searle, J.R. (1992) *The Rediscovery of the Mind*. Cambridge: MIT Press.

Talvitie, V. and Tiitinen, H. (2006) 'From the repression of contents to the rules of the (narrative) self: A present-day cognitive view of the "Freudian phenomenon" of repressed contents', *Psychology and Psychotherapy: Theory, Research and Practice*, 79, 164–181.

Teasdale, J.D. (1997) 'The transformation of meaning: The interacting cognitive subsystems approach', in M. Power and C. Brewin (Eds), *The Transformation of Meaning in Psychological Therapies*. Chichester: Wiley.

Turner, M. (1996) *The Literary Mind: The Origins of Thought and Language*. New York: Oxford University Press.

White, M. (2007) *Maps of Narrative Practice*. New York: Norton.

White, M. and Epston, D. (1990) *Narrative Means to Therapeutic Ends*. New York: Norton.

ELEVEN Behavioural Activation

JOE CURRAN, DAVID EKERS, DEAN MCMILLAN AND
SIMON HOUGHTON

Historical Development of Behavioural Activation

Behavioural activation (BA) is treatment for depression and has a long history growing from the writings of Skinner (Skinner, 1953) focused upon the role of the environment and understanding peoples responses to it. Early behavioural theories of depression, such as those of Ferster (1973) and Lewinsohn (1974) took the basic principle of operant conditioning, suggesting the frequency of a behaviour is determined by its consequences, and applied it to our understanding of depression. These models pointed to negative reinforcement of avoidance behaviours and low rates of response-contingent positive reinforcement and used them to explain how people become and remain depressed (outlined later in this chapter). Interventions derived from these models were focused upon increasing access to sources of positive reinforcement. To do this they monitored the links between behaviour and mood and used activity scheduling and a number of additional behavioural techniques (such as social skills training and problem solving) to coach people to modify their relationship with their environment. This increased contact with potentially 'anti-depressant' experiences and was often focused upon 'pleasant events' (MacPhillamy and Lewinsohn, 1982). Initial evaluations of these reasonably straightforward approaches showed encouraging results in early trials (Brown and Lewinsohn, 1984) .

Despite these promising findings, purely behavioural treatments soon lost favour. The emergence of cognitive approaches to depression, most notably in the form of Beck's cognitive therapy treatment (CT) (Beck et al., 1979), soon came to eclipse purely behavioural approaches. This dominance occurred in the absence of compelling evidence of the superiority of cognitive-based treatments over BA. For example, Zeiss et al. (1979) found no significant differences between cognitive and behavioural techniques as treatment strategies for depression. Although there were some exceptions (e.g. Shaw 1977), there was far from definitive evidence of the superiority of cognitive treatments over purely behavioural approaches. The rise of cognitive approaches led to diminished interest in behavioural models, which were no longer seen as adequate explanations of human behaviour and functioning. This shift in focus to the central importance of thinking became the main psychological approach to understanding and treating depression. Cognitive behaviour therapy (CBT) or cognitive therapy (CT) thus became the focus of research agendas and was considered the first-line psychological treatment for depression. Cognitive treatments still retained behavioural strategies such as self-monitoring and activity scheduling in their treatment packages (Beck et al., 1979), used as experiments to loosen assumptions regarding control of mood and thus the behavioural theory was lost. Throughout the 1980s and early 1990s there could be said to have existed clinical hegemony where CBTs dominance was maintained, and the promise of a simple and effective behavioural intervention for depression was largely forgotten.

The resurgence of interest in purely behavioural approaches came with the seminal trial of Jacobson et al. (1996). Jacobson, while working on an earlier trial involving CT, had noticed that much of the change in this intervention occurred early on in treatment when straightforward behavioural treatment strategies, such as activity scheduling, were used (Jacobson and Gortner, 2000). While cognitive theory suggested that cognitive techniques aimed at modifying underlying cognitive structures were responsible for the effects of CT, this observation indicated a possible alternative explanation: improvements in depression that occur in CT may be a result of basic behavioural interventions which bring back contact with positive reinforcers in the person's environment. The trial of Jacobson et al. (1996) used a component analysis design in which the full form of CT, including behavioural techniques, thought challenging and schema work, was compared with an intervention consisting of behavioural technique and thought challenging but not schema work, and BA alone. The main finding of the study – a finding that caused considerable controversy (Jacobson and Gortner, 2000) – was that there were no significant differences in outcome between the three treatments. This finding triggered a renewed interested in purely behavioural approaches, particularly because they offered the possibility of providing a simple and parsimonious treatment relative to other psychological interventions (Jacobson and Gortner, 2000). Interest in this finding has grown, particularly following replication and extension of the initial Jacobson et al. trial (Dimidjian et al., 2006), as well as the independent development of other behavioural approaches for depression, notably BA treatment for depression (BATD) (Lejuez et al., 2001). More recently there have been a number of meta-analyses supporting the efficacy of behavioural approaches to depression and this renewed interest (Cuijpers et al., 2007; Ekers et al., 2008; Mazzucchelli et al., 2009).

Much of the research and development of behavioural treatments for depression have come from the USA. The UK had taken behavioural theories and developed their use in anxiety disorders over a number of years (Marks, 2000); however, this development did not extend to depression, where CT remained the focus of clinical and research activity. More recently with the interest in single-strand treatments and stepped care increasing, BA has become increasingly used in the UK and is now recognised as an effective and valuable treatment of depression (National Institute of Clinical Excellence, 2009).

Theoretical Underpinnings of BA

Major Theoretical Concepts

BA takes a functional analytic perspective in formulating the development and maintenance of depression (Martell et al., 2001). This means that the function of the person's presenting behaviour is of interest rather than what it looks like, or the form it takes. Many behaviours that are displayed when a person becomes depressed appear logical or understandable, serving a helpful function in the context of the whole of the person's life and experience at that time. When conceptualising the maintenance of depression within a BA framework, five particular environmental contingencies are important to observe:

1   Increased rates of negative reinforcement of avoidant behaviour.
2   Reduced positive reinforcement of non-depressed behaviour.
3   Increased positive reinforcement of depressed behaviour.
4   A punishing/aversive environment.
5   Response cost (see Table 11.1).

Function Over Form

An important consideration in BA, as in all behavioural approaches, is that of 'function over form': in other words, the consequences that reliably follow specific behaviour(s) are more important than how they appear (Martell et al., 2001). This is because a key aspect of behavioural theory, operant conditioning, asserts that these consequences will determine the probability of the behaviour occurring again. Therefore, if we can understand what maintains behaviour we are able to help a person arrange an environment that will increase the frequency of some behaviours, or decrease the frequency of others. In everyday language we might consider function as the purpose of a behaviour or the reason the person does something, although it is more technically correct to speak of consequences that have reliably followed the behaviour in the past that have maintained it or have increased the probability of it occurring again.

Applying this to the depressed behaviours of crying, withdrawal, avoidance, complaining, we could note their presence and seek to reduce them. However, from a behaviour analytic point of view, following Ferster (1973),

Table 11.1   Definition of behavioural concepts used in BA

Process	Consequence of behaviour	Example
Positive reinforcement	Something's added to the person's environment or experience that increases the likelihood of it reoccurring.	Rewards Praise Money Medals Achievement
Negative reinforcement	Something's removed from the person's environment or experience that increases the likelihood of it reoccurring.	Removal of anxiety, discomfort Escape from demands Reduction of pressure
Punishment	Something's added to the person's environment or experience that reduces the likelihood of it reoccurring.	Pain Noise Additional of any unpleasant experience
Response cost	Something's removed from the person's environment or experience that reduces the likelihood of it reoccurring.	Fines 'Time-out' procedures The naughty step

reducing the frequency of behaviour requires us to attend to its function, that is, the consequences that are maintaining it. On some occasions these behaviours will be functioning as avoidance, as they may lead to the reduction or termination of difficult feelings or situations (such as stopping a difficult task). This avoidance also functions to reduce opportunities to engage in behaviour that will be positively reinforced. The awareness of these processes can then help the BA therapist and client plan alternative behaviours based on function, rather than just 'do something different'. It is important to note that not all instances of the depressed behaviours described above, and others, mean that a person is avoiding something, only that our analysis allows for us to understand the consequences for each individual on each occasion.

What is important here is that a particular type of behaviour can take several forms (such as the range of behaviour exhibited by a depressed person), and can have several functions (in terms of the contingencies described above), both of which will vary across individuals and, depending on the context of the behaviour, vary within individuals. This highlights the importance of individual functional analysis as an assessment tool, so that both client and clinician can get a detailed understanding of what the person is doing or not doing, and what the range of consequences are (internal and external) that account for this. These consequences are considered in more detail below, after we discuss another important aspect of BA, namely the role of thinking.

Thinking as behaviour

As thinking is something that a person does, it is viewed as behaviour. This reasonably straightforward point has sometimes been obscured by the misconceived idea that all behavioural approaches insist that only publicly observable behaviour can be studied and that all other responses ignored, despite this never being part of Skinner's approach (e.g. verbal behaviour). In the variety of behaviourism underpinning BA, thinking can be considered 'private behaviour' that is observable to the person doing it. This 'audience of one' means that it is possible to employ some of the methods of behavioural assessment and treatment with thinking as part of a comprehensive behavioural approach.

In BA, thoughts that may precede some actions are viewed as part of a sequence of behaviours that influence each other, and are not considered *causes* of behaviour (Hayes and Brownstein, 1986). When helping a person carry out a functional analysis of their own behaviour, we may notice that a specific thought, such as 'I'm a failure' when attempting to complete a task, is followed by a range of responses such as stopping the task, withdrawal, isolation and 'feeling sad'. Using our 'function over form' maxim, we can see that this thought, on this occasion, has functioned to cease ongoing behaviour, and it is this stopping, rather than the thought, that may be producing the 'feeling'. In this example, if this were noticed to be an established pattern across settings or contexts, the BA therapist would work towards helping the person change the function of the thought – that is, a trigger to stopping the activity – by carrying on even if the thought were present so that the task is completed (and therefore an important source of positive reinforcement is contacted see below). This can be contrasted with more content-oriented therapies that may seek to change the form of the thought; that is, changing 'I'm a failure' into something more balanced and helpful.

The thinking process targeted in BA is that of rumination, which whilst having some helpful functions (such as problem solving) can function to reduce engagement with a meaningful, rewarding life.

How Client Problems are Conceptualised

Increased Rates of Negative Reinforcement of Avoidant Behaviour
Much behaviour observed in patients with depression can be seen to function as attempts to reduce aversive experience. This may be either to directly eliminate discomfort or to prevent a current experience from becoming more uncomfortable. This process of negative reinforcement is most commonly observed as the function of avoidance behaviours. Withdrawal from work, social contact, family and friends will often be an understandable response to feeling low in mood, anxious or physically lethargic and are commonly learned responses to sources of discomfort throughout a person's life. When the person becomes depressed and experiences the wide range of physical, emotional and cognitive symptoms that typically identify depression, these avoidant responses can become more than a temporary coping strategy to a transient aversive experience, but rather they can become the primary method of responding to day-to-day

experiences. When this pattern of avoidance becomes the primary response to life experience, the reinforcement will likely become continuous and so the depressed person finds it increasingly difficult to reverse this pattern.

Reduced Positive Reinforcement of Non-Depressed Behaviour

A consequence of increased avoidance when depressed is that the person is likely to also reduce their contact with naturally occurring positive reinforcement from their environment. Withdrawal from contingencies of positive reinforcement will likely lead to increased symptoms of depression as the person gains less and less reward for their efforts in general life. Behaviour such as social contact or work may become more difficult and more anxiety provoking as a consequence of symptoms such as poor concentration or memory, and so they may lose their positively reinforcing quality. Aspects of life that may add quality to experience, such as wider family contact, relationships with a partner, children or parents, may lose their positively reinforcing nature, for example being shown less direct affection as a result of withdrawal. A reduced appetite may lead to less enjoyment of food, or difficulties concentrating may make previously enjoyed entertainments less satisfying.

Increased Positive Reinforcement of Depressed Behaviour

Together with the already described pattern of increased avoidance and a poorer experience of previously enjoyed activity, the person with depression will likely begin to receive positive reinforcement for depressed behaviour. Actions such as resting more, taking time off work and being less active in general often become more common. These behaviours can look like attempts to cope with difficult symptoms and may be explicitly encouraged by other people in the person's environment, or by the sense of benefit the person receives from these actions. These actions may be reinforced directly by friends and relatives, work colleagues or health professionals through encouraging the person to 'take it easy' or 'get some rest', or through simple sympathetic statements such as 'It doesn't matter about that' or 'Do it when you feel up to it'. This positive reinforcement may be continuous initially as the person struggles to cope, again making changes once well-established all the more difficult.

A Punishing or Aversive Environment

Often accompanying increased avoidance, reduced reward from previously reinforcing actions and the positive reinforcement of efforts to cope with symptoms, the person will experience their environment as more aversive or punishing than they did previously. The person's continued efforts to manage symptoms through the methods already described above may lead to environmental contingencies changing in function if not in how they appear. Work may become more difficult and attempts to cope may lead to the person's performance being adversely affected, which in turn may make work even more difficult. Similarly, where depressed behaviour was initially reinforced by friends and relatives, over time this contingency may change as the person does not quickly recover and their avoidance stops being viewed as understandable short-term strategy.

Response Cost

Once the depressed person has established a pattern of avoidance of discomfort as a primary method of coping with symptoms of depression they will likely experience efforts to reverse these behaviour patterns as more difficult than they remember them being in their past. These activities then can be said to have a cost in the sense that changed responses seem to have a greater cost than benefit and so efforts to change become aversive experiences in themselves. For example efforts to reverse physical inactivity by re-starting a previously well-practised exercise routine may lead to a greater effort being expended and the person feeling physically worse after the exercise than before. This process of efforts to change the response being punished may then lead to these new activities not being maintained.

Schedules of Reinforcement

Although there is little empirical work in the area of depression, it may be helpful to consider the patterns of reinforcement that are present in a person's life. Behaviour does not need to be followed by 'reward or punishment' every time that it occurs; patterns of reinforcement delivery that are associated with prolonged occurrence of behaviour are those in which reinforcement comes seemingly intermittently (a variable ratio schedule). Applied to depression, this means that any of the behaviours outlined above may be being maintained because they have worked at some times in the person's history, and/or are being reinforced intermittently by their current environment.

We can use the schedules of reinforcement in two ways in clinical work. First, when helping to plan activities in the early part of therapy with a person it may be helpful to attempt to devise a continuous schedule, so that each occurrence is followed by a consequence that will lead to it happening again (such as task completion, satisfaction, 'sense of achievement'). This schedule is particularly helpful at initiating behaviour, and is one of the reasons we grade activity or break tasks down into component parts, noting that 'success breeds success'. This is similar to the behavioural process of 'shaping' in which successive approximations of the target behaviour are reinforced. However, as schedules of reinforcement that are intermittently reinforced are the hardest to extinguish, there is an argument for intermittently reinforcing behaviour that has become established so that it is maintained in the absence of continuous reinforcement. Everyday life does not usually lead to the occurrence of each behaviour in

BA model

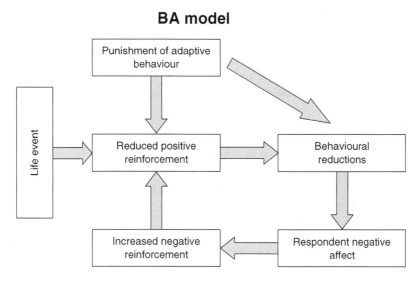

Figure 11.1 Mechanism of BA for depression (adapted from J. Kanter, see Manos et al., 2010)

a chosen area being followed by a reinforcing consequence (i.e. every work day isn't always full of achievement, praise, satisfaction and interpersonal harmony), therefore we aim to have balance in schedules and contingencies present.

Moving away from Internal Deficit Models of Depression
From the above it can be seen that a behavioural account of a person's depression is one that places the condition firmly within an interrupted relationship with their environment rather than due to faulty thinking, neurotransmitter problems or unconscious conflict. It is not due to something being 'wrong' inside but an understandable pattern emerging based upon events in one's world. Therefore treatment does not try to put something right inside to facilitate change but instead manipulates person–environment interactions to make things right over time. Simply put, we ask people not to 'wait to feel right to do things' but 'to do thing to feel right'.

Stable and Diverse Sources of Reinforcement
A final point to make when planning BA treatment (Kanter et al., 2009) is that sources of positive reinforcement in a person's life are most helpful if they are stable (the activity and reinforcing effects are repeatable) and diverse (what Kanter describes as 'not putting all of one's eggs into one basket': p. 35).

See Figure 11.1 one for a diagram of the behavioural model of depression.

Practical Applications

The Therapeutic Relationship

As in all cognitive behavioural therapies, developing a strong therapeutic relationship is vital in delivering effective behavioural activation. Within all models of behavioural activation the patient is being asked to give up well-practised and safe behaviours in favour of new behaviours with uncertain outcomes. It is crucial, then, that the therapist engenders trust in the patient very early in the treatment. Initial sessions promote this development of trust by the therapist using a range of interpersonal skills to demonstrate empathic understanding of the patient's current experience. The therapist offers a credible understanding of the patient's problem by developing an explanation for the development and continuation of the patient's symptoms in terms of a behavioural case formulation, and presenting a clear rationale for the treatment proposed. Throughout the course of behavioural activation the therapist will observe and identify behaviours within the session that may be examples of the patient's problem, and use their own behaviour (verbal and non-verbal) to try to decrease their frequency. Similarly, the therapist will attempt to identify desired changes in the patient's behaviour in session and reinforce these.

Treatment Strategies

In a recent review Kanter et al. (2010) identified several component techniques that have formed part of BA treatment packages since the 1970s. These consisted of activity monitoring, assessment of goals and values, activity scheduling, skills training, relaxation training, contingency management, procedures targeting verbal behaviour (i.e. cognition) and procedures targeting avoidance. Of note, the only components that were constant over the seven treatment manuals reviewed were activity monitoring and scheduling, raising some questions as to the 'active' components in BA. The similarity between behavioural activation approaches and activity scheduling that forms part of Beck et al.'s (1979) cognitive therapy shouldn't be overlooked here, as Beck's work largely drew from Peter Lewinsohn and colleagues approach, although framed it in cognitive terms, noted above. Of course, as will have already have been gathered, the theoretical rationales of behaviourally and cognitively oriented approaches for the use of activity monitoring and scheduling is markedly different.

Of the main approaches to the application of BA as described above that have a body of published data on their effectiveness in clinical settings, we now focus on two of those most recently developed, and describe a further one that combines several key behavioural activation procedures.

The first of these, known commonly as behavioural activation, was described as a stand-alone treatment by Martell et al. (2001). They focus on the functional aspects of depressive behaviour, and the interaction between the person and their environment over time. This model is primarily concerned with identifying environmental triggers to ineffective coping responses linked to the maintenance of depressive emotional states. As such, primary symptoms of depression such as lethargy or low mood are not the focus of BA. Instead, the client is directed to pay attention to their responses to these symptoms, their attempts to cope, as the target of change strategies. In this model, then, the identification of behavioural avoidance, and its function, is crucial and treatment is delivered in 24 sessions over 16 weeks (Dimidjian, 2006).

The second approach, behavioural activation treatment for depression (BATD), was developed by Lejuez and colleagues (2001; Lejuez et al., In press). BATD is based on an application behavioural matching theory to depression (Hernstein, 1970) suggesting that 'time and effort allocated to exhibiting depressed relative to non-depressed (or healthy) behaviour is directly proportional to the relative value of reinforcement obtained for depressed versus non-depressed behaviour' (Hopko et al., 2003: 704–705). This model predicts that increased contact with the reinforcement of healthy (non-depressed) behaviour, or reduced contact with the reinforcers of depressed behaviour, will have the effect of decreasing depressed behaviour and increasing non-depressed behaviour. The BATD model is described by Hopko and colleagues as being delivered in an 8–15 session protocol (Hopko et al., 2003).

An additional behavioural activation approach, as yet largely unevaluated as a complete treatment package, involves a synthesis of the components of BA approaches. This approach is termed 'stepped behavioural activation' (Kanter et al., 2009) and will be described in more detail in the next section.

Major Treatment Techniques

In this section we will consider the treatment techniques in each of the major approaches to BA discussed above.

Martell's BA

The first sessions of BA are used to develop a rapport with the patient, describe the treatment rationale, and help the patient begin to develop and increased awareness and understanding of their attempts to cope with symptoms of depression through their behaviour. The first strategy used in BA is activity and mood monitoring, where patients are asked to keep a daily diary of their main activity hour by hour, together with a brief description of their mood state at the time. The data recorded in the activity and mood monitoring is then used as the basis for initial case formulation, identifying general activity level, breadth or restriction of activity, range and intensity of emotion and whether there is any links between specific activities and mood. The next step in BA is applying a functional analytic view to avoidance behaviour. In BA, this is translated into an acronym, TRAP: Trigger, Response, Avoidance Pattern. Once the patient and therapist can observe these patterns of avoidance, the focus moves to helping the patient to re-engage in various healthy behaviours through the development of alternative coping strategies or TRAC: Trigger, Response, Alternative Coping. The general approach then in BA is to use scheduling and functional analysis to reduce avoidance and increase contact with positive reinforcement from a person's environment. As such the identification of specific goals and alternative coping strategies should be identified in collaboration with the client linking to their particular values. BA encourages the use of techniques such as grading activities, therapist modelling, mindfulness training, skills training, problem solving and mental rehearsal as methods of engaging with positive reinforcement and replace avoidance with 'healthy behaviours', the goal of therapy.

BATD

Similarly to BA, the initial sessions of BATD are used to help establish a strong therapeutic relationship between the patient and therapist, identifying the reinforcement patterns within the patient's environment, and describing the treatment rationale. BATD then employs a 'systematic activation approach' with the specific goal of increasing the frequency and subsequent reinforcement of healthy behaviour. As in BA, patients are asked to monitor their activities, but unlike BA they are not asked to describe mood states alongside their behaviour. Information from the activity monitoring is used to orient the patient to the quality and quantity of their activities, and to provide ideas for activities to focus on during treatment. The focus of BATD then moves on to identifying goals in major valued areas of life such as relationships, education, employment, hobbies and recreation, general health issues, spirituality and so on. After these values identification and goal-setting procedures, the patient is asked to select 15 activities and put them into a hierarchy based on each activity's difficulty in achieving. The patient is then directed to work progressively through the hierarchy, agreeing specific weekly goals with the therapist in relation to frequency and duration of each activity to be performed. Patients are also helped to identify weekly rewards designed to be an incentive for completing their goals each week.

'Stepped BA'

Kanter et al. (2009) begin with an assessment of the person's history and explanation of the treatment rationale in the first session. This is then supplemented with the commencement of activity monitoring and an assessment of the person's values, a process that has been integrated from acceptance and commitment therapy (ACT) (Hayes et al., 1999) that is also used by Hopko and colleagues. Sessions two to four continue activity monitoring and complete the values assessment, leading to the development of an activity hierarchy that the person is then encouraged working up to one step at a time. This 'simple activation' is focused on in the next sessions and the person's response monitored through functional assessment. If there is no response to simple activation, Kanter et al. (2009) suggest using the results of the functional assessment to determine the area for subsequent focus. The functional assessment, linking directly to functional analysis procedures, explores the antecedents – behaviour – and consequences of simple activation tasks. The first area for consideration is identifying whether problems exist in the antecedents to carrying out activation, such as forgetting to do the task. If this is noticed, then some stimulus control procedures can be used, such as setting up reminders in the person's environment (e.g. Post-It notes), or involving others. The second area to explore is whether the person has the skills necessary for them to carry out the activation tasks. If such repertoire deficits are identified, specific skills training exercises of activities can be developed to enable them to carry out the behaviours necessary to obtain reinforcement. Examples here would be the use of social skills related to interaction with others, such as making (or refusing) requests or helping the person acquire problem-solving skills. The third area in the functional assessment is separated into either public environmental consequences or private environmental consequences. The public environmental consequences of simple activation are those that are directly observable, such as escape or the reactions of others, and are therefore able to be manipulated. If these are identified as problematic, then Kanter and colleagues suggest using contingency management procedures to provide rewarding consequences for behaviours. This may involve the use of praise, enjoyable activity or access to highly rewarding activity (e.g. one's favourite foodstuffs) as a consequence of a simple activation task. Contracting with oneself or with a supportive partner of friend may be used here, and the use of mild aversive stimuli or response cost procedures could be used here. Although the use of these arbitrary reinforcers has a place in behavioural activation approaches (Kanter et al., 2009; Martell et al., 2001), it is preferable for behaviour to be maintained by natural reinforcers, that is, those that automatically follow in the person's own environment. The private environmental consequences of activation that could become problematic in simple activation refer to the occurrence and avoidance of feelings and thoughts that the person may experience as aversive (e.g. anxiety) or may reduce the probability of them engaging in the activation task again (thoughts such 'What's the point?'). If these consequences are identified, then what Kanter and colleagues term 'mindful valued activation' is recommended. Here, the person and therapist first explore avoidance patterns and their impact (in terms of negative reinforcement) before returning to the values assessment completed earlier so that the focus remains on what really matters for them, and identifying the values that are being worked towards as part of each activation task (e.g. contacting old friends may be difficult and anxiety provoking but is necessary if one is to live towards one's value of 'being a good friend'). It is worth noting here that when one is working towards what really matters, difficult feelings and thoughts might arise as part of the process. Then, rather than seek to change or modify their feelings or thoughts, the person is encouraged to activate in their presence. They are then introduced to various techniques and processes that are similar to mindfulness that encourage non-judgemental awareness of these difficult thoughts and feelings (see Baruch et al., In press, for two specific examples).

Overcoming Obstacles to Client Progress

In our view, the functional assessment procedure used by Kanter and colleagues is a valuable tool to use if obstacles to client progress need to be overcome. By returning to basic behavioural principles (i.e. the tree-term contingency), is it possible to develop an understanding of the difficulties that may arise in therapy. One obstacle frequently encountered is homework compliance. By viewing 'homework compliance' as operant behaviour, therapist and client can work together to explore the antecedents to not doing the agreed homework, the actual behaviour carried out, or the consequences. In doing this, clear environmental factors (including the person's own private environment) that would contribute to an increase in homework compliance can be identified and attributions of the causes of behaviour to internal causes (e.g. poor motivation) can be avoided.

A second point to make here is that there are many methods congruent with the practice of behavioural activation for helping clients overcome a lack of progress. If a therapist considers that a person would benefit from intervention that does not form part of the treatment manual with which they are working, it would be helpful to think functionally about the clinical work ('Is this working to increase the person's access increased rates of positive reinforcement?'), rather than an excessive focus on its form ('Am I doing it right?'). Here, any of the BA components identified earlier could reasonably be employed. Two specific areas of focus we now consider are the use of goal setting and values and delivery of the intervention in groups.

Goal setting and Values
In the models of BA described, all patients should have clearly defined goals. In Martell's BA these should be related to reversing patterns of avoidance, whereas BATD would suggest goals should be activities which bring about a sense of pleasure or accomplishment. Values differ from goals in that they are used to describe a direction for life rather than the end point or target. Using a tool such as the valued living questionnaire (Hayes et al., 1999) can help patients take a step back to examine broad areas of their life and help the patient select activities likely to provide positive reinforcement.

Groups
It has been suggested that there are additional benefits to patients from the social interaction inescapable within a group setting (Houghton et al., 2008).

Social isolation is not reinforced in a group setting, whereas use of interpersonal skills, relationship building, problem solving and helping others are generally positively reinforced by other group members. In group approaches based on both Martell's BA and BATD the occurrence of such behaviours within the group may help patients practice skills that they can then take into their wider lives.

Case Example: Beth

How the client's problems were conceptualised

Beth was a 30-year-old single professional woman referred for therapy by her GP. At initial assessment her main problem was depression in the form of persistent low mood, lack of energy, feelings of guilt, reduced activity and reduced interest or pleasure in her usual activities, poor appetite and low libido. Symptoms had been present for six months following a prolonged period of stress at work due to ever increasing performance targets and disruptions in her relationship with her partner. She had tried to deal with these issues herself, but reported that she had failed and now no longer 'bothered trying'. She had a marked reduction in activity and ability to enjoy things the way she used to do. She avoided social situations, including having her friends to visit as she didn't want them to see her this way. She had stopped previous hobbies of going to the gym, playing badminton, learning Spanish, and was on sick leave from work. She scored 40 on the Beck Depression Inventory-II, indicative of severe depression.

Assessment

As part of the assessment process, Beth kept a diary of her activity and mood over a two-week period. This consisted of a simple form that asked Beth to write down the main activity she had engaged in for each hour of the day along with a rating (between 0 and 10) of her mood during that time. An excerpt of Beth's activity diary is reproduced in Table 11.2. This process identified that Beth was engaging in a limited range of activities, particularly when compared to the range of things she was doing prior to experiencing depression. Her week chiefly consisted of 'sitting around the house', 'watching TV', 'worrying', 'looking for jobs on the internet', 'thinking about ringing my friends'. This was a marked change from her usual range of activities that included frequent socialising, holidays, sports and exercise, learning and work. The range of emotions identified was limited in that the predominant feelings reported were 'sad', 'low', 'upset' and 'frustrated'.

When planning therapy a key question was whether Beth's depressed mood needed to change before she could begin to engage in more meaningful, rewarding activities. Consistent with the outside-in approach of behavioural activation, we approached Beth's problem from the perspective that if we could work towards helping her change and improve the quality of her activities in everyday life she might begin to notice improvements in her mood.

(Continued)

(Continued)

Table 11.2 Excerpt from Beth's activity diary

Day/Date: Wednesday 15th October

Time	Activity	Main Mood description and rating (0 = Depressed: 10 = Happy)
5 a.m.	Woke up – stayed in bed thinking.	Low (2/10)
6 a.m.	Went downstairs, tried to read.	Frustrated (3/10)
7 a.m.	Made myself get washed and dressed.	A bit better (5/10)
8 a.m.	Watched TV.	Bored (3/10)
9 a.m.	Walked to the shop and back.	Anxious (4/10)
10 a.m.	Came home.	Relieved but pleased (6/10)
11 a.m.	Mum rang – said she would pay some bills for me.	Reassured (5/10)
12 midday	Tried to make a sandwich.	Bored (3/10)
1 p.m.	Looking for jobs on the internet.	Hopeful then anxious (4/10)
2 p.m.	Looking at irrelevant stuff on the internet.	Distracted (5/10)
3 p.m.	Sitting around worrying that I won't get a job.	Sad (3/10)
4 p.m.	Started tidying the house but couldn't be bothered.	Fed up (3/10)
5 p.m.	Planned to ring Lucy – kept putting it off.	Frustrated (5/10)
6 p.m.	Rang Lucy – had a good chat.	A bit happy for a while (6/10)
7 p.m.	Tried to spend time with partner – he fell asleep on the couch.	Upset (3/10)
8 p.m.	Watched TV – couldn't concentrate.	Bored, sad, empty (2/10)
9 p.m.	Watched TV – couldn't concentrate.	Bored 2/10
10 p.m.	Went to bed – couldn't get off to sleep.	Frustrated and low 2/10

Formulation

More detailed behavioural assessment explored Beth's specific behavioural patterns, with the consequences of her behaviour being the focus of particular attention.

Beth's experience can be formulated using the BA model above (in Figure 11.2). Her life events of stress at work and disruptions in her relationship are examples of the changes in the contingencies or reinforcement that may be associated with the experience of depression. The reduction in both her engagement in and enjoyment of her usual activities, along with the reductions in positive feedback at work, are examples of reduced *positive reinforcement*, particularly of non-depressed

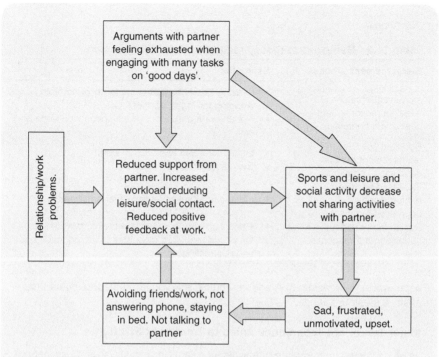

Figure 11.2   BA model of depression related to Beth

behaviour. Leaving or avoiding difficult situations as a way of reducing discomfort are illustrations of the *negative reinforcement* process, and her attempts to try to address her situation being followed by feeling worse either through the addition of some unpleasant consequence or feeling worse are both examples of *punishment* processes (the latter more accurately described as *response cost*). As noted above, these processes combined, and the behavioural reductions they engender, all elicit the moods, symptoms and behaviours that come to be called 'depression' as part of a natural (respondent) response to changes in life circumstances and contingencies of reinforcement. An outline of behavioural theory related to Beth's depression is given in Table 11.3.

The Therapeutic Relationship

At this stage of therapy it was particularly important to maintain a therapeutic relationship and convey empathic understanding that Beth's behaviours were attempts to manage her mood. Beth found this validating and helped her begin to engage with the approach. Also important in this regard was the observation that some features of her environment, such as work and relationships, may have played a contributory factor in the development and maintenance of her problem. This was outlined in the formulation and shared with Beth; her response to this was 'It's not all me'. This was validating of previous attempts to

(Continued)

(Continued)

Table 11.3 Behavioural theory related to Beth's depression

Reinforcement process	Examples
Increased rates of negative reinforcement of avoidant behaviour	• Leaving situations that became uncomfortable. • Avoiding talking to partner. • Not answering the door or telephone when people call.
Reduced positive reinforcement of non-depressed behaviour	• Little praise and feedback at work. • Ever increasing workload.
Increased positive reinforcement of depressed behaviour	• Increased attention from mother and friends.
Punishment of adaptive behaviour and response cost	• Rows with partner when she tries to talk to him. • On occasional good days tries to do too much and ends up feeling worse.

cope whilst increasing her understanding and belief that she could make positive steps to change.

Major Treatment Techniques Allied to Treatment Strategies

As we had begun to formulate that avoidance (in all its forms) was playing a central role in the maintenance of Beth's problem (through both negative reinforcement and reducing opportunities to engage with sources of positive reinforcement), we worked on TRAPs (described above), two examples of which are:

Trigger:	Think about partner's affair.
Response:	Feel angry, guilty and worthless.
Avoidance **P**attern:	Avoid talking to him.

Trigger:	Phone call from HR.
Response:	Dread, panic, 'They'll pressure me to go back to work'.
Avoidance **P**attern:	Switch the phone off.

As Beth developed her awareness of her own behaviour through the use of the TRAPs she started noticing the wide range of activities that she used as avoidance. These began with what to her were obvious behaviours, such a leaving a situation and not answering the door or telephone to others, for example asking for help with tasks, or putting things off. Interestingly, and consistent with the BA literature, she began to view some things she did, such as making herself busy, watching TV or 'thinking things through too much' as avoidance behaviours in some circumstances. This last observation relates well to the 'functions of thinking' aspect of BA covered earlier on, and will be returned to below.

As an alternative to TRAPs, the next session looked at helping Beth develop alternatives to avoidance. This was initiated using the TRACs acronym, and an example of Beth's worksheet is:

Trigger:	Thinking about partner's affair.
Response:	Feel guilty, hurt and worthless.
Alternative **C**oping:	Talk to him about how I feel.

Trigger:	Phone call from HR.
Response:	Dread, panic, 'They'll pressure me to go back to work'.
Alternative **C**oping:	Answer the phone, arrange a time for them to call me back.

The second important emphasis of therapy was increasing the range of positively reinforced activity, such as returning to the things she was doing (or equivalent ones) that gave her a sense of reward, satisfaction, pleasure or elevated mood. From her list of activities, exercise was a useful starting point as the benefits of exercise on depression have been noted (Veale and Wilson, 2007). Again, the one-step-at-time approach remained important so that early attempts were positively reinforced, increasing the probability of repeating the activity.

Working with Beth's Thinking

Beth frequently identified lots of thoughts about herself that she viewed as important, such as 'I'm no good' and 'Things will never work out for me'. Rather than focus on the content of these thoughts (and seek to change them), Beth and her BA therapist explored the process of thinking this way and the impact on her ability to continue working towards her goals.

Beth noticed that when her mood was low she spent long periods of time dwelling on these thoughts, and several others, with the consequence she would not be engaging in meaningful activity. This would lead to her viewing time as being wasted, a trigger for more episodes of prolonged thinking about how she was not able to do things.

At this stage it was helpful to notice the process of 'dwelling on thoughts' viewed as a process of rumination. Initially, as with behaviours, Beth completed a 'dwelling on thoughts/rumination' diary, specifically noting things that were happening before she started thinking this way, how she was thinking, and then the consequences. Two particular issues are important here: first, although there is a particular focus on the process of thinking over the content of thoughts, it remains important to notice and acknowledge these thoughts as important aspects of a person's experience that may be experienced as distressing. Ignoring this may lead to the therapist as being inattentive, un-empathic or invalidating. Second, it's important to be aware that not all consequences of ruminative thinking are necessarily unhelpful or limiting as it can lead to effective problem-solving strategies (Watkins, 2008).

To help Beth work with rumination a range of approaches were explored with her. Specifically, we helped her consider the consequences of rumination by asking herself 'How is dwelling on this issue helpful for me?'. If she noticed unhelpful consequences on either mood or her behaviour in the current setting (such engaging with a current activity), she developed the idea of 'doing something else' that included 'taking my mind off this right now'. This approach was particularly helpful when she found herself ruminating on her thoughts and feelings about her partner's

(Continued)

(Continued)

affair, as it helped her decide whether her thinking was having a problem-solving focus, or whether it was removing her from engaging in her current environment usefully. Beth would often use a TRAP worksheet, with 'dwelling on my situation' as an avoidance pattern and alternative coping as 'do something else'. To help engagement with her current environment as an alternative to rumination, some 'attention to experience' activities (Martell et al., 2001) were developed. These took the form of developing an awareness of the sensory aspects of her current environment, using all senses, and paying deliberate attention to these rather than internal ruminations.

Overcoming obstacles to progress

Working with Beth to help her implement her alternative coping required taking a step-by-step approach, rather than doing it all straightaway (termed 'all-or-nothing behaviour' or the 'Nike' approach of 'Just do it') (Martell et al., 2010). This was particularly important in approaching her partner, which required breaking the activity into component parts, such as developing smaller regular patterns of communication about everyday topics in the first stages.

Working with Beth using BA took 16 sessions and resulted in her engaging in a wider range of activities that she experienced as rewarding or pleasurable, such as increased socialisation, as well as engaging in things that were difficult but important to her, such as addressing key issues in her relationship with her partner. Importantly, she found the BA approach useful in understanding the workplace patterns, and her responses to them, that preceded her depression. This led to a career change to train as teacher of English as a second language, with the aim of working overseas in a Spanish-speaking country. Her BDI-II at the end of therapy was 18 (mild depression), and 10 (not depressed) at one-month follow-up.

Research Status

As described above, the resurgence of interest in behavioural treatment for depression has much to do with the evidence of its effectiveness that has accrued over the last two decades. Of particular note is the seminal randomised trial of Jacobson et al. (1996) and the replication and extension of that trial (Dimidjian et al., 2006). These led to a number of meta-analyses examining the efficacy of this intervention (Cuijpers et al., 2007; Ekers et al., 2008; Mazzucchelli et al., 2009).

Efficacy at Post-Treatment

Three meta-analyses have focused specifically on the efficacy of behavioural activation; all found that BA was more effective than control arms (e.g. wait list) at post-treatment, with effect sizes ranging from 0.70 (Ekers et al., 2008) to 0.87 (Cuijpers et al., 2007). A key comparison, particularly given the interest generated in behavioural activation since the Jacobson et al. (1996) trial, is that with cognitive therapy. All three meta-analyses failed to find a difference at post-treatment between the two interventions, and the differences as estimated by effect sizes were negligible in all cases. The absence of a difference was maintained when the comparison was restricted to those studies in which the samples met criteria for major depressive disorder (Mazzucchelli et al., 2009). There was, however, some evidence of variation in the quality of the studies included in these comparisons (Ekers et al., 2008). In the Ekers et al. (2008) meta-analysis, for example, 7 out of 12 studies failed to meet pre-determined quality assessment criteria relating to measurement selection, measurement, performance and attrition. One possibility is that the inclusion of poorer-quality studies masked a genuine difference between the two treatments. However, heterogeneity between studies was not large and the pooled effect size did not appear to be influenced by methodological characteristics (Ekers et al., 2008).

Two of the meta-analyses also directly compared behavioural activation with a range of interventions for depression other than CT. Mazzucchelli et al. (2009) identified 17 studies that compared BA with a non-CT intervention. At post-treatment, a medium-sized difference was found favouring BA. However, the other interventions in this comparison included treatment as usual and 'non-active' psychological interventions designed to control non-specific factors. Any superiority may be a function of the inclusion of such interventions moderating the group effect (Wampold et al., 1997). The comparison between BA and brief psychotherapy by Ekers et al. (2008) is of interest because all three studies in this comparison used psychodynamic therapy that was intended to be therapeutic. This comparison found a clear advantage for BA relative to psychodynamic therapy, although caution regarding this finding was recommended as the number of included studies was small.

Comparisons of the effectiveness of BA against antidepressant medication are limited. The Dimidjian et al. trial (2006) found an SSRI (Paroxetine) provided up to a maximum dose of 50 mg per day (mean dosage by week 12: 35.17 mg, sd = 12.08 mg) to have no significant difference to BA a post-treatment but superior durability over time (Dobson et al., 2008).

Efficacy at Follow-Up

Evidence on the long-term effectiveness of BA relative to other therapeutic approaches is limited, particularly at longer durations of follow-up. However, what evidence there is suggests that there are no substantial significant differences between BA and other treatment approaches. For example, Mazzucchelli et al. (2009) examined trials comparing BA and CT that contained follow-up data at 1–3, 4–6, 7–12 and 13–24 months and found effect sizes that were small and non-significant at each comparison point. The comparison for the longest follow-up, 13–24 months, was, however, based on just two studies (Dobson et al., 2008, Gortner et al., 1998).

Efficacy of BA and Severity of Depression

Proponents of BA identify its simplicity relative to interventions, such as CT, as a strength of the approach. More practical strategies may be needed for severe depression because the person may struggle to engage in complex or demanding cognitive tasks characteristic of CT or, for that matter, other psychological interventions. Beck himself, in the original description of CT for depression (Beck et al., 1979), recognised the importance of behavioural techniques in this regard (p. 117). As the severity of depression increases, so too do deficits in a number of areas of cognition (McDermott and Ebmeier, 2009).

The Dimidjian et al. (2006) trial reported results separately for high-severity and low-severity depression. For the high-severity group, both the BA and the antidepressant groups showed a greater rate of between-session change in symptoms, as measured by the Beck Depression Inventory-II (Beck et al., 1996) and the a modified version of the Hamilton rating scale for depression (Hamilton, 1960) than the CT group, whereas there were no significant differences in the rate of response between the three groups for those people classified as having low-severity depression. Furthermore, among the more severely depressed group there was some indication that the participants who had received BA had better outcomes at post-treatment than those receiving antidepressants and CT, though this was not on every comparison made. For example, 76 per cent of the BA group met criteria for response (at least a 50 per cent improvement in symptoms) or remission (scoring below a pre-determined 'non-clinical' cut-off point), which compares to 48 per cent of the CT group and 49 per cent of the antidepressant group on the Beck Depression Inventory-II, a finding that fell just short of conventional tests of significance. There were no differences in terms of the proportion meeting either response or remission for the HRSD; however, the BA group were more likely to meet remission criteria on this measure than the two other groups.

Two meta-analyses examined the relationship between severity and outcome. Mazzucchelli et al. (2009) found no effect of self-reported pre-treatment severity on effect sizes in a comparison of BA with other psychological treatments including CT. In contrast, Ekers et al. (2008) found an association between larger effect sizes for BA relative to CT in studies with a higher baseline depression severity. However, this review included data from the Dimidjian et al. trial, one of the larger trials in the studies reviewed, and the extent to which this finding is being carried by this single study is unclear.

The Parsimony Argument

A related claim is that BA, because it is simpler to deliver, can be delivered by therapists with less training, which may therefore make it the psychological treatment of choice because of associated cost-effectiveness. For proponents of behavioural activation this is one of its most attractive features, one that could transform the way depression is treated (Jacobson and Gortner, 2000); surprisingly, then, the evidence for this claim is currently limited.

Evidence is emerging, however, that BA can be delivered effectively by health professionals with no or minimal previous psychotherapeutic experience or training. Ekers et al. (2011) compared BA to treatment as usual, with the BA condition delivered by two mental health nurses with no previous formal training or experience in the delivery of psychological interventions. The training for BA was limited to five days, with one hour of supervision a week. Despite this, BA produced substantial improvements relative to treatment as usual in depression and functioning similar to those seen in trials included in previous meta analysis delivered by experienced therapists. The treatment in this study was based on combination of strategies described in Martell et al. (2003) and Lejuez et al. (2001), and is one of the more complex variants of BA. The fact that the generic mental health workers could be trained to deliver this competently in a short time may provide some evidence that even the more complex forms of BA represent a parsimonious effective psychological intervention for depression. Head-to-head comparisons of BA delivered in this way and treatments such as CT with matched therapy duration and the modelling of therapist effects are required to expand knowledge in this area.

Summary of Evidence Base

Behavioural activation is an effective treatment for depression that compares well with other psychological interventions at post-treatment. The evidence for the effectiveness of BA over the longer term is based on a smaller number of studies, particularly for follow-ups in excess of one year, but what evidence there is also suggests that BA performs well. The existing literature also provides some indication, though by no means definitive, that BA is particularly beneficial for more severe depression. While there is some evidence that BA can be delivered effectively by health professionals with only brief training, there is still work to be done to compellingly demonstrate the claims made about the parsimony of BA relative to other forms of psychological treatment.

Suggested Further Reading

Ekers, D., Richards, D. and Gilbody, S. (2008) 'A meta-analysis of randomized trials of behavioural treatment of depression', *Psychological Medicine*, 38(5): 611–623.

Kanter, J., Busch, A. and Rusch, L. (2009) *Behavioural Activation*. London: Routledge.

Kanter, J., Manos, R., Bowe, W. Baruch, D., Busch, A. and Rusch, L. (2010) 'What is behavioural activation? A review of the empirical literature', *Clinical Psychology Review*, 30: 608–620.

Martell, C.R., Addis, M.E. and Jacobson, N.S. (2003) *Depression in Context: Strategies for Guided Action*. New York: Norton.

Martell, C., Dimidjian, S. and Herman-Dunn, R. (2010) *Behavioral Activation for Depression: A Clinicians Guide*. New York: Guilford Press.

References

Baruch, D., Kanter, J., Bowe, W. and Pfennig, S. (In press) 'Improving homework compliance in career counselling with a behavioral activation functional assessment procedure: A pilot study', *Cognitive Behavioural Practice*.

Beck, A.T., Rush, A.J., Shaw, B.F. and Emery, G. (1979) *Cognitive Therapy of Depression*. New York: Guilford Press.

Beck, A.T., Steer, R.A. and Brown, G.K. (1996) *Manual for the Beck Depression Inventory-II*. San Antonio, CA: Psychological Corporation.

Brown, R. and Lewinsohn, P. (1984) 'A psychoeducational approach to the treatment of depression: Comparison of group, individual, and minimal contact procedures', *Journal of Consulting and Clinical Psychology*, 52(5): 774–783.

Cuijpers, P., Van Straten, A. and Warmerdam, L. (2007) 'Behavioral activation treatments of depression: A meta-analysis', *Clinical Psychology Review*, 27(3): 318–326.

Dimidjian, S., Hollon, S.D., Dobson, K.S., Schmaling, K.B., Kohlenberg, R.J., Addis, M.E., Gallop, R., McGlinchey, J.B., Markley, D.K. and Gollan, J.K. (2006) 'Randomized trial of behavioral activation, cognitive therapy, and antidepressant medication in the acute treatment of adults with major depression', *Journal of Consulting and Clinical Psychology*, 74(4): 658–670.

Dobson, K.S., Hollon, S.D., Dimidjian, S., Schmaling, K.B., Kohlenberg, R.J., Gallop, R., Rizvi, S.L., Gollan, J.K., Dunner, D.L. and Jacobson, N.S. (2008) 'Randomized trial of behavioral activation, cognitive therapy, and antidepressant medication in the prevention of relapse and recurrence in major depression', *Journal of Consulting and Clinical Psychology*, 76(3): 468.

Ekers, D., Richards, D. and Gilbody, S. (2008) 'A meta-analysis of randomized trials of behavioural treatment of depression', *Psychological Medicine*, 38(5): 611–623.

Ekers, D., Richards, D., McMillan, D., Bland, M. and Gilbody, S. (2011) 'Behavioural activation delivered by the non specialist: Phase II randomised controlled trial', *British Journal of Psychiatry*, 198(1): 66–72.

Ferster, C.B. (1973) 'A functional analysis of depression', *American Psychologist*, 28(10): 857–870.

Gortner, E.T., Gollan, J.K., Dobson, K.S. and Jacobson, N.S. (1998) 'Cognitive-behavioral treatment for depression: Relapse prevention', *Journal of Consulting and Clinical Psychology*, 66(2): 377–384.

Hamilton, M. (1960) 'A rating scale for depression', *Journal of Neurology, Neurosurgery and Psychiatry*, 23(1): 56–62.

Hayes, S. and Brownstein, A. (1986) 'Mentalism, behavior-behavior relations and a behavior analytic view of the purposes of science', *The Behavior Analyst*, 9: 175–190.

Hayes, S., Strosahl, K. and Wilson, K.L.G.P. (1999) *Acceptance and Commitment Therapy: An Experiential Approach to Behaviour Change*. London: Guilford Press.

Hernstein, R. (1970) 'On the law of effect', *Journal of the Experimental Analysis of Behavior*, 13: 243–266.

Hopko, D., Lejuez, C., Ruggiaro, K. and Eifert, G. (2003) 'Contemporary behavioural activation treatments for depression: Procedures, principles and progress', *Clinical Psychology Review*, 23: 699–717.

Houghton, S., Curran, J. and Saxon, D. (2008) 'An uncontrolled evaluation of group behavioural activation for depression', *Behavioural and Cognitive Psychotherapy*, 35: 235–239.

Jacobson, N.S. and Gortner, E.T. (2000) 'Can depression be de-medicalized in the 21st century: Scientific revolutions, counter-revolutions and the magnetic field of normal science', *Behaviour Research and Therapy*, 38(2): 103–117.

Jacobson, N.S., Dobson, K.S., Truax, P.A., Addis, M.E., Koerner, K., Gollan, J.K., Gortner, E. and Prince, S.E. (1996) 'A component analysis of cognitive-behavioral treatment for depression', *Journal of Consulting and Clinical Psychology*, 64(2): 295–304.

Kanter, J., Busch, A. and Rusch, L. (2009) *Behavioural Activation*. London: Routledge,

Kanter, J., Manos, R., Bowe, W., Baruch, D., Busch, A. and Rusch, L. (2010) 'What is behavioural activation? A review of the empirical literature', *Clinical Psychology Review*, 30: 608–620.

Lejuez, C.W., Hopko, D.R. and Hopko, S.D. (2001) 'A brief behavioral activation treatment for depression: Treatment manual', *Behavior Modification*, 25(2): 255–286.

Lejuez, C., Hopko, D., Acierno, R., Daughters, S. and Pagoto, S. (In press) 'Ten year revision of the Brief Behavioral Activation Treatment Manual for Depression (BATD): Revised Treatment Manual (BATD-R)', *Behaviour Modification*.

Lewinsohn, P.M. (1974) 'A behavioral approach to depression', in R.J. Friedman and M.M. Katz (Eds), *Psychology of Depression: Contemporary Theory and Research*. Oxford: Wiley. pp. 157–185.

MacPhillamy, D. and Lewinsohn, P. (1982) 'The pleasant events schedule: Studies in reliability, validity and scale intercorrelation', *Jourrnal of Consulting and Clinical Psychology*, 50: 363–380.

Manos, R., Kanter, J. and Busch, A. (2010) 'A critical review of the assessment strategies to measure the behavioral activation model of depression', *Clinical Psychology Review*, 30: 547–561.

Marks, I. (2000) 'Forty years of psychosocial treatments', *Behavioural and Cognitive Psychotherapy*, 28(4): 323–334.

Martell, C., Addis, M. and Jacobson, N. (2001) *Depression in Context: Strategies for Guided Action*. New York: Norton.

Martell, C.R., Addis, M.E. and Jacobson, N.S. (2003) *Depression in Context: Strategies for Guided Action*. New York: Norton.

Martell, C., Dimidjian, S. and Herman-Dunn, R. (2010) *Behavioral Activation for Depression: A Clinicians Guide*. New York: Guilford Press.

Mazzucchelli, T., Kane, R. and Rees, C. (2009) 'Behavioral activation treatments for depression in adults: A meta-analysis and review', *Clinical Psychology: Science and Practice*, 16(4): 383–411.

McDermott, L.M. and Ebmeier, K.P. (2009) 'A meta-analysis of depression severity and cognitive function', *Journal of Affective Disorders*, 119(1–3): 1–8.

National Institute of Clinical Excellence (2009) *Management of Depression in Primary and Secondary Care*. London: NICE.

Shaw, B.F. (1977) 'Comparison of cognitive therapy and behavior therapy in the treatment of depression', *Journal of Consulting and Clinical Psychology*, 45(4): 543–551.

Skinner, B. (1953) *Science and Human Behavior*. Oxford: MacMillan.

Veale, D. and Wilson, R. (2007) *Manage Your Mood*. London: Robinson.

Wampold, B.E., Mondin, G.W., Moody, M., Stich, F., Benson, K. and Ahn, H. (1997) 'A meta-analysis of outcome studies comparing bona fide psychotherapies: Empirically, "all must have prizes"', *Psychological Bulletin*, 122(3): 203–215.

Watkins, E. (2008) 'Constructive and unconstructive repetitive thought', *Psychological Bulletin*, 134: 163–206.

Zeiss, A.M., Lewinsohn, P.M. and Muñoz, R.F. (1979) 'Nonspecific improvement effects in depression using interpersonal skills training, pleasant activity schedules, or cognitive training', *Journal of Consulting and Clinical Psychology*, 47(3): 427–439.

TWELVE   The Transdiagnostic Approach to CBT

WARREN MANSELL

This chapter will propose that by identifying the commonalities in cognitive and behavioural processes that maintain symptoms across a wide range of psychological disorders (the transdiagnostic approach), we are led to a new integrative therapy that overlaps somewhat with earlier work within the fields of counselling and psychodynamic therapy. I will propose that what is often dismissed as a non-specific ingredient of therapy – the 'Dodo bird effect' – is actually a highly specific cognitive-interpersonal process harnessed by effective psychological therapies (Mansell, 2011). At the heart of this integrative approach is the formulation of intrapersonal (cognitive) and interpersonal (social) control. Essentially, it is proposed that inter- and intra-personal control are closely related, and that the balance of control within a therapy session reflects the way that the client and therapist relate to their own mental states (commonly known as metacognition); they are flip sides of the same coin. Effective psychological therapy helps the client to restore control over their own life as a whole through becoming aware of their overarching personal goals and values and letting go of perpetuating a habitual pattern of rigid control over their thoughts, feelings, behaviour and the behaviour of other people. Therapy therefore aims to provide a safe testing ground in which the client can effectively reprioritise their overarching life goals in the face of the disturbing effects of their own thoughts and feelings, and the responses of others. I will propose that a transdiagnostic, or universal, form of CBT developed in this way may be more easily trainable and adaptable to different client groups than the disorder-specific approaches currently practised.

Historical Development of the Approach

In order to understand the development of the transdiagnostic approach, it is necessary to trace the origins of the talking therapies to before the diagnostic system took root. The apocryphal story described below illustrates how the methods of contemporary therapies have their origins in many earlier accounts of how to alleviate human suffering:

> A woman came to see Buddha because she was at a loss with grief over her dead baby, refusing to let go of his corpse, long after he had passed away. She asked Buddha to take away her grief. He said he would do so if she could merely bring him a single poppy seed. But the poppy seed must be given to her by a household that is untouched by grief. Therefore the woman went to search for such a household, going from door to door around the village. At the end of her search she did not have a single poppy seed. Yet she learned how many people had lost loved ones, she heard stories of how they had coped with their loss, and she began to face her own grief.

Through the eyes of a cognitive behavioural therapist, the above story might be seen as a 'behavioural experiment', as a 'reality testing' exercise or as 'guided exposure' to previously avoided emotions. But of course, these are terms that are provided after the fact – people were facing their fears and shifting their ways of thinking long before modern psychotherapy. Arguably, the roots of psychotherapy lie in religion and philosophy rather than innovations from the last century of modern psychology (de Botton, 2000; de Silva, 1984; Gilbert, 2010).

Nevertheless, it is in more recent times that the term 'psychotherapy' has emerged. The talking therapies and the classification of the 'disorders' of distress have been evolving in tandem from the turn of the 19th century to the present day. We now have around 350 different psychological disorders and at least that many different forms of counselling and psychotherapy. Therefore, at the beginning of modern psychotherapy, there was a simpler classification system, and a similar therapy was provided to a range of presenting problems. This could be termed a 'prediagnostic' phase. Yet, even as the diagnostic system expanded, the talking therapies remained universal. For example, within the cognitive field, Albert Ellis (1962) targeted his rational therapy at alleviating psychological distress in general. At around the same time, Carl Rogers (1951) developed person-centred counselling using a theoretical framework that applied to all.

In contrast, Aaron T. Beck, a psychiatrist and psychoanalyst familiar with the diagnostic system, wished to treat depression (Beck, 1967). His 'cognitive therapy' was initially applied to this problem alone, yet throughout the 1980s and 1990s it came to be diversified and applied to many different disorders, each with its own model (e.g. Clark, 1986; Clark and Wells, 1995). It is these models that were successfully evaluated in controlled trials to inform the guidelines for the practice of CBT across the globe. Maybe predictably, clinical researchers within the field of CBT began to see the commonalities across disorders that were the initial inspiration for prediagnostic psychotherapies.

In 2003, Chris Fairburn and colleagues published a cognitive model applied across the eating disorders, which was described as 'transdiagnostic' (Fairburn et al., 2003). Shortly after, a group of CBT researchers in the UK, led by Allison Harvey and involving myself, Ed Watkins and Roz Shafran, published the culmination of a three-year review into 'transdiagnostic processes' (Harvey et al., 2004). We identified 12 cognitive and behavioural processes that research studies had shown maintained people's distress and were shared across a range of different psychological disorders. These processes included hypervigilance for threat, selective memory, avoidance behaviour and biases in reasoning. For example, recurrent negative thinking, in the form of worry and rumination, was elevated relative to non-clinical controls in people with depression, various anxiety disorders, eating disorders, chronic pain and psychotic disorders. Furthermore, recurrent negative thinking prospectively predicts psychological distress in the form of anxiety, depression, alcohol use and even persecutory delusions (Murray et al., 2002; Nolen-Hoeksema et al., 2007; Segerstrom et al., 2000; Startup et al., 2007). Yet, similar evidence is available for many of the other cognitive and behavioural processes that were identified by Harvey et al. (2004). This raises the question of what each of these processes are really measuring and how they may overlap with one another.

Therefore, in a more recent article, we felt it was important to spell out the conceptual foundations of the transdiagnostic approach to guide future developments (Mansell et al., 2009). The transdiagnostic approach to CBT simply states that there are significant benefits to formulating and treating the cognitive and behavioural processes that are shared across different disorders. It does not provide the theory or the therapy to carry this out. There are many candidate theories and therapies that could be applied in this way (Mansell et al., 2009). The field of 'transdiagnostic CBT' is burgeoning at present, with several international groups of researchers and clinicians making significant progress in developing and testing forms of transdiagnostic CBT (e.g. Barlow et al., 2004; McManus et al., 2010; Norton et al., 2004). One important direction for this research is to establish whether the processes that are shared across disorders can be simplified from the dozen or so that have been identified. It is encouraging to see increasing evidence that there is little difference in statistical terms between different processes such as 'rumination', 'safety behaviours', 'thought suppression' and 'experiential avoidance', – they are all closely correlated, and research studies suggest it is this shared variable that is linked to psychological distress (e.g. Aldao and Nolen-Hoeksema, 2010; Field and Cartwright-Hatton, 2008; Mansell et al., 2007; Patel, 2010; Schwannauer, 2007).

It is possible that the factor identified in the above studies also overlaps with the processes that were identified within the wider fields of psychotherapy and counselling (Higginson et al., 2011). However, it is hard to find these similarities when there is such a diverse use of terminology. For example, how does one compare and contrast 'avoidance', 'defences' and 'conditions of worth'? Surely a deeper level of scientific theory is required to judge whether there are commonalities across these disciplines?

Theoretical Underpinnings

As stated above, the transdiagnostic approach is not a theory; it is an empirical exercise with implications for theory development. In fact, it lends itself to a number of different theoretical approaches that are covered in some detail elsewhere (Mansell et al., 2009). In this chapter, I spell out the underpinnings of one of these approaches – perceptual control theory (PCT) (Powers, 1973; Powers et al., 1960). PCT has the advantage of not being a psychological theory. It is derived from control engineering and uses specific terms with operationalised definitions. It is therefore not aligned to any one discipline within psychology and provides a level of explanation that has the capacity to unite diverse approaches with very different terms. Anyone who has struggled to differentiate the terms 'belief', 'attitude', 'assumption', 'rule' and 'value' will appreciate the advantages of a clean slate.

Major Theoretical Concepts

Control

The phenomenon of control underpins the PCT approach. Echoing the process of homeostasis in biology and the approach of early psychology (Dewey, 1896; James, 1890; Morell, 1853), PCT proposes that living organisms are self-regulating; to live is to control. It places 'purpose' and 'volition' as central in any living system. This echoes, among others, the emphasis of cybernetics (Wiener, 1948), person-centred psychology (Rogers, 1951), attachment theory (Bowlby, 1969) and the approach of Alfred Adler (Dyslin, 1994). The direct origins of PCT actually lie in the field of control engineering. Our reliance on the ingenuity of artificial control systems such as factory production lines, incubators, steam engine valves and amplifiers validate this approach to understanding the phenomenon of control.

Within PCT, control is achieved through a process of *negative feedback*. The individual *perceives* the current state of its experience (e.g. ambient temperature is 5 degrees), *compares* this with its desired value (e.g. 20 degrees) and *acts* to reduce this discrepancy or error (e.g. move indoors). This process continues until the error reaches zero, whereby no further action is necessary. These systems are seen to underlie all purposeful behaviour, from simple motor control, to maintaining proximity to a caregiver, to pursuing personal goals such as 'to be a good worker'.

Hierarchical Organisation

We need to regulate the diverse range of experiences that matter to us and balance them in a co-ordinated fashion. PCT states that we manage this through hierarchy of control. The idea that the mind is organised in a hierarchical fashion, from surface to deep structures, permeates psychology (e.g. Beck, 1967; Botvinick, 2008; Hayek, 1952). However, PCT is precise about the nature of the levels in a hierarchy, their relationship with one another, and their function. At the bottom of the hierarchy we control the *intensities* of our momentary experience through subtle changes in muscle tension. At the next level up we co-ordinate these intensities to experience desired sensations, such as the feeling of touching skin. At the level above this we co-ordinate our *sensations* to experience desired *configurations* of sensations, such as the shape of another person's hand in ours. These levels continue upwards through several further levels to *programs*, such as 'driving home', that depend on organising patterns of lower-level experiences according to 'if ... then ...' rules (see later). Programs are then organised to allow the control of more abstract experiences we control, such as our adherence to certain *principles* such as 'honesty', which in turn inform our *system concepts* such as our sense of identity.

Conflict

Within any control system, *conflict* is one of the most inevitable and yet potentially destructive features; it is observed when two or more of a person's goals interfere or inhibit one another. Conflict is at the heart of a range of psychological theories (see Higginson et al., 2011). For example, ambivalence, as a form of cognitive dissonance, underpins the approach of motivational interviewing (W.R. Miller, 1996); the behavioural treatment of phobia involves navigating the balance between approaching and avoiding the feared stimulus; and importantly, the development of an attachment relationship involves balancing the conflict between exploration and safety seeking (Bowlby, 1969). PCT proposes that a key role of an upper layer of control in a hierarchy is to set the goals for the two conflicting systems; it develops in order to regulate and manage this conflict, and it needs to be accessed in therapy in order to reduce the conflict.

Reorganisation

Reorganisation is the learning process within PCT. It reduces the error (loss of control) caused by prolonged conflict. In some ways it operates like operant conditioning, in that random trial-and-error changes are utilised. However, unlike conditioning, and in common with theories of insight and problem-solving such as those within Gestalt psychology (e.g. Kohler, 1927), reorganisation operates on the internal properties of the control systems rather than on any specific behaviour (see also Huether et al., 1999). According to PCT, to resolve long-term loss of control, reorganisation needs to be directed to the regions in a hierarchy that will reduce the conflict – namely, the level that is above the conflicting systems – and allowed to make random changes until the conflict is reduced and the individual eventually regains control.

How Client Problems Are Conceptualised

Within PCT, the top levels of the hierarchy are critical as these set the standards for those below. When a person feels in control of their own lives, this means that they set perceptions for themselves at a high levels (e.g. to be a good parent) that can be flexibly achieved through applying a range of principles and, in turn, programs at lower levels that are coherent with one another and sensitive to feedback from their current experience. To do so, the person needs to sustain their attention both on their long-term goals and to present-moment feedback to these goals. Many therapeutic accounts emphasise the importance of raising awareness of the present moment (e.g. Carey, 2011; Fogel, 2009; Greenberg et al., 1996; Kabat-Zinn, 1991; Rogers, 1946; Stern, 2004; Wells, 2000). From a PCT perspective, this is essential for a number of reasons. First, feedback from perceptual signals in the present moment is an essential component of a working control system – the client's mind and body in the session. Second, shifts of awareness to higher-level systems ('background thoughts') need to be noticed and maintained to facilitate their reorganisation. Third, focusing on the present moment allows the therapist to regularly check that the client feels in control as the topic of conversation changes ('Is this a problem for you?', 'Is this what you want to discuss today?', 'How is it going talking about this?').

PCT proposes that chronic psychological distress is a product of problems caused when people do not allow themselves to allocate their attention across levels in this adaptive manner (cf. Watkins, 2011). Instead, they are focused on pursuing and maintaining low-level or concrete experiences (e.g. to never feel anxious; to restrict eating) that undermine their capacity to achieve their long-term goals (e.g. to assert themselves; to get support from other people). This is termed *arbitrary control* (Mansell, 2005; Powers, 1973).

From a PCT perspective, it is arbitrary control that reflects the most problematic feature of the cognitive and behavioural processes that have been identified as transdiagnostic. For example, 'avoidance' is only a problem that maintains psychological distress when it conflicts with a valued goal, such as the person with agoraphobia whose avoidance of the outside world leads to a restriction in their lives. There are many contexts in which 'avoidance' is not a problem and can actually be a very adaptive process – it is advantageous to avoid crossing a motorway and to avoid a situation of domestic violence, for example. Thus, it is the interference or inhibition of important, overarching goals that is critical. In particular, arbitrary control is most pernicious when it conflicts with the following processes:

- *Awareness of the problem* – By definition, when people engage in arbitrary control, they are not aware of the fact that this process is interfering with their life goals. Many individuals will be aware of the impact at other times, which accounts for why they seek therapy – to try to reverse the destructive, habitual patterns of which they are aware when stepping outside the problem situation. However, many people will remain unaware of the fact their attempts at control are impacting on their lives – they cannot 'step outside the problem'. The therapist may describe this as 'denial' of their problems even though it is simpler than that according to PCT – by definition, the root of all chronic problems remain, to some degree, outside awareness. Thus, lack of awareness of the problem remains a challenge for any therapist – to attempt to raise awareness in the client's mind of the nature of their problems.

- *Restricting the process of change* – Clearly, it is critical for people with long-term psychological problems to make changes in their lives. However, the process of change involves a range of experiences that can be resisted – uncertainty, shifts in emotion and occasional mistakes are just some examples. Where a person's rigid attempts at control obstruct the change process itself, this is clearly a problem – examples include perfectionism and emotion suppression.
- *Sense of self-worth and acceptance* – Classically, Carl Rogers proposed that where the individual behaves according to other people's conditions of worth and acceptance, this leads to an alienated sense of self that characterises chronic psychological distress (Rogers, 1951). There is a range of processes that compromise self-worth, such as attempts to avoid rejection, engaging in self-criticism and following other people's standards rather than following one's own goals.
- *Survival goals* – For many people in distress, their attempts at control can escalate to the degree that it threatens their survival. Self-harm, food restriction and suicide are pertinent examples.

In the next section I will discuss how an effective talking therapy can begin to reverse arbitrary control alongside the pernicious effects described above, and replace it with attempts at control that are more flexible and adaptive.

Practical Applications

The Therapeutic Relationship

A PCT approach immediately allows us to formulate 'control' within any relationship. According to PCT, and in line with other theories of child development (e.g. Bowlby, 1969), a good early relationship with a caregiver allows a child to be in control of their experiences and provides a safe place for the child to make mistakes and learn from them – essentially to 'play' with new ideas and perspectives. This continues into adult life. Where a second person tries to inflict their own goals on the individual (i.e. to control them for their own ends), conflict occurs. This is arbitrary control in an interpersonal context. If this controlling person is unimportant in the first person's life, they can be avoided and there is no longer a problem. However, it is the special case where the controlling person is also someone who also meets the goals of the individual (e.g. in providing safety, shelter and support) that internal conflict occurs: 'Do I stay with this person or find someone else?', even more importantly, 'Do I continue to treat myself in the way I have learned from this person, or do I treat myself differently?'

The therapeutic relationship provides a unique opportunity for a client *not* to be the subject of arbitrary control by other people. This is a well-known tenet of person-centred counselling (Rogers, 1951). Yet, the cognitive therapist also promotes client control. The session is led by the client's problem list; the relationship is explicitly collaborative and deviations from this are noted and reflected upon. Thus, PCT may help explain why these interpersonal features of CBT seem so integral, even though they are not a central part of cognitive theory (Mansell, 2008). The challenge of any therapy is how to *balance* maintaining the client's sense of control with the important process of also encouraging change – whether this is through facing a new feared object, questioning a negative thought, reflecting the client's statements, or sharing a formulation of the their problems. Within PCT, the goal is to manage this balancing act as mindfully as possible, so that the therapist does not 'get in the way' (Carey, 2006), and yet manages to help the client gear their attention towards the present-moment perceptual feedback that informs higher-level goals. Within PCT, it is not so important whether conflicting control systems are situated within the same person or within two individuals. Therefore, the balance of control in a session is likely to reflect and affect the balance of control a person takes to their own internal experiences.

Strategies of Treatment

There is increasing evidence that psychotherapies which apparently follow different theoretical models vary very little, or to a modest degree, in their level of effectiveness (e.g. Tolin, 2010; Ward et al., 2000). A PCT approach would regard this as inevitable as each different therapy would be attempting to address the same core process of change, with somewhat varying degrees of efficiency. Essentially, the skill a therapist brings to the session is to provide an environment that allows the client to consider their overarching goals and how they can be implemented in the moment, alongside the disruptions and changes that this may entail. According to this approach, effective transdiagnostic CBT engages the clients in a collaborative and graded process of deciding what to bring into mind and explore at this moment in time. Over the course of therapy, attending to and sustaining awareness on deeper problems, whatever their nature or terms of reference (e.g. strong emotions, deeply held beliefs, schemata, cherished goals, recurrent habits, distressing imagery) should help the client to re-evaluate how to manage their own problems. Within this approach, it is the change that accompanies addressing the deeper problems as they are manifested in the present moment, alongside the associated feelings, which is critical to long-term recovery (Mansell, 2011). Nevertheless, clients need to navigate towards this point in a way that allows them to feel in control, and it is this process of the client understanding their process of change that maintains their engagement in therapy or other forms of help.

In essence, the methods that the therapist uses to try to help the client explore their problem will naturally vary in how much they compromise each client's own ability to control their experiences at that moment. For example, an anxious client may feel pushed into thinking of 'the worst thing that could happen' through the downward arrow technique and therefore temporarily feel out of control. An emotionally distant client being questioned in the same way may answer it with a pre-rehearsed response that fails to get them to consider what they are really worried will happen and therefore feel that they have too much control over the session to learn anything from it. Thus, it seems that effective therapy involves keeping the client in a zone where they feel sufficiently in control to feel safe, but slightly out of control, or uncertain, to begin to consider their problem (cf. Grawe, 2006).

Major Treatment Techniques

A form of cognitive therapy derived from PCT known as 'method of levels' (MOL) is designed to help clients restore control in the ways described here (Carey, 2006). There are a range of resources available on this approach elsewhere (Carey, 2006, 2008; Mansell, 2009). Essentially, MOL is a process of questioning that encourages the client to talk about their problem in detail, and to notice 'background thoughts' about their problem which are thought to reflect their underyling goals and values. Within this chapter, rather than explaining MOL, I will discuss how the subtleties of control in a therapy session can be conceptualised within any therapy. In MOL, the form of questioning will typically lead to a restored balance where the client feels sufficiently in control to talk about and explore their problems. Figure 12.1 illustrates a hypothesised formulation based on PCT of how this could be managed in a CBT, counselling or psychotherapy session.

In Figure 12.1, the balance of control between the therapist and client, from the client's perspective, is illustrated as four sections of a circle. Towards the outside of the circle represents where this balance of control in therapy is coupled with a greater degree of conflict in higher-order goals, whereas towards the inside of the circle this balance of control in the session is coupled with a lesser degree of conflict in higher-order goals and therefore less overall distress. In order to re-establish a collaborative balance, the therapist needs to help direct the client towards the centre of the circle. It is important that the therapist is curious to find out from the client how they are feeling about the process of therapy at the moment, and adapting it accordingly. For example, if the client feels vulnerable and intruded upon

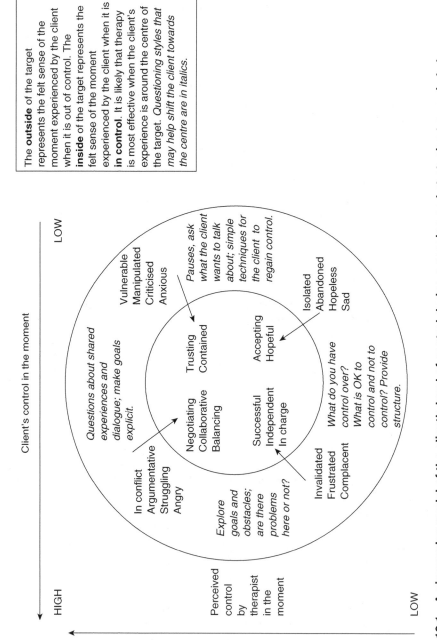

The **outside** of the target represents the felt sense of the moment experienced by the client when it is out of control. The **inside** of the target represents the felt sense of the moment experienced by the client when it is **in control**. It is likely that therapy is most effective when the client's experience is around the centre of the target. *Questioning styles that may help shift the client towards the centre are in italics.*

Client's control in the moment

HIGH

LOW

Perceived control by therapist in the moment

LOW

Questions about shared experiences and dialogue; make goals explicit.

Vulnerable
Manipulated
Criticised
Anxious

Pauses, ask what the client wants to talk about; simple techniques for the client to regain control.

In conflict
Argumentative
Struggling
Angry

Negotiating
Collaborative
Balancing

Trusting
Contained

Accepting
Hopeful

Isolated
Abandoned
Hopeless
Sad

Successful
Independent
In charge

What do you have control over? What is OK to control and not to control? Provide structure.

Explore goals and obstacles; are there problems here or not?

Invalidated
Frustrated
Complacent

Figure 12.1   A circumplex model of the client's level of control during a session and strategies to regain balance

by the therapist's questions, the therapist may find that pausing for longer and granting the client more control over what is talked about will be beneficial. Conversely, clients who manage to talk fluently without openly discussing their problems may benefit from questions that help them to refocus on the problem they came to discuss in the session.

Table 12.1 summarises the occasions on which the balance of control can stray from a balanced collaborative, exploratory stance. It provides a control theory explanation, some concrete examples of interventions, and also illustrates drawbacks of each of these strategies.

Essentially, these strategies suggest that change is best facilitated in an environment in which the client can feel in control yet is willing to consider the uncertainties and conflicts surrounding their problem. Interpersonal situations in which they are controlled by others (e.g. being told how to behave), or in which they are allowed to control their own awareness in ways that distract them from their problems, or make them worse (e.g. allowed to engage in worry or thought suppression), do not provide this opportunity. The therapist, sensitive to this balance of control, helps the client to navigate their way to the root of their difficulties whilst getting in the way of this process as little as possible – but just enough to keep up the process of change. According to this view, many superficially different techniques are actually similar as they each allow an individual to balance their conflicting goals in the moment: to approach or avoid a snake; to suppress or accept a feeling of anger; to weigh up their work versus family priorities; to follow or ignore an urge to binge; to push away or face a traumatic memory (see also Carey, 2011). As a therapist learns to be more aware of this intrapersonal balance of control within the client, the better he or she is able to titrate their own behaviour to maintain a helpful interpersonal balance of control between the two of them.

The wealth of techniques available to the contemporary CBT therapist can prove very confusing, especially with clients presenting with complex problems and ongoing loss of control over their mood, thoughts and behaviour. Indeed, when comparing CBT to earlier forms of counselling and psycho-therapy, CBT can seem awash with tools and techniques that can often obstruct its key principles. A control theory approach may provide some clarity as to how certain CBT strategies have their effects, when one considers the hierarchical nature of control. According to PCT, there are 11 levels of perceptual goals (Powers, 1998). However, to try to draw links with CBT, four layers will be distinguished:

1 *Low-level perceptual control*: At the lowest layer (actually formed of several levels in Powers' theory) is the control of perceptual experience, including physical sensations, visual and auditory perception. This is critical for any carefully co-ordinated action such as walking, talking and gesture. It would also manage any immediate therapeutic technique that is trained in vivo, such as grounding interventions or applied relaxation.

Table 12.1 A control theory framework for understanding circumstances where the balance of control strays from collaborative exploration

Locus of control during session	Circumstances	Control theory explanation	Examples	Limitations
Client in control	1. Therapist is requested to provide help	Client uses therapist as a *feedback function* to achieve goals.	Writing letters to official bodies (e.g. councils, solicitors); liaising with other health professionals.	The client may not find their own ways of helping themselves across situations.
	2. Therapist provides information	Client lacks *reference values* for goals.	Providing information, e.g. the effects of hyperventilation; the common occurrence of intrusive thoughts.	Information may be incorrect, excessively influenced by the therapist's goals, and/or rejected by client.
	3. Therapist facilitates a change in the environment	Client is experiencing an *uncontrollable disturbance*.	Help to re-house client; access a safe haven during domestic abuse.	The client may still create or select a similar problematic environment; a less aversive environment may not be available.
IDEAL: Balance of control between client and therapist	Therapy	*Reorganisation* of higher level goals is a trial-and-error process that requires periods of control and yet some loss of control.	Answering therapist's questions; sustaining awareness on previously avoided experiences and emotions; reflection; decentering; reprioritising; shifting perspectives; restructuring.	Client may feel out of control if questions are perceived as too intrusive; client may not change if questions fail to target the important conflicting goals.
Therapist in control	1. Limits to resources	The therapist's capacity to facilitate the client's control is compromised, creating *conflict*.	Lack of time; arbitrary limits set by services (e.g. time and duration of sessions); lack of therapist training and expertise; over-medication.	Limits may be so constraining and arbitrary as to prevent change or create further problems.
	2. Client looms out of control rapidly	When looming out of control, control systems need to stabilise at least temporarily through *arbitrary control*.	Grant client more choice of topic; work on a less sensitive problem; grounding techniques; applied relaxation; soothing techniques; build up hypothetical, 'healthy' self to be tried out at a later stage; provide reassurance.	The client may not report they feel they are losing control; techniques may not work and create more conflict.
	3. Immediate and significant perceived risk	Therapist holds and exercises a *principle* to protect others from actual harm.	Prioritising discussion of reasons for living; medication; hospital admission; police.	The therapist may utilise methods of control that disrupt engagement and cause further problems.

2 *Program control*: Going upward from the low level, the layers culminate in the *program* level. It is here that arrangements and changes in the lower levels are managed as discrete programs of goals that follow an 'if ... then ...' structure (Powers, 1973). It seems to correspond most closely to the coping strategy level within Beck's (1967) cognitive theory. Interestingly, this is the level within PCT that seems to be studied in closer detail by other theories, such as TOTE (G.A. Miller et al., 1960) and implementation intentions (Gollwitzer, 1999), and is regarded as the focus of awareness for much of the time (Carver and Scheier, 1982). According to PCT, although it appears sometimes as though programs of behaviour are 'triggered' by an environmental cue, these cues are actually set by the individual in order to delegate control of multiple programs to different environmental contexts and are mediated via the lower layers of the hierarchy described earlier. This level of control is likely to be utilised when clients are helped to implement their plans and organise routines.

3 *Principle control*: Above the program level is the principle level, which corresponds most closely to the level of attitudes, or 'rules for life'. People's principles determine different programs depending on the current situation. At this level, people consider their rules of living and their attitudes that are common to a range of situations, for example to be 'honest', 'reliable' or 'strong'.

4 *System concept*: The highest layer is known as the system concept, and approximates to a person's self-concept as well as their sense of other systems, such as their workplace or family. Systems are built from sets of principles. Ultimately, it is at this highest level at which truly autonomous control is exercised by the adult client. According to PCT, changes in organisation that do not permeate to an adult client's system concept of their self in the world are unlikely to persist in the long term.

As stated already, the levels of control normally interface with the physical environment via the levels in between. However, they can also be disconnected from the levels below and operate in an *imagination mode* – an 'as if', *mental simulation* of the world at various levels of abstraction (Powers, 1973; Pezzulo and Castelfranchi, 2009). This occurs, for example, during the control of mental imagery, thinking, planning and self-talk, and thus is virtually ubiquitous during therapy. Indeed, the degree to which the client is engaging the imagination mode would determine how little they are striving to control their current situation – the therapy session. Thus, one of the first markers of the client's loss of control is often their switching to trying to control the therapist rather than their own internal perceptions. Conversely, helping the client to engage in the imagination mode in a controllable way is likely to foster flexibility and, ultimately, change.

The levels of control that are used in therapy may correspond to the level at which a psychological intervention has its effects, which is illustrated in

Hierarchy of control to be modified

Therapeutic techniques facilitating change at different levels

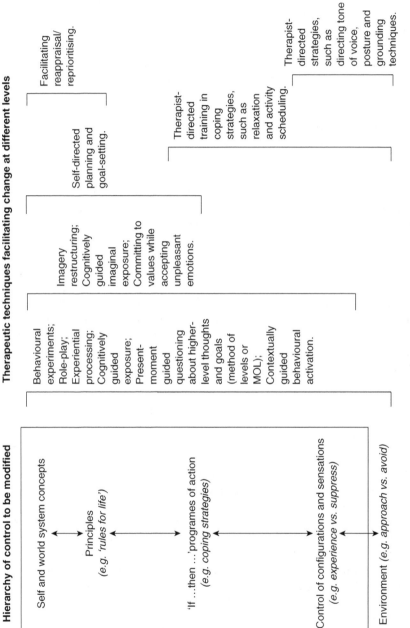

Figure 12.2 A control theory hypothesis for the mode of change of different therapy techniques

Figure 12.2. In principle, those interventions that utilise the higher levels of control and permeate through all levels via feedback with the immediate environment would be more effective in the long term, whereas those techniques that utilise lower levels will have a more instant positive effect, and yet have the capacity to circumvent the client's own personal goals, thereby potentially exacerbating the level of goal conflict. Successful therapy may involve both kinds of intervention used flexibly and collaboratively.

Overcoming Obstacles to Client Progress

Within CBT, obstacles are often tackled by discussing them openly in therapy and looking at any functional reasons for them (e.g. 'I avoided today's session because I thought you would make me talk about my feelings'). This leads to a return to the client's goals for therapy, so that these problems are prioritised. For example, a client may want to learn how to manage their feelings better before talking about the trauma they experienced. The transdiagnostic approach guided by PCT would not differ greatly, but the theory may help to conceptualise why this approach should help.

There is a tension in PCT with regard to what is seen as an 'obstacle'. On one hand, the theory acknowledges that the client needs to establish control and learn to self-regulate their own access to therapy. Thus, what appears to the therapist as an 'obstacle' may be the client's own attempts at control. This needs to be considered. On the other hand, when an 'obstacle' results from the client engaging in arbitrary control, this implies that he or she is disregarding and inhibiting their own higher-level, personal goals. These obstacles are therefore the same as the maintenance processes described earlier, such as self-criticism, fear of change and risk-taking. A PCT approach would formulate each of these as the client's attempt to regain control over an important experience. Therefore, therapy is directed at trying to understand the process, and in particular the higher-order goals that the person is attempting to fulfil through them. The client can then be helped to analyse whether the process is helping to achieve this goal or not, and to weigh this up against the drawbacks of their arbitrary control. When the client is helped to see the underlying purpose behind the behaviour, this enables them to be more flexible, and in the words of William James (1890), 'pursue fixed ends though variable means'. The clinical example below spells out this approach in more detail.

Case Example: Jane

Jane was a school teacher who came for help with her depression, which was always worse during term time. She reported poor sleep, uncontrollable worry and a fear of close relationships, both with new friends and potential partners. She

(Continued)

(Continued)

described herself as a perfectionist and as being self-critical, an enduring style of relating to herself that she developed as a child. No formal diagnoses were made, but generalised anxiety, recurrent depression and social anxiety would describe her presenting problems. Jane was seen as part of a trial into method of levels (MOL), and she consented to her sessions being used anonymously.

The Therapeutic Relationship

Jane engaged well with the therapy from the first session and rated her satisfaction for each session at 8 out of 10 or above. She seemed to find self-reflection relatively easy to do and yet also an emotionally painful process. Unlike some clients, it seemed straightforward to maintain a balance of control that was collaborative and in the spirit of guided discovery. When Jane became upset during many sessions, it was natural for the therapist to offer her a tissue, and to ask if she was OK to continue. In PCT terms, this may have helped her to feel grounded and safe at times when she felt out of control (top right quadrant of Figure 12.1). Consistent with PCT, at the end of each session, Jane was asked for feedback on the therapy and given the choice to suggest a change in the approach (see S.D. Miller et al., 2007). She did not take up these offers.

Strategies of Treatment

The MOL therapy aimed at allowing Jane to remain in control at the same time as focusing regularly and frequently on her current thoughts and feelings, with the aim of helping her to view her problems from 'a higher level'. This strategy would be applied whatever the current problem described. For example, when Jane described her self-criticism ('being hard on myself'), the therapist asked her about this process: whether it was going on right now how it was working for her; what the voice sounded like; how she decided how 'hard' to be on herself; whether she was ever soft on herself; whether she was only hard on herself or to other people too. The goal was to access the level above the self-criticism that is regulating its use across contexts and help her to regain control over it, with the expectation that she would then use it in circumstances in which it fulfilled her goals, and cease to use it, or modify it, in situations in which it compromised her goals.

Major Treatment Techniques

As described above, MOL uses only questioning as a technique. However, these questions can appear very different depending on the content of the session. For example, when clients provide a metaphorical description of their problem, this provides a good opportunity to explore the present moment perception as it emerges. In one of many examples, Jane described her tendency to not open up to people as a 'wall' in front of her. The therapist explored this with her literally (see Carey, 2006; Stott et al., 2010). How far does the wall extend? Is the wall complete? Can you see over the wall or not? Is this image changing or staying the same? After this discussion, Jane had transformed her image to one of a stone 'keep' around her, with 'arrow slits' to see other people, and she started to realise the paradox of this wall – that she does it to protect herself, but that it isolates her at the same time.

At other times in the sessions, the questioning accessed the present moment in other ways: for example, asking about her smiles or changes in tone of voice; asking how what she says sounds to her as she says it; and occasionally more direct questions to access higher-order goals: 'What makes this important for you?' Nevertheless, at all times the strategy is the same: to sustain attention on conflicting feedback to higher level control systems and to do this in a way that maximises the client's own control over the session.

Overcoming Obstacles to Client Progress

Despite good engagement, there were clear obstacles to progress, which were essentially the same as the processes being tackled. For example, Jane reported always wanting to find a 'quick fix' to a problem and wanting to be absolutely certain about the solution. She struggled to accept that her current problem would take time and involve uncertainty. The therapist helped her to quantify how much uncertainty she could accept as she went though therapy. Another obstacle seemed to be that Jane would 'tell herself' something (e.g. 'I must try to be myself more'), and even say it out loud in the session, and yet at the same time 'feel' in the opposite way – that trying to be herself would be too difficult to manage. A side of her was taking control of her problem without accepting the uncertainty on other side – this would be reflected as at the bottom left quadrant in Figure 12.1. Therefore, the questioning would lean towards reminding her of the other side that felt reserved about making changes with the aim of restoring a more balanced perspective. The way this was managed in one session is illustrated below:

Jane:　　I sometimes feel like my life is on autopilot – a life full of rushed things.

Therapist:　Do you want the autopilot there or not?

Jane:　　Some of the time yes, but I would like to have more control about what I do [*laughs*].

Therapist:　What made you laugh just then?

Jane:　　Well, a lot of this down to me, allowing time and space to think about things. I control that, but not at rate I am comfortable with. I need to learn to control it just enough.

Therapist:　And what is the level that is just enough for you?

Jane:　　I feel that I put too much effort into things and I am not feeling my real self.

Therapist:　How much of your real self do you feel right now, at the moment?

Jane:　　It seems like forever ago I last felt like myself.

Therapist:　Is any of that self here now or not?

Jane:　　[*long pause*] Not a great amount. It's like the enjoyable, happy self has been taken over by scary, working self.

Therapist:　And what it the balance right now between those?

Jane:　　Its 75 per cent scary self and 25 per cent normal human being. [*pause*]. But what I like now is that I can see that happening. I never

(Continued)

(Continued)

	used to see how bad I was getting but I can see that now. I need to make time to be myself again.
Therapist:	Do you need to make time or is that happening now?
Jane:	I think it makes me feel calmer to think about myself now. Normally I go through the day and get on with it and don't think about myself at all. I need to listen to myself more.
Therapist:	As you are saying that to me, was the scary side of yourself agreeing with that or not?
Jane:	[*laughs*] No! That's quite a challenge isn't it, but I am good at challenges. I'll have to see how it goes. It seems straightforward sat in here but not when at work outside of here.
Therapist:	What is the difference between the two?
Jane:	I think it would take ten hours to do it outside here!
Therapist:	Ten hours? Is that about the time you think it would take?
Jane:	It feels like it would need a long time but perhaps it wouldn't. It made me think yesterday that I was saying to my pupils in teaching they need to be more positive about themselves and what they need – and yet I don't listen to myself at all. I need to listen to myself more. Maybe that's my target for this week – to stop and listen to myself.
Therapist:	How is it going with these two sides of yourself now?
Jane:	This good side of myself feels calm. The other side doesn't need to go away totally, because I think I need it sometimes. I just need to manage it better.

This session preceded an improvement in the next session. Jane reported that she was more able to notice when she was being hard on herself and 'let it go'. She still struggled at term time but reported that her awareness of her tendencies to criticise herself and her new ability to accept uncertainty were proving fruitful, and she experienced less depression than in previous periods of this kind. Other people had commented on the positive change. Her social anxiety dropped progressively over the initial sessions, although she had not fulfilled her goal of starting a new relationship at the time of writing.

Research Status

There is a variety of research that informs the approach described here. First, the evidence for the existence of transdiagnostic processes is robust, as established by the comprehensive review (Harvey et al., 2004). The evidence that these processes share common variance is also emerging, as described earlier. Similarly, basic science of perceptual control theory is supported by a number of experimental and computer studies (Powers, 2008). The challenge lies in three other factors: dissemination, the PCT formulation of distress, and controlled trials.

There is little awareness or acceptance that the evidence for the transdiagnostic approach is so robust. The method of classifying disorders and treating them according to the diagnosis are very much established within the way our services are organised, especially secondary and tertiary care. Similarly, the evidence for the validity of PCT over stimulus-response accounts of behaviour is established (e.g. Powers, 1978) and yet rarely cited; the challenge is one of dissemination (Mansell, 2009).

One focus for future research lies in evaluating a PCT model of psychological distress and recovery. For example, one study asked participants to report on their higher order goals (reasons) for expressing, and for suppressing, different emotions (anger, anxiety, excitement). When participants rated the reasons for both expressing and suppressing an emotion as important (i.e.conflict between high-level goals), they experienced more problems with that emotion, which in turn related to general psychological distress (Kelly et al., In preparation). In addition, there needs to be further research testing the efficacy and efficiency of MOL and other transdiagnostic approaches in controlled trials. A transdiagnostic approach does not generally claim a more efficacious treatment than other approaches – there is good evidence that disorder-based CBT is highly effective, even in the presence of comorbidity and in real-world (non-trial) settings (e.g. Gillespie et al., 2002). Instead, it typically claims a tighter link between theory and practice, greater flexibility for complex cases, and more efficient training and delivery without the need for extended assessment sessions. Whether these advantages outweigh the advantages of maintaining the current diagnostic method (including limiting the upheaval of systemic change in the mental health system) is an open question.

Conclusions

This chapter has introduced the transdiagnostic approach to CBT and spelt out its implications for counselling and psychotherapy as a whole. There is a real promise for convergence between different therapeutic approaches that incorporates an understanding of both cognitive (intrapersonal) and social (interpersonal) processes of control as they interface in a therapeutic engagement. I have made the case here that the framework of perceptual control theory provides this opportunity as it operationalises the notion of control, provides a multi-layered structure familiar to a variety of psychological approaches, and it leads to specific implications for a novel therapy in the form of MOL and ways of informing existing therapeutic practice.

Suggested Further Reading

Carey, T.A. (2008) 'Perceptual control theory and the method of levels: Further contributions to a transdiagnostic perspective', *International Journal of Cognitive Therapy*, 1: 237–255.

Harvey, A.G., Watkins, E.R., Mansell, W. and Shafran, R. (2004) *Cognitive Behavioural Processes across Psychological Disorders: A Transdiagnostic Approach to Research and Treatment*. Oxford: Open University Press.

Higginson, S., Mansell, W. and Wood, A.M. (2011) 'An integrative mechanistic account of psychological distress, therapeutic change and recovery: The perceptual control theory approach', *Clinical Psychology Review*, 31: 249–259.

Mansell, W. (2012) 'Working with comorbidity in CBT: The transdiagnostic control theory model (TCTM)', in W. Dryden (Ed.), *The CBT Handbook*. London: Sage.

Mansell, W., Harvey, A.G., Watkins, E.R. and Shafran, R. (2009) 'Conceptual foundations of the transdiagnostic approach', *Journal of Cognitive Psychotherapy*, 23: 6–19.

For further information on PCT, see www.pctweb.org.

References

Aldao, A. and Nolen-Hoeksema, S. (2010) 'Specificity of cognitive emotion regulation strategies: A transdiagnostic examination', *Behaviour Research and Therapy*, 48: 974–983.

Barlow, D.H., Allen, L.B. and Choate, M.L. (2004) 'Toward a unified treatment for emotional disorders', *Behavior Therapy*, 35: 205–230.

Beck, A.T. (1967) *Depression: Clinical, Experimental and Theoretical Aspects*. New York: Harper & Row.

Botvinick, M.M. (2008) 'Hierarchical models of behavior and prefrontal function', *Trends in Cognitive Sciences*, 12: 201–208.

Bowlby, J. (1969) *Attachment*. London: Hogarth.

Carey, T.A. (2006) *Method of Levels: How to Do Psychotherapy without Getting in the Way*. Hayward, CA: Living Control Systems Publishing.

Carey, T.A. (2008) 'Perceptual control theory and the method of levels: Further contributions to a transdiagnostic perspective', *International Journal of Cognitive Therapy*, 1: 237–255.

Carey, T.A. (2011) 'Exposure and reorganization: The what and how of effective psychotherapy', *Clinical Psychology Review*, 31: 236–248.

Carver, C.S. and Scheier, M.F. (1982) 'Control theory: A useful conceptual framework for personality, social, clinical and health psychology', *Psychological Bulletin*, 92: 111–135.

Clark, D.M. (1986) 'A cognitive approach to panic', *Behaviour Research and Therapy*, 24: 461–470.

Clark, D.M. and Wells, A. (1995) 'A cognitive model of social phobia' in R.G. Heimberg, M.R. Liebowitz, D.A. Hope and F.R. Schneier (Eds), *Social Phobia: Diagnosis, Assessment and Treatment*. New York: Guilford Press. pp. 69–93.

De Botton, A. (2000) *Consolations of Philosophy*. London: Hamish Hamilton.

De Silva, P. (1984) 'Buddhism and behaviour modification', *Behaviour Research and Therapy*, 22: 661–678.

Dewey, J. (1896) 'The reflex arc concept in psychology', *Psychological Review*, 3: 357–370.

Dyslin, C.W. (1994) 'Perceptual control theory: A model of volitional behaviour in accord with the ideas of Alfred Adler', *Journal of Individual Psychology*, 54: 24–40.

Ellis, A. (1962) *Reason and Emotion in Psychotherapy*. Secaucus, NJ: Citadel Press.

Fairburn, C.G., Cooper, Z. and Shafran, R. (2003) 'Cognitive behaviour therapy for eating disorders: A 'transdiagnostic' theory and treatment', *Behaviour Research and Therapy*, 41: 509–528.

Field, A.P. and Cartwright-Hatton, S. (2008) 'Shared and unique factors in social anxiety', *International Journal of Cognitive Therapy*, 1: 206–222.

Fogel, A. (2009) *The Psychophysiology of Self-Awareness*. New York: WW Norton.

Gilbert, P. (2010) *The Compassionate Mind*. London: Constable and Robinson.

Gillespie, K., Duffy, M., Hackmann, A. and Clark, D.M. (2002) 'Community based cognitive therapy in the treatment of post-traumatic stress disorder following the Omagh bomb', *Behaviour Research and Therapy*, 40: 345–357.

Gollwitzer, P.M. (1999) 'Implementation intentions: Strong effects of simple plans', *American Psychologist*, 54: 493–503.

Grawe, K. (2006) *Neuropsychotherapy: How the Neurosciences Inform Effective Psychotherapy*. Hove: Lawrence Erlbaum.

Greenberg, L.S., Rice, L.N. and Elliott, R. (1996) *Facilitating Emotional Change: The Moment-by-Moment Process*. New York: Guilford Press.

Harvey, A.G., Watkins, E.R., Mansell, W. and Shafran, R. (2004) *Cognitive Behavioural Processes Across Psychological Disorders: A Transdiagnostic Approach to Research and Treatment*. Oxford: Oxford University Press.

Hayek, F.A. (1952) *The Sensory Order: An Inquiry into the Foundations of Theoretical Psychology*. Chicago, IL: University of Chicago Press.

Higginson, S., Mansell, W. and Wood, A.M. (2011) 'An integrative mechanistic account of psychological distress, therapeutic change and recovery: The perceptual control theory approach', *Clinical Psychology Review*, 31: 249–259.

Huether, G., Doering, S., Ruger, U., Ruther, E. and Schlussler, G. (1999) 'The stress-reaction process and the adaptive modification and reorganization of neuronal networks', *Psychiatry Research*, 87: 83–95.

James, W. (1890) *The Principles of Psychology*. New York: Dover.

Kabat-Zinn, J. (1991) *Full Catastrophe Living: Using the Wisdom of Your Body and Mind to Face Stress, Pain and Illness*. New York: Delacorte Press.

Kelly, R.E., Samad, M., Mansell, W. and Wood, A. (In preparation) *Conflict and Rigid Control During Emotional and Behavioural Self-Regulation Predicts Emotional Distress*.

Kohler, W. (1927) *The Mentality of Apes*. (E. Winter, Trans.) London: Routledge.

Mansell, W. (2005) 'Control theory and psychopathology: An integrative approach', *Psychology and Psychotherapy: Theory, Research and Practice*, 78: 141–178.

Mansell, W. (2008) 'The seven C's of CBT: A consideration of the future challenges for cognitive behavioural therapy', *Behavioural and Cognitive Psychotherapy*, 36: 641–649.

Mansell, W. (2009) 'Perceptual control theory as an integrative framework and method of levels as a cognitive therapy: What are the pros and cons?', *The Cognitive Behavioural Therapist*, 2: 178–196.

Mansell, W. (2011) 'Editorial: Core processes in psychopathology: Does the Dodo bird effect have wings', *Clinical Psychology Review*, 31: 189–192.

Mansell, W., Drummond, K., Faruq, M. and Bird, T. (2007) 'Investigating and extending the transdiagnostic approach'. Paper presented at the British Association of Behavioral and Cognitive Psychotherapies, Brighton.

Mansell, W., Harvey, A.G., Watkins, E.R. and Shafran, R. (2009) 'Conceptual foundations of the transdiagnostic approach', *Journal of Cognitive Psychotherapy*, 23: 6–19.

McManus, F., Shafran, R. and Cooper, Z. (2010) 'What does a "transdiagnostic" approach have to offer the treatment of anxiety disorders?', *British Journal of Clinical Psychology*, 49: 491–505.

Miller, G.A., Galanter, E. and Pribram, K.H. (1960) *Plans and the Structure of Behavior*. New York: Holt, Rinehart and Winston.

Miller, S.D., Duncan, B.L., Brown, J., Sorrell, R. and Chalk, M.B. (2007) 'Using formal client feedback to improve outcome and rentention', *Journal of Brief Therapy*, 5: 19–28.

Miller, W.R. (1996) 'Motivational interviewing: Research, practice and puzzles', *Addictive Behaviors*, 21: 835–842.

Morell, J.D. (1853) *Elements of Psychology*. London: Pickering.

Murray, J., Ehlers, A. and Mayou, R.A. (2002) 'Dissociation and post-traumatic stress disorder: Two prospective studies of motor vehicle accident survivors', *British Journal of Psychiatry*, 180: 363–368.

Nolen-Hoeksema, S., Stice, E., Wade, E. and Bohon, C. (2007) 'Reciprocal relations between rumination and bulimic, substance abuse and depressive symptoms in female adolescents', *Journal of Abnormal Psychology*, 116: 198–207.

Norton, P.J., Hayes, S.A. and Hope, D.A. (2004) 'Effects of a transdiagnostic group treatment for anxiety on secondary depressive disorders', *Depression and Anxiety*, 20: 198–202.

Patel, T. (2010) *The Development of a Scale to Measure Cognitive Behavioural Processes Across a Range of Psychological Disorders*. Unpublished doctoral thesis, University of East London.

Pezzulo, G. and Castelfranchi, C. (2009) 'Thinking as the control of imagination: A conceptual framework for goal-directed systems', *Psychological Research*, 73: 559–577.

Powers, W.T. (1973) *Behavior: The Control of Perception*. Montclair, NJ: Benchmark Publications.

Powers, W.T. (1978) 'Quantitative analysis of purpose systems: Some spadework at the foundations of scientific psychology', *Psychological Review*, 85: 417–435.

Powers, W.T. (1998) *Making Sense of Behaviour: The Meaning of Control*. Montclair, NJ: Benchmark Publications.

Powers, W.T. (2008) *Living Control Systems III: The Fact of Control*. New Canaan, CT: Benchmark Publications.

Powers, W.T., Clark, R.K. and McFarland, R.L. (1960) 'A general feedback theory of human behaviour: Part II', *Perceptual and Motor Skills*, 11: 309–323.

Rogers, C. (1946) 'Significant aspects of client-centred therapy', *American Psychologist*, 1: 415–422.

Rogers, C. (1951) *Client-centred Counselling*. London: Constable.

Schwannauer, M. (2007) 'Cognitive, interpersonal and psychological factors influencing vulnerability, treatment outcome and relapse in bipolar affective disorders'. Unpublished doctoral thesis, University of Edinburgh.

Segerstrom, S.C., Tsao, J.C.I., Alden, L.E. and Craske, M.G. (2000) 'Worry and rumination: Repetitive thought as a concomitant and predictor of negative mood', *Cognitive Therapy and Research*, 24: 671–688.

Startup, H., Freeman, D. and Garety, P.A. (2007) 'Persecutory delusions and catastrophic worry in psychosis: Developing the understanding of delusion distress and persistence', *Behaviour Research and Therapy*, 45: 523–537.

Stern, D.N. (2004) *The Present Moment in Psychotherapy and Everyday Life*. New York: Norton.

Stott, R., Mansell, W., Salkovskis, P.M., Lavender, A. and Cartwright-Hatton, S. (2010) *An Oxford Guide to Metaphors in CBT: Building Cognitive Bridges*. Oxford: Oxford University Press.

Tolin, D.F. (2010) 'Is cognitive-behavioral therapy more effective than other therapies? A meta-analytic review', *Clinical Psychology Review*, 30, 710–720.

Ward, E., King, M., Lloyd, M., Bower, P., Sibbald, B., Farrelly, S., Gabbay, M., Tarrier, N. and Addington-Hall, J. (2000) 'Randomised controlled trial of non-directive counselling, cognitive-behaviour therapy and usual general practitioner care for patients with depression. I: Clinical effectiveness', *British Medical Journal*, 321: 1383–1388.

Watkins, E.R. (2011) 'Dysregulation in the level of goal and action identification across disorders', *Clinical Psychology Review*, 31: 260–278.

Wells, A. (2000) *Emotional Disorders and Metacognition: Innovative Cognitive Therapy*. Chichester: Wiley.

Wiener, N. (1948) *Cybernetics: Control and Communication in the Animal and the Machine*. Cambridge, MA: MIT Press.

Index

Note: page numbers in *italics* refer to case examples.